Mental
Retardation
SOURCEBOOK

Health Reference Series

First Edition

Mental Retardation
SOURCEBOOK

*Basic Consumer Health Information about
Mental Retardation and Its Causes, Including
Down Syndrome, Fetal Alcohol Syndrome,
Fragile X Syndrome, Genetic Conditions,
Injury, and Environmental Sources:*

*Along with Preventive Strategies, Parenting
Issues, Educational Implications, Health Care
Needs, Employment and Economic Matters,
Legal Issues, a Glossary, and a Resource Listing
for Additional Help and Information*

Edited by
Joyce Brennfleck Shannon

Omnigraphics

615 Griswold Street • Detroit, MI 48226

Bibliographic Note

Because this page cannot legibly accommodate all the copyright notices, the Bibliographic Note portion of the Preface constitutes an extension of the copyright notice.

Beginning with books published in 1999, each new volume of the *Health Reference Series* will be individually titled and called a "First Edition." Subsequent updates will carry sequential edition numbers. To help avoid confusion and to provide maximum flexibility in our ability to respond to informational needs, the practice of consecutively numbering each volume will be discontinued.

Edited by Joyce Brennfleck Shannon

Health Reference Series

Karen Bellenir, *Series Editor*
Peter D. Dresser, *Managing Editor*
Joan Margeson, *Research Associate*
Dawn Matthews, *Verification Assistant*
Margaret Mary Missar, *Research Coordinator*
Jenifer Swanson, *Research Associate*

Omnigraphics, Inc.

Matthew P. Barbour, *Vice President, Operations*
Laurie Lanzen Harris, *Vice President, Editorial Director*
Kevin Hayes, *Production Coordinator*
Thomas J. Murphy, *Vice President, Finance and Comptroller*
Peter E. Ruffner, *Senior Vice President*
Jane J. Steele, *Marketing Consultant*

Frederick G. Ruffner, Jr., Publisher

© 2000, Omnigraphics, Inc.

Library of Congress Cataloging-in-Publication Data

Mental retardation sourcebook : basic consumer health information about mental retardation and its causes, including down syndrome, fetal alcohol syndrome, Fragile X syndrome, genetic conditions, injury ... / edited by Joyce Brennfleck Shannon.-- 1st ed.
    p. cm. -- (Health reference series)
    Includes bibliographical references and index.
    ISBN 0-7808-0377-9 (lib. bdg. : alk. paper)
    1. Mental retardation--Popular works. 2. Mentally handicapped children--Popular works. 3. Consumer education. I. Shannon, Joyce Brennfleck. II. Series.

RC570 .M4227 2000
616.85'884--dc21

00-021692

∞

This book is printed on acid-free paper meeting the ANSI Z39.48 Standard. The infinity symbol that appears indicates that the paper in this book meets that standard.

Printed in the United States

Table of Contents

Part IV: Preventing Mental Retardation

Part V: Family Life

Part VI: Education

Part VII: Specific Health Care Issues

Part VIII: Important Economic Matters for Mentally Retarded Individuals

Part IX: Legal Concerns of the Mentally Retarded and Their Families

Part X: Additional Help and Information

Preface

About This Book

According to figures derived from the most recently available census data, an estimated 6.2 to 7.5 million U.S. citizens suffer the effects of mental retardation. The numbers suggest that mental retardation is 10 times more common than cerebral palsy, 25 times more common than blindness, and 28 times more common than neural tube defects, such as spina bifida. In fact, one out of every ten American families is directly affected by mental retardation.

Despite its prevalence, however, mental retardation is often misunderstood. It is a disorder that causes developmental, learning, and social difficulties. It is not a disease, nor should it be confused with mental illness. The three most common causes of mental retardation are Down syndrome, fragile X syndrome, and fetal alcohol syndrome.

- Down syndrome, which is caused by a chromosomal abnormality, occurs in approximately one of every 800-1,000 births. More than 350,000 people in the United States have Down syndrome.

- Fragile X syndrome is a genetically inherited form of mental retardation. Its characteristics are observed in approximately one of every 1,000 male births and in one of every 2,500 female births.

- Fetal alcohol syndrome, caused by maternal alcohol use during pregnancy, occurs in an estimated one out of every 750 live births, or about 5,000 infants annually.

This *Sourcebook* provides basic consumer health information about mental retardation, its causes, and prevention strategies. Topics such as parenting issues, educational implications, health care needs, employment and economic matters, and legal issues are included. A glossary helps define terms used by health-care providers, educators, lawmakers, attorneys, and advocates. A directory of organizational resources featuring up-to-date contact information, including websites and E-mail addresses, and a list of other reading material offer additional help to readers seeking further information.

How to Use This Book

This book is divided into parts and chapters. Parts focus on broad areas of interest. Chapters are devoted to single topics within a part.

Part I: Mental Retardation: Definition and Diagnosis presents the basic criteria used to determine mental retardation and the normal range of developmental activities for children.

Part II: Three Major Causes of Mental Retardation describes Down syndrome, fragile X syndrome, and fetal alcohol syndrome. It offers strategies for parents, clinical information, and explains the danger of drinking alcohol during pregnancy.

Part III: Other Causes of Mental Retardation looks at other genetic conditions with less prevalence; developmental disorders, including autism and spina bifida; environmental issues such as chemicals, poverty, and cultural deprivation; and injuries caused by brain trauma or shaken baby syndrome.

Part IV: Preventing Mental Retardation presents proven health care strategies and environmental and safety practices that can reduce the number of people affected by mental retardation.

Part V: Family Life presents information for parents and caregivers concerning issues of day-to-day life within the home and community for families that include a person with mental retardation.

Part VI: Education gives an overview of the Individuals with Disabilities Education Act (IDEA), including the 1997 Final Regulations. Also addressed are early interventions, parental and student rights in the education process, assistive technology, and transition education from school to work and community life.

Part VII: Specific Health Care Issues reviews the relatiohsip between mental retardation and other issues, such as general physical fitness and aging, sexual abuse, Alzheimer's disease, Human Immunodeficiency Virus (HIV)/Acquired Immune Deficiency Syndrome (AIDS), managed care, and long-term services.

Part VIII: Important Economic Matters for Mentally Retarded Individuals looks at employment, social security disability benefits, future planning through trusts, and appropriate housing options for people with mental retardation.

Part IX: Legal Concerns of the Mentally Retarded and Their Families gives an overview of guardianship needs, rights and responsibilities, and the status of a person with mental retardation in our justice system.

Part X: Additional Help and Information provides a glossary, contact information for organizations and support groups, and a listing of books, videos, and newsletters.

Bibliographic Note

This volume contains documents and excerpts from publications issued by the following U.S. government agencies: Administration for Children and Families (ACF), Administration on Developmental Disabilities (ADD), Department of Education, ERIC Clearinghouse on Disabilities and Gifted Education, Food and Drug Administration (FDA), National Highway Traffic Safety Administration (NHTSA), National Information Center for Children and Youth with Disabilities (NICHCY), National Institute on Alcohol Abuse and Alcoholism (NIAAA), National Institute on Drug Abuse (NIDA), National Institute of Mental Health (NIMH), National Institute of Neurological Disorders and Stroke (NINDS), Office of Behavioral and Social Sciences Research (OBSR), Office of Medical Applications of Research (OMAR), and the Social Security Administration (SSA).

In addition, this volume contains copyrighted documents from the following organizations and individuals: American Association on Mental Retardation (AAMR), Center for the Study of Autism, *Genetic Drift Newsletter*, National Angelman Syndrome Foundation, National Down Syndrome Society, National Organization on Fetal Alcohol Syndrome, National Tuberous Sclerosis Association, The Nemours Foundation, Prader-Willi Syndrome Arizona Association, The Arc, and

Williams Syndrome Association. A copyrighted article from *Roots and Wings* is also included.

Full citation information is provided on the first page of each chapter. Every effort has been made to secure all necessary rights to reprint the copyrighted material. If any omissions have been made, please contact Omnigraphics to make corrections for future editions.

Acknowledgements

Special thanks to the many organizations, agencies, and individuals who have contributed materials for this *Sourcebook* and to Karen Bellenir, Maria Franklin, Joan Margeson, Dawn Matthews, and the rest of the team for their assistance. This book is dedicated to the mentally retarded individuals who have shared their lives and friendship with me.

Note from the Editor

This book is part of Omnigraphics' *Health Reference Series*. The series provides basic information about a broad range of medical concerns. It is not intended to serve as a tool for diagnosing illness, in prescribing treatments, or as a substitute for the physician/patient relationship. All persons concerned about medical symptoms or the possibility of disease are encouraged to seek professional care from an appropriate health care provider.

Our Advisory Board

The *Health Reference Series* is reviewed by an Advisory Board comprised of librarians from public, academic, and medical libraries. We would like to thank the following board members for providing guidance to the development of this series:

Dr. Lynda Baker, Associate Professor of Library and
Information Science, Wayne State University, Detroit, MI

Nancy Bulgarelli,
William Beaumont Hospital Library, Royal Oak, MI

Karen Imarasio,
Bloomfield Township Public Library, Bloomfield Township, MI

Karen Morgan,
Mardigian Library, University of Michigan-Dearborn,
Dearborn, MI

Rosemary Orlando,
St. Clair Shores Public Library, St. Clair Shores, MI

Health Reference Series *Update Policy*

The inaugural book in the *Health Reference Series* was the first edition of *Cancer Sourcebook* published in 1992. Since then, the Series has been enthusiastically received by librarians and in the medical community. In order to maintain the standard of providing high-quality health information for the lay person the editorial staff at Omnigraphics felt it was necessary to implement a policy of updating volumes when warranted.

Medical researchers have been making tremendous strides, and the challenge to stay current with the most recent advances is one our editors take seriously. Each decision to update a volume will be made on an individual basis. Some of the considerations will include how much new information is available and the feedback we receive from people who use the books. If there's a topic you would like to see added to the update list, or an area of medical concern you feel has not been adequately addressed, please write to:

Editor
Health Reference Series
Omnigraphics, Inc.
615 Griswold
Detroit, MI 48226

The commitment to providing on-going coverage of important medical developments has also led to some technical changes in the *Health Reference Series*. Beginning with books published in 1999, each new volume will be individually titled and called a "First Edition." Subsequent updates will carry sequential edition numbers. To help avoid confusion and to provide maximum flexibility in our ability to respond to informational needs, the practice of consecutively numbering each volume will be discontinued.

Part One

Mental Retardation: Definition and Diagnosis

Chapter 1

Mental Retardation Defined

People with mental retardation are those who develop at a below average rate and experience difficulty in learning and social adjustment. The regulations for the Individuals with Disabilities Education Act (IDEA) provide the following technical definition for mental retardation:

> "Mental retardation means significantly subaverage general intellectual functioning existing concurrently with deficits in adaptive behavior and manifested during the developmental period, that adversely affects a child's educational performance."

"General intellectual functioning" is typically measured by an intelligence test. Persons with mental retardation usually score 70 or below on such tests. "Adaptive behavior" refers to a person's adjustment to everyday life. Difficulties may occur in learning, communication, social, academic, vocational, and independent living skills.

Mental retardation is not a disease, nor should it be confused with mental illness. Children with mental retardation become adults; they do not remain "eternal children." They do learn, but slowly, and with difficulty.

Probably the greatest number of children with mental retardation have chromosome abnormalities. Other biological factors include (but are not limited to): asphyxia (lack of oxygen); blood incompatibilities

"General Information about Mental Retardation," Fact Sheet Number 8, National Information Center for Children and Youth with Disabilities (NICHCY), February 1999.

3

between the mother and fetus; and maternal infections, such as rubella or herpes. Certain drugs have also been linked to problems in fetal development.

Incidence

Some studies suggest that approximately 1% of the general population has mental retardation (when both intelligence and adaptive behavior measures are used). According to data reported to the U.S. Department of Education by the states, in the 1996-97 school year, 594,025 students ages 6-21 were classified as having mental retardation and were provided services by the public schools. This figure does not include students reported as having multiple disabilities or those in non-categorical special education pre-school programs who may also have mental retardation.

Characteristics

Many authorities agree that people with mental retardation develop in the same way as people without mental retardation, but at a slower rate. Others suggest that persons with mental retardation have difficulties in particular areas of basic thinking and learning such as attention, perception, or memory. Depending on the extent of the impairment—mild, moderate, severe, or profound—individuals with mental retardation will develop differently in academic, social, and vocational skills.

Educational Implications

Persons with mental retardation have the capacity to learn, to develop, and to grow. The great majority of these citizens can become productive and full participants in society.

Appropriate educational services that begin in infancy and continue throughout the developmental period and beyond will enable children with mental retardation to develop to their fullest potential.

As with all education, modifying instruction to meet individual needs is the starting point for successful learning. Throughout their child's education, parents should be an integral part of the planning and teaching team.

In teaching persons with mental retardation, it is important to:

- Use concrete materials that are interesting, age-appropriate, and relevant to the students;

4

- Present information and instructions in small, sequential steps and review each step frequently;

- Provide prompt and consistent feedback;

- Teach these children, whenever possible, in the same school they would attend if they did not have mental retardation;

- Teach tasks or skills that students will use frequently in such a way that students can apply the tasks or skills in settings outside of school; and

- Remember that tasks that many people learn without instruction may need to be structured, or broken down into small steps or segments, with each step being carefully taught.

Children and adults with mental retardation need the same basic services that all people need for normal development. These include education, vocational preparation, health services, recreational opportunities, and many more. In addition, many persons with mental retardation need specialized services for special needs. Such services include diagnostic and evaluation centers; special early education opportunities, beginning with infant stimulation programs and continuing through preschool; and educational programs that include age-appropriate activities, functional academics, transition training, and opportunities for independent living and competitive employment to the maximum extent possible.

Resources

Smith, R. (Ed.). (1993). *Children with Mental Retardation: A Parents' Guide*. Rockville, MD: Woodbine House. Telephone: 1-800-843-7323.

Trainer, M. (1991). *Differences in Common: Straight Talk on Mental Retardation, Down Syndrome, and Life*. Rockville, MD: Woodbine House. Telephone: 1-800-843-7323.

Organizations

The Arc
National Organization on Mental Retardation
1010 Wayne Ave, Suite 650
Silver Spring, MD 20910
Tel: 301-565-3842

Fax: 301-565-3843
E-mail: thearc@metronet.com
URL: http://www.thearc.org

American Association on Mental Retardation (AAMR)
444 N. Capitol Street N.W., Suite 846
Washington, D.C. 20001-1512
Tel: 202-387-1968
Toll-free: 800-424-3688
Fax: 202-387-2193
URL: http://www.aamr.org

National Down Syndrome Congress
1605 Chantilly Drive, Suite 250
Atlanta, GA 30324
Tel: 404-633-1555
Toll-free: 800-232-6372
E-mail: NDSCcenter@aol.com
URL: http://www.carol.net/~ndsc

National Down Syndrome Society
666 Broadway, Suite 810
New York, NY 10012
Tel: 212-460-9330
Toll-free: 800-221-4602
E-mail: info@ndss.org
URL: http://www.ndss.org

National Information Center for Children and Youth with Disabilities (NICHCY)
P.O. Box 1492
Washington, DC 20013-1492
E-mail: nichcy@aed.org
URL: http://www.nichcy.org
Tel: 800-695-0285 (Voice/TTY)

Chapter 2

Is This Normal? Human Growth and Development

Children grow and develop at different rates. This chapter shows the ages by which most young children develop certain abilities. It is normal for a child to do some things later than the ages noted here. If your child fails to do many of these at the ages given, or you have questions about his or her development, talk with your child's doctor or other health care provider.

Table 2.1. Indicators of Normal Development

Age: birth-3 months

> **Skills or Abilities, Awareness and Thinking:**
> Responds to new sounds
> Follows movement of hands with eyes
> Looks at objects and people
> **Communication:**
> Coos and makes sounds.
> Smiles at mother's voice
> **Movement:**
> Waves hands and feet
> Grasps objects
> Watches movement of own hands

Adapted from "Growth and Developmental Milestones," Maryland Infants and Toddlers Program, Baltimore, MD, 1995, NIH Publication No. 97-4023, September 1997.

Age: birth-3 months (continued)

Social:
Enjoys being tickled and held
Makes brief eye contact during feeding
Self-help:
Opens mouth to bottle or breast and sucks

Age: 3-6 months

Skills or Abilities, Awareness and Thinking:
Recognizes mother
Reaches for things
Communication:
Turns head to sounds and voices
Begins babbling
Imitates sounds
Varies cry
Movement:
Lifts head and chest
Bangs objects in play
Social:
Notices strangers and new places
Expresses pleasure or displeasure
Likes physical play
Self-help:
Eats baby food from spoon
Reaches for and holds bottle

Age: 6-9 months

Skills or Abilities, Awareness and Thinking:
Imitates simple gestures
Responds to name
Communication:
Makes nonsense syllables like gaga
Uses voice to get attention
Movement:
Crawls
Stands by holding on to things
Claps hands

Moves objects from one hand to the other
Social:
Plays peek-a-boo
Enjoys other children
Understands social signals like smiles or harsh tones
Self-help:
Chews
Drinks from a cup with help

Age: 9-12 months

Skills or Abilities, Awareness and Thinking:
Plays simple games
Moves to reach desired objects
Looks at pictures in books
Communication:
Waves bye-bye
Stops when told "no"
Imitates new words
Movement:
Walks holding on to furniture
Deliberately lets go of an object
Makes marks with a pencil or crayon
Social:
Laughs aloud during play
Shows preference for one toy over another
Responds to adult's change in mood
Self-help:
Feeds self with fingers
Drinks from cup

Age: 12-18 months

Skills or Abilities, Awareness and Thinking:
Imitates unfamiliar sounds and gestures
Points to a desired object
Communication:
Shakes head to mean "no"
Begins using words
Follows simple commands

Age: 12-18 months (continued)

Movement:
Creeps upstairs and downstairs
Walks alone
Stacks blocks

Social:
Repeats a performance laughed at
Shows emotions like fear or anger
Returns a kiss or hug

Self-help:
Moves to help in dressing
Indicates wet diaper

Age: 18-24 months

Skills or Abilities, Awareness and Thinking:
Identifies parts of own body
Attends to nursery rhymes
Points to pictures in books

Communication:
Uses two words to describe actions
Refers to self by name

Movement:
Jumps in place
Pushes and pulls objects
Turns pages of book one by one
Uses fingers and thumb

Social:
Cries a bit when parents leave
Becomes easily frustrated
Pays attention to other children

Self-help:
Zips
Removes clothes without help
Unwraps things

Age: 24-36 months

Skills or Abilities, Awareness and Thinking:
Matches shapes and objects
Enjoys picture books
Recognizes self in mirror
Counts to ten

Communication:
Joins in songs and rhythm
Uses three-word phrases
Uses simple pronouns
Follows two instructions at a time

Movement:
Kicks and throws ball
Runs and jumps
Draws straight lines
Strings beads

Social:
Pretends and plays make believe
Avoids dangerous situations
Initiates play
Attempts to take turns

Self-help:
Feeds self with spoon
Uses toilet with some help

Chapter 3

Diagnosing and Identifying Mental Retardation

What Is Mental Retardation?

An individual is considered to have mental retardation based on the following three criteria: intellectual functioning level (IQ) is below 70-75; significant limitations exist in two or more adaptive skill areas; and the condition is present from childhood (defined as age 18 or less) (AAMR, 1992).

What Are the Adaptive Skills Essential for Daily Functioning?

Adaptive skill areas are those daily living skills needed to live, work, and play in the community. They include communication, self-care, home living, social skills, leisure, health and safety, self-direction, functional academics (reading, writing, basic math), community use, and work.

Adaptive skills are assessed in the person's typical environment across all aspects of an individual's life. A person with limits in intellectual functioning who does not have limits in adaptive skill areas may not be diagnosed as having mental retardation.

Reprinted with permission, "Introduction to Mental Retardation," © 1998, The Arc.

How Many People Are Affected by Mental Retardation?

The Arc reviewed a number of prevalence studies in the early 1980s and concluded that 2.5 to 3 percent of the general population have mental retardation (The Arc, 1982).

Based on the 1990 census, an estimated 6.2 to 7.5 million people have mental retardation. Mental retardation is 10 times more common than cerebral palsy and 28 times more prevalent than neural tube defects such as spina bifida. It affects 25 times as many people as blindness (Batshaw, 1997).

Mental retardation cuts across the lines of racial, ethnic, educational, social, and economic backgrounds. It can occur in any family. One out of ten American families is directly affected by mental retardation.

How Does Mental Retardation Affect Individuals?

The effects of mental retardation vary considerably among people, just as the range of abilities varies considerably among people who do not have mental retardation. About 87 percent will be mildly affected and will be only a little slower than average in learning new information and skills. As children, their mental retardation is not readily apparent and may not be identified until they enter school. As adults, many will be able to lead independent lives in the community and will no longer be viewed as having mental retardation.

The remaining 13 percent of people with mental retardation, those with IQs under 50, will have serious limitations in functioning. However, with early intervention, a functional education and appropriate supports as an adult, all can lead satisfying lives in the community.

How Is Mental Retardation Diagnosed?

The AAMR process for diagnosing and classifying a person as having mental retardation contains three steps and describes the system of supports a person needs to overcome limits in adaptive skills.

The first step in diagnosis is to have a qualified person give one or more standardized intelligence tests and a standardized adaptive skills test, on an individual basis.

The second step is to describe the person's strengths and weaknesses across four dimensions. The four dimensions are:

1. Intellectual and adaptive behavior skills

2. Psychological/emotional considerations

3. Physical/health/etiological considerations

4. Environmental considerations

Strengths and weaknesses may be determined by formal testing, observations, interviewing key people in the individual's life, interviewing the individual, interacting with the person in his or her daily life, or a combination of these approaches.

The third step requires an interdisciplinary team to determine needed supports across the four dimensions. Each support identified is assigned one of four levels of intensity—intermittent, limited, extensive, pervasive.

Intermittent support refers to support on an "as needed basis." An example would be support that is needed in order for a person to find a new job in the event of a job loss. Intermittent support may be needed occasionally by an individual over their life span, but not on a continuous daily basis.

Limited support may occur over a limited time span such as during transition from school to work or in time-limited job training. This type of support has a limit on the time that is needed to provide appropriate support for an individual.

Extensive support in a life area is assistance that an individual needs on a daily basis that is not limited by time. This may involve support in the home and/or support in work. Intermittent, limited, and extensive supports may not be needed in all life areas for an individual.

Pervasive support refers to constant support across environments and life areas and may include life-sustaining measures. A person requiring pervasive support will need assistance on a daily basis across all life areas.

What Does the Term "Mental Age" Mean When Used to Describe the Person's Functioning?

The term mental age is used in intelligence testing. It means that the individual received the same number of correct responses on a standardized IQ test as the average person of that age in the sample population.

Saying that an older person with mental retardation is like a person of a younger age or has the "mind" or "understanding" of a younger person is incorrect usage of the term. The mental age only refers to the intelligence test score. It does not describe the level and nature of the person's experience and functioning in aspects of community life.

What Are the Causes of Mental Retardation?

Mental retardation can be caused by any condition which impairs development of the brain before birth, during birth, or in the childhood years. Several hundred causes have been discovered, but in about one-third of the people affected, the cause remains unknown. The three major known causes of mental retardation are Down syndrome, fetal alcohol syndrome, and fragile X syndrome.

The causes can be categorized as follows:

- **Genetic conditions**—These result from abnormality of genes inherited from parents, errors when genes combine, or from other disorders of the genes caused during pregnancy by infections, overexposure to x-rays, and other factors. More than 500 genetic diseases are associated with mental retardation. Some examples include PKU (phenylketonuria), a single gene disorder also referred to as an inborn error of metabolism because it is caused by a defective enzyme. Down syndrome is an example of a chromosomal disorder. Chromosomal disorders happen sporadically and are caused by too many or too few chromosomes, or by a change in structure of a chromosome. Fragile X syndrome is a single gene disorder located on the X chromosome and is the leading inherited cause of mental retardation.

- **Problems during pregnancy**—Use of alcohol or drugs by the pregnant mother can cause mental retardation. Recent research has implicated smoking in increasing the risk of mental retardation. Other risks include malnutrition, certain environmental contaminants, and illnesses of the mother during pregnancy, such as toxoplasmosis, cytomegalovirus, rubella, and syphilis. Pregnant women who are infected with HIV may pass the virus to their child, leading to future neurological damage.

- **Problems at birth**—Although any birth condition of unusual stress may injure the infant's brain, prematurity and low birth weight predict serious problems more often than any other conditions.

- **Problems after birth**—Childhood diseases such as whooping cough, chicken pox, measles, and Hib disease which may lead to meningitis and encephalitis can damage the brain, as can accidents such as a blow to the head or near drowning. Lead, mercury, and other environmental toxins can cause irreparable damage to the brain and nervous system.

- **Poverty and cultural deprivation**—Children in poor families may become mentally retarded because of malnutrition, disease-producing conditions, inadequate medical care, and environmental health hazards. Also, children in disadvantaged areas may be deprived of many common cultural and day-to-day experiences provided to other youngsters. Research suggests that such under-stimulation can result in irreversible damage and can serve as a cause of mental retardation.

Can Mental Retardation Be Prevented?

During the past 30 years, significant advances in research have prevented many cases of mental retardation. For example, every year in the United States, we prevent:

- 250 cases of mental retardation due to phenylketonuria (PKU) by newborn screening and dietary treatment;

- 1,000 cases of mental retardation due to congenital hypothyroidism thanks to newborn screening and thyroid hormone replacement therapy;

- 1,000 cases of mental retardation by use of anti-Rh immune globulin to prevent Rh disease and severe jaundice in newborn infants;

- 5,000 cases of mental retardation caused by Hib diseases by using the Hib vaccine;

- 4,000 cases of mental retardation due to measles encephalitis thanks to measles vaccine; and untold numbers of cases of mental retardation caused by rubella during pregnancy thanks to rubella vaccine (Alexander, 1998).

Other interventions have reduced the chance of mental retardation. Removing lead from the environment reduces brain damage in children. Preventive interventions such as child safety seats and bicycle helmets reduce head trauma. Early intervention programs with high-risk infants and children have shown remarkable results in reducing the predicted incidence of subnormal intellectual functioning.

Finally, early comprehensive prenatal care and preventive measures prior to and during pregnancy increase a woman's chances of preventing mental retardation. Pediatric AIDS is being reduced by AZT treatment of the mother during pregnancy, and dietary supplementation with folic acid reduces the risk of neural tube defects.

Research continues on new ways to prevent mental retardation, including research on the development and function of the nervous system, a wide variety of fetal treatments, and gene therapy to correct the abnormality produced by defective genes.

References

American Association on Mental Retardation. (1992). *Mental Retardation: Definition, Classification, and Systems of Supports*, 9th Edition. Washington, DC.

Alexander, D. (1998). *Prevention of Mental Retardation: Four Decades of Research. Mental Retardation and Developmental Disabilities Research Reviews*. 4: 50-58

Batshaw, M. (1997). *Children with Disabilities*. Baltimore: Paul H. Brookes Publishing Co.

The Arc. (1982). *The Prevalence of Mental Retardation*. (out-of-print).

The Arc
National Organization onMental Retardation
1010 Wayne Avenue, Suite 650
Silver Spring, MD 20910
Tel: 301-565-3842
TDD: 301-565-3843
E-mail: thearc@metronet.com
URL: http://www.thearc.org

Part Two

Three Major Causes of Mental Retardation

Chapter 4

Down Syndrome

Contents

Section 4.1

Parent and Professional Information

Parent and Professional Information

Down syndrome affects people of all ages, races, and economic levels. It is the most frequently occurring chromosomal abnormality, occurring once in approximately every 800 to 1,000 live births. Over 350,000 people in the United States alone have Down syndrome.

For centuries, people with Down syndrome have been alluded to in art, literature, and science. It wasn't until the late 19th century, however, that John Langdon Down, an English physician, published an accurate description of a person with Down syndrome. It was this scholarly work, published in 1866, which earned Down the recognition as the "father" of the syndrome. Although other people had previously recognized the characteristics of the syndrome, it was Down who described the condition as a distinct and separate entity.

Throughout the 20th century, advances in medicine and science enabled researchers to investigate the characteristics of people with Down syndrome. In 1959, the French physician, Jerome Lejeune, identified Down syndrome as a chromosomal anomaly. Instead of the usual 46 chromosomes present in each cell, Lejeune observed 47 in the cells of individuals with Down syndrome. It was later determined that an extra partial or complete 21st chromosome results in the characteristics associated with Down syndrome.

Down Syndrome—A Genetic Condition

The human body is made of cells; all cells contain a center, called a nucleus, in which genetic material is stored. This genetic material, known as genes, carries the codes responsible for all our inherited characteristics.

Genes are grouped along rod-like structures called chromosomes. Normally, the nucleus of each cell contains 23 pairs of chromosomes, half of which are inherited from each parent.

In Down syndrome, however, the cells usually contain not 46, but 47 chromosomes; with the extra chromosome being a number 21. This excess genetic material, in the form of additional genes along the 21st chromosome, results in Down syndrome.

Because 95 percent of all cases of Down syndrome occur because there are three copies of the 21st chromosome, it is referred to as "trisomy 21."

Chromosomes may be studied by examining blood or tissue cells. Individual chromosomes are identified, stained, and numbered from largest to smallest. The visual display of the chromosomes is known as a karyotype.

The Causes of Down Syndrome

Down syndrome is usually caused by an error in cell division called non-disjunction. However, two other types of chromosomal abnormalities, mosaicism and translocation, are also implicated in Down syndrome—although to a much lesser extent. Regardless of the type of Down syndrome which a person may have, all people with Down syndrome have an extra, critical portion of the number 21 chromosome present in all, or some, of their cells. This additional genetic material alters the course of development and causes the characteristics associated with the syndrome.

Nondisjunction is a faulty cell division which results in an embryo with three number 21 chromosomes instead of two. Prior to, or at, conception, a pair of number 21 chromosomes, in either the sperm or the egg, fail to separate. As the embryo develops, the extra chromosome is replicated in every cell of the body. This faulty cell division is responsible for 95 percent of all cases of Down syndrome.

Why nondisjunction occurs is currently unknown, although it does seem to be related to advancing maternal age. Many people are surprised to find out that 80 percent of children born with Down syndrome are born to women under 35 years of age. This is because younger women have higher fertility rates. It does not contradict the fact that the incidence of births of children with Down syndrome increases with the age of the mother.

Although nondisjunction can be of paternal origin, this occurs less frequently. Because this error in cell division is often present in the egg prior to conception, and women are born with their complete store of eggs, it has been postulated that some environmental factors may be implicated in nondisjunction. However, despite years of research, the cause (or causes) of nondisjunction, is still unknown. There seems to be no connection between any type of Down syndrome and parents' activities before or during pregnancy.

Mosaicism occurs when nondisjunction of the 21st chromosome takes place in one of the initial cell divisions after fertilization. When this occurs, there is a mixture of two types of cells, some containing 46 chromosomes and some containing 47. Those cells with 47 chromosomes contain an extra 21st chromosome. Because of the "mosaic" pattern of the cells, the term mosaicism is used. Mosaicism is rare, being responsible for only one to two percent of all cases of Down syndrome.

Some research has shown that individuals with mosaic Down syndrome are less affected than those with trisomy 21; however, broad generalizations are not possible due to the wide range of abilities that people with Down syndrome possess.

Translocation is a different type of chromosomal problem and occurs in only three to four percent of people with Down syndrome. Translocation occurs when part of the number 21 chromosome breaks off during cell division and attaches to another chromosome. While the total number of chromosomes in the cells remains 46, the presence of an extra part of the number 21 chromosome causes the features of Down syndrome. As with nondisjunction trisomy 21, translocation occurs either prior to or at conception.

Unlike nondisjunction, maternal age is not linked to the risk of translocation. Most cases are sporadic, chance events. However, in about one-third of cases, one parent is a carrier of a translocated chromosome. For this reason, the risk of recurrence for translocation is higher than that of nondisjunction. Genetic counseling can be sought to determine the origin of the translocation.

Risk of Having a Second Child with Down Syndrome

In general, it is estimated that the risk of having a second child with trisomy 21 or mosaic Down syndrome is about 1 in 100. The risk is higher if one parent is a carrier of a translocated cell.

Prenatal Tests to Detect Down Syndrome

There are two types of procedures available to pregnant women: screening tests and diagnostic tests. Screening tests estimate the risk of the fetus having Down syndrome; diagnostic tests tell whether or not the fetus actually has the condition.

The most commonly used screening tests are the Triple Screen and the Alpha-fetoprotein Plus. These tests measure quantities of various substances in the blood (alpha-fetoprotein, human chorionic gonadotropin, and unconjugated estriol) and together with the woman's age, estimate her risk of having a child with Down syndrome. These screening tests are typically offered between fifteen and twenty weeks of gestation.

Screening tests are of limited value and are often performed in conjunction with a detailed sonogram. These tests are only able to accurately detect about sixty percent of fetuses with Down syndrome. Many women who undergo these tests will be given false-positive readings, and some women will be given false-negative readings.

The procedures available for prenatal diagnosis of Down syndrome are chorionic villus sampling (CVS), amniocentesis, and percutaneous umbilical blood sampling (PUBS). Each one of these procedures carries a small risk of miscarriage as tissue is extracted from the placenta or the umbilical cord to examine the fetus' chromosomes. The procedures are about 98 to 99 percent accurate in the detection of Down syndrome. Amniocentesis is usually performed between 12 and 20 weeks of gestation, CVS between eight and 12 weeks, and PUBS after 20 weeks.

Diagnosis of Down Syndrome in a Newborn

The diagnosis of Down syndrome is usually suspected after birth as a result of the baby's appearance. It is a particularly difficult time, coupled with the natural stresses of childbirth. Although there is no easy way to be informed, most families agree that having the baby present, being together, and being told as soon as possible is the best way to proceed.

There are many physical characteristics which form the basis for suspecting an infant has Down syndrome. Many of these characteristics are found, to some extent, in the general population of individuals who do not have Down syndrome. Hence, if Down syndrome is suspected, a karyotype will be performed to ascertain the diagnosis. Some infants with Down syndrome have only a few of these traits, while others have many. Among the most common traits are:

- Muscle hypotonia, low muscle tone
- Flat facial profile, a somewhat depressed nasal bridge and a small nose

- Oblique palpebral fissures, an upward slant to the eyes

- Dysplastic ear, an abnormal shape of the ear

- Simian crease, a single deep crease across the center of the palm

- Hyperflexibility, an excessive ability to extend the joints

- Dysplastic middle phalanx of the fifth finger, fifth finger has one flexion furrow instead of two

- Epicanthal folds, small skin folds on the inner corner of the eyes

- Excessive space between large and second toe

- Enlargement of tongue in relationship to size of mouth

Medical Problems of Babies Born with Down Syndrome

Children with Down syndrome are at increased risk for certain health problems. Congenital heart defects, increased susceptibility to infection, respiratory problems, obstructed digestive tracts, and childhood leukemia occur with greater frequency among children who have Down syndrome. However, advances in medicine have rendered most of these health problems treatable and the majority of people born with Down syndrome today have a life expectancy of approximately 55 years.

Adults with Down syndrome are at increased risk for Alzheimer's disease. Whereas approximately six percent of the general population will develop the disease, the figure is about 25 percent for people with Down syndrome. Many individuals with Down syndrome have the changes in the brain associated with Alzheimer's, but do not necessarily develop the clinical disorder.

Down Syndrome Affects Development

Most people with Down syndrome have some level of mental retardation; however, the level usually falls into the mild to moderate range and is not indicative of the many strengths and talents that each individual possesses. Children with Down syndrome learn to sit, walk, talk, play, toilet train, and do most other activities—only somewhat later than their peers without Down syndrome. Because speech is often delayed, careful attention should be paid to the child's hearing, as retention of fluid in the inner ear is a very common cause of hearing and speech difficulties.

Early intervention services, which begin shortly after birth, help children with Down syndrome develop to their full potential. Quality educational programs, along with a stimulating home environment, and good medical care enable people with Down syndrome to become contributing members of their families and communities.

People with Down syndrome are highly responsive to their physical and social environment. Those who receive good medical care and are included in the activities of the community can be expected to adapt successfully—to attend school, make friends, find work, participate in decisions which affect them, and make a positive contribution to society.

People with Down syndrome have the same emotions and needs as their peers and deserve the same opportunities.

The Future for People with Down Syndrome

People with Down syndrome are people first. They may have some of the characteristics generally associated with this condition, but they are overwhelmingly unique and must be treated as individuals. Over the past few decades, beginning with Section 504 of The Rehabilitation Act of 1973, continuing with The Education for All Handicapped Children Act of 1975, and culminating with the passage of the Americans with Disabilities Act in 1991, people with Down syndrome have been granted equal protections under federal law.

Ensuring equal treatment and access to services is a struggle that every family of a child with Down syndrome faces. Daily, these individuals strive to accomplish the same goals as everyone else: self-fulfillment, pride in their achievements, inclusion in the activities of the community, and the challenge of reaching their full potential.

Daily, people with Down syndrome venture out into the community: to schools, jobs, and leisure activities. Some live with family, some with friends, and some independently. They form ongoing interpersonal relationships and some may marry. Women with Down syndrome are fertile and can have children.

The opportunities available to people with Down syndrome today have never been greater. However, it is only through the collective efforts of parents, professionals, and concerned citizens that acceptance is becoming widespread. It is the goal of the National Down Syndrome Society to ensure that all people with Down syndrome are provided the opportunity to achieve their full potential in all aspects of community life.

Questions and Answers about Down Syndrome

What Impact Does Down Syndrome Have on Society?

Individuals with Down syndrome are becoming increasingly integrated into society and community organizations, such as school, health care systems, work forces, and social and recreational activities.

Individuals with Down syndrome possess varying degrees of mental retardation, from very mild to severe. Most people with Down syndrome have IQs in the mild to moderate range of mental retardation.

Due to advances in medical technology, individuals with Down syndrome are living longer than ever before. In 1910, children with Down syndrome were expected to survive to age nine. With the discovery of antibiotics, the average survival age increased to 19 or 20. Now, with recent advancements in clinical treatment, as many as 80 percent of adults with Down syndrome reach age 55, and many live even longer.

In the United States, approximately 350,000 families are affected by Down syndrome. Approximately 5,000 children with Down syndrome are born each year. As the mortality rate associated with Down syndrome is decreasing, the prevalence of individuals with Down syndrome in our society will increase. Some experts project that the number of people with Down syndrome will double in the next 10 years. More and more Americans will interact with individuals with this genetic condition, increasing the need for widespread public education and acceptance.

Is Down Syndrome Transmitted from the Mother or Father?

The additional genetic material which causes Down syndrome can originate from either the father or the mother. Approximately five percent of the cases have been traced to the father.

Who Has the Highest Risk of Having a Child with Down Syndrome?

Down syndrome affects people of all races and economic levels. Women age 35 and older have a significantly increased risk of having a child with Down syndrome. A 35-year-old woman has a one in 400 chance of conceiving a child with Down syndrome and this chance increases gradually to one in 110 by age 40. At age 45 the incidence becomes approximately one in 35.

Since many couples are postponing parenting until later in life, the incidence of Down syndrome conceptions is expected to increase. Therefore, genetic counseling for parents is becoming increasingly important. Still, many physicians are not fully informed about advising their patients about the of incidence of Down syndrome, advancements in diagnosis, and the protocols for care and treatment of babies born with Down syndrome.

Why Is It Important to Raise Children with Down Syndrome at Home?

A greater understanding of Down syndrome and advancements in treatment of Down syndrome-related health problems have allowed people with Down syndrome to enjoy fuller and more active lives.

Children raised at home and included in all aspects of community life can best reach their potential and function in society with a greater degree of independence. Parental love, nurturing, and support, as well as early intervention programs, educational opportunities, and community involvement, have a direct relationship to the degree that a person with Down syndrome is able to achieve his/her potential.

Why Are Medical Researchers Following Down Syndrome Work so Closely?

Down syndrome is a developmental disorder. As researchers learn more about the molecular genetics and other aspects of Down syndrome, they also obtain valuable information about human development and can advance the study of many biological processes.

In addition, individuals with Down syndrome have a higher incidence of certain medical problems and the study of Down syndrome may yield important breakthroughs in those areas. Research in Down syndrome provides a way for looking at many important problems:

- **Heart disease:** Up to 50 percent of individuals with Down syndrome are born with congenital heart defects. The majority of heart defects in children with Down syndrome can now be surgically corrected with resulting long-term health improvements. However, scientists continue to search for the cause of this problem and look for means of prevention.

- **Alzheimer's disease:** Estimates vary, but it is reasonable to conclude that 25 percent or more of individuals with Down syndrome over the age of 35 will develop the clinical signs and symptoms of Alzheimer's-type dementia.

• **Leukemia:** Individuals with Down syndrome have a 15 to 20 times greater risk of developing leukemia. The majority of cases are categorized as acute megakaryoblastic leukemia, which tends to occur in the first three years of life, and for which there is a high cure rate. A transient form of leukemia is also seen in newborns with Down syndrome, disappearing spontaneously during the first two to three months of life.

Why Hasn't Down Syndrome Received Much Attention in the Past?

Even though Dr. Jerome Lejeune discovered in 1959 that it was an extra 21st chromosome that caused Down syndrome, it is only in the last few years that a focus has been placed on the study of the 21st chromosome. Why? Because we now have the technology to isolate specific genes and genetic material.

The momentum is increasing. Chromosome 21 is the first chromosome to be fully mapped and is a prototype for the federally funded genome mapping project. Up to 1,000 genes exist on the 21st chromosome. We have already identified between 30 to 35 genes and gene products—and new findings are occurring rapidly.

Researchers continue to look for the genes related to the development of intelligence and the physical characteristics associated with Down syndrome. Once identified, it is hoped that the biochemical process which causes Down syndrome can be decoded, leading to the development of an intervention and cure.

Section 4.2

Myths and Truths about Down Syndrome

Reprinted with the express consent and approval of the National Down Syndrome Society, © 1999. Through education, research, and advocacy, NDSS works to ensure that all people with Down syndrome have the opportunity to achieve their full potential in community life. For more information call 800-221-4602 or visit www.ndss.org.

Myth: Down syndrome is a rare genetic disorder.

Truth: Down syndrome is the most commonly occurring genetic condition. One in every 800 to 1,000 live births is a child with Down syndrome, representing approximately 5,000 births per year in the United States alone. Today, Down syndrome affects more than 350,000 people in the United States.

Myth: Most children with Down syndrome are born to older parents.

Truth: Eighty percent of children born with Down syndrome are born to women younger than 35-years-old. However, the incidence of births of children with Down syndrome increases with the age of the mother.

Myth: People with Down syndrome are severely retarded.

Truth: Most people with Down syndrome have IQs that fall in the mild to moderate range of retardation. Children with Down syndrome are definitely educable and educators and researchers are still discovering the full educational potential of people with Down syndrome.

Myth: Most people with Down syndrome are institutionalized.

Truth: Today people with Down syndrome live at home with their families and are active participants in the educational, vocational, social, and recreational activities of the community. They are integrated into the regular education system, and take part in sports, camping, music, art programs, and all the other activities of their communities. In addition, they are socializing with people with and without disabilities, and as adults are obtaining employment and living in group homes and other independent housing arrangements.

Myth: Parents will not find community support in bringing up their child with Down syndrome.

Truth: In almost every community of the United States there are parent support groups and other community organizations directly involved in providing services to families of individuals with Down syndrome.

Myth: Children with Down syndrome must be placed in segregated special education programs.

Truth: Children with Down syndrome have been included in regular academic classrooms in schools across the country. In some instances they are integrated into specific courses, while in other situations students are fully included in the regular classroom for all subjects. The degree of mainstreaming is based in the abilities of the individual; but the trend is for full inclusion in the social and educational life of the community.

Myth: Adults with Down syndrome are unemployable.

Truth: Businesses are seeking young adults with Down syndrome for a variety of positions. They are being employed in small and medium sized offices: by banks, corporations, nursing homes, hotels, and restaurants. They work in the music and entertainment industry, in clerical positions, and in the computer industry. People with Down syndrome bring enthusiasm, reliability, and dedication to their jobs.

Myth: People with Down syndrome are always happy.

Truth: People with Down syndrome have feelings just like everyone else in the population. They respond to positive expressions of friendship and they are hurt and upset by inconsiderate behavior.

Myth: Adults with Down syndrome are unable to form close interpersonal relationships leading to marriage.

Truth: People with Down syndrome date, socialize, and form ongoing relationships. Some are beginning to marry. Women with Down syndrome can and do have children, but there is a 50 percent chance that their child will have Down syndrome. Men with Down syndrome are believed to be sterile, with only one documented instance of a male with Down syndrome who has fathered a child.

Myth: Down syndrome can never be cured.

Truth: Research on Down syndrome is making great strides in identifying the genes on chromosome 21 that cause the characteristics of Down syndrome. Scientists now feel strongly that it will be possible to improve, correct, or prevent many of the problems associated with Down syndrome in the future.

Periodicals and Newsletters

Update
Quarterly newsletter of the National Down Syndrome Society
666 Broadway
New York, NY 10012
Tel.: 800-221-4602

News & Views
Quarterly, full-color magazine for and by teens and young adults with Down syndrome, edited by actor and NDSS National Goodwill Ambassador, Chris Burke.
Published by the National Down Syndrome Society
666 Broadway
New York, NY 10012
Tel.: 800-221-4602

Exceptional Parent
Magazine for parents and professionals published eight times annually by the Psy-Ed Corporation. Subscription information available from
Exceptional Parent
P.O. Box 3000, Dept. EP
Denville, NJ 07834
Tel.: 800-562-1973

Down Syndrome News
Newsletter available from the National Down Syndrome Congress
7000 Peachtree-Dunwoody Rd., NE
Building #5, Suite 100
Atlanta, GA 30328
Tel.: 800-232-6372

Editor's Note: Chapter 47—Books, Videos, and Newletters contains a detailed listing of materials that give further information about Down syndrome.

Chapter 5

Clinical Information about Down Syndrome

The documents in this chapter are reprinted with the express consent and approval of the National Down Syndrome Society. Through education, research, and advocacy, NDSS works to ensure that all people with Down syndrome have the opportunity to achieve their full potential in community life. For more information call 800-221-4602 or visit www.ndss.org.

Contents

Editor's Note: Chapter 36—Alzheimer's Disease addresses Alzheimer's Disease and Down syndrome.

Section 5.1

The Heart and Down Syndrome

"The Heart and Down Syndrome," by Dr. Langford Kidd, Helen B. Taussig Professor, Director Division of Pediatric Cardiology, Johns Hopkins University, reprinted with permission © 1998, National Down Syndrome Society.

The Heart and Down Syndrome

Approximately half of all infants born with Down syndrome have a heart defect. Many of these defects have serious implications and it is important to understand them and how they may adversely affect the child so that we may provide the most appropriate medical care.

What Are the Most Common Heart Defects in Children with Down Syndrome?

The most common defects are Atrioventricular Septal Defect (formally called Endocardial Cushion Defect), Ventricular Septal Defect, Persistent Ductus Arteriosus, and Tetralogy of Fallot.

What Is an Atrioventricular Septal Defect?

An Atrioventricular Septal Defect is caused by a failure of tissue to come together in the heart during embryonic life. This results in a large opening in the center of the heart, usually with a hole between the two pumping chambers (a Ventricular Septal Defect) and between the two collecting chambers (an Atrial Septal Defect) as well as abnormalities of the two atrioventricular valves, the mitral and tricuspid valves. This defect occurs in nearly 60% of the children with Down syndrome who are born with congenital heart disease. In less severe cases, Ventricular Septal Defects and Atrial Septal Defects can also occur separately.

What Is Persistent Ductus Arteriosus?

The ductus arteriosus is a channel between the pulmonary artery and the aorta which during fetal life diverts blood away from the lungs. After birth this channel usually closes on the first day of life. If it does not close, it is termed "persistent" and results in an increased flow of blood into the lungs.

What Is Tetralogy of Fallot?

This is a term given to a heart condition in which there is both a Ventricular Septal Defect and a narrowing of the passage from the right ventricle to the lungs causing Pulmonary Stenosis. The Pulmonary Stenosis causes the blue blood in the right ventricle to cross the Ventricular Septal Defect into the aorta and produces what is commonly called a "blue baby."

What Are the Effects of Atrioventricular Septal Defect, Ventricular Septal Defect, and Persistent Ductus Arteriosus?

These defects result in increased blood flow going to the lungs as the blood goes through the septal defects or the ductus from the high pressure left heart into the low pressure right heart. This flooding of the lungs results in a buildup of pressure in the pulmonary circulation and this higher pressure and high flow leads to damage to the pulmonary circulation and pulmonary hypertension. In the first few months of life, signs of heart failure may be prominent with rapid breathing and failure to grow and gain weight. Later, progressive damage to the blood vessels and the lungs may result in reversal of the shunt and blueness of the skin (cyanosis).

What Is the Relationship of Heart Defects to the Respiratory System?

The lungs of children with Down syndrome do not develop as fully as in the general population. Consequently, the growth of blood vessels throughout the lungs is limited. The narrowed arteries of the lungs hold potential for long-lasting damage in the face of increased pressure and flow of blood through the lungs.

How Are the Defects Diagnosed?

Some children with Down syndrome and major heart defects will present with heart failure, difficulty breathing, and failure to thrive in the newborn period; however, because in some children the defect may not be at first apparent, it is important that all children born with Down syndrome, even those who have no symptoms of heart disease, should have an echocardiogram in the first two or three months of life.

What Is the Recommended Treatment?

Heart surgery to correct the defects is recommended and it must be done before age five or six months in order to prevent lung damage. Although the complexity of the defects raises the risk of surgery slightly above that of surgery on children without Down syndrome, successful surgery will allow many of the affected children to thrive as well as any child with Down syndrome who is born with a normal heart. There may be residual defects (such as imperfect valves, in cases of Atrioventricular Septal Defect), but their effect on health is often minimal.

What Are the Guidelines for Choosing a Hospital?

Look for a medical center in a major metropolitan area which has experience in open heart surgery on infants, and experience in operating on infants with Down syndrome in particular. A hospital that conducts at least 10 such operations a year, with a good survival rate, would be considered an experienced hospital.

What Should Be Considered in Selecting a Surgical Team?

Again, experience, together with the parents' rapport with the physician, should be the determining factor in the choice. It is important that an experienced anesthesiologist be selected, as children with Down syndrome often have airway problems.

- Congenital cardiac defects occur in up to 50 percent of children with Down syndrome.

- Early diagnosis via echocardiogram is crucial within the first two months of life, even if no symptoms are present.

- The majority of heart defects in children with Down syndrome can be surgically corrected with resulting long-term health improvements.

- Experience and success are the key factors in selecting a hospital and surgical team for heart surgery on infants with Down syndrome.

Section 5.2

Endocrine Conditions in Down Syndrome

"Endocrine Conditions in Down Syndrome," by Dr. Ernest McCoy, Professor of Pediatrics, University of Alberta, reprinted with permission © 1998, National Down Syndrome Society.

Endocrine Conditions in Down Syndrome

Individuals with Down syndrome have a higher incidence of endocrine problems than the general population. The endocrine system refers to a set of glands which includes the thyroid, adrenal, and pituitary glands.

What Is Hypothyroidism?

Hypothyroidism results from a malfunctioning thyroid gland, which decreases the synthesis of the hormone thyroxin. Thyroxin is the hormone that promotes growth of the brain and other body tissue.

How Common Is Hypothyroidism?

Hypothyroidism is the most common endocrine problem in children with Down syndrome. One study showed these individuals to be 28 times more prone to congenital hypothyroidism than the general population. It is estimated that approximately 10 percent of children with Down syndrome have congenital or acquired thyroid disease. Incidence of thyroid disease in adults with this genetic disorder varies from 13 to 50 percent. Hypothyroidism can occur at any time from infancy through adulthood.

How Is Hypothyroidism Diagnosed?

All individuals with Down syndrome should be tested for hypothyroidism at birth and at periodic intervals (at least every two years) thereafter. The indicators of hypothyroidism—enlarged tongue, constipation, and poor circulation—are also found in individuals who are

39

not hypothyroid, so the blood test for thyroid function is an important diagnostic test. As the thyroid hormone affects normal development of the brain, testing of infants is particularly crucial.

What Treatment Exists for Hypothyroidism?

The thyroid hormone, thyroxin, is readily replaced through medication.

What Is Hyperthyroidism?

In this case, the thyroid gland is overactive. Symptoms are swelling in the neck, abnormal sweating, and rapid pulse rate. No evidence exists as to whether hyperthyroidism is more prevalent in individuals with Down syndrome than in the general population.

Are People with Down Syndrome More Prone to Diabetes?

There is not sufficient data available at this point to know if there is increased risk for children with Down syndrome to develop type one diabetes as compared to the rate for their peers in the general population. However, research suggests that individuals who develop one type of endocrine autoimmune disorder, such as thyroiditis, are more likely to develop a second disorder, such as type one diabetes.

What Is the Status of Research on Use of the Growth Hormone for Children with Down Syndrome?

Use of growth hormone for children with Down syndrome is still in experimental stages. There are reports of increased rates of growth in children with Down syndrome who received the hormone for a brief period; however, these reports were not controlled studies, so there is no scientific evidence that long-term administration of the hormone would increase final height.

Can Any Growth Hormone Be Administered to Any Down Syndrome Child?

At present, doctors are licensed to prescribe growth hormone for individuals with Down syndrome only when there is a demonstrated deficiency of that hormone. It is strongly advised that such treatment be obtained only through a clinical trial until long-term benefits are demonstrated.

Section 5.3

The Neurology of Down Syndrome

"The Neurology of Down Syndrome," by Dr. Ira Lott, Professor of Pediatrics, University of California at Irvine, reprinted with permission © 1998, National Down Syndrome Society (NDSS).

The Neurology of Down Syndrome

Neurology, the study of the human nervous system and its disorders, is important in the clinical care treatment of a person with Down syndrome. The nervous system is always affected in Down syndrome; among the most common involvements of the nervous system are developmental disabilities (retardation in mental development and motor capabilities), hypotonia, atlantoaxial dislocation, and seizures.

What Does the Term "Developmental Disabilities" Mean in Relation to Down Syndrome?

This term refers to incomplete development of the brain, which leads to both mental retardation and to slowed and/or incomplete mastery of physical coordination.

What Is Known about Brain Pathology in Regard to Developmental Difficulties?

Pathology in the Down syndrome brain includes a slightly smaller brain size for age, a shorter diameter for the anterior-posterior brain measurement, an unusually steep slope to the posterior portions of the brain, and an insufficiently developed superior temporal gyrus. It is not known in what way these features contribute to the developmental disabilities of Down syndrome.

Has Any Progress Been Made in the Pathology of the Down Syndrome Brain Through Research?

Research in this area is being actively pursued, especially since it may yield clues to Alzheimer's disease and to the neuroscientific effects on learning and memory.

Is IQ (Intelligence Quotient) a Meaningful Measure in Down Syndrome?

No. IQ is not an adequate measure of the functional status of people with Down syndrome. For example, individuals with Down syndrome may have difficulty with grammar, but understand individual words, or have a sense of when to speak, at a par with their mental age.

What Can Be Done to Help People with Down Syndrome to Achieve Their Full Potential in the Face of Such Disabilities?

A variety of intervention programs, designed to begin in infancy and continue throughout learning years, help children with Down syndrome maximize their capabilities.

What Is Hypotonia?

Hypotonia refers to the reduced muscle tone that occurs in virtually all infants with Down syndrome. It is commonly seen in the flexor group, muscles which act to flex a joint. The muscle weakness ranges from mild to moderate to severe.

How Is Hypotonia Diagnosed?

Common hypotonic symptoms are a lagging head when the child is pulled into a sitting position and arching of the back when carried upright or lying on the stomach. In addition, hypotonic children will tire more easily and adopt movement patterns requiring the least expenditure of energy.

Are There Any Effective Interventions for Hypotonia?

Hypotonic conditions tend to improve with age. Gross motor programs offered by occupational and physical therapists have been shown to diminish hypotonic symptoms. These programs improve large body movements, such as walking, turning, sitting, standing, and climbing stairs. Enrollment of children in an early intervention program which includes gross motor programs is recommended at the earliest feasible age, generally between four and six weeks of age.

What is Atlantoaxial Dislocation?

Atlantoaxial dislocation refers to a problem caused by hypotonia. The ligaments at the first two cervical vertebra are more relaxed than they should be, putting the individual at risk of spinal cord compression and injury.

How Common Is Atlantoaxial Dislocation?

The cervical spine instability occurs in 10 to 20 percent of children with Down syndrome; however, actual spinal compression is rare.

What Are the Symptoms of Atlantoaxial Dislocation?

If symptoms are present, they include neck pain, change in gait, onset of weakness in the extremities, spasticity, limited neck movement, and bowel/bladder incontinence (particularly after toilet training has been accomplished). However, most children with x-ray evidence of atlantoaxial dislocation have no apparent symptoms.

What Preventive Measures Should Be Taken?

Since most children with atlantoaxial dislocation do not exhibit symptoms, lateral cervical x-rays are recommended for all children with Down syndrome after age two. If the instability is present, but there are no symptoms, the appropriate precaution is to limit "high risk" activities which might over-stress the neck. These activities include high-jumping, diving, gymnastics, trampoline, and butterfly strokes in swimming. To devise a safe exercise program for a symptom-free child with atlantoaxial dislocation, consult your doctor.

Is There Any Treatment for Atlantoaxial Dislocation?

If symptoms are present, the atlantoaxial joint can be surgically fused.

What Is the Incidence of Seizures in Down Syndrome?

In the young child with Down syndrome, seizures are no more common than in the general population. Beginning at age 20-30, the incidence of seizure disorder rises substantially in the Down syndrome population. Research is ongoing as to whether the frequencies of seizures in individuals with Down syndrome is related to the aging of the brain.

What Is the Typical Seizure for a Person with Down Syndrome?

Seizures for individuals with Down syndrome commonly look like epileptic seizures: jerking of arms and legs and loss of consciousness.

Seizures can also take a mixed form, with staring spells and momentary lapses of attention.

What Is the Treatment for Seizures?

Seizures can be controlled with standard anti-convulsant medication.

Section 5.4

Sexuality in Down Syndrome

"Sexuality in Down Syndrome," by Dr. William Schwab, Associate Professor, Department of Family Medicine and Practice, University of Wisconsin, reprinted with permission © 1998, National Down Syndrome Society (NDSS).

Sexuality in Down Syndrome

Human sexuality encompasses an individual's self-esteem, interpersonal relationships, and social experiences relating to dating, marriage, and the physical aspects of sex. Sex education, appropriate for the developmental level and intellectual attainment of individuals with Down syndrome, helps in engendering healthy sexuality, preventing unwanted pregnancy and diseases, and in alleviating other problems related to sexual function.

Do Individuals with Down Syndrome Have Sexual Feelings?

In the past, sexuality was not considered an issue for young people with Down syndrome because of the inaccurate belief that mental retardation was equivalent to permanent childhood. In fact, all people with Down syndrome do have intimacy needs, and it is important that these be recognized and planned for in education, residential, and other programs and settings.

Do Children with Down Syndrome Develop Physically the Same Way as Their Peers in the General Population?

Children with Down syndrome experience the same sequence of physical and hormonal changes associated with puberty as other children their age.

Do Children with Down Syndrome Experience the Emotional Upheavals Characteristic of Adolescence?

The emotional changes characteristic of adolescence are also present in children with Down syndrome, and may be intensified by social factors. Any adolescent who lives in the community, attends school, and is exposed to media inevitably develops an awareness of sexuality. Teenagers and young adults with Down syndrome often express interest in dating, marriage, and parenthood. They can be expected to experience typical adolescent changes in mood and outlook.

What Kind of Sex Education Is Appropriate for Individuals with Down Syndrome?

To be effective, education must be individualized and understandable, focusing not only on the physical reproductive aspects, but also positioning sexuality within the context of all interpersonal relationships. An ideal curriculum will ensure that the individual's understanding of relationships, sexual intercourse, and parenting is factual, realistic, and socially acceptable.

How Can Healthy Sexuality Be Encouraged for Individuals with Down Syndrome?

Creating an environment conducive to healthy sexual expression must be considered in designing educational, vocational, recreational, and residential programs. Positive sexual awareness can only develop through self-esteem, understanding of social relationships, and personal interaction/communication skills. All these factors influence how intimacy needs are met.

Do Women with Down Syndrome Have Any Special Needs or Concerns in Regard to Birth Control?

Women with Down syndrome are fertile and may use any method of contraception without added medical risk. The method chosen will depend on personal preference, ability to use the contraceptive effectively, and possible side effects. Surgical sterilization may also be performed without added risk for women with Down syndrome who are in stable medical condition; however, availability of this procedure to women who are developmentally disabled may be controlled by state law.

Are There Any Special Needs for Individuals with Down Syndrome in Regard to Disease Prevention?

Men and women with Down syndrome have the same susceptibility to sexually transmitted diseases as the rest of the population. Use of condoms during sexual intercourse is the best known form of protection against AIDS, herpes, and other sexually transmitted diseases.

How Can a Person with Down Syndrome Be Protected Against Sexual Abuse?

It is highly recommended that age-appropriate education in protective behaviors should begin in childhood and be reinforced throughout the life of the person with Down syndrome. Individuals with Down syndrome must be taught the boundaries of normal physical interactions in the social sphere, as well as the self-assertion skills to enlist help if necessary.

Female Sexuality in Down Syndrome

Do Girls with Down Syndrome Have Normal Menstrual Periods?

Menstruation for girls with Down syndrome is no different than for their peers in the general population. On the average, they begin menstruating at age 12.5, but may begin as early as age 10 or as late as age 14 without being in any way abnormal. Most girls with Down syndrome have regular cycles with the same minor irregularities typical of their peer group.

If a Women with Down Syndrome Experiences Major Irregularities of the Menstrual Cycle, What Problems Will This Point to Other than Pregnancy?

Alterations in a previously regular cycle may be due to the normal process of aging, or may be a sign of emerging hyperthyroidism. Ongoing irregularity of menstrual cycle warrants medical examination.

If a Woman with Down Syndrome Becomes Pregnant, Will the Baby Be Normal?

At least half of all women with Down syndrome do ovulate and are fertile. Between 35 and 50 percent of children born to mothers with Down syndrome will have trisomy 21 or other developmental difficulties.

When Is the Onset of Menopause for Women with Down Syndrome?

Menopause may occur at a wide range of ages. Typically it takes place after age 40.

Male Sexuality in Down Syndrome

Are Males with Down Syndrome Fertile?

Scientific information about the fertility of men with Down syndrome is limited. While most textbooks indicate that no man with Down syndrome is known to have fathered a child, geneticists in England recently reported a case in which the paternity of a man with Down syndrome was confirmed. It is likely that additional cases will be recognized—especially as more men have the opportunity to live in the community and develop intimate relationships. It is not known if the offspring of men with Down syndrome are more likely to have Down syndrome or other anomalies. It does seem clear that, in general, men with Down syndrome have a lower overall fertility rate than that of other men of comparable ages. An individual's status can be partially assessed by having a semen analysis done, but this may not be definitive. Therefore, if a couple desires pregnancy prevention, contraception should always be used.

Does the Boy with Down Syndrome Mature Later Than His Peer Group in the General Population?

The onset of puberty in boys may be slightly delayed, but this is not a major factor. Genital anatomy is comparable to that of boys who do not have Down syndrome.

Section 5.5

Vitamin Therapies, Piracetam, and Cosmetic Surgery

National Down Syndrome Society Position Statements on Vitamin Related Therapies, Use of Piracetam, and Cosmetic Surgery for Children with Down Syndrome, reprinted with permission © 1998, National Down Syndrome Society (NDSS).

Vitamin Related Therapies

The National Down Syndrome Society cautions parents that the administration of the vitamin related therapies, e.g. the vitamin/mineral/amino acid/hormone/enzyme combination, has not been shown to be of benefit in a controlled trial, that the rationale advanced for these therapies is unproved, and that the previous use of these therapies has not produced any scientifically validated significant results. Moreover, the long-term effects of chronic administration of many of the ingredients in these preparations are unknown.

Despite the large sums of money which concerned parents have spent for such treatments in the hope that the conditions of their child with Down syndrome would be bettered, there is no evidence that any such benefit has been produced.

Use of Piracetam

Recently, information from nationally televised programs and mass mailings has suggested that children with Down syndrome may benefit from treatment with amino acid supplements and a drug known as Piracetam. Piracetam is a psychoactive drug that some believe may improve cognitive function, but this theory has not been clinically tested. The American College of Medical Genetics has most recently announced that it is not aware of any definitive scientific proof that either treatment is beneficial.

The National Down Syndrome Society does not recommend the use of drugs that have not undergone rigorous research for individuals with Down syndrome. An appropriate scientific study must be a blind

48

trial that compares results in individuals who have taken the drug with individuals who have been given a placebo. Such studies have not been done for Piracetam.

Because of the absence of solid scientific research to support the efficacy of these therapies and the lack of approval by the Food and Drug Administration for the sale of Piracetam in the United States, the National Down Syndrome Society does not recommend the use of Piracetam for children with Down syndrome.

The National Down Syndrome Society supports the American College of Medical Genetics' call for establishing well-designed randomized trials of each of these modalities to determine what, if any, benefits they may offer to children with Down syndrome.

Surgery for Children with Down Syndrome

The decision to have cosmetic surgery is always a personal one, and the National Down Syndrome Society (NDSS) supports people with Down syndrome and their families in their individual choices. However, NDSS believes that such a decision should be an informed one made by the family with the help of doctors, counselors, and other interested parties.

For 20 years, NDSS has worked for inclusion and acceptance for all people with Down syndrome. Today more than ever, people with Down syndrome learn in regular classrooms, are employed in a variety of jobs, and interact in many different ways in the larger community. NDSS believes in supporting individuals with Down syndrome through full inclusion in the community, and not attaching a stigma to their physical features.

The goal of inclusion and acceptance is mutual respect based on who we are as individuals, not how we look. Altering a child's appearance as a means of encouraging acceptance does not change the reality of the disability.

In fact, some education experts believe that the physical characteristics of Down syndrome may offer visual cues to people about an individual's disability, and thus foster an easier acceptance and understanding of that disability. Many families believe that to alter their child's facial features would be to disrespect his or her individuality and that an important part of that individuality is the condition of Down syndrome.

It should be noted that cosmetic surgery is performed on a very small number of people with Down syndrome. NDSS advises parents considering cosmetic surgery to become educated about all aspects of the procedure as well as the physical, social and psychological consequences for their child, and to make an informed decision based on this knowledge.

Chapter 6

Inclusive Education for Children with Down Syndrome

Creative approaches to inclusive schooling are being discovered throughout the United States every day as parents and educators work together to meet the unique needs of their students. Today it is common to see youngsters with Down syndrome, in every part of the country, included in their neighborhood schools. Boys and girls, in rural, urban, and suburban locations, at the preschool, elementary, and secondary level are able to enjoy the company of their peers and the activities of the regular school setting.

Inclusion in the regular classroom is only one of the many options available to children with Down syndrome. It is, however, an important one. This chapter is designed to familiarize you with the philosophy and practice of inclusion.

Inclusion Is...

A Philosophy. It is a belief in every person's inherent right to participate fully in society. Inclusion implies acceptance of differences. It means making room for a person who would otherwise be excluded. Translating this philosophy into reality is a process that requires collaboration, teamwork, flexibility, a willingness to take risks, and support from a whole array of individuals, services, and institutions.

Reprinted with the express consent and approval of the National Down Syndrome Society © 1999. Through education, research, and advocacy, NDSS works to ensure that all people with Down syndrome have the opportunity to achieve their full potential in community life. For more information call 800-221-4602 or visit www.ndss.org.

A Practice. It is the educational process by which all students, even those with disabilities, are educated together, with sufficient support, in age-appropriate, regular education programs in their neighborhood schools. The goal of inclusive education is to prepare all students for productive lives as full, participating members of their communities.

Evolving. As people learn more about inclusion, they understand that "full inclusion" means that students with Down syndrome are part of the regular education system even if their curricular goals and needs differ from those of their classmates.

Rewarding for all people involved. When inclusion is carried out appropriately, research has demonstrated benefits to students with Down syndrome as well as to their peers. Friendships develop, students without disabilities learn to appreciate differences and students with disabilities are more motivated. All of this is carried home and into the community.

Inclusion Is Not...

A Passing Fad. Numerous federal district court decisions have affirmed the right of students with Down syndrome to attend regular classes full time when the educational benefits for the student warrant such a placement. Inclusion, with its focus on outcomes, is the spirit of the Individuals with Disabilities Education Act (IDEA) and the trend for the future.

Dumping. It does not mean that a child with special needs is placed in a classroom without adequate support and appropriate services. It does not mean that undue burdens are placed on teachers and peers. Thoughtful planning, continual monitoring, and sufficient support are all part of successful inclusion programs.

Easy. Parents, educators, peers, and administrators are all partners in the inclusion process and must work together to make it successful. On-going problem solving is involved.

Mainstreaming. Inclusion is more than mainstreaming. Mainstreaming implies that a child from a special education class visits the regular class for specific, usually non-academic, subjects. Inclusion means that a student with special needs is part of the regular class, even if he or she receives occasional services in another setting.

What Makes Inclusion Successful?

- **A commitment to the philosophy** of inclusion and a belief in the equal value of all students must be shared by everyone. Many school districts make explicit mention in their mission statements that the educational goals of students with disabilities are of equal value to those of other students.

- **Accountability** assures that all individuals, at the district, building, and classroom level delegate tasks appropriately and fulfill their responsibilities. The department of special education should have clearly defined policies for program implementation.

- **Careful assessment and planning** guarantees that the student's curriculum is appropriate; adequate support is provided; and long and short-term goals are met. Assessment should focus on the child's strengths and parents should actively participate in the design of the Individualized Education Program (IEP).

- **Collaboration** requires that all participants be equal partners. Teachers will be working together in and out of the classroom; peers will become allies and friends; and parents will continually be interacting with the school system. The need for teamwork is constant and only through cooperative effort does inclusion work.

- **Flexibility** must be present at every stage of the inclusion process. Because teaching models are often altered, curriculum adaptations made, and unique needs addressed, all participants must be willing to accept compromise and try new situations.

- **Funding** must be available for the necessary support services. Some research has shown that districts which are implementing inclusion are not spending more than their segregated counterparts; rather, they are shifting costs.

- **Good leadership** sets the tone for the entire process. Principals and superintendents must convey a positive attitude towards inclusion and foster a supportive environment in which new and challenging situations are dealt with in a flexible manner. Teachers who have the encouragement and backing of their supervisors are often the most successful initiators of change.

- **Social skills and peer relationships** are two of the most important foundations for, and by-products of, inclusion. Peers are positive role models for speech and appropriate behavior. As allies and friends, peers offer support in and out of the classroom: in cooperative learning situations; in peer support groups; and in after-school activities. Friendships develop which extend beyond the classroom.

- **Support** includes everything necessary to meet the goals established in the IEP. Additional personnel may be present in the classroom; peers may form a support network; curricula may be adapted; teaching methods may change; physical accommodations may be made; and therapies may be given. Support can be extensive or minimal, depending on the needs of the particular student. For teachers, support may mean encouragement from supervisors; collaboration with peers; team teaching; feedback from parents; or access to the many resources available on inclusion.

- **Transition planning** alleviates potential problems. Before the school year begins, teachers and staff should have appropriate training; the student with Down syndrome should be familiar with his or her surroundings; and peers should receive orientation. Knowledge about Down syndrome and the abilities of people with Down syndrome will lessen the apprehension of teachers and classmates.

What Can You Do to Foster Your Child's Inclusion?

- **Become aware of your rights under federal and state laws**. Learn about IDEA and what it means for your child. If you request an appropriate inclusion program, your school system is required to provide it. A child cannot be placed in a more restrictive environment unless the school system has shown that inclusion was unsuccessful despite the provision of appropriate support and services.

- **Communicate with the school system**. Help administrators and teachers develop methods that will work well. Provide insight and awareness regarding the needs and goals of your child.

- **Learn about successful inclusion practices**. Contact parents, organizations, and schools that have made inclusion work. Write for information from the growing number of national organizations that have a proven commitment to inclusion. Form support networks. Avail yourself of the numerous publications and videos available.

- **Participate in the design of your child's IEP**. The goals and objectives listed in the IEP will determine not only what your child is taught, but how and where that teaching will take place.

Since the passage of Public Law 94-142 in 1975, educational options for children with Down syndrome have expanded greatly. IEPs are now provided for all children with special needs; parent involvement in the planning process is sought; and advocacy and support is widely available. Inclusion represents the latest effort to provide all children with the best education possible in the diversity of their neighborhood school.

Additional Information

For more information about materials to help you along the road to inclusion, or parent groups that may have experience working with schools, contact

National Down Syndrome Society
666 Broadway
New York, NY 10012

Terminology

Cooperative Learning—A group of students with diverse skills and traits working together. This promotes collaboration, teamwork and an appreciation of differences while fostering long-term relationships.

IDEA—The federal law supporting special education and related service programming for children and youth with disabilities. Also referred to as Public Law 101-476, IDEA reauthorized and expanded the provisions guaranteed under Public Law 94-142 in 1990.

Public Law 94-142—The Education for All Handicapped Children Act of 1975. This law mandates a free appropriate public education (FAPE) for all children with disabilities; education in the least restrictive environment (LRE); and individualized education programs. It ensures due process rights and is the core of federal funding for special education. It was renamed and amended in 1990 and is now known as IDEA.

FAPE—A free appropriate public education refers to special education and related services which are provided at public expense to meet the educational goals defined in the child's IEP.

IEP—The individualized education program is the written plan for each school year which delineates the goals and special services necessary to meet the child's needs. Parents, teachers, and administrators take part in the preparation of the child's IEP for the academic year.

LRE—The Least Restrictive Environment provision of the IDEA states that to the maximum extent appropriate, children with disabilities are educated with children who do not have disabilities "and that special classes, separate schooling, or other removal of ... children from the regular educational environment occurs only when the nature or severity of the handicap is such that education in regular classes with the use of supplementary aids and services cannot be achieved satisfactorily."

Teaching—A broad term referring to different groupings of teachers. One common method is to have a regular education teacher team up with a general education teacher and together be responsible for all the children of the class. All team teaching is based on shared responsibility and collaboration.

Nationwide Study Finds Inclusive Education Rewarding for All Involved

The inclusion of students with Down syndrome in typical classrooms is a more rewarding experience than expected for both students and classmates, according to a recently released national study.

Inclusion is the educational process by which all students, with or without disabilities, are educated together, with sufficient support, in age-appropriate, regular education programs in their neighborhood schools. Support is often provided in a "push-in" (in-class aid), or "pull-out" (visits to a resource room) basis.

The majority of teachers who participated in the nationwide study, commissioned by the National Down Syndrome Society (NDSS) and conducted by Gloria Wolpert, Ed.D., reported that entire classes benefit from working with a student with Down syndrome. Almost all teachers who responded found inclusion enjoyable, with some calling it the single most interesting and rewarding experience of their careers.

The NDSS study was conducted to determine the success, or lack of success, of inclusive practices, and to identify the common characteristics of the most successful programs. The study included a nationwide survey of parents and teachers. Overall, both parents and teachers find current inclusive practices successful, but there is room for improvement. The study found that more appropriate teacher preparation and more time for conferences between teachers, therapists, parents, and support personnel would be beneficial to all involved.

Factors which directly affect the success of an inclusive experience, as measured by both parents and teachers, include a match of teacher personality and style to the skills of a student. Teachers who are flexible, willing to modify classroom materials, and who utilize hands-on learning tools are the bests catalysts for achievement.

Those parents whose children with Down syndrome had friends in class rated the inclusion experience the most successful and reported great benefits in the areas of communication, self esteem, and independence. Teacher preparation is important for success, but surprisingly, formal training from the school district does not appear to be relevant.

A copy of the Educational Challenges Inclusion Study, which includes suggestions for classroom practice, can be obtained by sending a check or money order for $10 to cover printing and postage, to the NDSS Educational Challenges Program, 666 Broadway, 8th Floor, New York, NY 10012-2317.

Editor's Note: A list of organizations, publications, and other materials that present a commitment to the philosophy and practice of inclusion is available in Chapter 47—Books, Videos, and Newsletters.

Chapter 7

Fetal Alcohol Syndrome: Drinking Can Hurt Your Baby

What Is Fetal Alcohol Syndrome?

Fetal Alcohol Syndrome (FAS) and Fetal Alcohol Effects (FAE) refer to a group of physical and mental birth defects resulting from a woman's drinking alcohol during pregnancy. FAS is the leading known cause of mental retardation. Other symptoms can include organ dysfunction, growth deficiencies before and after birth, central nervous dysfunction resulting in learning disabilities and lower IQ, and physical malformities in the face and cranial areas. In addition, children may experience behavioral and mental problems, which progress into adulthood.

FAE is a lesser set of the same symptoms, which make up FAS. Babies affected by alcohol can have any or all of these symptoms. FAS and FAE are widely under-diagnosed. Some experts believe that between 1/3 and 2/3 of all special education children have been irreversibly affected by alcohol in some way. At least 5,000 infants are born each year with FAS; another 50,000 children show symptoms of FAE.

If you drink wine, beer, or liquor when you are pregnant, your baby could develop FAS. A baby with FAS can suffer from mental retardation,

---

This chapter includes text from "What Is FAS?" and "FAS Fact Sheet," © 1998, reprinted with permission of The National Organization on Fetal Alcohol Syndrome; "Fetal Alcohol Syndrome," *Alcohol Alert* No. 13-1991, National Institute on Alcohol Abuse and Alcoholism (NIAAA), July 1991; and "Facts about Alcohol Use During Pregnancy," © 1992, reprinted with permission of The Arc.

59

central nervous dysfunction, organ dysfunction, and facial abnormalities. These disabilities will last a lifetime. No amount of alcohol has been proven safe to consume during pregnancy. FAS and FAE are 100% preventable when a pregnant woman abstains from alcohol.

Thirty to forty percent of babies whose mothers drink heavily throughout pregnancy have the syndrome. FAS/FAE is a problem found in all races and socio-economic groups. FAS and FAE are widely under-diagnosed.

All communities nationwide, and especially high-risk women in their childbearing years, need better information about the dangers of drinking during pregnancy. But most health care providers are unfamiliar with and untrained in the issues of substance abuse among pregnant women. FAS/FAE is widely misdiagnosed and under-diagnosed less than 10% of medical schools require students to complete a course on the proper diagnosis and referral of individuals with alcoholism and other drug additions.

FAS/FAE produces irreversible physical, mental, and emotional effects. Behavioral and mental problems of FAE children can be just as severe as those of FAS children. Many children with FAS/FAE are not able to understand cause and effect relationships and long-term consequences. The institutional and medical costs for one child with FAS are $1.4 million over a lifetime.

Important Facts about Fetal Alcohol Syndrome

No amount of alcohol consumption during pregnancy is known to be safe.

- FAS is the leading known cause of mental retardation, surpassing both Spina Bifida and Down's Syndrome. (*Journal of the American Medical Association*, 1991)

- At least one of every five pregnant women uses alcohol and/or other drugs. (*Substance Abuse and the American Woman*, Center on Addiction and Substance Abuse, Columbia University, June 5, 1996)

- Alcohol produces by far the most serious neurobehavioral effects in the fetus when compared to other drugs including heroin, cocaine, and marijuana. Annual cost estimates for FAS and related conditions in the United States range from $75 million to $9.7 billion. (*Fetal Alcohol Syndrome: Diagnosis, Epidemiology, Prevention and Treatment, Institute of Medicine*, 1996)

- The Centers for Disease Control and Prevention reported a six-fold increase in the percentage of babies born with FAS over the past fifteen years. Since the Centers began tracking FAS, the rate has increased from 1 case per 10,000 live births in 1979 to 6.7 cases per 10,000 live births in 1993. (*The New York Times*, April 7, 1995)

- Over three times as many women used alcohol during pregnancy than used illegal drugs. (National Institute on Drug Abuse, 1994)

- Each year more than 5,000 are born with FAS and nearly 50,000 babies are born with Fetal Alcohol Effects (FAE), a condition characterized by symptoms similar to but less severe than FAS. (*Public Health Education Information Sheet*, March of Dimes, 1992)

- Fewer that 57% of Americans under the age of 45 have even heard of FAS. Of those, less than 25% can correctly identify it as a set of birth defects while the rest think it means being born intoxicated or addicted to alcohol. (*National Health Interview Survey*, U.S. Department of Health and Human Services, 1985)

- An average of one to two reported drinks per day has been linked to decreased birth-weight, growth abnormalities, and behavioral problems. (*Alcohol Problems in Women*, 1984)

- The probability of having a child with FAS increases with the amount and frequency of alcohol consumed. Whenever a pregnant woman stops drinking, she reduces the risk of having a baby with FAS. (*Alcohol Health and Research World*, The National Institute on Alcohol Abuse and Alcoholism, 1995)

- The latest estimate for the U.S. is a rate of 19.5 per 10,000 live births, although estimates run as high as 30 per 10,000—about 12,000 babies a year. (*Substance Abuse and the American Woman*, Center on Addiction and Substance Abuse, Columbia University, June 5, 1996)

- A 100% misdiagnosis rate was reported in a Houston hospital study of 48 newborns known to have alcoholic mothers. By age one, six of the infants had significant signs of FAS but none had been diagnosed at birth. (*Little, Bertis, Snell, Laura*, 1990)

- A federally funded study in four U.S. southern communities found that only 65% of women were asked by a physician or nurse about alcohol or drug use during their most recent pregnancy. Further, although most of the women who were asked acknowledged substance abuse, only 3% were referred to treatment. (*Shelly Geshan, Southern Regional Project on Infant Mortality*, 1993).

- A national panel convened by the Josiah Macy Jr. Foundation found that most doctors do not even try to identify problems by asking patients questions about alcohol and drug habits, and do not know how to respond if they do find evidence of dependency. The panel called for an increase in mandatory training on substance abuse for medical residents as the first step toward improving treatment. (*The New York Times*, February 14, 1996)

- A National Center for Health Statistics study found that doctors appear less likely to tell black women to quit drinking and smoking during pregnancy than they are to tell white women. Pregnant black women were thirty percent more likely than white women to report that they had never been told to quit drinking, and twenty percent more likely to report that they had not been told to quit smoking. (*The New York Times*, January 19, 1994)

History and Research of Fetal Alcohol Syndrome

In 1973, Jones and Smith (1) coined the term "fetal alcohol syndrome" (FAS) to describe a pattern of abnormalities observed in children born to alcoholic mothers. It was originally postulated that malnutrition might be responsible for these defects. However, the pattern of malformation associated with FAS is not seen in children born to malnourished women, and alcohol has been found to be acutely toxic to the fetus independently of the effects of malnutrition (2,3).

Criteria for defining FAS were standardized by the Fetal Alcohol Study Group of the Research Society on Alcoholism in 1980 (4), and modifications were proposed in 1989 by Sokol and Clarren (5). The proposed criteria are:

1. prenatal and/or postnatal growth retardation (weight and/or length below the 10th percentile)

2. central nervous system involvement, including neurological abnormalities, developmental delays, behavioral dysfunction, intellectual impairment, and skull or brain malformations

3. a characteristic face with short palpebral fissures (eye openings), a thin upper lip, and an elongated, flattened midface and philtrum (the groove in the middle of the upper lip).

Sokol and Clarren (5) suggested the term "alcohol-related birth defects" (ARBD) to describe anatomic or functional abnormalities attributed to prenatal alcohol exposure. The term "possible fetal alcohol effect(s)" (FAE) indicates that alcohol is being considered as one of the possible causes of a patient's birth defects. In the view of Sokol and Clarren, the frequent use of this term to indicate a birth defect judged milder than FAS is incorrect, although others continue to use it that way (5).

Mental handicaps and hyperactivity are probably the most debilitating aspects of FAS (6), and prenatal alcohol exposure is one of the leading known causes of mental retardation in the Western World (7). Problems with learning, attention, memory, and problem solving are common, along with uncoordination, impulsiveness, and speech and hearing impairment (8,6). Deficits in learning skills persist even into adolescence and adulthood (6,9).

It is generally accepted that the adverse effects of prenatal alcohol exposure exist along a continuum, with the complete FAS syndrome at one end of the spectrum and incomplete features of FAS, including more subtle cognitive-behavioral deficits, on the other. Thus, infants with suboptimal neurobehavioral responses may later exhibit subtle deficits in such aspects of daily life as judgment, problem solving, and memory (6).

Studies of the incidence of FAS are complicated by methodological problems. Data have been collected in various ways:

1. in the catchment approach, birth defects are monitored at the time of birth only

2. in retrospective studies, children are identified as having FAS at some time after birth

3. in prospective studies, children are followed over time and assessed at various intervals from birth onward.

Catchment data tend to underestimate FAS incidence because the neonatal period is a difficult time to detect FAS. Not only are facial features associated with the syndrome difficult to recognize, but the central nervous system dysfunction, including mental retardation, may not be identified until several years after birth (5,10,11). On the

63

other hand, retrospective and prospective studies may overestimate FAS incidence by over-sampling populations where FAS incidence is unusually high (10). Analyses are further complicated by the unreliability of self-reports of maternal drinking (12).

Catchment data on the incidence of FAS are derived from the Birth Defects Monitoring Program of the Centers for Disease Control (CDC) (13). Based on data from 1,500 hospitals, CDC reported the nationwide incidence of FAS to be 0.3–0.9 per 10,000 births (excluding Native Americans). In contrast, Abel and Sokol (10) surveyed 19 published epidemiologic studies worldwide. The overall rate from all studies was 1.9 cases per 1,000 live births. The average for retrospective studies surveyed by Abel and Sokol was 2.9 per 1,000, compared with 1.1 per 1,000 for prospective studies. Most reported cases in the United States came from study sites where the mothers were black or Native American and of low socioeconomic status. The estimated rate at these sites was 2.6 per 1,000 compared with 0.6 per 1,000 from other study sites, where the mothers were predominantly white and of middle socioeconomic status (10).

According to the CDC catchment study, incidences of FAS per 10,000 total births for different ethnic groups were as follows: Asians 0.3, Hispanics 0.8, whites 0.9, blacks 6.0, and Native Americans 29.9 (13). Because of differences in study design, the ratios among the various ethnic groups derived from the CDC catchment data cannot be used to estimate FAS incidence for different ethnic groups as obtained from prospective and retrospective studies. Among Native Americans, the incidence of FAS varies among different cultures. Health units serving principally Navajo and Pueblo tribes report an FAS prevalence similar to that for the overall U.S. population, while for Southwest Plains Indians, a much higher prevalence was reported (1 case per 102 live births) (14). Several factors, such as cultural influences, patterns of alcohol consumption, nutrition, and metabolic differences have been suggested to play a role in this difference (15).

In the case of blacks, the risk of FAS remains about sevenfold higher than for whites, even after adjustment for the frequency of maternal alcohol intake, occurrence of chronic alcohol problems, and parity (number of children borne) (16). This raises the question of some kind of genetic susceptibility, the nature of which is unknown.

Apart from epidemiology, the key questions in FAS research include, How much alcohol is too much? and, When is the fetus at greatest risk? The major problem in addressing these questions is the lack of a specific physiological measure that accurately reflects alcohol consumption. There is no biological marker currently available to measure alcohol intake, and self-reports of alcohol consumption may be unreliable, perhaps especially so during pregnancy (17). Morrow-Tlucak and colleagues (18) found that women with more-serious alcohol-related problems are those more likely to underreport their alcohol consumption when interviewed during pregnancy.

While it is apparent that children who meet the criteria for FAS are born only to those mothers who consume large amounts of alcohol during pregnancy, studies have reported neurobehavioral deficits and intrauterine growth retardation in infants born to mothers who reported themselves to be moderate alcohol consumers during pregnancy (19,20,21). In a prospective study of 359 newborns, Ernhart and colleagues (22) found a trend toward increasing head and facial abnormalities with increasing embryonic alcohol exposure. An effect occurred at even the lowest reported levels of alcohol intake, so that a clear threshold (minimum amount of alcohol to produce an effect) could not be defined (22).

Given the range of defects that result from prenatal alcohol exposure, the search for an overall threshold for fetal risk may be unreasonable. Instead, each abnormal outcome in brain structure and function and growth might have its own dose-response relationship (23). Animal research has shown that different profiles of alcohol-related birth defects are related to critical periods for specific aspects of fetal development (3). Thus, heavy alcohol consumption throughout pregnancy results in a wide variety of effects characteristic of FAS, while episodic binge drinking at high levels results in partial expression of the syndrome, with the abnormalities being unique to the period of exposure (24). Vulnerability of individual organ systems may be greatest at the time of their most rapid cell division (25).

An important strategy for preventing alcohol-related birth defects is the development of better screening techniques to identify women at high risk for heavy alcohol consumption throughout their pregnancy. Currently available laboratory tests for detecting biochemical markers of heavy drinking are not as sensitive as self-report screening instruments, whereas the latter are complicated by denial (12).

A possible way to overcome denial might be to inquire about past, rather than present, drinking. This is suggested by the results of a study showing that self-reports of first trimester drinking made at the seventh month of pregnancy are often higher than those made at the fourth month (26). The researchers suggested that women may feel safer reporting higher levels of drinking farther away from the event. Although this strategy may not reveal a drinking problem until relatively late in pregnancy, intervention at this time is still useful. While abstaining during the second trimester does not eliminate the risk of fetal abnormalities, it does seem to mitigate some of the behavioral effects that may occur shortly after birth (27,20).

Sokol and colleagues (12) developed a simple and brief questionnaire to help circumvent denial and underreporting of heavy drinking by pregnant women. The test instrument, referred to as T-ACE, correctly identified 69 percent of the "risk drinkers" (defined as those consuming 1 ounce of absolute alcohol per day, equivalent to two standard drinks per day) out of a cohort of 971 pregnant women. T-ACE was found to be superior to other standard instruments used for detecting alcohol abuse, such as MAST and CAGE. The test is brief, and may be administered easily in prenatal clinics and obstetricians' offices. Its key feature is a tolerance ("T") question, "How many drinks does it take to make you feel 'high?'" (Tolerance is acquired by drinking.) Clinical experience suggests that questions about tolerance are less apt to be perceived by lay persons as an indication of drinking, and are therefore less likely to trigger denial (12). A more reliable indicator of heavy drinking awaits the development of objective biochemical markers.

References

1. Jones, K.L., & Smith, D.W. Recognition of the fetal alcohol syndrome in early infancy. *Lancet* 2:999-1001, 1973.

2. Phillips, D.K.; Henderson, G.I.; & Schenker, S. Pathogenesis of fetal alcohol syndrome: Overview with emphasis on the possible role of nutrition. *Alcohol Health & Research World* 13(3):219-227, 1989.

3. Randall, C.L. Alcohol as a teratogen: A decade of research in review. *Alcohol and Alcoholism Suppl.* 1:125-132, 1987.

4. Rosett, H.L. A clinical perspective of the fetal alcohol syndrome. *Alcoholism: Clinical and Experimental Research* 4(2):119-122, 1980.

5. Sokol, R.J., & Clarren, S.K. Guidelines for use of terminology describing the impact of prenatal alcohol on the offspring. *Alcoholism: Clinical and Experimental Research* 13(4):597-598, 1989.

6. Streissguth, A.P.; Sampson, P.D.; & Barr, H.M. Neurobehavioral dose-response effects of prenatal alcohol exposure in humans

from infancy to adulthood. *Annals of the New York Academy of Sciences* 562:145-158, 1989.

7. Abel, E.L., & Sokol, R.J. Fetal alcohol syndrome is now leading cause of mental etardation. *Lancet* 2:1222, 1986.

8. Streissguth, A.P., & LaDue, R.A. Psychological and behavioral effects in children prenatally exposed to alcohol. *Alcohol Health & Research World* 10(1):6-12, 1985.

9. Streissguth, A.P.; Aase, J.M.; Clarren, S.K.; Randels, S.P.; LaDue, R.A.; & Smith, D.F. Fetal alcohol syndrome in adolescents and adults. *Journal of the American Medical Association* 265(15):1961-1967, 1991.

10. Abel, E.L., & Sokol, R.J. Incidence of fetal alcohol syndrome and economic impact of FAS-related anomalies. *Drug and Alcohol Dependence* 19:51-70, 1987.

11. Little, B.B.; Snell, L.M.; Rosenfeld, C.R.; Gilstrap, L.C.; & Gant, N.F. Failure to recognize fetal alcohol syndrome in newborn infants. *American Journal of Diseases of Children* 144(10):1142-1146, 1990.

12. Sokol, R.J.; Martier, S.S.; & Ager, J.W. The T-ACE questions: Practical prenatal detection of risk-drinking. *American Journal of Obstetrics and Gynecology* 160(4):863-870, 1989.

13. Chavez, G.F.; Cordero, J.F.; & Becerra, J.E. Leading major congenital malformations among minority groups in the United States, 1981-1986. *Journal of the American Medical Association* 261(2):205-209, 1989.

14. May, P.A.; Hymbaugh, K.J.; Aase, J.M.; & Samet, J.M. Epidemiology of fetal alcohol syndrome among American Indians of the Southwest. *Social Biology* 30(4):374-387, 1983.

15. Aase, J.M. The fetal alcohol syndrome in American Indians: A high risk group. *Neurobehavioral Toxicology and Teratology* 3(2):153-156, 1981.

16. Sokol, R.J.; Ager, J.; Martier, S.; Debanne, S.; Ernhart, C.; Kuzma, J.; & Miller, S.I. Significant determinants of susceptibility to alcohol teratogenicity. *Annals of the New York Academy of Sciences* 477:87-102, 1986.

17. Ernhart, C.B.; Morrow-Tlucak, M.; Sokol, R.J.; & Martier, S. Underreporting of alcohol use in pregnancy. *Alcoholism: Clinical and Experimental Research* 12(4):506-511, 1988.

18. Morrow-Tlucak, M.; Ernhart, C.B.; Sokol, R.J.; Martier, S.; & Ager, J. Underreporting of alcohol use in pregnancy: Relationship to alcohol problem history. *Alcoholism: Clinical and Experimental Research* 13(3):399-401, 1989.

19. Little, R.E.; Asker, R.L.; Sampson, P.D.; & Renwick, J.H. Fetal growth and moderate drinking in early pregnancy. *American Journal of Epidemiology* 123(2):270-278, 1986.

20. Coles, C.D.; Smith, I.E.; Lancaster, J.S.; & Falek, A. Persistence over the first month of neurobehavioral differences in infants exposed to alcohol prenatally. *Infant Behavior and Development* 10:23-37, 1987.

21. Russell, M. Clinical implications of recent research on the fetal alcohol syndrome. *Bulletin of the New York Academy of Medicine* 67(3):207-222, 1991.

22. Ernhart, C.B.; Sokol, R.J.; Martier, S.; Moron, P.; Nadler, D.; Ager, J.W.; & Wolf, A. Alcohol teratogenicity in the human: A detailed assessment of specificity, critical period, and threshold. *American Journal of Obstetrics and Gynecology* 156(1):33-39, 1987.

23. Clarren, S.K.; Bowden, D.M.; & Astley, S.J. Pregnancy outcomes after weekly oral administration of ethanol during gestation in the pig-tailed macaque (Macaca nemestrina). *Teratology* 35(3):345-354, 1987.

24. Kotkoskie, L.A., & Norton, S. Cerebral cortical morphology and behavior in rats following acute prenatal ethanol exposure. *Alcoholism: Clinical and Experimental Research* 13(6):776-781, 1989.

25. Weiner, L., & Morse, B.A. FAS: Clinical perspectives and prevention. In: Chasnoff, I.J., ed. *Drugs, Alcohol, Pregnancy and Parenting*. Boston: Kluwer Academic Publishers, 1989. pp. 127-148.

26. Robles, N., & Day, N.L. Recall of alcohol consumption during pregnancy. *Journal of Studies on Alcohol* 51(5):403-407, 1990.

27. Coles, C.D.; Smith, I.; Fernhoff, P.M.; & Falek, A. Neonatal neurobehavioral characteristics as correlates of maternal alcohol use during gestation. *Alcoholism: Clinical and Experimental Research* 9(5):454-460, 1985.

28. Serdula, M.; Williamson, D.F.; Kendrick, J.S.; Anda, R.F.; & Byers, T. Trends in alcohol consumption by pregnant women: 1985 through 1988. *Journal of the American Medical Association* 265(7):876-879, 1991.

Questions and Answers about Pregnancy and Alcohol

What Is Meant in Warnings to Pregnant Women Not to Drink Alcohol?

Research has shown that even small levels of alcohol consumed during pregnancy may affect the fetus in damaging ways. In pregnant women, alcohol is not only carried to all organs and tissues, but also to the placenta, where it easily crosses through the membrane separating maternal and fetal blood systems. In this way, alcohol is transported directly to the fetus and to all its developing tissues and organs.

When a pregnant woman drinks an alcoholic beverage, the concentration of alcohol in her unborn baby's bloodstream is the same level as her own. Unlike the mother, however, the liver of a fetus cannot process alcohol at the same adult's rate of one ounce every two hours. High concentrations of alcohol, therefore, stay in the fetus longer, often for up to 24 hours. In fact, the unborn baby's blood alcohol concentration is even higher than the mother's during the second and third hour after a drink is consumed.

What Kind of Damage Can Occur to the Fetus from Alcohol Consumption by the Mother?

There are two degrees of damage that can occur. The most severe is Fetal Alcohol Syndrome (FAS). The Fetal Alcohol Syndrome Study Group of the National Council on Alcoholism outlines minimal criteria for the diagnosis of FAS as being, "evidence of abnormalities in three specific areas: growth, central nervous system functions, and facial characteristics."

Fetal Alcohol Effects (FAE) include less severe birth defects in the same areas. In both FAS and FAE, birth defects are caused when a woman drinks alcohol during pregnancy. FAS and FAE form the single largest class of birth defects that are 100 percent preventable.

Is There a Safe Amount of Alcohol that a Pregnant Woman Can Drink?

The best advice is not to drink during pregnancy. We do not know what is a safe level at this time, and it may vary considerably with different individuals. The adverse effects of alcohol may vary with the stage of pregnancy and the amount of alcohol consumed on each occasion. There appears to be no difference in the type of alcoholic beverage (beer, wine, hard liquor) and its effects during pregnancy. Early exposure presents the greatest risk for serious physical defects, and later exposure increases the chances of neurological and growth deficiencies or miscarriage.

- **The First Trimester**—This appears to be the most critical time when abnormal features can be caused. Alcohol may affect the way cells grow and arrange themselves as they multiply, altering tissue growth in the part of the fetus that is developing at the time of exposure. The brain is particularly sensitive to alcohol that diminishes the number of cells growing in the brain. Consequently, the brain is smaller and often its neurons are found in the wrong places. The early loss of cells in the developing fetus may help explain overall retarded growth and low birth weight in babies with FAS.

- **Second Trimester**—Miscarriage is a major risk during this time. There may be times of fetal distress related to binge drinking (irregular periods of heavy drinking).

- **Third Trimester**—During this period the fetus normally undergoes rapid and substantial growth. Alcohol can impair this growth. This is also the time of greatest brain development. Research with animals indicates the brain and central nervous system are at great risk during the third trimester.

How Common Are FAS and FAE?

Full-blown FAS occurs in an estimated one out of every 750 live births. Less severe FAE occurs in approximately 10 to 12 live births out of 1,000 (36,000 babies per year). Among known alcohol-abusing women, however, FAS occurs in 30 percent of recorded live births.

What Are the Problems of Children Born with These Disorders?

Typically, children born with FAS and FAE have the following symptoms:

* Low birth weight and failure throughout their lives to catch up to their peers in physical growth.

* Head:
  Small head size
  Narrow eye slits
  Flat midface
  Low nasal ridge
  Loss of groove between nose and upper lip

* Central nervous system:
  Mental retardation
  Alcohol withdrawal at birth
  Poor sucking response
  Sleep disturbances
  Restlessness and irritability
  Developmental delays
  Short attention span
  Learning disabilities

* Organs and body parts:
  Muscle problems
  Bone and joint problems
  Genital defects
  Heart defects
  Kidney defects

Do All Children with FAS/FAE Have Mental Retardation?

No. A recent study of 61 adolescents and adults with FAS or FAE revealed IQ scores ranging from 20 to 105, with an average of 68. Fifty-eight percent of these individuals had an IQ score of 70 or below (Streissguth, et al., 1991).

Can FAS Be Treated?

Birth defects related to alcohol use are permanent. Surgery can repair some of the physical problems, and schools and day care centers offer programs to improve mental and physical development. However, children born with FAS remain below average in physical and mental development throughout their lives.

How Can FAS Be Prevented?

Recent studies have shown that pregnant women will reduce or cease their alcohol intake if they are made aware of the harmful effects of alcohol on their babies. However, the most critical period of the fetus is in the first trimester when the mother may not even suspect she is pregnant. For such women, an early warning system is imperative. The best advice for a woman who drank before she knew she was pregnant is to stop drinking for the remainder of her pregnancy and get regular prenatal care.

Why Do Some Women Who Drink during Pregnancy Have Normal Children?

Not all women who drink, even those who drink heavily, during pregnancy will have children with FAS. FAS is one end of the spectrum of outcomes associated with drinking. Some children born to drinkers appear normal at birth, but as they grow, the less obvious physical, intellectual, and psychological problems resulting from alcohol exposure during pregnancy can become evident. At this time, there is not a known safe level of alcohol consumption during pregnancy.

Can a Father's Drinking Cause FAS?

A father's drinking during or before pregnancy does not directly cause FAS. However, women's drinking behavior is influenced by the drinking behavior of their partners, families, and communities. A partner can play an important role in helping the pregnant woman refrain from alcohol consumption during pregnancy. Families and friends can also be a powerful influence.

What about Adults with FAS, Will Their Children Also Have FAS?

FAS is not a genetic (inherited) disorder. Unless the mother drinks during the pregnancy, her children should not have FAS.

What about Other Drugs? Do They Cause FAS?

No drug or medication should be taken during pregnancy without first consulting a doctor. By definition, alcohol is the cause of FAS.

We do not know whether other drugs might contribute to some of the physical, intellectual, and psychological problems seen in individuals with FAS.

Why Is It Especially Important to Educate Young People about FAS?

There are rising numbers of teen pregnancies and teens who use alcohol.

Statistics illustrate the problems: According to McDonald's Corporation, the average age of beginning alcohol use is 12.5. The National Council on Alcoholism has said that nearly 100,000 10- and 11-year olds get drunk at least once a week.

The 1985 Statistical Abstract developed by the U.S. Department of Commerce showed there were 239,000 pregnancies of girls between the ages of 14 and 18.

Given the estimates of the incidence of FAS and FAE, more than 3,300 babies, born to teenagers, might be affected by FAS or FAE in one year.

References

Streissguth, A.P., et al. (1991). "Fetal Alcohol Syndrome in Adolescents and Adults." *JAMA*. Vol. 265, No. 15.

Additional Information

Alcoholics Anonymous (AA)
Check your local phone book for listings in your area
URL: http://www.alcoholicsanonymous.org

National Council on Alcoholism and Drug Dependence
12 West 21st Street
New York, NY 10010
Tel: 800-622-2255
URL: http://www.ncadd.org

National Institute on Alcohol Abuse and Alcoholism
6000 Executive Boulevard, Suite 409
Bethesda, MD 20892-7003
Tel: 301-443-3860
URL: http://www.niaaa.nih.gov

National Organization on Fetal Alcohol Syndrome
1819 H Street, NW, Suite 750
Washington, DC 20006
Tel: 800-944-9662
URL: http://www.nofas.org

The Arc
National Organization on Mental Retardation
1010 Wayne Ave, Suite 650
Silver Spring, MD 20910
Tel: 301-565-3842
Fax: 301-565-3843
E-mail: thearc@metronet.com
URL: http://www.thearc.org

Chapter 8

Strategies for Parents and Caregivers of Children with Fetal Alcohol Syndrome

Keys to working successfully with FAS/FAE children are structure, consistency, variety, brevity, and persistence. Because these children lack internal structure, caretakers need to provide external structure for them. It is important to be consistent in response and routine so that the child feels the world is predictable. Because of serious problems maintaining attention, it is important to be brief in explanations and directions, but also to use a variety of ways to get and keep their attention. Finally, we must repeat what it is we want them to learn, over and over again.

Many FAS children:

- Have difficulty structuring work time.
- Show impaired rates of learning.
- Experience poor memory.
- Have trouble generalizing behaviors and information.
- Act impulsively.
- Exhibit reduced attention span or is distractible.
- Display fearlessness and are unresponsive to verbal cautions.

- Demonstrate poor social judgment.
- Cannot handle money age appropriately.
- Have trouble internalizing modeled behaviors.
- May have differences in sensory awareness (Hypo or Hyper).
- Language production higher than comprehension.
- Show poor problem solving strategies.

Effective strategies include:

- Fostering independence in self-help and play.
- Give your child choices and encourage decision-making.
- Focus on teaching daily living skills.
- Encourage the use of positive self talk.
- Have child get ready for next school day before going to bed.
- Establish a few simple rules. Use identical language to remind them of the rules. "This is your bed, this is where you are supposed to be."
- Establish routines so child can predict coming events.
- Give child lots of advance warning that activity will soon change to another one.
- For unpredictable behavior at bedtime/mealtime, establish a firm routine.
- Break their work down into small pieces so they do not feel overwhelmed.
- Be concrete when teaching a new concept. Show them.

Discipline:

- Set limits and follow them consistently.
- Change rewards often to keep interest in reward getting high.
- Review and repeat consequences of behaviors. Ask them to tell you consequences.
- Do not debate or argue over rules already established. "Just do it."
- Notice and comment when your child is doing well or behaving appropriately.
- Avoid threats.

- Redirect behavior.
- Intervene before behavior escalates.
- Avoid situations where child will be overstimulated.
- Have child repeat back their understanding of directions.
- Protect them from being exploited. They are naive.
  Have pre-established consequences for misbehavior.

What Are the Implications for Adoptive and Biological Parents?

Patients with fetal alcohol syndrome typically have multiple handicaps and require special medical, educational, family, and community assistance. Their caretakers need medical information, peer support, financial assistance, and respite care. Many children are alcohol exposed in utero but are placed as normal, healthy infants. These children may require lifelong, expensive, intensive care and intervention to reach their potential. Alcohol use and abuse affects us all. Society at large and the adoption community in particular must educate themselves to the very special needs of alcohol affected children.

Patients with Fetal Alcohol Syndrome and Their Caretakers

Physical Characteristics

Patients with FAS are of short stature, slight build, and have a small head. Typically they are below the third to tenth percentile compared to national norms. A pattern of dysmorphic facial features characterizes these persons as well, and include 1) short eye openings; 2) a short, upturned nose; 3) smooth area between the nose and mouth; and 4) a flat midface and thin upper lip. The facial patterns made FAS patients recognizable although not grossly malformed. In addition, these patients can display other physical anomalies including 1) minor joint and limb abnormalities; 2) cardiac defects; 3) dental anomalies; and 4) vision and hearing problems.

Intellectual Capabilities

A considerable range of intellectual functioning is found among patients with FAS. In a report of twenty cases of varying severity, Ann P. Streissguth and colleagues reported a range of IQ scores from 16 to 105 with a mean IQ of 65. Severity of the syndrome was related to IQ, with the most severely affected children having the lowest IQ scores.

Behavioral Characteristics

There are many behavioral characteristics which differentiate FAS patients from other mentally retarded individuals. Socially, they tend to be very outgoing and socially engaging, yet they are frequently seen by others as intrusive, overly talkative, and generally unaware of social cues and conventions. Poor social judgment and poor socialization skills are common: many patients are hungry for attention, even negative. Due to their social immaturity, they have difficulty establishing friendships, especially with children of the same age. The potential for both social isolation and exploitation of individuals with FAS is very evident. Hyperactivity is frequently cited as a problem for young children who characteristically have short attention spans. Many also have memory problems, thus creating further setbacks to adaptive functioning and academic achievement later on.

Needs of the Patient with FAS

Medical Needs

Patients with FAS/FAE typically have complex medical needs associated with their higher than average congenital anomalies. Infants are at risk for central nervous system problems, including a weak suck and feeding and sleeping difficulties as well as failure to thrive. Birth control and sex education for adolescents with FAS are additional areas of medical concern. As adolescents, these children tend to be sexually curious, yet often lack understanding of socially appropriate sexual behavior. Thus, they are at higher than average risk for sexual victimization due to their impulsive behavior and poor social judgment.

Educational Needs

Children with FAS/FAE have special educational needs. Even very young infants can benefit from early stimulation programs to help with intellectual and motor development. These programs are now widely available, with some even offered at home by traveling therapists and educators. Preschoolers often have a range of developmental and language delays as well as signs of hyperactivity, irritability, and distractibility. Preschool programs which follow individualized educational plans are helpful for the child as well as for the parents who gain valuable respite time to regroup from the intense demands of these children.

Appropriate placement in special education classes beginning in elementary school is often necessary for children with FAS/FAE. A small classroom setting with clear guidelines and a great deal of individual attention can maximize the intellectual capabilities of these learners. Although intensive remedial education has not been shown to increase the intellectual capabilities of children with FAS/FAE, it may prevent further deterioration. Many patients with fetal alcohol syndrome reach an academic plateau in high school. Many will be unable to hold a regular job. Nonetheless, all of these students need to know basic life skills, including money management, safety skills, interpersonal relating, and so forth. These tasks will enrich their adult lives and allow them a degree of independence. The addition of such a life-skills component to the special education curricula for FAS students can be invaluable. Wherever possible and appropriate, vocational training should be part of the high school experience. Unfortunately, most vocational and technical institutes beyond high school will offer a curriculum too academically rigorous for developmentally delayed individuals.

Family Needs

Patients with FAS/FAE are at a higher than average risk for physical and sexual abuse and neglect when raised in their families of origin. These children need a supportive, loving home environment with clear guidelines and clear lines of communication in order to develop to their fullest potential. When foster (or adoptive) placement is necessary, the greatest progress is made by calm, low key individuals, who are secure and comfortable with themselves and live stable and predictable lives. Families who treat the FAS child as normally as possible, combining loving acceptance with firm limit setting seem more satisfied than do those who have high performance expectations.

Due to their poor social judgment, underdeveloped independent living skills, and impaired intellectual functioning, most FAS children will require a structured, sheltered living situation throughout their lives. The most severely affected may require a completely supervised and sheltered environment. For more functional patients, a group home or halfway house for developmentally disabled adults may be appropriate if continued residence with a family is not possible or desirable.

Needs of the Caretaker

The parent, biological, foster, or adoptive of a child with FAS assumes a responsibility far beyond that normally associated with parenting. The constellation of physical, intellectual, and behavioral characteristics that typifies patients with FAS can create a very demanding situation for any family. The children often require constant supervision. Parents require an extraordinary amount of energy, love, and most of all, consistency. Therefore, these parents need support in their efforts. This support can often be provided by the social service network to help prevent the burnout that often accompanies high-stress parenting situations.

Those parenting FAS/FAE children need information about fetal alcohol syndrome in order to understand the physical, intellectual, and behavioral concomitants of the child's diagnosis. Parents must have a realistic view of the child's functioning in order to develop reasonable expectations and plan appropriate interactions for the child in order to minimize management problems. A well-run parent support group set up around the needs of those parenting handicapped children can be an ideal vehicle for parents to share information, gain support, and overcome the feeling of being "the only one" experiencing problems.

Many caretakers of children with FAS/FAE will require some form of financial assistance as well. Adoption of FAS patients, as with other special needs children, can mean high costs and low subsidies for families. The recent emphasis on adoption of special needs children has focused on this problem and is attempting to address these issues. An advocacy-oriented caseworker can be an invaluable resource in helping potential foster and adoptive families identify available financial resources and negotiate their way through the maze of paperwork often required.

Need for Respite Care

Many parents and foster parents of FAS/FAE children could benefit from respite care, yet few receive it and most don't even know about existing programs which might serve them. The daily stress and demands generated by these children can easily trigger parental burnout. Once a parent support group is operative, a rotating system of informal, needs-based respite care can be arranged among participating families in some cases.

The Need for Advocacy

Children and parents dealing with the problems of FAS/FAE need strong advocates. Advocacy must come from both the parents and the professionals involved. Their different spheres of influence and different roles must combine to ensure that the needs of both parent and child are being met. Despite the many problems of patients with FAS/FAE, these individuals have a great capacity for love and contribution to family and community. The challenge of caretakers and service providers alike is to help these children harness their potential and find their place in the world.

Chapter 9

Fragile X Syndrome: X-Linked Inheritance

Introduction

Fragile X syndrome is the most common genetically-inherited form of mental retardation currently known. In addition to intellectual disability, some individuals with Fragile X display common physical traits and characteristic facial features, such as prominent ears. Children with Fragile X often appear normal in infancy but develop typical physical characteristics during their lifetime. Mental impairment may range from mild learning disability and hyperactivity to severe mental retardation and autism. This genetic syndrome is caused by a defect on the X chromosome. Because of scientific advances, improvements in genetic testing, and increased awareness, the number of children diagnosed with Fragile X has increased significantly over the last decade.

A substantial research effort led to the 1991 discovery of FMR-1 (Fragile X mental retardation), the gene that when damaged causes Fragile X. Although the normal function of the FMR-1 gene is not fully understood, it appears to be important early in development. The mechanism by which the normal FMR-1 gene is converted into an altered, or mutant, gene capable of causing disease symptoms involves an increase in the length of the gene. A small region of the gene, CGG, undergoes repeated duplications, forming deoxyribonucleic acid (DNA) repeats that result in a longer gene. The lengthened DNA region is

Excerpts from "Facts about Fragile X Syndrome," National Institute of Child Health and Development (NICHD).

susceptible to a chemical modification process called DNA methylation. When the number of repeats is small (less than 200) the individual often has no signs of the disorder. However, in individuals with a larger number of repeats, the characteristics that are typical of Fragile X are observed. In families that exhibit Fragile X, both the number of repeats and the length of the chromosome increase with succeeding generations. The severity of the symptoms increases with the increasing length of the repeated region.

Fragile X Exhibits X-Linkage

The effect of X-linkage is that the frequency of the syndrome is greater in males than in females. To understand the mechanism of X-linkage some background information on the organization of human chromosomes is needed. Human females typically have two X chromosomes, and human males have one X and one Y chromosome. A female who inherits a chromosome carrying the Fragile X gene from either parent is likely to inherit a normal X chromosome from the other parent. The normal X chromosome could provide the normal gene function and mask the presence of the Fragile X gene in a female. In that case, the female would still possess the Fragile X gene and be capable of passing it on to her offspring, but she would not exhibit symptoms. She would be a "carrier." On the other hand, a male who inherits the Fragile X gene from his mother would inherit a Y chromosome and not a normal X chromosome from his father, and therefore a male with one copy of the gene is likely to show symptoms. We do not yet have a complete understanding of the mechanism of genetic transmission of Fragile X. For example, it is not known why approximately one-fifth of males who carry mutated forms of FMR-1 are either unaffected or only mildly affected. In some cases, a single copy of the Fragile X gene is sufficient to cause the syndrome in females. The situation is made more complex by the fact that the intensity of the symptoms increases with succeeding generations. The observable characteristics of Fragile X occur in approximately 1 in 1,000 male births and 1 in 2,500 female births. On a normal X chromosome, the FMR-1 region of the chromosome contains 50 or fewer copies of the CGG repeat. This same region may be repeated hundreds or even thousands of times in individuals with Fragile X. Researchers have made a surprising correlation between the number of DNA repeats and the degree of clinical impairment. Individuals with between 50 and 20 repeats are often carriers of Fragile X who have mild symptoms or no symptoms at all. When the number of repeats increases, the chemical modification process called DNA methylation is more likely to occur. It is this chemical modification that appears to inactivate the FMR-1 gene, leading to deficits in cognitive processing. Why methylation of this region of DNA leads to the symptoms of Fragile X is not understood. Mental impairment in Fragile X appears to correlate with DNA containing more than 200 repeats. In that case, most males are impaired and 50 percent of females show some learning disabilities. However, there are exceptions, including individuals with enormous numbers of repeats who have no apparent impairment.

Inheritance

In normal individuals the FMR-1 gene is passed on, in stable fashion, from the parent to the offspring. In Fragile X individuals, the repeated sequences not only expand abnormally, but are unstable and the degree of impairment in offspring may vary. The Fragile X mutation appears to increase in length as it is inherited by succeeding generations. This phenomenon is known as "genetic anticipation." Eventually, the mutation reaches a critical number of repeats and causes Fragile X syndrome. For example, a male may have normal IQ, no Fragile X symptoms, and a short region of DNA repeats at the Fragile X region of his X chromosome. This individual, called a "transmitting" male, may have a daughter with 50 to 200 repeats. At that stage the condition is considered a "premutation" as there still may be no apparent symptoms. This daughter, a "carrier," might have a son with 1,000 repeats and the full blown Fragile X syndrome. If a woman is a carrier, each of her children has a 50 percent chance of inheriting her Fragile X gene. Each time her Fragile X gene is inherited, it is likely to have expanded in length. A daughter who inherits the gene will be a carrier with some chance of impairment; a son who inherits the gene has an 80 percent likelihood of developing Fragile X syndrome.

Testing for Fragile X Carriers

A simple test is now available that can determine if a woman is carrier of the Fragile X gene. A drop of blood can be taken from the woman's finger and analyzed quickly and inexpensively. If a woman who is found to be a carrier is pregnant, she can arrange for testing of the fetus, as described below. For a woman with a family history of retardation, testing before pregnancy will help determine if she is at risk.

Prenatal Testing

Three prenatal tests can determine if Fragile X is present in the fetus. Chorionic villi sampling (CVS) involves extracting a tiny amount of fetal tissue at 9 to 11 weeks of pregnancy. CVS is not widely used and carries a 1-2 percent risk of miscarriage following the procedure.

Amniocentesis is the removal and analysis of a small sample of fetal cells from the amniotic fluid. Amniocentesis is widely available and involves a lower risk of miscarriage. However, amniocentesis cannot be done until the 15th to 18th week of pregnancy and it usually takes an additional 2 to 4 weeks for the cells to grow and be analyzed. So a woman may have to wait until the 17th to 22nd week of her pregnancy to have the results of this test.

The third method, percutaneous umbilical blood sampling (PUBS), is the most accurate method and can be used to confirm the results of CVS or amniocentesis. However, PUBS is not widely available, PUBS is not done until the 18th to 22nd week and carries the greatest risk of miscarriage.

Chapter 10

Diagnosing and Treating Fragile X Syndrome

Individuals with Fragile X may have a cluster of physical, behavioral, mental, and other characteristics. These symptoms may vary in number and degree among affected children. In the best of circumstances, early identification of a child with Fragile X and subsequent treatment involves a team of professionals. These might include a speech and language pathologist, an occupational therapist (perhaps even a specialist in sensory integration), a physical therapist, a special education teacher, a genetics counselor, and a psychologist.

Physical Characteristics

Males with Fragile X have some common physical characteristics: a long narrow face; large or prominent ears; and macroorchidism (enlarged testicles). More than 80 percent of males with Fragile X develop at least one of these features, but often not until after puberty. Other physical characteristics of males with Fragile X are double-jointed fingers, flat feet, puffy eyelids, and "hollow chest." These physical features may indicate an underlying abnormality of the connective tissue, although no specific connective tissue defect has been detected. Females with Fragile X syndrome do not exhibit most of the physical characteristics found in males with Fragile X, although they often have large or prominent ears.

"Facts about Fragile X Syndrome," National Institute of Child Health and Development (NICHD).

Behavioral Characteristics

The most prevalent behavioral characteristics of children with Fragile X are attention problems and hyperactivity, known as attention-deficit hyperactivity disorder (ADHD). ADHD is frequently treated with medication, generally central nervous system stimulants such as methylphenidate (Ritalin), permoline (Cylert) and dextroamphetamine (Dexedrine). Because these drugs have side effects that include irritability and poor appetite, alternatives such as amantadine and clonidine may be appropriate. Amantadine has been used with surprising success to treat hyperactivity and attention difficulties in children with low IQs, for whom stimulants are generally less effective.

Fragile X children with ADHD may benefit from the addition of tricyclic antidepressants or a major tranquilizer such as thioridazine (Mellaril). Because mood swings and temper tantrums present major difficulties for children with Fragile X, psychotherapeutic medications such as Lithium and more recently fluoxetine (Prozac) have helped control aggression and outbursts. Anticonvulsants such as carbanazepine or valproate, used if seizures are present, can also help treat behavior problems, including aggression in males with Fragile X.

Children with Fragile X have strong reactions to changes in their environment, and their heightened anxiety can compound their behavioral difficulties. They appear to have an underlying disability related to processing external stimuli, called sensory integration (see Additional Therapies). Extreme hypersensitivity to their environment makes is difficult for them to screen out stimuli such as noise, lights, or odors. This, in turn, often provokes emotional outbursts or tantrums.

Some of the other behaviors associated with Fragile X are similar to those of autism, including hand flapping, hand biting, poor eye contact, and tactile defensiveness (responding negatively to being touched). However, one strength of males with Fragile X is their great sociability and friendliness, in contrast to autistic children, who appear unable to relate to others. Researchers recommend that autistic children be screened for Fragile X.

Mental Impairment

Mental retardation associated with Fragile X is similar to that of Down syndrome in that most of those affected fall somewhere in the

88

middle range of impairment. There are differences between males and females with Fragile X with respect to their mental impairment.

Many females with Fragile X syndrome are learning disabled in math, but perform exceptionally well in reading and spelling. In addition, one-third of females with Fragile X have mental disabilities similar to those associated with schizophrenia, such as dependence on odd forms of communication and preference for social isolation. Males with Fragile X appear to differ in mental development from both females with Fragile X and children with other kinds of developmental delays who exhibit learning disabilities. Males with Fragile X may actually achieve more than some other developmentally disabled children with higher IQ scores. It is important for educators to understand the particular difficulties of males with Fragile X. They appear to process information in simultaneous fashion; this causes difficulty when they are taught skills that require sequential processing of information, such as reading. For males with Fragile X, learning often involves seeing the whole in order to understand the parts.

Speech, Language, and Learning Disabilities

Speech and language present special difficulties. Children with Fragile X often speak in rapid bursts or repeat words (called echolalia). For males with Fragile X, the primary language difficulty is perseveration. Perseveration is the inability to complete a sentence because of continuous repetition of words at the end of a phrase. Another language-based behavior displayed by males with Fragile X is talking inappropriately and incessantly about one topic. This particular difficulty distinguishes males with Fragile X from individuals with other forms of mental retardation or autism. Speech problems are made worse in situations where the child must have eye contact with another person or when the child becomes anxious, leading researchers to suspect some underlying relationship between difficulties with language and difficulties with sensory processing.

Medical Problems

Although most children with Fragile X do not have serious physical problems, they are at greater risk for certain types of moderate medical problems than are normal children. For example, they often suffer recurrent otitis media (inner ear infections), which should be treated as early as possible to prevent it from becoming a source of language difficulties. Common eye problems include myopia (near-sightedness) and a high incidence of "lazy eye." Orthopedic difficulties related to flat feet and joint laxity may occur. Twenty percent of males with Fragile X are prone to seizures, including petit mal, grand mal, and temporal lobe seizures. In addition, many children with Fragile X have digestive disorders, such as gastroesophageal reflux, which causes gagging, regurgitation, and discomfort.

Education of Children with Fragile X

Even at a young age, children with Fragile X tend to be good at imitation and to be very social. Consequently, they can benefit immensely from early intervention programs and prolonged contact with children who are developing normally. Congressional legislation (Public Law 99-457) mandates early intervention services for children with developmental delays, ages 3 to 5 years; in some states this includes younger children. (For help finding local programs see Additional Information section.)

Parents and educators should be aware that many children with Fragile X achieve above the level that would have been predicted from measured IQ, and it is important for parents and educators to help these children reach their maximum potential. Children with Fragile X with an IQ above 70 generally do best when mainstreamed into a well-organized classroom environment with individualized help from special education experts and other professionals. Cooperative instruction, using peers to help teach, often relieves some of the stress of the classroom environment and the teacher-child relationship.

Additional Therapies

To counter the sensory integration difficulties of children with Fragile X, a wide range of strategies has been employed. Minimizing exposure to noise and odors may prevent overstimulation. Therapeutic calming techniques, such as music therapy, can also be used. It may be helpful to make special efforts to provide structure in the immediate environment and in day-to-day activities. Children with Fragile X often develop their own routines. Occupational therapists specializing in sensory integration therapy can work with children with Fragile X to help them organize environmental stimuli and to improve their response to formal education.

The strength of their visual memory means that children with Fragile X process information better when they are presented with whole pictures rather than when information is presented orally or sequentially, as in normal reading. As a result, use of pictures, message boards, calculators, and other visual devices may be helpful. Some children with Fragile X learn sign language, a visual system. Computer software is now available for learning basic concepts in language and math using high-interest visual themes.

Psychology professionals warn against the tendency to assume that all characteristics of a child with Fragile X stem directly from the Fragile X syndrome. The emotional difficulties of an individual with Fragile X may include insecurity and anxiety related to having a disability.

These strategies are only a few that specialists have developed to help children with Fragile X. Parents and other individuals working with these children should make use of their assets, such as their positive outlook on life and love of other people. Children with Fragile X should be encouraged to express their feelings openly even when they have difficulty using words.

Future Research

Since the discovery of the Fragile X gene in 1991, there has been tremendous progress in the understanding of this disorder. Preimplantation genetic screening, using molecular genetic screening of in vitro fertilized embryos followed by implantation of embryos that are free of the disorder, may be available to would-be parents in the near future.

Some affected families argue that not enough research is being conducted on the treatment of Fragile X. In response, experts explain that it is difficult to treat Fragile X without first understanding more about the biology of the condition and the meaning of the DNA expansions. It has been particularly difficult to investigate these questions in the absence of an animal model. The nature of the Fragile X mutation may itself be a source of the difficulty scientists are having in developing an animal model of the disease. The excess genetic material of the Fragile X defect is so voluminous and so fragile that inserting the Fragile X DNA into animal cells has been a problem for laboratory scientists. However, there has been some recent progress in this area, and continued research is likely to bring success.

Once an animal model is developed, researchers will be able to learn more about the basis of the Fragile X mutation and the mechanisms that contribute to its unstable character. Ongoing analysis of the FMR-1 gene and its protein product may help researchers understand the normal function of this protein and perhaps find a way to intervene when its functioning goes awry.

Additional Information

National Fragile X Foundation
1441 York St., Suite 303
Denver, CO 80206-2127
Tel: 303-333-6155
Toll-free: 800-688-8765

Provides assistance and advice to parents and professionals, works to increase awareness and encourage research. Publishes and sells brochures, information packets, a quarterly newsletter, and the International Fragile X Directory that provides a list of Fragile X testing sites, resource centers, and groups worldwide.

FRAXA Research Foundation, Inc.
P.O. Box 0935
West Newbury, MA 01985-0935
Tel: 508-462-1990

FRAXA is a tax-exempt public charity, run by parents of children with Fragile X syndrome. FRAXA's goal is to accelerate research aimed at the specific treatment with Fragile X syndrome by direct funding of promising research projects and by raising awareness of this disease.

National Fragile X Advocate
Avanta Publishing Company
P.O. Box 17023
Chapel Hill, NC 27516-1702
Toll-free: 800-434-0322

Bimonthly subscription newsletter, 16 pages.

Part Three

Other Causes of
Mental Retardation

Chapter 11

Genetic Conditions

Contents

Section 11.1

Genetic Causes of Mental Retardation

Reprinted with permission © 1996, The Arc. Produced by The Arc's Human Genome Education Project, Sharon Davis, Ph.D., Principal Investigator and Leigh Ann Reynolds, Project Associate. Reviewed by Stacie R. Rosenthal, M.S., Mary Simmons, M.S., and Gail Brookshire, M.S., genetic counselors with Children's Medical Center of Dallas.

What Is Genetics?

Genetics is "the science that studies the principles and mechanics of heredity, or the means by which traits are passed from parents to offspring" (Glanze, 1996). Through genetics a number of specific disorders have been identified as being genetically caused. One example is fragile X syndrome, a common genetic cause of mental retardation, which is caused by the presence of a single non-working gene (called the FMR-1 gene) on a child's X chromosome.

Genetics originated in the mid-19th century when Gregor Mendel discovered over a ten year period of experimenting with pea plants that certain traits are inherited. His discoveries provided the foundation for the science of genetics. Mendel's findings continue to spur the work and hopes of scientists to uncover the mystery behind how our genes work and what they can reveal to us about the possibility of having certain diseases and conditions. The scientific field of genetics can help families affected by genetic disorders to have a better understanding about heredity, what causes various genetic disorders to occur, and what possible prevention strategies can be used to decrease the incidence of genetic disorders.

Can a Person's Genes Cause Mental Retardation?

Some genetic disorders are associated with mental retardation, chronic health problems, and developmental delay. Because of the complexity of the human body, there are no easy answers to the question of what causes mental retardation. Mental retardation is attributable to any condition that impairs development of the brain before birth, during birth, or in the childhood years (The Arc, 1993).

As many as 50 percent of people with mental retardation have been found to possess more than one causal factor (AAMR, 1992). Some research has determined that in 75 percent of children with mild mental retardation the cause is unknown (Kozma & Stock, 1993).

The field of genetics has important implications for people with mental retardation. Over 350 inborn errors of metabolism have been identified, most of which lead to mental retardation (Scriver, 1995). Yet, the possibility of being born with mental retardation or developing the condition later in life can be caused by multiple factors unrelated to our genetic make-up. It is caused not only by the genotype (or genetic make-up) of the individual, but also by the possible influences of environmental factors. Those factors can range from drug use or nutritional deficiencies to poverty and cultural deprivation.

How Often Is Mental Retardation Inherited?

Since the brain is such a complex organ, there are a number of genes involved in its development. Consequently, there are a number of genetic causes of mental retardation. Most identifiable causes of severe mental retardation (defined as an IQ of 50 or less) originate from genetic disorders. Up to 60 percent of severe mental retardation can be attributed to genetic causes making it the most common cause in cases of severe mental retardation (Moser, 1995). People with mild mental retardation (defined as an IQ between 50 and 70-75) are not as likely to inherit mental retardation due to their genetic make-up as are people with severe mental retardation. People with mild mental retardation are more likely to have the condition due to environmental factors, such as nutritional state, personal health habits, socioeconomic level, access to health care, and exposure to pollutants and chemicals, rather than acquiring the condition genetically (Nelson-Anderson & Waters, 1995). Two of the most common genetically transmitted forms of mental retardation include Down syndrome (a chromosomal disorder) and fragile X syndrome (a single-gene disorder).

What Causes Genetic Disorders?

Over 7,000 genetic disorders have been identified and catalogued, with up to five new disorders being discovered every year (McKusick, 1994). Genetic disorders are typically broken down into three types: chromosomal, single-gene and multifactorial.

Chromosomal disorders affect approximately 7 out of every 1,000 infants. The disorder results when a person has too many or too few chromosomes, or when there is a change in the structure of a chromosome. Half of all first-trimester miscarriages or spontaneous abortions occur as a result of a chromosome abnormality. If the child is born, he or she usually has multiple birth defects and mental retardation. Most chromosomal disorders happen sporadically. They are not necessarily inherited (even though they are considered to be genetic disorders). In order for a genetic condition to be inherited, the disease-causing gene must be present within one of the parent's genetic code. In most chromosomal disorders, each of the parents' genes are normal. However, during cell division an error in separation, recombination, or distribution of chromosomes occurs. Examples of chromosomal disorders include Down syndrome, Trisomy 13, Trisomy 18, and Cri du chat.

Single-gene disorders (sometimes called inborn errors of metabolism or Mendelian disorders) are caused by non-working genes. Disorders of metabolism occur when cells are unable to produce proteins or enzymes needed to change certain chemicals into others, or to carry substances from one place to another. The cell's inability to carry out these vital internal functions often results in mental retardation. Approximately 1 in 5,000 children are born with defective enzymes resulting in inborn errors of metabolism (Batshaw, 1992). Although many conditions are generally referred to as "genetic disorders," single-gene disorders are the most easy to identify as true genetic disorders since they are caused by a mutation (or a change) within a single gene or gene pair.

Combinations of multiple gene and environmental factors leading to mental retardation are called multifactorial disorders. They are inherited but do not share the same inheritance patterns typically found in single-gene disorders. It is unclear exactly why they occur. Their inheritance patterns are usually much more complex than those of single gene disorders because their existence depends on the simultaneous presence of heredity and environmental factors. For example, weight and intelligence are traits inherited in this way (Batshaw, 1992). Other common disorders, including cancer and hypertension, are examples of health problems caused by the environment and heredity. Multifactorial disorders are very common and cause a majority of birth defects. Examples of multifactorial disorders include heart disease, diabetes, spina bifida, anencephaly, cleft lip and cleft palate, clubfoot, and congenital heart defects.

How Are Genetic Disorders Inherited?

Genetic disorders can be inherited in much the same way a person can inherit other characteristics such as eye and hair color, height, and intelligence. Children inherit genetic or hereditary information by obtaining genes from each parent. There are three common types or modes of inheritance: dominant, recessive, and X-linked (or sex-linked).

Dominant inheritance occurs when one parent has a dominant, disease-causing gene which causes abnormalities even if coupled with a healthy gene from the other parent. Dominant inheritance means that each child has a 50 percent chance of inheriting the disease-causing gene. An example of dominant inheritance associated with mental retardation is tuberous sclerosis.

Recessive inheritance occurs when both parents carry a disease-causing gene but outwardly show no signs of disease. Parents of children with recessive conditions are called "carriers" since each parent carries one copy of a disease gene. They show no symptoms of having a disease gene and remain unaware of having the gene until having an affected child. When parents who are carriers give birth, each child has a 25 percent chance of inheriting both disease genes and being affected. Each child also has a 25 percent chance of inheriting two healthy genes and not being affected, and a 50 percent chance of being a carrier of the disorder, like their parents. Examples of disorders which are inherited recessively and are also associated with mental retardation include phenylketonuria (PKU) and galactosemia.

X-linked or sex-linked inheritance affects those genes located on the X chromosome and can be either X-linked recessive or X-linked dominant. The X-linked recessive disorder, which is much more common compared to X-linked dominant inheritance, is referred to as a sex-linked disorder since it involves genes located on the X chromosome. It occurs when an unaffected mother carries a disease-causing gene on at least one of her X chromosomes. Since females have two X chromosomes, they are usually unaffected carriers because the X chromosome that does not have the disease-causing gene compensates for the X chromosome that does. Therefore, they are less likely than males to show any symptoms of the disorder unless both X chromosomes have the disease-causing gene. If a mother has a female child, the child has a 50 percent chance to inherit the disease gene and be a carrier and pass the disease gene on to her sons (March of Dimes, 1995). On the other hand, if a mother has a male child, he has a 50 percent chance of inheriting the disease-causing gene since he has only one

X chromosome. Consequently, males cannot be carriers of X-linked recessive disorders. If a male inherits an X-linked recessive disorder, he is affected. Some examples of X-linked inheritance associated with mental retardation include fragile X syndrome, Hunter syndrome, Lesch Nyhan syndrome, and Duchenne muscular dystrophy.

Can Genetic Disorders Which Cause Mental Retardation Be Fixed?

In the past, only a few genetic disorders could be detected and treated early enough to prevent disease. However, the Human Genome Project, an international project among scientists to identify all the 60,000 to 100,000 genes within the human body, is significantly increasing our ability to discover more effective therapies and prevent inherited disease (National Center for Human Genome Research, 1995). As more disease-causing genes are identified, scientists can begin developing genetic therapies to alter or replace a defective gene.

However, the development of gene therapies is still in the infancy stage. Gene therapy (also called somatic-cell gene therapy) is a procedure in which "healthy genes" are inserted into individuals to cure or treat an inherited disease or illness. Although there is a role for gene therapy in the prevention of mental retardation, it will most likely benefit only those people who have single-gene disorders, such as Lesch-Nyhan disease, Gaucher disease, and phenylketonuria (PKU) that cause severe mental retardation (Moser, 1995). Gene therapy is far less likely to provide treatment of mild mental retardation that accounts for 87 percent of all cases of mental retardation (The Arc, 1993).

References

AAMR (1992). *Mental retardation: Definition, classification, and systems of supports*, 9th edition.

Batshaw, M.L. & Perret, Y.M. (1992). *Children with disabilities: A medical primer* (3rd ed.). Baltimore: Paul H. Brookes Publishing Co.

Glanze, W. (Ed.). (1996). The signet Mosby medical encyclopedia (revised edition). New York: Penguin Books Ltd.

Kozma, C. & Stock, J. (1992). "What is mental retardation." In Smith, R.S. *Children with Mental Retardation: A Parent's Guide*. Maryland: Woodbine House.

March of Dimes (1995). *Birth defects.* (Publication No. 09-026-00). White Plains, New York: Author.

McKusick, V.A. (1994). Mendelian Inheritance in Man. *Catalogs of Human Genes and Genetic Disorders. (Eleventh edition).* Baltimore: Johns Hopkins University Press.

Moser, H. G. (1995) A role for gene therapy in mental retardation. *Mental Retardation and Developmental Disabilities Research Reviews: Gene Therapy,* 1, 4-6.

National Center for Human Genome Research, National Institutes of Health. (1995). *The Human Genome Project: From Maps to Medicine* (NIH Publication No. 95-3897). Bethesda, MD.

Scriver, C. R. (1995). *The metabolic and molecular bases of inherited disease. (Seventh edition).* New York: McGraw-Hill.

The Arc (1993). "Introduction to mental retardation." *Q&A.* Arlington, Texas: Author.

Section 11.2

Angelman Syndrome

Reprinted with permission © 1998, National Angelman Syndrome Foundation. This document was developed by the Angelman Syndrome Foundation with assistance from the Raymond C. Philips Unit, Division of Genetics, Department of Pediatrics, University of Florida.

Introduction

In 1965, Dr. Harry Angelman, an English physician, first described three children with characteristics now known as the Angelman Syndrome (AS)[1]. He noted that all had a stiff, jerky gait, absent speech, excessive laughter, and seizures. Other cases were eventually published[2-8] but the condition was considered to be extremely rare and many physicians doubted its existence. The first reports from North America appeared in the early 1980s[9-10] and within the last five years many new reports have appeared.[11-15] Dr. Angelman relates the following regarding his discovery of this syndrome.[16]

The history of medicine is full of interesting stories about the discovery of illnesses. The saga of Angelman's Syndrome is one such story. It was purely by chance that nearly thirty years ago three handicapped children were admitted at various times to my children's ward in England. They had a variety of disabilities and although at first sight they seemed to be suffering from different conditions I felt that there was a common cause for their illness. The diagnosis was purely a clinical one because in spite of technical investigations, which today are more refined, I was unable to establish scientific proof that the three children all had the same handicap. In view of this I hesitated to write about them in the medical journals. However, when on holiday in Italy I happened to see an oil painting in the Castelvecchio museum in Verona called, "A Boy with a Puppet." The boy's laughing face and the fact that my patients exhibited jerky movements gave me the idea of writing an article about the three children with a title of Puppet Children. It *was not* a name that pleased all parents but it served as a means of combining the three little patients into a single group. Later the name was changed to Angelman syndrome. This article was published in 1965 and after some initial interest lay almost forgotten until the early eighties.

The precise incidence of AS is unknown but in the United States and Canada, the Angelman Syndrome Foundation is aware of approximately 1000 individuals, so the disorder is not extremely rare. AS has been reported throughout the world among divergent racial groups. In North America, the great majority of known cases seem to be of Caucasian origin. Although the exact incidence of AS is unknown an estimate of between 1 in 15,000 to 1 in 30,000 seems reasonable.

Developmental and Physical Features

Angelman syndrome is usually not recognized at birth or in infancy since the developmental problems are nonspecific during this time. Parents may first suspect the diagnosis after reading about AS or meeting a child with the condition. The most common age of diagnosis is between three and seven years when the characteristic behaviors and features become most evident. A summary of the developmental and physical findings has recently been published[17] for the purpose of establishing clinical criteria for the diagnosis and these are listed below. All of the features do not need to be present for the diagnosis to be made and the diagnosis is often first suspected when the typical behaviors are recognized.

Developmental History and Laboratory Findings

- Normal prenatal and birth history with normal head circumference; absence of major birth defects
- Developmental delay evident by 6–12 months of age
- Delayed but forward progression of development (no loss of skills)
- Normal metabolic, hematologic, and chemical laboratory profiles
- Structurally normal brain using MRI or CT (may have mild cortical atrophy or dysmyelination

Clinical Features

Consistent (100%)

- Developmental delay, functionally severe
- Speech impairment, minimal or no use of words; receptive, and non-verbal communication skills higher than verbal ones
- Movement or balance disorder, usually ataxia of gait and/or tremulous movement of limbs
- Behavioral uniqueness: any combination of frequent laughter/ smiling; apparent happy demeanor; easily excitable personality, often with hand flapping movements; hypermotoric behavior; short attention span

Frequent (More Than 80%)

- Delayed, disproportionate growth in head circumference, usually resulting in microcephaly (absolute or relative) by age 2
- Seizures, onset usually <3 years of age
- Abnormal EEC, characteristic pattern with large amplitude slow-spike waves

Associated clinical features (occurring 20–80%) of AS are described under "Medical and Developmental Problems."

Chromosome 15

For several decades the chromosome study of AS revealed no abnormalities but with the development of improved methods a very small deleted area was found in chromosome 15. Newer molecular methods now demonstrate a deletion in about 70% of individuals with AS. The deleted area, although extremely small, is actually quite large when viewed at the molecular level. It is believed to be about 3.5 million molecules in length, enough of a distance to contain many genes.

The deleted region on chromosome 15 is known to contain genes that are activated or inactivated depending upon the chromosome's parent of origin (the 15 chromosome inherited from the mother might have a gene that is turned on but the same gene inherited from the father's 15 might be turned off). Because the deletions seen in AS only occur on the chromosome 15 given by the mother, it is believed the gene is turned on only on the maternal chromosome. No AS gene/s have yet been isolated although this may be forthcoming soon. Disruption of genes that are active on the paternally derived 15 is now known to cause another mental retardation disorder termed the Prader-Willi syndrome (PWS). The PWS gene/s are actually located close to the AS gene, but they are different.

After the discovery of the chromosome deletion, another rare cause of AS was discovered. This cause was due to the child having both 15 chromosomes inherited from the father, a condition termed paternal uniparental disomy (UPD) In this case, there is no deletion, but the child is still missing the active AS gene because the paternal-derived chromosomes 15 only have "turned off" AS genes on them.

Furthermore, there are also some families having two or more children with AS. In many of these families it was then shown that the AS children always inherited the same maternal chromosome 15's but inherited different paternal 15's indicating that the inherited maternal chromosome may have a mutation on it. Two genetic mechanisms have now been identified whereby AS can be inherited from the mother: mutations in Imprinting Control (IC) region and mutations in the putative AS gene which is called ubiquitin-protein ligase E3A (UBE3A).[18,19] The UBE3A gene is believed to be the causative gene in AS, and all of the other genetic mechanisms that are associated with AS (see below) appear to cause inactivations or absence of this gene. UBE3A is an enzymatic component of a complex protein degradation system termed the ubiquitin-proteasome pathway.[20] This pathway is located in the cytoplasm of all cells. This pathway involves the action of a small protein molecule, ubiquitin, which can be attached to proteins thereby causing them to be degraded. However, we currently do not know what brain proteins the UBE3A enzyme is normally supposed to be degrading.

We also now know that there is an region on chromosome 15 that can control or turn on or off the action of the UBE3A gene. This control region is called the Imprinting Center (IC) and the small mutations have been identified in this area that can cause AS.[21] The IC appears to be able to exert its effect on UBE3A from a distant location, but how this regulation happens is not yet known.

All of these discoveries have now led to the realization that there are several genetic "classes" or mechanisms that cause AS and all generally lead to the typical clinical features observed in AS although minor differences may occur between groups. These mechanisms are summarized in Table 11.1.

Table 11.1. Genetic Classes of Angelman Syndrome

Class No.	Genetic Cause	Percent of AS Caused	Description of Cause
1	Large common deletions	70-75%*	Includes deletion of the P gene, so hypopigmentation is common
2	Other chromosome abnormalities	2%	Unusual chromosome rearrangements can cause absence of the 15q11-13 region
3	Paternal uniparental disomy	4%	Inheritance of both paternal 15's, no maternal 15 present
4	Imprinting center mutation	1%	Rare occurrence
5	UBE3A mutation	3-5%	Newest identified mechanism. True incidence not yet established
6	Unknown	15%	All of the above mechanisms should be ruled out by genetic testing before assignment to this group.

*Estimated frequency of cases. These numbers vary slightly from study to study.

Medical and Developmental Problems

Seizures

More than 90% are reported to have seizures but this may be an over-estimation because medical reports tend to dwell on the more severe cases. Less than 25% develop seizures before 12 months of age. Most have onset before 3 years, but occurrence in older children or in teenagers is not exceptional.[13] The seizures can be of any seizure type (i.e. major motor involving jerking of all extremities; absence type involving brief periods lack of awareness), and may require multiple anticonvulsant medications. Seizures may be difficult to recognize or distinguish from the child's usual tremulousness, hyperkinetic limb movements, or attention deficits. The typical EEG is often more abnormal than expected and it may suggest seizures when in fact there are none.

There is no agreement as to the optimal seizure medication, but there are patterns of use that are more frequent. Anticonvulsant medications used for minor motor seizures (valproic acid, clonazepam, etc.) are more commonly prescribed than are ones for major motor seizures (diphenylhydantoin, phenobarbital, etc.). Single medication use is preferred but seizure breakthrough is common. Some children with uncontrollable seizures have been placed on a ketogenic diet, but it is uncertain if this is beneficial. Children with AS are at risk for medication over-treatment because their movement abnormalities or attention deficits can be mistaken for seizures and because EEG abnormalities can persist even when seizures are controlled.

Gait and Movement Disorders

Hyperkinetic movements of the trunk and limbs have been noted in early infancy[19] and jitteriness or tremulousness may be present in the first 6 months of life. Voluntary movements are often irregular, varying from slight jerkiness to uncoordinated coarse movements that prevent walking, feeding, and reaching for objects. Gross motor milestones are delayed; sitting usually occurring after age 12 months and walking is often delayed until age 3 or 4 years.[13,15]

In early childhood, the mildly impaired child can have almost normal walking. There may be only mild toe-walking or an apparent prancing gait. This may be accompanied by a tendency to lean or lurch forward. The tendency to lean forward is accentuated during running and, in addition, the arms are held uplifted. For these children, balance and coordination does not appear to be a major problem. More severely affected children can be very stiff and robot-like or extremely

106

shaky and jerky when walking. Although they can crawl fairly effectively, they may "freeze up" or appear to become anxious when placed in the standing position. The legs are kept wide based and the feet are flat and turned outward. This, accompanied by uplifted arms, flexed elbows, and downward turned hands, produces the characteristic gait of AS. Some children are so ataxic and jerky that walking is not possible until they are older and better able to compensate in their motor skills for the jerkiness; about 10% may fail to achieve walking.[23] In situations where AS has not been diagnosed, the nonspecific diagnosis of cerebral palsy is often given to account for the abnormal walking. Physical therapy is usually helpful in improving ambulation and sometimes bracing or surgical intervention may be needed to properly align the legs.

Hyperactivity

Hyperactivity is probably the most typical behavior in AS. It is best described as hypermotoric with a short attention span. Essentially all young AS children have some component of hyperactivity[15] and males and females appear equally affected. Infants and toddlers may have seemingly ceaseless activity, constantly keeping their hands or toys in their mouth, moving from object to object. In extreme cases, the constant movement can cause accidental bruises and abrasions. Grabbing, pinching, and biting in older children have also been noted and may be heightened by the hypermotoric activity. Persistent and consistent behavior modification helps decrease or eliminate these unwanted behaviors.

Attention span can be so short that social interaction is prevented because the AS child cannot attend to facial and other social cues. In milder cases, attention may be sufficient enough to learn sign language and other communication techniques. For these children, educational and developmental training programs are much easier to structure and are generally more effective. Observations in young adults suggest that the hypermotoric state decreases with age. Most AS children do not receive drug therapy for hyperactivity although some may benefit from use of medications such as methylphenidate (Ritalin). Use of sedating agents such as phenothiazines is not recommended due to their potency and side effects.

Laughter and Happiness

It is not known why laughter is so frequent in AS. Even laughter in normal individuals is not well understood. Studies of the brain in

AS, using MRI or CT scans, have not shown any defect suggesting a site for a laughter-inducing abnormality. Although there is a type of seizure associated with laughter, termed gelastic epilepsy, this is not what occurs in AS. The laughter in AS seems mostly to be an expressive motor event; most reactions to stimuli, physical or mental, are accompanied by laughter or laughter-like facial grimacing. Although AS children experience a variety of emotions, apparent happiness predominates.

The first evidence of this distinctive behavior may be the onset of early or persistent social smiling at the age of 1-3 months. Giggling, chortling, and constant smiling soon develop and appear to represent normal reflexive laughter but cooing and babbling are delayed or reduced. Later, several types of facial or behavioral expressions characterize the infant's personality. A few have pronounced laughing that is truly paroxysmal or contagious and "bursts of laughter" occurred in 70% in one study.[15] More often, happy grimacing and a happy disposition are the predominant behaviors. In rare cases, the apparent happy disposition is fleeting as irritability and hyperactivity are the prevailing personality traits; crying, shrieking, screaming, or short guttural sounds may then be the predominant behaviors.

Speech and Language

Some AS children seem to have enough comprehension to be able to speak, but in even the highest functioning, conversational speech does not develop. Clayton-Smith[23] reported that a few individuals spoke 1-3 words, and in a survey of 47 individuals, Buntirix et al.[15] reported that 39% spoke up to 4 words, but it was not noted if these words were used meaningfully. Children with AS caused by uniparental disomy or extremely small deletions may have higher verbal and cognitive skills; at times use of 10-20 words may occur, although pronunciation may be awkward."[16]

The speech disorder in AS has a somewhat typical evolution. Babies and young infants cry less often and have decreased cooing and babbling. A single apparent word, such as "mama," may develop around 10-18 months but it is used infrequently and indiscriminately without symbolic meaning. By 2-3 years of age, it is clear that speech is delayed but it may not be evident how little the AS child is verbally communicating; crying, and other vocal outbursts may also be reduced. By 3 years of age, higher functioning AS children are initiating some type of non-verbal language. Some point to body parts and indicate some of their needs by use of simple gestures, but they are much better at following and understanding commands. Others, especially those with severe seizures or extreme hyperactivity cannot be attentive enough to achieve the first stages of communication, such as establishing sustained eye contact. The nonverbal language skills of AS children vary greatly, with the most advanced ones able to learn some sign language and to use such aids as picture-based communication boards.

Mental Retardation and Developmental Testing

Developmental testing is compromised by the attention deficit, hyperactivity, and lack of speech and motor control. In such situations, test results are invariably in the severe range of functional impairment. More attentive children can perform in the moderate range and a minority can perform in some categories, like receptive social skills, in the mildly impaired range. As we learn more about the different genetic classes of AS it appears that patients with uniparental disomy have less severe clinical manifestations than those with large deletions.[24]

It is known that the cognitive abilities in AS are higher than indicated from developmental testing. The most striking area where this is evident is in the disparity between understanding language and speaking language. Because of their ability to understand language, AS children soon distinguish themselves from other severe mental retardation conditions. Young adults with AS are usually socially adept and respond to most personal cues and interactions. Because of their interest in people they establish rewarding friendships and communicate a broad repertoire of feelings and sentiments, enriching their relationship to families and friends. They participate in group activities, household chores, and in the activities and responsibilities of daily living. Like others, they enjoy most recreational activities such as TV, sports, going to the beach, etc.

There is a wide range however in the developmental outcome so that not all individuals with AS attain the above noted skills. A few will be more impaired in terms of their mental retardation and lack of attention, and this seems especially the case in those with difficult to control seizures or those with extremely pronounced ataxia and movement problems. Fortunately, most children with AS do not have these severe problems, but even for the less impaired child, inattentiveness and hyperactivity during early childhood often give the impression that profound functional impairment is the only outcome possible. However, with a secure home and consistent behavioral intervention and stimulation, the AS child begins to overcome these problems and developmental progress occurs.

Hypopigmentation

When AS is caused by the large deletion, skin and eye hypopigmentation usually results. This occurs because there is a pigment gene, located close to the AS gene, that is also missing. This pigment gene produces a protein (called the P protein) that is believed to be crucial in melanin synthesis. Melanin is the main pigment molecule in our skin. In some children with AS, this hypopigmentation can be so severe that a form of albinism is suspected. In those with uniparental disomy or very small deletions, this gene is not missing and normal skin and eye pigmentation is seen. AS children with hypopigmentation are sun sensitive, so use of a protective sun screen is important. Not all AS children with deletions of the P gene are obviously hypopigmented, but may only have relatively lighter skin color than either parent.

Strabismus and Ocular Albinism

Surveys of AS patients demonstrate 30–60% incidence of strabismus. This problem appears to be more common in children with eye hypopigmentation, since pigment in the retina is crucial to normal development of the optic nerve pathways. Management of strabismus in AS is similar to that in other children: evaluation by an ophthalmologist, correction of any visual deficit, and where appropriate, patching and surgical adjustment of the extraocular muscles. The hypermotoric activities of some AS children will make wearing of patches or glasses difficult.

CNS Structure

The brain in AS is structurally normal although occasional abnormalities have been reported. The most common Mid or CT change, when any is detected, is mild cortical atrophy (i.e. a small decrease in the thickness of the cortex of the cerebrum) and/or mildly decreased myelination (i.e. the more central parts of the brain appear to have a slight degree of diminished white matter).[13,15] Several detailed microscopic and chemical studies of the brain in AS have been reported but the findings generally have been nonspecific or the number of cases have been too few to make meaningful conclusions.

Sleep Disorders

Parents report that decreased need for sleep and abnormal sleep/ wake cycles are characteristic of AS. Sleep disturbances have been reported in AS infants and abnormal sleep/wake cycles have been studied in one AS child who benefited from a behavioral treatment program. Many families construct safe but confining bedrooms to accommodate disruptive nighttime wakefulness. Use of sedatives such as chloral hydrate or diphenhydramine (Benadryl) may be helpful if wakefulness excessively disrupts home life. Recently, administration of 0.3 mg melatonin one hour before bed time, has been shown to be of help in some children but should not be given in the middle of the night if the child awakens.[25] Nevertheless, most AS infants and children do not receive sleep medications and those who do usually do not require long term use.

Feeding Problems and Oral-Motor Behaviors

Feeding problems, are frequent but not generally severe and usually manifest early as difficulty in sucking or swallowing.[13,15,22] Tongue movements may be uncoordinated with thrusting and generalized oral-motor lack of coordination. There may be trouble initiating sucking and sustaining breast feeding. Bottle feeding may prove easier. Frequent spitting up may be interpreted as formula intolerance or gastroesophageal reflux. The feeding difficulties often first present to the physician as a problem of poor weight gain or as a "failure to thrive" concern. Infrequently, severe gastroesophageal reflux may require surgery.

AS children are notorious for putting everything in their mouths. In early infancy, hand sucking (and sometimes foot sucking) is frequent. Later, most exploratory play is by oral manipulation and chewing. The tongue appears to be of normal shape and size, but in 30–50%, persistent tongue protrusion is a distinctive feature. Some have constant protrusion and drooling while others have protrusion that is noticeable only during laughter. Some infants with protrusion eventually have no noticeable problem during later childhood (some seem to improve after oral-motor therapy). For the usual AS child with protruding tongue behavior, the problem remains throughout childhood and can persist into adulthood. Drooling is frequently a persistent problem, often requiring bibs. Use of medications, such as scopolamine to dry secretions usually does not provide an adequate long term effect.

111

Physical Growth

Newborns appear to be physically well formed, but by 12 months of age some show a deceleration of cranial growth which may represent relative or absolute microcephaly (absolute microcephaly means having a head circumference in the lower 2.5 percentile). The prevalence of absolute microcephaly varies from 88% [13] to 34% [12] and may be as low as 25% when nondeletion cases are also included.[11] Most AS individuals however have head circumferences less than the 25th percentile by age 3 years, often accompanied by a flattened back of the head. Average height is lower than the mean for normal children but most AS children will plot within the normal range. Final adult height has ranged from 4 foot 9 inches to 5 foot 10 inches in a series of 8 adults with AS. Familial factors will influence growth so that taller parents have AS children that tend to be taller than the average AS child. During infancy weight gain may be slow due to feeding problems but by early childhood most AS children appear to have near normal subcutaneous fat. Obesity is rare but by late childhood some increased weight gain can occur.[23]

Education

The severe developmental delay in AS mandates that a full range of early training and enrichment programs be made available. Unstable or nonambulatory children may also benefit from physical therapy. Occupational therapy may help improve fine motor and oral-motor control. Special adaptive chairs or positioners may be required at various times, especially for hypotonic or extremely ataxic children. Speech and communication therapy is essential and should focus on nonverbal methods of communication. Augmentative communication aids, such as picture cards or communication boards, should be used at the earliest appropriate time.

Extremely active and hypermotoric AS children will require special provisions in the classroom and teacher aides or assistants may be needed to integrate the child into the classroom. AS children with attention deficits and hyperactivity need room to express themselves and to "grapple" with their hypermotoric activities. The classroom setting should be structured, in its physical design and its curricular program, so that the active AS child can fit in or adjust to the school environment. Individualization and flexibility are important factors. Consistent behavior modification in the school and at home can enable the AS child to be toilet trained (schedule-trained), and to perform most self help skills related to eating, dressing, and performing general activities in the home.

Young Adulthood

During adolescence, puberty may be delayed by 1-3 years but sexual maturation occurs with development of normal secondary sexual characteristics. Some weight gain can be evident in this period but frank obesity is rare. Young AS adults continue to learn and are not known to have significant deterioration in mental abilities. Physical health in AS appears to be remarkably good. For many, seizure medications can be discontinued in the early adolescent or adult years.[10,15] AS individuals with severe ataxia may lose their ability to walk if ambulation is not encouraged. Scoliosis can develop in adolescence and is especially a problem in those that are nonambulatory. Scoliosis is treated with early bracing to prevent progression, and surgical correction or stabilization may be necessary for severe cases. Life span does not appear to be dramatically shortened and the National Angelman Syndrome Foundation is aware of a 58-year-old woman with AS and of many AS individuals in their third or fourth decades of life.

Laboratory Testing for AS

In the child in whom the AS diagnosis is suspected, a high resolution chromosome analysis is often first performed to insure that no other chromosome disorder is present, since features such as mental delay, microcephaly, or seizures can be seen in other chromosome abnormalities. Concurrent with the chromosome test, a fluorescent *in situ* hybridization (FISH) analysis is usually ordered. This is a newly developed test that uses molecular tags to detect the deletion on chromosome 15. The tags are directly applied to the chromosome and it is examined under a microscope after special stains are applied. The FISH test is far superior to the usual chromosome test. The child with AS should have their chromosomes 15 fully studied to insure that they are structurally normal; a maternal chromosome study as well provides additional confirmation that the maternal chromosome 15 is structurally normal. In the diagnostic testing for AS, some laboratories now offer a "DNA methylation" test in conjunction with chromosome and FISH testing. The methylation test can detect the large common deletion type of AS, as well as those with uniparrental disomy or defects in the imprinting center (IC). Confirmation of uniparental disomy needs to be made by additional molecular testing (usually, study of parental sequencing in the IC area). About 80-85% of individuals with AS will be diagnosed by a combination of these tests, but there still remain 15-20% who will have some genetic testing. Some individuals in this latter group, perhaps less than 20%, will be found however to have mutations in the UBE3A gene. At this time, molecular analysis for UBE3A and IC mutations is not commercially available but is being performed in some research labs.

Genetic Counseling

About 70-75% of cases of AS are caused by spontaneously occurring large common deletions or by uniparental disomy. To our knowledge, recurrence has not been reported for these groups and recurrence risk is estimated to be less than 1%. Prenatal diagnosis is available by use of cytogenetic or molecular testing.

Individuals with AS due to IC mutations have either inherited this mutation from a normal mother or have received the mutation spontaneously (i.e., not inherited). In the former case the theoretical recurrence risk is 50% and in the latter (i.e., spontaneous mutation) the risk is believed to be less than 1%.

Those with AS due to UBE3A mutations, as is the case with IC mutations, have either received the mutation from a normal mother or acquired it by spontaneous mutation. Recurrence risk is felt to be 50% in the former and less than 1% in the latter. When IC or UBE3A mutations have been molecularly characterized, prenatal diagnosis is available via molecular testing. Cases of AS that are associated with a structurally abnormal chromosome 15 (i.e., a chromosome translocation) may have an increased risk for recurrence. In these instances, the recurrence risk must be based upon the specific chromosome abnormality and what is known about its risk of recurrence. Prenatal diagnosis by cytogenetic and/or molecular techniques is generally available in these instances.

Estimating recurrence risks is very difficult for individuals with AS who have normal genetic studies (i.e., have none of the above etiologies). Familial occurrence in this group does occur, so it is apparent that the recurrence risk for AS is higher than it is for those with, for example, a typical large common deletion. Until more is known about this group, caution is warranted during genetic counseling since the theoretical recurrence risk can be as high as 50% (if one assumes that undetected AS-causing mutations has been inherited from the mother).

It should be noted that the customary chromosome study, performed during routine prenatal diagnosis is often interpreted as normal in AS fetuses with deletions, since the small abnormalities on chromosome 15 would not be detected by this type of study. Specialized chromosome 15/FISH studies are needed for prenatal diagnosis in cases where the testing seeks to establish normal chromosome 15 structure. Also, fetal ultrasound offers no help in detecting physical abnormalities related to AS since the affected fetus is expected to be well formed. Amniotic fluid volume and alpha-feto-protein levels also appear normal.

Because of the complexities of evaluating recurrence risk, genetic counseling from an expert familiar with AS is advised.

References

1. Angelman, H. "Puppet" children: A report on three cases. *Dev Med Child Neurol.* l965;7:681-688.

2. Bower BD, Jeavons PM. The "happy puppet" syndrome. *Arch Dis Child.* 1967;42:298-302.

3. Berg, JM and Pakula, Z. Angelman's ("happy puppet") syndrome. *Am J Dis Child.* 1972; 123:72-74.

4. Berggreen, S. "Happy puppet" syndrome. *Ugeskr Laeger.* 1972; 134:1174.

5. Kibel MA, Burness FR, The "happy puppet" syndrome. *Centr Afr J Med.* 1973; 19:91-93.

6. Mayo 0, Nelson MM, Townsend, HRA. Three more "happy puppets". *Dev Med Child Neural.* 1973;1S:63-74.

7. Moore JR, Jeavons PM. The "happy puppet" syndrome: Two new cases and a review of five previous cases. *Neuropaediatrie.* 1973;4: 172-179.

8. Elian M. Fourteen happy puppets. *Clin Pediatr.* 1975; 14:902-908.

9. Pashayan H, Singer W, Dove C, Eisenberg E, Seto B. The Angelman syndrome in two brothers. *Am J Med Genet.* 1982;13:295-298.

10. Williams CA, Frias IL. The Angelman ("happy puppet") syndrome. *Am J Med Genet.* 1982; 11:543-460.

11. Clayton-Smith J and Pembrey ME. Angelman syndrome. *J Med Genet*. 1992;29(6):412-415.

12. Saitoh, S., Harada, N., Jinno, Y., et al. Molecular and clinical study of 61 Angelman syndrome patients. *Am J Med Genet*. 1994;52: 158-163.

13. Zori RT, Hendrickson J, Woolven S, Whidden EM, Gray B, Williams CA. Angelman syndrome: clinical profile. *J Child Neuro*. 1992;7(3):279-280.

14. Chan CTJ, Clayton-Smith J, Cheng XJ, et al. Molecular mechanisms in Angelman syndrome: a survey of 93 patients. *J Med Genet*. 1993;30:895-902.

15. Buntinx IM, Ilunnekam RCM, Brouwer OF, Stroink H, Beuten J, Mangelsehots K, Fryns JP. Clinical profile of Angelman syndrome at different ages. *Am J Med Genet*. 1995;56: 176-183.

16. Angelman H (1991): personal correspondence

17. Williams CA, Angelman H, Clayton-Smith J, Driscoll DJ, Hendrickson JE, Knoll JHM, Magenis RE, Schinzel A, Wagstaff J, Whidden EM, Zori RT. Angelman syndrome: Consensus for diagnostic criteria. *Am J Med Genet*. 1995;56:237-238.

18. Kishino T, Lalande M, Wagstaff J. UBE3A/E6-AP mutations cause Angelman syndrome. *Nature Genet*. 1997;15:70-73

19. Matsuura T, Sutcliffe JS, Fang P. et al. De novo truncations mutations in E6-AP ubiquitin-protein ligase gen (UBE3A) in Angelman syndrome. *Nature Genet*. 1997;15:74-77.

20. Mitch WE, Goldberg AL. Mechanisms of Muscle Wasting The Role of the Ubiquitin-Proteasome Pathway. *NEJM*. 1996;335:58-64

21. Saitoh S, Buiting K, Cassidy S, et al. Clinical Spectrum and Molecular Diagnosis of Angelman and prader-Willi Syndrome Patients With an Imprinting Mutation. *Am J Med Genet*. 1997;68:195-206

22. Fryburg JS, Breg WR, Lindgren V. Diagnosis of Angelman Syndrome in infants. *Am J Med Genet*. 1991;38:58-64.

23. Clayton-Smith, J. Clinical research on Angelman syndrome in the United Kingdom: observations on 82 affected individuals. *Am J Med Genet.* l993;46(1): 12-15.

24. Bottani A, Robinson 'VP, DeLozier-Blanchet CD, et al. Angelman syndrome due to paternal uniparental disomy of chromosome 15: A milder phenotype? *Am J Med Genet.* 1994;51:35-40.

25. Wagstaff J. Genetic and Clinical Studies of Angelman Syndrome. Angelman Syndrome Foundation Medial and Scientific Symposium. July 3, 1997, Seattle, Washington.

Additional Information

National Angelman Syndrome Foundation, USA
414 Plaza Drive, Suite 209
Westmont, IL 60550
Tel:800-432-6435
Fax: 630-655-0391
E-Mail: asf@adminsys.com
URL: http://chem-faculty.ucsd.edu/harvey/asfsite/

Section 11.3

Phenylketonuria (PKU)

What Is PKU?

PKU, which stands for Phenylketonuria, is an inherited metabolic disease (also called an inborn error of metabolism) that leads to mental retardation and other developmental disabilities if untreated in infancy. With an inborn error of metabolism, the body is unable to produce proteins or enzymes needed to convert certain toxic chemicals into nontoxic products, or to transport substances from one place to another (Glanze, 1996).

The body's inability to carry out these vital internal functions may result in neurological damage. In the case of PKU, the amino acid called phenylalanine accumulates. As phenylalanine builds up in the bloodstream, it causes brain damage. Infants with untreated PKU appear to develop typically for the first few months of life, but by twelve months of age most babies will have a significant developmental delay and will be diagnosed with mental retardation before school entry.

How Is PKU Inherited?

PKU is inherited as a single-gene disorder. Single-gene disorders are caused by a mutant or abnormal gene. They can be inherited in one of three patterns: autosomal dominant, autosomal recessive, and X-linked. PKU is an autosomal recessive disorder. Each parent of a child with PKU carries one defective gene for the disorder and one normal gene. In a recessive condition, an individual must have two defective genes in order to have the disorder. Individuals with only one copy of a defective gene are called "carriers," show no symptoms of having the disease, and usually remain unaware of their status until they have an affected child. In order for a child to inherit PKU, both parents must be PKU carriers. When this occurs, there is a one in four chance of their producing an affected child with each pregnancy. Boys and girls are equally at risk of inheriting this disorder.

How Is PKU Diagnosed?

Before the 1960s, most infants born with PKU developed mental retardation and cerebral palsy. Although treatment for PKU using a low phenylalanine diet was first described in the 1950s, the inability to detect PKU early in the child's life limited effective treatment.

The first newborn screening test was developed by Dr. Robert Guthrie in 1959 specifically to test for PKU. This simple, yet very effective and economical test was developed to screen newborn infants for PKU before leaving the hospital. Today, all states routinely screen newborns for PKU. To test for PKU, the infant's heal is pricked and a few drops of blood are taken. This blood sample is then tested in a state laboratory for abnormal amounts of phenylalanine.

The normal phenylalanine level is less than 2 mg/dl. Those with phenylalanine levels of 20.0 milligrams per deciliter (mg/dl) or higher are considered likely to have "classical" PKU (Yanicelli, Davidson & vanDoornick, 1986). Infants with these high levels are further tested to confirm the diagnosis before treatment is started. Some infants will have more modest elevations of blood phenylalanine and are said to have "mild hyperphenylalanemia." Today many clinicians believe that any child with a phenylalanine level greater than 6 or 8 mg/dl should be treated with a modified phenylalanine restricted diet.

Is Testing for PKU 100 Percent Accurate?

Experts recommend that testing for PKU should be done when the infant is at least twenty-four hours of age but less than seven days old. If an infant is tested too soon after birth, there is a chance that some cases of PKU will be missed as the phenylalanine level will not have risen yet. Now that many hospitals are discharging mothers and infants twenty-four hours after birth, there is a greater likelihood of this happening. The American Academy of Pediatrics recommends that infants receiving the test during the first twenty-four hours of life be retested at two to three weeks of age during their first postnatal pediatric visit (March of Dimes, 1994).

How Is PKU Treated?

Although PKU is not preventable, its symptoms can often be treated successfully through the use of a carefully regimented diet. The diet consists of foods that have a restricted phenylalanine content. Babies are given a special formula that contains very low phenylalanine levels; then they gradually progress to eating certain vegetables and other foods that are low in phenylalanine. Affected children must have their blood tested regularly to ensure the presence of the correct level of phenylalanine.

Foods recommended for those affected by PKU contain small amounts of protein, such as fruits and vegetables, limited amounts of cereal and grain products, and special low protein products available through mail-order. High protein foods such as meat, fish, eggs, poultry, dairy products, nuts, peanut butter, legumes, soy products, and products containing Nutrasweet should be avoided (Yannicelli, Davidson & vanDoornick, 1986).

The food program used to treat those with PKU is quite expensive, typically costing up to $10,000 a year or more. Although health departments may pay for the formula in some states and mandated insurance coverage may cover the cost in other states, most insurance companies do not cover the cost of treatment for children/adults with PKU because it is considered nutritional rather than medical therapy. While phenylalanine restricted diets have proven to be highly effective

119

in preventing mental retardation, it is now recognized that there may still be subtle cognitive deficits. Usually the individual has a normal IQ, but the incidence of attention deficit hyperactivity disorder (ADHD) and learning disabilities is higher compared to those children who do not have PKU (Yanicelli, Davidson & vanDoornick, 1986).

Do Those Affected by PKU Have to Stay on a Regimented Diet All Their Lives?

It was believed in the past that children could discontinue the diet when they turned five to six years old. Recent studies have found that children with PKU who did stop the diet in early childhood did not develop as rapidly as children who remained on the diet. They also had more learning disabilities, behavioral problems, and other neurological problems. Thus, until research provides alternative treatments, all persons with PKU should remain on a restricted diet indefinitely in order to maintain a safe level of phenylalanine (believed to be in the range of 2-6 mg/dl) (Schuett, 1996).

What Happens When Women with PKU Have Children?

When women with PKU who are not receiving dietary therapy become pregnant, their high levels of phenylalanine can damage their unborn child, causing mental retardation and other congenital defects. High levels of phenylalanine are extremely toxic to the brain of a fetus. Thus, although the child does not have PKU, he or she will have sustained brain damage from the toxic effects of phenylalanine in utero (in the womb). This is known as "Maternal PKU."

More than 90 percent of infants born to women with PKU who are not on a specialized diet will have mental retardation, and may also have small head size (microcephaly), heart defects, and low birth weight. These infants cannot be treated with a special diet since they do not have PKU. Therefore, women who have PKU should be on a phenylalanine restricted diet at least one year before pregnancy and should stay on the diet while breast-feeding to increase the chance of having a healthy child (Levy, 1988).

Are Other Rare Metabolic Disorders Associated with Mental Retardation Being Screened For as Well as PKU?

Dr. Guthrie's newborn screening test for PKU sparked the testing for other rare metabolic disorders associated with mental retardation:

congenital hypothyroidism, galactosemia, homocystinuria, biotinidase deficiency, and maple syrup urine disease. While all states and the District of Columbia screen for PKU, only some states screen for the other metabolic conditions (The Arc, 1994).

The development of a screening test for PKU was a significant step toward preventing mental retardation caused by metabolic disorders. Unfortunately, there remain more than 100 rare metabolic disorders that lead to mental retardation for which newborn screening is currently unavailable (McKusick, 1994).

Quick Facts

Condition: Phenylketonuria (PKU)

Link to mental retardation: Brain damage leading to mental retardation that occurs in children with PKU due to high blood levels of phenylalanine that is not properly metabolized (broken down).

Primarily affects: Newborns; more common among North European descent, less common among Jewish, Asian, and African-American families.

Symptoms: Typical appearance during first few months after birth but at three-five months the baby will lose interest in its surroundings and have mental retardation by twelve months of age. It may often be irritable, restless, or destructive. Other symptoms include dry skin or rashes, a strong, musty body odor, and convulsions.

Incidence: One in every 12,000 to 15,000 babies is born with PKU in the U.S.

Cause: An inherited disorder caused by a build up of an amino acid called phenylalanine that, if left untreated, causes mental retardation. The higher the level of phenylalanine within the body, generally the more severe the disability.

Treatment: A low-protein diet consisting of foods that have little or no phenylalanine can decrease the high levels of phenylalanine and prevent the occurrence of mental retardation. All babies in the U.S. are routinely screened for PKU.

For More Information

National PKU News
206-525-8140
E-mail: pkunews@workmail.com

Children's PKU Network
(619) 233-3202

The Arc
National Organization on Mental Retardation
1010 Wayne Ave, Suite 650
Silver Spring, MD 20910
Tel: 301-565-3842
Fax: 301-565-3843
E-mail: thearc@metronet.com
URL: http://www.thearc.org

References

Glanze, W. (Ed.). (1996). *The signet Mosby medical encyclopedia (revised edition)*. New York: Penguin Books Ltd.

Levy, H.L. (1988). Maternal phenylketonuria. *Progress in Clinical and Biological Research*, 281, 227-242.

March of Dimes (1994). PKU (Phenylketonuria): Public health information sheet. *The March of Dimes Birth Defects Foundation*. White Plains, New York.

McKusick, V.A. (1994). Mendelian inheritance in man. *Catalogs of Human Genes and Genetic Disorders. (Eleventh edition)*. Baltimore: Johns Hopkins University Press.

Schuett, V. (1996). What is PKU? *National PKU News* [On-line]. Available: http://www.wolfenet.com/~kronmal/pkuintro.htm.

The Arc (April, 1994) Newborn screening to prevent mental retardation. *Q&A*. Arlington, Texas.

Yannicelli, Davidson & vanDoornick (1986). Diet intervention for the late-treated adult with PKU. *Inherited Metabolic Diseases Clinic*. Denver, Colorado.

Section 11.4

Prader-Willi Syndrome

The following text is reprinted with permission of the Prader-Willi Syndrome Arizona Association: "What Is Prader-Willi Syndrome?" © 1998; "Imagine..." by Teresa Kellerman © 1997; "Family Dynamics: Relationships Within the Family," © 1997; and "Ask Miss Willi Nilli," © 1998.

What Is Prader-Willi Syndrome (PWS)?

Prader-Willi Syndrome (PWS) is a group of symptoms caused by a genetic defect in Chromosome 15. This uncommon condition occurs in about one in every 15,000 births, and was first described by Drs. Prader, Labhart, and Willi in 1956.

Symptoms of Prader-Willi Syndrome include many but not necessarily all of the following:

- **Central Nervous System** malfunction includes impaired body control and mental retardation with an average IQ around 70. Dysfunction of the hypothalamus affects physical growth, sexual development, appetite, temperature control, and emotional stability.

- **Hypotonia** during infancy with poor motor control, weak cry, and poor sucking ability. Although children get stronger as they grow older, muscle tone usually remains lower than normal.

- **Short stature**, with adults reaching about five feet. Small hands and feet, narrow forehead.

- **Insatiable appetite** begins somewhere between age 2 and 5 years. Since individuals with PWS have a metabolism which is only 60% of normal, they require fewer calories to maintain weight. An uncontrolled preoccupation with food usually leads to obesity, serious health problems, and early death unless access to food is strictly controlled. With adequate supervision and careful control of food intake, persons with PWS can maintain healthy weight.

- **Scratching and skin picking** due to increased pain tolerance and decreased sensory input.

- **Behavior difficulties** beginning in early childhood and persisting throughout adult life, includes temper tantrums, stubbornness, non-compliance, and resistance to transitions. Most persons with PWS show signs of obsessive-compulsive disorder (OCD), apart from their obsessions with food. OCD symptoms in PWS include ordering and arranging, concerns with symmetry, rewriting, and a compulsion to tell or ask the same thing over and over.

Prader-Willi Syndrome occurs when the deletion is in the *paternal* chromosome 15. When the deletion occurs in the *maternal* chomosome 15, the result is a totally different disability called Angelman's Syndrome, with a very different set of symptoms.

Imagine What It Would Be Like if You Were Born with Prader-Willi Syndrome

Imagine that your desire to get food is so strong that you would do anything to get it, even crawl out of your bedroom window in the middle of the night to walk to the store several miles away.

Imagine that you are hungry all the time, and that you are on a diet, all the time, and that you can only eat about half as much as everybody else, not to lose weight, but just so you don't gain weight. Imagine that if you do gain weight, you will have to go on an even stricter diet, getting about as many calories in one day as there are in just one cheeseburger and fries. Boy, would you like to have a cheeseburger and fries! But that's not in your diet. You are told that your diet is very important, because if you gain weight you could get really sick and die, because your heart can't handle the burden of obesity. Imagine that everybody in your group is going on a hike, and you want to go, but you know you will get tired easily, because your muscle tone is not really good, but you don't want to be left behind, so you go along, and it's really hard for you to keep up with everybody. And when you stop for lunch, the person next to you has a big sandwich with mayonnaise and cheese and roast beef and five cookies and potato chips, and the person sitting on the other side of you has 3 granola bars and trail mix with nuts and a candy bar. And you have two skinny slices of diet bread with mustard and a thin slice of ham, and a rice cake, and a teeny apple. You think that candy bar looks really good, and you watch that candy bar, because maybe it will get set down, and maybe you can get your hands on it, and maybe it would taste so good, and you can't think about anything else but that candy bar.

Imagine that you find a $20 bill laying on the ground, and you pick it up and put it in your pocket and don't tell anybody, because maybe you can buy some candy bars with it some time when no one is looking. But you get found out and you are accused of stealing, and nobody believes that you just found it.

Imagine that when you see a little scab on your arm, you just have to scratch it, you can't help it, you just have to! And when it bleeds, you get in trouble. And you try really hard to leave it alone, but you can't! And sometimes it takes over a year for sores to heal.

Imagine that when you want something to eat you have to ask, and then you usually get told "no" or you get carrot sticks, and you can't eat what you want because there is a lock on the refrigerator and on the pantry too. But you know if there were no locks, you would get more food, and gain weight and get sick. So you really don't mind if the food is locked up. At least you don't have to worry about getting food like you used to before there were locks, and you would wait until the middle of the night to get up and go get food without anyone knowing. You feel safe with the food locked up.

Imagine that there's something you like to do and you're really good at it, like working jig-saw puzzles. And you have one that is a thousand pieces, and you've been working on it for days, and you want to put it together all by yourself, because it's your puzzle and you know where all the pieces go, and then someone else puts pieces in for you, and you take it all apart to start over, and you get yelled at, and you are told you are stubborn, but it's your puzzle, and you just want to work it yourself.

Imagine that you are going to the movies, and everybody else is getting popcorn and candy, but you can only have a diet pop, but you have to sit there and smell everybody else's popcorn and chocolate, and watch them eat, and hear them munch. You really wish you could have a giant tub of popcorn like that guy over there! And you see a piece of popcorn that someone dropped and you pick it up and someone tries to grab it from you but you are faster then they are and you eat it, and they get mad at you, but it was worth it because that one little piece tasted so good. Better than the air popped stuff.

Imagine that you have a hard time expressing your feelings and you get mad easily, but only when things aren't fair. Only when someone breaks a promise. Only when you're not getting what you think you need or deserve.

Imagine that when you can't say what you want to say and you scream and hit. You wonder why you get in trouble for hollering when everybody else is hollering too! Or sometimes you just sit and refuse, and nobody can make you move. You know you feel better when you take your medicine, but you don't want to take your medicine. You don't know why, you just don't want to take it. When you refuse to take your medicine, you get in trouble. But when someone in charge forgets to give you your medicine and you lose control, then you are the one who gets in trouble.

Imagine that you have family and friends who understand you. Imagine that your teacher, your case manager, your care provider, your doctor, all understand PWS. They know you are different, but they know you are special too. Imagine how lucky you would be!

Family Dynamics: Relationships within the Family

Parent/Child Relationships

The primary care giver during infancy, usually the Mom, has an intense bond with the PWS child who had to be fed so carefully, to be nourished in order to get the underweight baby to gain weight. First having to feed with a gavage tube, then trying to get the baby to suck enough, taking an hour or two just to get a few ounces down.

The lack of facial affect, due to poor muscle tone, interferes with normal interaction between parent and baby, so the parent doesn't get that warm feeling of having the baby smile back. This happens later, and is so fleeting! Of course, later in life, the same child may be a drama star!

A great deal of energy is focused on getting the PWS baby to eat, respond, and move, usually with no diagnosis until later.

When the child leaves infancy and enters the second stage of PWS, the parent is suddenly faced with trying to keep the same child from eating too much! Along with behavior problems like tantrums and skin picking, there is a lot of guilt and self-doubt, until there is a diagnosis.

As long as the child lives in the home, a great deal of energy is spent on keeping the environment safe, and even with locks or alarms, the parent must be extremely vigilant. This cannot be avoided and is very draining.

The PWS child is so driven to get food, that the interaction between the child and the food giver, usually Mom, is replete with tantrums, arguing, manipulation, etc. The relationship is intense and requires a lot of energy.

Sibling Relationships

The siblings are sometimes unfairly and unwittingly given too much responsibility for the child with PWS, being asked to watch out for the child in the parents' absence. The siblings may be subjected to low-calorie meals and locked refrigerators. This can lead to resentment. Sometimes an older sibling can have a locked bedroom with a personal refrigerator to give more personal freedom.

The siblings are sometimes unintentionally ignored falsely assuming that the child with PWS is more important than they are because of the time and energy that goes into coping with PWS syndrome. Allowing the sibling to verbalize their feelings in a non-judgmental setting can be helpful.

In junior high years, siblings may be embarrassed by PWS behaviors, and may show hostility toward the child they used to tolerate. Often, teens desire more privacy and distance from the child with PWS. This usually dissipates later. Offer a teen the chance to "sit" for the child with PWS, for pay, and with the option to decline. Make arrangements for respite sitters so the teen doesn't feel obligated.

Studies show that a sibling of a child with a disability may feel greater pressure to perform and succeed. Older siblings may feel that they are responsible or will be responsible for the care of the child with PWS. This is a great burden, even if it is not expressly implied. This could invoke fear and resentment. Plans should be made for a guardian to be named in the parents' will other than a sibling under the age of 25. This should be communicated to the children. If and when parents choose a sibling to be named as guardian, this should be discussed frankly and openly before it is legalized.

Parents Supporting Each Other

Often one parent is the strict and the other is lenient. One parent may seek information while the other may deny there is a disability. It is important that each parent support the other, and that both get as much information as possible, and that both become involved in parent support groups (or start one!).

It is extremely difficult to find a respite sitter that is qualified and willing. Sometimes a good sitter just can't be found, and a parent can become isolated.

It is important for the care giver to talk with people. It is helpful if the case manager and others on the team can be supportive listeners.

There is a tendency to let PWS take over the family, and the parent who is less active in the care may feel neglected or shut out, while the parent giving care may feel overwhelmed and unsupported. Studies show that parents of children with PWS have greater stress than parents of children with any other disability. Counseling is always helpful and sometimes necessary.

Questions and Answers

Note: The following suggestions are not to be taken as professional advice. If you have questions about medications or treatment, please consult a physician who knows about PWS. Suggestions on nutrition can be confirmed by consulting a nutritionist. All information here is based on expertise of professionals who have extensive knowledge of PWS.

I Have Begun to Count Calories for My Child, Age 13, Who Has PWS. How Much Fat Should There Be in Her Diet?

I'm so glad you will be counting calories. Kids with PWS usually like to count up all the numbers. Most nutritionists suggest that the diet consist of approximately 25% fat calories, 25% calories of protein, and 50% carbohydrates. For a 1,000-calorie-a-day diet, intake should consist of 27.7 grams of fat, 62.5 grams of protein, and 125 grams of carbohydrates. The usual prescription for age 10 and over for maintenance is 1200-1400 calories a day, and 1,000 calories a day for weight loss plus vitamins with minerals.

My Child Likes to Eat a Lot, But 1,000 Calories Is Not Very Much. What Should I Do?

Quantity is very important to a person with PWS, so just pile the plate high with salad greens and veggies. Spread it around the plate. Serve many small servings instead of a few large large servings. There are some great recipes that make large servings with few calories.

Skin Picking Has Become a Real Problem. What Can I Do to Get Him to Stop?

Skin picking in persons with PWS is neurological in origin, and the person has little control over the urge to pick. The high pain tolerance, the decreased sensation on certain areas of the skin, and out-of-balance neurochemicals in the brain all contribute to the tendency to pick. One technique that seems to work quite well is Sensory Integration Therapy, treatment that can be prescribed upon evaluation of your child by an occupational therapist. Until you get professional advice, here are some things you can do:

- Provide your child with lots of touching, to the back and shoulders and arms. Back rubs help a great deal.

- Use brisk rubbing on the skin, almost like warming up after coming in from the cold. This increases circulation and gives greater input to the brain from the skin. This helps to normalize processing of the central nervous system. This brisk rubbing has an effect that lasts about 2-1/2 hours, so this can be done several times a day.

If these are done consistently, you will probably see a marked decrease in picking. It has been known to eradicate skin picking completely.

Why Has My Child, Age 12, Become Aggressive?

Consult a specialist in behavior management. While the tendency to have tantrums is neurological in nature and the person with PWS lacks total control over this tendency, sometimes offering external motivation can help give them a certain amount of control. Find out what your child really wants, then contract with him/her to get it. Be positive, focusing on the behavior you want, in this case respect of others and appropriate expression of feelings. Make the contract fair, so that it is not too hard for the child to succeed. Have a daily contract for behavior that is healthy and safe, with an additional weekly reward for 5 out of 7 successful days. Remember, that studies show that children are less likely to exhibit aggressive behavior if they have not witnessed or experienced aggression first. This means that the behavior of role models and family members should be non-aggressive, and TV programs should be monitored for violent content.

How Do I Teach My Child Peaceful Problem Solving?

Help your child to verbalize her feelings. If she is angry, tell her, "You look like you are really angry, tell me what is upsetting you". Listen without getting hooked into an argument. A little empathy can go a long way. People with PWS get angry about situations they perceive to be unjust, whether it is real or imagined, it's all the same to them. Little things are as important as major issues. Offer a notebook and pen, and ask her to write down all the things that she feels angry about at that moment. Allow her to call someone who will be willing to listen. Promise to do something about the situation, such as "I will call so-and-so tomorrow and we will set up a meeting". Negotiate! This really works. Offer a compromise so that the child feels like a winner. Usually, with negotiation, you can come up with a solution that makes everyone happy. Try to anticipate when there will be a problem, and negotiate ahead of time, before the anger erupts. It takes time and effort, but it's worth it.

Section 11.5

Tuberous Sclerosis

Reprinted with permission © "Tuberous Sclerosis: Facts You Need to Know," National Tuberous Sclerosis Association (NTSA), and "Questions and Answers about Tuberous Sclerosis," by Vicky Holets Whittemore © reprinted with permission of the NTSA.

Tuberous Sclerosis: Facts You Need to Know

- At least one child born each day will be affected with Tuberous Sclerosis (TS). Current estimates place TS-affected births at 1 in 5,800.

- Nearly one million people world-wide are know to have Tuberous Sclerosis.

- Tuberous Sclerosis effects can be mild to severe. Tumors can grow on any body organ, but most strike the brain, kidneys, heart, lungs, and skin.

- Defects on two separate genes have been found to cause Tuberous Sclerosis. Only one of the genes needs to be affected for TS to be present. The defect in Chromosome 16 was discovered in December 1993. The defect in Chromosome 9 was discovered in August 1997.

- The TS genes 9 and 16 are believed to both act to suppress tumor growth in the body. When those genes are defective, tumors are not suppressed, and Tuberous Sclerosis results.

- Tuberous Sclerosis is genetically transmitted as an autosomal dominant disorder. This means that only one parent need have the gene and each child has a 50% chance of inheriting TS.

- Only one-third of Tuberous Sclerosis cases are, at this point, known to be genetically transmitted. The other two-thirds are believed to be a result of spontaneous mutation, with researchers believing the mutation occurs in individual sperm and egg cells prior to conception. The cause of these mutations is a mystery.

- A TS genetic diagnostic test is under development. Diagnosis is currently made after MRI, CT Scan, ultrasound, echocardiogram, EKG, ophthalmoscope, and Wood's Lamp evaluation. A recent study showed diagnosis takes an average 90 days with consultation of at least three specialists.

- The most common first symptoms of Tuberous Sclerosis are white spots and seizures, with up to 80% of TS-affected individuals experiencing seizures at some point in their life. Medication provides relief for some, but not all, TS individuals. Surgery provides improvement in frequency of seizures for some.

- TS is the largest known genetic cause of epilepsy. Seizures result from brain tubers or lesions (small patches in the brain that don't develop normally.)

- Tuberous Sclerosis is now the second largest identifiable genetic cause of autism.

- Tuberous Sclerosis affects on the brain can also produce behavioral problems such as aggression, uncontrollable rage, or hyperactivity in mild to severe forms.

- Tuberous Sclerosis can cause destruction of kidneys, lungs, heart, or other affected organs.

- Some individuals develop malignant kidney tumors.

- Over 60% of individuals with Tuberous Sclerosis cannot function independently.

- There are many undiagnosed cases of Tuberous Sclerosis. This is due to the obscurity of the disease and the mild form symptoms may take in some people. TS is as common as ALS (Lou Gehrig's Disease) but virtually unknown by the general population.

* People with mild cases of Tuberous Sclerosis can produce a child that is severely affected.

* Advancements in treatments are bringing new hope to those with TS. Surgery to remove tumors is helping to preserve kidney function and the function of other affected organs. Technology is developing to pinpoint the exact portions of the brain stimulating seizures. In some cases those portions can be surgically removed to relieve seizure frequency without impact on function or intelligence.

Questions and Answers about Tuberous Sclerosis

Can I Catch Tuberous Sclerosis from Another Person?

No you cannot "catch" tuberous sclerosis from someone, but you can inherit it from your parents if they have the disorder. Tuberous sclerosis is an autosomal dominant genetic disorder which means if a parent has the tuberous sclerosis gene, each offspring of the person has a 50% chance of inheriting it.

Where Is the Gene for Tuberous Sclerosis?

There are actually two genes that can cause tuberous sclerosis. One of the genes (the TSC1 gene) is located on chromosome 9 and is called the hamartin gene. The other gene (the TSC2 gene) is located on chromosome 16 and is called the tuberin gene. Researchers are now trying to determine what these genes do and how a defect in these genes causes tuberous sclerosis.

Is There a Genetic Test (Prenatal Test) for Tuberous Sclerosis?

No, a genetic test for tuberous sclerosis is not yet available. Even though the TSC2 gene has been located, it will take two or three more years of research to develop a genetic test for the gene. The researchers have to find out what changes in the gene actually cause tuberous sclerosis and refine their methods to pick out these gene defects.

How Can so Many Different Organs Be Affected by Tuberous Sclerosis?

Researchers speculate that the defect in the tuberous sclerosis genes causes problems in cells in many different organs because the genes are important for cell function very early in the life of the fetus. At the earliest stages there are only a few cells that make up the fetus. A defect in these early stages can lead to problems in many different organs.

What Is the Normal Life Expectancy of an Individual with Tuberous Sclerosis?

Individuals with tuberous sclerosis can live long, productive lives and will die from the same things everyone else does—heart disease, cancer, strokes, etc. There can be complications from the disease in some organs such as the kidneys and brain that can lead to difficulties and even death, but with modern medical techniques, individuals with tuberous sclerosis can look forward to excellent health care and long lives.

What Is the Average Age at Diagnosis of Individuals with Tuberous Sclerosis?

This figure is not known. Sixty to eighty percent of individuals will have seizures at some point in their life. Many individuals with tuberous sclerosis present to their doctor because they develop seizures, and will subsequently be diagnosed with tuberous sclerosis. Seizures can start at any time, from infancy to adulthood. Seizures in individuals with tuberous sclerosis are often intractable (do not respond to anti-epileptic drugs), so they will go through life having seizure after seizure every day. With new anti-epileptic drugs coming onto the market, and new advances in brain surgery for seizures, there is hope for all individuals with tuberous sclerosis.

Are the Tumors That Form in the Brain, Heart, Kidneys, and Eyes Cancerous?

No, the tumors that form in these organs are benign, but may cause problems. Tumors that grow in the brain can block the flow of cerebral spinal fluid in the spaces (ventricles) in the brain. This can lead to behavior changes, nausea, headaches, or a number of other symptoms. In the heart, the tumors are usually at their largest at birth, and then decrease in size as the individual gets older. These heart tumors, called cardiac rhabdomyomas, can cause problems at birth if they are blocking the flow of blood, or causing severe arrhythmia problems. The tumors in the kidney (renal angiomyolipoma) can become so large as to eventually take over all of the normal kidney function. In the past, the patient was left until they developed kidney failure. Today, doctors are more aggressive and remove individual tumors before they get too large and compromise healthy kidney tissue. The tumors in the eyes are not as common, but can present problems if they grow and block too much of the retina.

For More Information

National Tuberous Sclerosis Association
8181 Professional Pl., #110
Landover, MD 20785
Toll-free: 800-225-6872
Fax: 301-459-0394

Section 11.6

Williams Syndrome

Reprinted with permission © 1997, Williams Syndrome Association.

Facts about Williams Syndrome

Williams syndrome is a rare genetic condition (estimated to occur in 1/20,000 births) which causes medical and developmental problems.

Williams syndrome is a genetic disorder that was first recognized as a distinct entity in 1961. It is present at birth, and affects males and females equally. It can occur in all ethnic groups and has been identified in countries throughout the world.

Common Facial Features of Williams Syndrome

Most young children with Williams syndrome are described as having similar facial features. These features which tend to be recognized by only a trained geneticist or birth defects specialist, include a small upturned nose, long philtrum (upper lip length), wide mouth, full lips, small chin, and puffiness around the eyes. Blue and green-eyed children with Williams syndrome can have a prominent "starburst" or white lacy pattern on their iris. Facial features become more apparent with age.

Heart and Blood Vessel Problems

The majority of individuals with Williams syndrome have some type of heart or blood vessel problem. Typically, there is narrowing in the aorta (producing supravalvular aortic stenosis—SVAS), or narrowing in the pulmonary arteries. There is a broad range in the degree of narrowing, ranging from trivial to severe (requiring surgical correction of the defect). Since there is an increased risk for development of blood vessel narrowing or high blood pressure over time, periodic monitoring of cardiac status is necessary.

Hypercalcemia (Elevated Blood Calcium Levels)

Some young children with Williams syndrome have elevations in their blood calcium level. The true frequency and cause of this problem is unknown. When hypercalcemia is present, it can cause extreme irritability or "colic-like" symptoms. Occasionally, dietary or medical treatment is needed. In most cases, the problem resolves on its own during childhood, but lifelong abnormality in calcium or Vitamin D metabolism may exist and should be monitored.

Low Birth Weight/Low Weight Gain

Most children with Williams syndrome have a slightly lower birth weight than their brothers or sisters. Slow weight gain, especially during the first several years of life, is also a common problem and many children are diagnosed with "failure to thrive." Adult stature is slightly smaller than average.

Feeding Problems

Many infants and young children have feeding problems. These problems have been linked to low muscle tone, severe gag reflex, poor suck/swallow, tactile defensiveness, etc. Feeding difficulties tend to resolve as the children get older.

Irritability (Colic During Infancy)

Many infants with Williams syndrome have an extended period of colic or irritability. This typically lasts from 4 to 10 months of age, then resolves. It is sometimes attributed to hypercalcemia. Abnormal sleep patterns with delayed acquisition of sleeping through the night may be associated with the colic.

Dental Abnormalities

Slightly small, widely spaced teeth are common in children with Williams syndrome. They also may have a variety of abnormalities of occlusion (bite), tooth shape or appearance. Most of these dental changes are readily amenable to orthodontic correction.

Kidney Abnormalities

There is a slightly increased frequency of problems with kidney structure and/or function.

Hernias

Inguinal (groin) and umbilical hernias are more common in Williams syndrome than in the general population.

Hyperacusis (Sensitive Hearing)

Children with Williams syndrome often have more sensitive hearing than other children. Certain frequencies or noise levels can be painful and/or startling to the individual. This condition often improves with age.

Musculoskeletal Problems

Young children with Williams syndrome often have low muscle tone and joint laxity. As the children get older, joint stiffness (contractures) may develop. Physical therapy is very helpful in improving muscle tone, strength, and joint range of motion.

Overly Friendly (Excessively Social) Personality

Individuals with Williams syndrome have a very endearing personality. They have a unique strength in their expressive language skills, and are extremely polite. They are typically unafraid of strangers and show a greater interest in contact with adults than with their peers.

Developmental Delay, Learning Disabilities, and Attention Deficit

Most people with Williams syndrome have some degree of intellectual handicap. Young children with Williams syndrome often experience developmental delays; milestones such as walking, talking, and toilet training are often achieved somewhat later than is considered normal. Distractibility is a common problem in mid-childhood, which appears to get better as the children get older.

Older children and adults with Williams syndrome often demonstrate intellectual "strengths and weaknesses." There are some intellectual areas (such as speech, long term memory, and social skills) in which performance is quite strong, while other intellectual areas (such as fine motor and spatial relations) are significantly deficient.

What Is the Cause of Williams Syndrome?

Williams syndrome is not caused by anything the parents did or did not do either before or during pregnancy. We know that most individuals with Williams syndrome are missing genetic material on chromosome #7 including the gene that makes the protein elastin (a protein which provides strength and elasticity to vessel walls.) It is likely that the elastin gene deletion accounts for many of the physical features of Williams syndrome. Some medical and developmental problems are probably caused by deletions of additional genetic material near the elastin gene on chromosome #7. The extent of these deletions may vary among individuals. In most families the child with Williams syndrome is the only one to have the condition in his or her entire extended family. However, the individual with Williams syndrome has a 50% chance of passing the disorder on to each of his or her children.

How Is Williams Syndrome Diagnosed?

Many individuals with Williams syndrome remain undiagnosed or are diagnosed at a relatively late age. This is of concern since individuals with Williams syndrome can have significant and possibly progressive medical problems. When the characteristics of Williams syndrome are recognized, referral to a clinical geneticist for further diagnostic evaluation is appropriate. The clinical diagnosis can be confirmed by a blood test. The technique known as fluorescent in situ hybridization (FISH), a diagnostic test of the DNA detects the elastin deletion on chromosome #7 in more than 98% of individuals with Williams syndrome.

Are Medical Problems Frequent in Williams Syndrome?

Williams syndrome can affect many different body organs. However, it is important to remember that no two individuals with Williams syndrome have exactly the same problems. Since some of the medical problems can develop over time, it is important that individuals with Williams syndrome receive ongoing medical monitoring and supervision. Despite the possibility of medical problems, most children and adults with Williams syndrome are healthy and lead active, full lives.

What Is the Outlook for Adults with Williams Syndrome?

The vast majority of adults with Williams syndrome master self-help skills and complete academic and/or vocational school. They are employed in a variety of settings (ranging from supervised to independent jobs). Many adults with Williams syndrome live with their parents; others live in supervised apartments and some are able to live on their own.

Who Should Care for Individuals with Williams Syndrome?

Given the complex nature of many of the problems found in individuals with Williams syndrome, many health and educational professionals should be involved in their care. Regular monitoring for potential medical problems is necessary and should be done by a physician familiar with the broad array of problems that can be seen in Williams syndrome.

Due to the intellectual "strengths and weaknesses," the expertise of developmental psychologists, speech and language pathologists, physical and occupational therapists, etc. who are familiar with Williams syndrome is recommended. Multi-disciplinary Williams syndrome teams, with professionals available in all of these areas, can be an effective adjunct to local resources. When a Williams syndrome clinic is not close by, it is necessary for the family to seek out professionals in their communities to provide this crucial input.

Additional Information

Williams Syndrome Association (WSA)
1316 N. Campbell, Suite 16
Royal Oak, MI 48067
Tel: 248-541-3630
Fax: 248-541-3631
E-mail: wsaoffice@aol.com

Williams Syndrome Foundation
University of California
Irvine, CA 92679-2310
Tel: 949-824-7259
URL: http://www.wsf.org

Chapter 12

Developmental Disorders

Contents

Section 12.1

Pervasive Developmental Disorders

National Information Center for Children and Youth with Disabilities
(NICHCY), Briefing Paper by Luke Y. Tsai, M.D., #FS20, January 1998.

Introduction

The term Pervasive Developmental Disorders was first used in the
1980s to describe a class of disorders. This class of disorders has in
common the following characteristics: impairments in social interaction,
imaginative activity, verbal and nonverbal communication skills, and
a limited number of interests and activities that tend to be repetitive.

The manual used by physicians and mental health professionals
as a guide to diagnosing disorders is the *Diagnostic and Statistical
Manual of Mental Disorders* (DSM). In DSM-IV, five disorders are
identified under the category of Pervasive Developmental Disorders:

1. Autistic Disorder

2. Rett's Disorder

3. Childhood Disintegrative Disorder

4. Asperger's Disorder, and

5. Pervasive Developmental Disorder Not Otherwise Specified or
   PDDNOS

Doctors are divided on the use of the term PDD. Many professionals use the term PDD as a short way of saying PDDNOS. Some doctors, however, are hesitant to diagnose very young children with a
specific type of PDD, such as Autistic Disorder, and therefore only use
the general category label of PDD This approach contributes to the
confusion about the term, because the term PDD actually refers to a
category of disorders and is not a diagnostic label. The appropriate
diagnostic label to be used is PDDNOS—Pervasive Developmental
Disorder Not Otherwise Specified—not PDD (the umbrella category
under which PDDNOS is found).

All the disorders that fall under the category of PDD share, to some extent, similar characteristics. To understand how the disorders differ and how they are alike, it's useful to look at the definition of each disorder.

Definition of the PDD Category and Its Five Specific Disorders

All types of PDD are neurological disorders that are usually evident by age 3. In general, children who have a type of PDD have difficulty in talking, playing with other children, and relating to others, including their family.

According to the definition set for in the DSM-IV, Pervasive Developmental Disorders are characterized by severe and pervasive impairment in several areas of development:

- social interaction skills;
- commuication skills; or
- the presence of stereotyped behavior, interests, and activities

The Five Types of PDD

Autistic Disorder, sometimes referred to as early infantile autism or childhood autism, is four times more common in boys than in girls. Children with Autistic Disorder have a moderate to severe range of communication, socialization, and behavior problems. Many children with autism also have mental retardation.

Rett's Disorder, also know as Rett Syndrome, is diagnosed primarily in females. In children with Rett's Disorder, development proceeds in an apparently normal fashion over the first 6 to 18 months at which point parents notice a change in their child's behavior and some regression or loss of abilities, especially in gross motor skills such as walking and moving. This is followed by an obvious loss in abilities such as speech, reasoning, and hand use. The repetition of certain meaningless gestures or movements is an important clue to diagnosing Rett's Disorder; these gestures typically consist of constant hand-wringing or hand-washing (Moeschler, Gibbs, & Graham 1990).

Childhood Disintegrative Disorder, an extremely rare disorder, is a clearly apparent regression in multiple areas of functioning (such as the ability to move, bladder and bowel control, and social and language skills) following a period of at least 2 years of apparently normal development. By definition Childhood Disintegrative Disorder can only be diagnosed if the symptoms are preceded by at least 2 years of normal development and the onset of decline is prior to age 10 (American Psychiatric Association, 1994).

Asperger's Disorder, also referred to as Asperger's or Asperger's Syndrome, is a developmental disorder characterized by a lack of social skills; difficulty with social relationships; poor coordination and poor concentration; and a restricted range of interests, but normal intelligence and adequate language skills in the areas of vocabulary and grammar. Asperger's Disorder appears to have a somewhat later onset than Autistic Disorder, or at least is recognized later. An individual with Asperger's Disorder does not possess a significant delay in language development; however, he or she may have difficulty understanding the subtleties used in conversation, such as irony and humor. Also, while many individuals with autism have mental retardation, a person with Asperger's possesses an average to above average intelligence (Autism Society of America, 1995). Asperger's is sometimes incorrectly referred to as "high-functioning autism."

Pervasive Developmental Disorder Not Otherwise Specified (PDDNOS). Children with PDDNOS either (a) do not fully meet the criteria of symptoms clinicians use to diagnose any of the four specific types of PDD above, and/or (b) do not have the degree of impairment described in any of the above four PDD specific types.

The Confusion of Diagnostic Labels

As discussed earlier, there is still some disagreement among professionals concerning the PDDNOS label. Some professionals consider "Autistic Disorder" appropriate only for those who show extreme symptoms in every one of several developmental areas related to autism. Other professionals are more comfortable with the term Autistic Disorder and use it to cover a broad range of symptoms connected with language and social dysfunction. Therefore, an individual may be diagnosed by one practitioner as having Autistic Disorder and by another practitioner as having PDDNOS (or PDD, if the practitioner is abbreviating for PDDNOS).

However, amidst all this confusion, it is very important to remember that, regardless of whether a child's diagnostic label is autism, PDDNOS, or MSDD, his or her treatment is similar.

144

The Cause of PDDNOS

Both behavioral and biological studies have generated sufficient evidence to suggest that PDDNOS is caused by a neurological abnormality—problems with the nervous system. However, no specific cause or causes have been identified.

While studies have found various nervous-system problems, no single problem has been consistently found, and exact causes are far from clear. This may be due to the current approach of defining PDDNOS based on behaviors (as opposed to, say, genetic testing). Hence, it is possible that PDDNOS is the result of several different conditions. If this is the case, it is anticipated that future studies will identify a range of causes.

The Symptoms and Signs of PDDNOS

Generally, children are 3 to 4 years old before they exhibit enough symptoms for parents to seek a diagnosis. There is no set pattern of symptoms and signs in children with PDDNOS. It is important to realize that a very wide range of diversity is seen in children with PDDNOS. All the items of behavior described in this section are common in these children, but a single child seldom shows all the features at one time. In other words, all children with PDDNOS do not have the same degree or intensity of the disorder. PDDNOS can be mild, with the child exhibiting a few symptoms while in the school or neighborhood environment. Other children may have a more severe form of PDDNOS and have difficulties in all areas of their lives. Because of the possibility that PDDNOS and Autistic Disorder are on a continuum, many clinical features described in the following section are very similar to those being described in the literature for Autistic Disorder.

Deficits in Social Behavior

Some infants with PDDNOS tend to avoid eye contact and demonstrate little interest in the human voice. They do not usually put up their arms to be picked up in the way that typical children do. They may seem indifferent to affection and seldom show facial responsiveness. As a result, parents often think the child is deaf. In children with fewer delays, lack of social responsiveness may not be obvious until well into the second or third year of life.

In early childhood, children with PDDNOS may continue to show a lack of eye contact, but they may enjoy a tickle or may passively accept physical contact. They do not develop typical attachment behavior, and there may seem to be a failure to bond. Generally, they do not follow their parents about the house. The majority of them do not show normal separation or stranger anxiety. These children may approach a stranger almost as readily as they do their parents. Many such children show a lack of interest in being with or playing with other children. They may even actively avoid other children.

In middle childhood, such children may develop a greater awareness or attachment to parents and other familiar adults. However, social difficulties continue. They still have problems with group games and forming peer relationships. Some of the children with less severe PDDNOS may become involved in other children's games.

As these children grow older, they may become affectionate and friendly with their parents and siblings. However, they still have difficulty understanding the complexity of social relationships. Some individuals with less severe impairments may have a desire for friendships. But a lack of response to other people's interests and emotions, as well as a lack of understanding of humor, often results in these youngsters saying or doing things that can slow the development of friendships.

Impairment in Nonverbal Communication

In early childhood, children with PDDNOS may develop the concrete gesture of pulling adults by the hand to the object that is wanted. They often do this without the typical accompanying facial expression. They seldom nod or shake their heads to substitute for or to accompany speech. Children with PDDNOS generally do not participate in games that involve imitation. They are less likely than typical children to copy their parents' activity.

In middle and late childhood, such children may not frequently use gestures, even when they understand other people's gestures fairly well. Some children do develop imitative play, but this tends to be repetitive.

Generally, children with PDDNOS are able to show joy, fear, or anger, but they may only show the extreme of emotions. They often do not use facial expressions that ordinarily show subtle emotion.

Impairment in Understanding Speech

Comprehension of speech in children with PDDNOS is impaired to varying degrees, depending on where the child is within the wide spectrum of PDDNOS. Individuals with PDDNOS who also have mental retardation may never develop more than a limited understanding of speech. Children who have less severe impairments may follow simple instructions if given in an immediate context or with the aid of gestures (e.g., telling the child to "put your glass on the counter," while pointing to the counter). When impairment is mild, only the comprehension of subtle or abstract meanings may be affected. Humor, sarcasm, and common sayings (e.g., "it's raining cats and dogs") can be confusing for individuals with the most mild PDDNOS.

Impairment in Speech Development

Many infants with PDDNOS do not babble, or may begin to babble in their first year but then stop. When the child develops speech, he or she often exhibits abnormalities. Echolalia (seemingly meaningless repetition of words or phrases) may be the only kind of speech some children acquire. Though echolalic speech might be produced quite accurately, the child may have limited comprehension of the meaning. In the past, it was thought that echolalia had no real function. More recent studies have found that echolalia can serve several functions, such as self-stimulation (when a child says words or phrases repeatedly without a communicative purpose—just because it feels good); as a step between a child being nonverbal and verbal; or as a way to communicate (Prizant & Rydell, 1993). Other children develop the appropriate use of phrases copied from others. This is often accompanied by pronoun reversal in the early stages of language development. For instance, when the child is asked "How are you?" he or she may answer "You are fine."

The actual production of speech may be impaired. The child's speech may be like that of a robot, characterized by a monotonous, flat delivery with little change in pitch, change of emphasis, or emotional expression.

Problems of pronunciation are common in young children with PDDNOS, but these often diminish as the child gets older. There may be a striking contrast between clearly enunciated echolalic speech and poorly pronounced spontaneous speech. Some children have a chanting or singsong speech, with odd prolongation of sounds, syllables, and words. A question-like intonation may be used for statements. Odd breathing rhythms may produce staccato speech in some children.

Abnormal grammar is frequently present in the spontaneous speech of verbal children with PDDNOS. As a result:

147

- phrases may be telegraphic (brief and monotone) and distorted;
- words of similar sound or related meaning may be muddled;
- some objects may be labeled by their use;
- new words may be coined; and
- prepositions, conjunctions, and pronouns may be dropped from phrases or used incorrectly.

When children with PDDNOS do develop functional speech, they may not use it in ordinary ways. Such children tend to rely on repetitive phrases. Their speech does not usually convey imagination, abstraction, or subtle emotion. They generally have difficulty talking about anything outside of the immediate context. They may talk excessively about their special interests, and they may talk about the same pieces of information whenever the same subject is raised. The most able persons can exchange concrete pieces of information that interest them, but once the conversation departs from this level, they can become lost and may withdraw from social contact. Ordinary to-and-fro conversational chatter is lacking. Thus, they give the impression of talking "at" someone, rather than "with" someone.

Unusual Patterns of Behavior

The unusual responses of children with PDDNOS to the environment take several forms.

Resistance to change. Many children are upset by changes in the familiar environment. Even a minor change of everyday routine may lead to tantrums. Some children line up toys or objects and become very distressed if these are disturbed. Efforts to teach new activities may be resisted.

Ritualistic or compulsive behaviors. Ritualistic or compulsive behaviors usually involve rigid routines (e.g., insistence on eating particular foods) or repetitive acts, such as hand flapping or finger mannerisms (e.g., twisting, flicking movements of hands and fingers carried out near the face). Some children develop preoccupations; they may spend a great deal of time memorizing weather information, state capitals, or birth dates of family members.

Abnormal attachments and behaviors. Some children develop intense attachments to odd objects, such as pipe cleaners, batteries, or film canisters. Some children may have a preoccupation with certain features of favored objects, such as their texture, taste, smell, or shape.

Unusual responses to sensory experiences. Many children may seem under-responsive or over-responsive to sensory stimuli. Thus, they may be suspected of being deaf or visually impaired. It is common for such young children to be referred for hearing and vision tests. Some children avoid gentle physical contact, yet react with pleasure to rough-and-tumble games. Some children carry food preferences to extremes, with favored foods eaten to excess. Some children limit their diet to a small selection, while others are hearty eaters who do not seem to know when they are full.

Disturbance of Movement

The typical motor milestones (e.g., throwing, catching, kicking) may be delayed but are often within the normal range. Young children with PDDNOS usually have difficulty with imitation skills, such as clapping hands. Many such children are very overactive, yet tend to become less overactive in adolescence. Children with PDDNOS may exhibit characteristics such as grimacing, hand flapping or twisting, toe walking, lunging, jumping, darting or pacing, body rocking and swaying, or head rolling or banging. In some cases the behaviors appear only from time to time; in other cases they are present continuously.

Intelligence and Cognitive Deficits

Generally, children with PDDNOS do very well on tests requiring manipulative or visual skills or immediate memory, while they do poorly on tasks demanding symbolic or abstract thought and sequential logic. The process of learning and thinking in these children is impaired, most particularly in the capacity for imitation, comprehension of spoken words and gestures, flexibility, inventiveness, learning and applying rules, and using acquired information. Yet, a small number of children with PDDNOS show excellent rote memory and special skills in music, mechanics, mathematics, and reading.

Because many children with PDDNOS are either without functional speech or otherwise cannot be tested, some people question the validity of testing their intelligence. Moreover, it has been observed that a number of these children show major improvements in other developmental areas during the follow-up period without a change in their tested IQ. Follow-up studies have also shown that retardation present at the time of initial diagnosis tends to persist. Those children with a low IQ show more severely impaired social development. They are more likely to display unusual social responses, such as touching or smelling people, ritualistic behavior, or self-injury.

Associated Features

The emotional expression of some children with PDDNOS may be flattened, excessive, or inappropriate to the situation. For no obvious reason, they may scream or sob inconsolably one time, yet giggle and laugh hysterically another time. Real dangers, such as moving vehicles or heights, may be ignored, yet the same child might seem frightened of a harmless object, such as a particular stuffed animal.

Diagnosing PDDNOS

The DSM-IV suggests that the diagnostic label of PDDNOS be used when there is a severe and pervasive impairment in the development of reciprocal social interaction, verbal and nonverbal communication skills, or the development of seemingly meaningless repetitive behavior, interests, and activities, but when the criteria are not completely met for a specific disorder within the category PDD (e.g., Autistic Disorder, Rett's Disorder, Asperger's Disorder). However, the DSM-IV framework has not offered specific techniques or criteria for diagnosing PDDNOS.

No Specific Test Available

Currently, no objective biological test, such as a blood test or an X-ray examination, can confirm a child's PDDNOS diagnosis. Diagnosing PDDNOS is complicated and much like putting together a jigsaw puzzle that does not have a clear border and picture. Therefore, it is reasonable to say that, when a PDDNOS diagnosis is made, it reflects the clinician's best guess. Obtaining an accurate diagnosis requires an assessment conducted by a well-trained professional who specializes in developmental disorders, usually a child psychiatrist, developmental pediatrician, pediatric neurologist, developmental pediatrician, child psychologist, developmental psychologist, or neuropsychologist.

PDDNOS Assessment

The purpose of PDDNOS assessment is twofold: to gather information to formulate an accurate diagnosis and to provide information that will form the basis of an appropriate intervention plan for the individual child and family. Assessment of PDDNOS usually includes the following elements:

Medical assessment. The medical evaluation should include a thorough birth, developmental, medical, and family history, and a full physical and neurological examination. Not all children with PDDNOS require laboratory tests such as a chromosome study, including a test for fragile X, an EEG (which measures the brain's electrical activity), or a brain scan such as MRI (an X-ray that gives a picture of the brain's anatomy). The primary care physician determines if these are needed. Although the cause of PDDNOS is generally unknown, the physician may discuss some medical conditions that do not cause PDDNOS but tend to be found in such children—for example, seizure disorder. Associated conditions can cause or worsen a child's problems.

Interviews with the parents, child, and child's teacher. A child with PDDNOS may exhibit different abilities and behaviors in different settings or situations. Parents and teachers can provide information about behaviors not observed during the formal testing sessions.

Behavior rating scales. Checklists of possible problems should be completed by parents or caretakers familiar with the child. Many diagnosticians use the checklist for autism. However, no scale has yet been developed specifically to determine the diagnosis of PDDNOS.

Direct behavioral observations. The child's behavior is recorded as it happens, and assessment results are often graphed to aid interpretation. This type of assessment can be carried out either in an artificial situation (e.g., a child taking an intelligence test) or in a natural situation (e.g., a child's home or classroom).

Psychological assessment. The psychologist uses standardized instruments to evaluate the child's cognitive, social, emotional, behavioral, and adaptive functioning. Parents learn in which areas of development their child exhibits delays.

Educational assessment. Both formal assessment (such as the use of standardized tests) and informal assessment (such as direct observation and interviewing the parents) should be used to evaluate the child on the following points:

* preacademic skills (e.g., shape and letter naming),
* academic skills (e.g., reading and arithmetic),
* daily living skills (e.g., toileting, dressing, eating), and
* learning style and problem-solving approaches.

Communication assessment. Formal testing, observational assessment, and interviewing the child's parents are all useful strategies for assessing communication skills. It is important to assess a range of communication skills, including the child's interest in communication, why (for what purpose) the child communicates, the content and context of the communication, how the child communicates (including facial expression, posture, gestures, etc.), and how well the child understands when others communicate with him or her. Assessment results should be used when designing a communication program for the child. This may incorporate one or more alternative forms to spoken communication, such as sign language and/or using a communication board (i.e., pointing to pictures to express oneself).

Occupational assessment. An occupational therapist may evaluate the child to determine the nature of his or her sensory integrative functioning: how the child's different senses—hearing, sight, taste, smell, touch—work together. Standardized tools are used to assess fine motor skills (such as using fingers to pick up small objects), gross motor skills (such as running and jumping), whether the child is right or left handed, and various visual skills (such as depth perception).

Evaluation summary. The professional evaluating a child will use all the information collected through these varying techniques to decide whether that child has a disability that falls under the category of PDD. Assessment and evaluation can be done through the child's local public school or a private practitioner.

Special Education and PDDNOS

By law, schools must make special services available to eligible children with disabilities. These services are called special education and related services (discussed more below). The law that requires this is the Individuals with Disabilities Education Act, or IDEA. Under the IDEA, school-aged children who are thought to have a disability must be evaluated by the public schools at no cost to parents. Based on the evaluation, a determination is made as to their eligibility for services.

IDEA defines categories of disability under which a child is considered eligible for services. These categories are: autism, deaf-blindness, hearing impairments including deafness, mental retardation, other health impairments, orthopedic impairments, serious emotional disturbance, specific learning disabilities, speech or language impairments, traumatic brain injury, visual impairments including blindness, or multiple disabilities. If permitted by the state and the local educational agency, a school may also provide services to a student, from age 3 through age 9, under the separate category of "developmental delay." Parents should check with their state department of special education to find out what guidelines their state uses.

It's important to realize that a child may have a disability and still not be eligible for special education and related services. For a child to be determined to be eligible, the child's disability must adversely affect his or her educational performance.

Special education is instruction that is specially designed to meet a child's unique educational needs. Related services can include a range of services that are provided to help the student benefit from his or her special education. Related services include (but are not limited to) such services as occupational therapy, speech therapy, or physical therapy. Both special education and related services must be provided at no cost to the parents; both can be extremely beneficial for children with PDDNOS.

Services to very young children are also covered under the IDEA. Through the Program for Infants and Toddlers with Disabilities, states make early intervention services available to eligible infants and toddlers (birth through two years). Not all services are free; some may be provided on a sliding-scale basis (in other words, according to the parents' ability to pay).

Early intervention services are designed to meet the developmental needs of the infant or toddler in areas such as their physical development, cognitive development, communication development, social or emotional development, or adaptive development. Services include (but are not limited to) such services as: family training and home visits, special instruction, speech-language pathology, vision services, and occupational therapy. To the maximum extent appropriate, early intervention services are to be provided in natural environments, including the home and community settings in which children without disabilities participate.

The IFSP and the IEP

The majority of school-aged children with PDDNOS will need some special education services, just as those who are younger will need early intervention services. If a school-aged child is found eligible for services, the parents and the school will develop an Individualized Education Program (IEP). This is a document that lists, among other things, the child's strengths and weaknesses, and what special education and related services the school will provide to address those needs. If the child is less than 3 years old, he or she will have an Individualized Family Service Plan, (IFSP). Parents can contact their state parent training and information center (PTI) or NICHCY for helpful information about IEP or IFSP development and the special education process.

Treatment of PDDNOS

On the whole, children with PDDNOS share the social and communicative disabilities found in children with Autistic Disorder. They often need services or treatments similar to those provided to children with autism.

Traditional Methods

No one therapy or method will work for all individuals with Autistic Disorder or PDDNOS. Many professionals and families will use a range of treatments simultaneously, including behavior modification, structured educational approaches, medications, speech therapy, occupational therapy, and counseling. These treatments promote more typical social and communication behavior and minimize negative behaviors (e.g., hyperactivity, meaningless, repetitive behavior, self-injury, aggressiveness) that interfere with the child's functioning and learning. There has been an increasing focus on treating preschool children with PDDNOS by working closely with family members to help the children cope with the problems encountered at home before they enter school. Many times, the earlier these children begin treatment, the better the outcome.

Addressing behavior issues. As children with PDDNOS struggle to make sense of the many things that are confusing to them, they do

154

best in an organized environment where rules and expectations are clear and consistent. The child's environment needs to be very structured and predictable.

Many times a behavior problem indicates that the child is trying to communicate something—confusion, frustration, or fear. Think of the child's behavior problem as a message to be decoded. Try to determine the possible cause of the behavior. Has the child's routine or schedule changed recently? Has something new been introduced that may be distressing or confusing the child? When a child's communication skills improve, behavior problems often diminish—the child now has a means of expressing what is bothering him or her, without resorting to negative behavior.

The use of positive behavioral support strategies for these children has proved effective. It is important to remember that:

1. Programs should be designed on an individual basis, because children vary greatly in their disabilities and abilities. Treatment approaches that work in certain cases may not work in others.

2. Children with PDDNOS have difficulty generalizing from one situation to another. The skills they have learned in school tend not to be transferred to the home or other settings. It is very important to be consistent in the treatment of a problem across all areas of the child's life—school, community, and home. This encourages generalization of behavior changes.

3. A home-community-based approach, which trains parents and special education teachers to carry out positive behavioral support strategies, can be instrumental in achieving maximum results.

Appropriate educational program. Education is the primary tool for treating PDDNOS. Many children with PDDNOS experience the greatest difficulty in school, where demands for attention and impulse control are virtual requirements for success. Behavioral difficulties can prevent some children from adapting to the classroom. However, with appropriate educational help, a child with PDDNOS can succeed in school.

The most essential ingredient of a quality educational program is a knowledgeable teacher. Other elements of a quality educational program include:

- structured, consistent, predictable classes with schedules and assignments posted and clearly explained;

- information presented visually as well as verbally;

- opportunities to interact with nondisabled peers who model appropriate language, social, and behavioral skills;

- a focus on improving a child's communications skills using tools such as communication devices;

- reduced class size and an appropriate seating arrangement to help the child with PDDNOS avoid distraction;

- modified curriculum based on the particular child's strengths and weaknesses;

- using a combination of positive behavioral supports and other educational interventions; and

- frequent and adequate communication among teachers, parents, and the primary care clinician.

Medical treatment. The primary aim of medical treatment of children with PDDNOS is to ensure physical and psychological health. A good preventive health care program should include regular physical checkups to monitor growth, vision, hearing, and blood pressure; immunization according to schedule; regular visits to the dentist; and attention to diet and hygiene. An effective medical treatment begins with a thorough medical assessment. The pretreatment assessment is essential for detecting existing medical conditions, such as a seizure disorder.

There is no one specific medication that helps all children with PDDNOS. Some medications have been found to be helpful, but for many children with autism or PDDNOS, medication levels need to be experimented with until the optimal combination and dosage are found. Since this differs with each child, there is no set medical treatment for children with PDDNOS but, rather, an individual medication regimen for each. Because of these complexities, in the eyes of many, medication therapy is viewed as a treatment to be used only when other types of treatment have been unsuccessful. It is important to note that medication can be effective and necessary for conditions that may coexist in children with PDDNOS, such as attention deficit disorder or obsessive compulsive disorder.

Parents' final decision on whether to use medication as part of their child's therapy is a personal one and should be respected and supported.

Medication should always be used in conjunction with other therapies, and its effects should be monitored through feedback from the child, parents, and teachers.

Psychological treatment. Counseling may be helpful to families to help them adjust to raising a child with a disability. If the child is already attending a school program, both parents and teachers need to be told of the symptoms of PDDNOS and how those symptoms may affect the child's ability to function at home, in the neighborhood, in school, and in social situations. Psychologists can also provide ongoing assessments, school consultation, case management, and behavior training. Some children also benefit from counseling from an experienced practitioner who knows about PDDNOS. Family teamwork can ease the burden on the primary home caregiver who needs a support system.

Other Therapies and Treatments

While exploring the treatment options available to help children with PDDNOS, parents and others may come across several therapies that can be used in conjunction with traditional ones. When considering one of these other therapies for a child, ask questions and carefully assess the program. It's important to ask for a written description of the program, including its length, the frequency of sessions, cost, and the rationale, philosophy, or purpose underlying the program. It's also important to investigate the credentials of the program director and staff and whether evidence exists to prove the effectiveness of the program, as well as the possible negative side effects. Here are some alternative programs available:

Facilitated communication. This is a method of encouraging people with communication impairments to express themselves. By providing physical assistance, a person, called a facilitator, helps the individual to spell words using a keyboard of a typewriter or computer or other letter display. Facilitation may involve hand-over-hand support or a simple touch on the shoulder. The individual with the impairment initiates the movement while the facilitator offers physical support.

Successful anecdotes of Facilitated Communication therapy have been reported and published over the past few years. They have also provoked considerable controversy, because generally they have not been supported by empirical research. It appears that Facilitated

Communication has the potential for becoming a useful technique for some children with PDDNOS, particularly those who are precocious readers and good with other forms of communication such as computer and signs, but who also are severely impaired in verbal expression skills.

Auditory integration therapy (AIT). AIT uses a device that randomly selects low and high frequencies from a music source (a cassette or CD player) and then sends these sounds through headphones to the child.

There are anecdotes about the positive effects from AIT. Some of the results that have been reported include diminished sensitivity to sounds, more spontaneous speech, more complex language development, answering questions on topic, more interaction with peers, and more appropriate social behavior.

However, significant results from a well-designed treatment study have not been available. It is still unclear how AIT works and whether people benefit from it.

Sensory integration therapy. Sensory integration is the nervous system's process of organizing sensory information for functional use. It refers to a normally occurring process in the brain that allows people to put sights, sounds, touch, taste, smells, and movements together to understand and interact with the world around them (Mailloux & Lacroix, 1992).

On the basis of assessment results, an occupational therapist who has been trained in sensory integration therapy guides an individual through activities that challenge his or her ability to respond appropriately to sensory stimulation. This type of therapy is directed toward improving how an individual's senses process stimulation and work together to respond appropriately. As with other therapies, no conclusive research demonstrates clear progress made through sensory integration therapy, but it is used in many areas.

The Lovaas method. This method (which is a type of Applied Behavior Analysis [ABA]), developed by psychologist Ivar Lovaas at UCLA, is an intensive intervention program originally designed for preschool-aged children with autism. It uses behavioral techniques—molding and rewarding desired behavior, and ignoring or discouraging undesirable actions—to achieve its goals. Generally, this method consists of 30 to 40 hours a week of basic language skills, behavior, and academic training. Therapy usually consists of 4 to 6 hours per day of one-on-one training,

5 to 7 days a week. Some research has shown remarkable progress in about 50% of the children receiving this therapy.

The Lovaas Method is getting wide attention, but, as with other therapies, it needs more study.

Vitamin therapy. Some anecdotal evidence has shown that Vitamin B6 and Magnesium help children with autism and PDDNOS. The rationale for this is that Vitamin B6 helps the formation of neurotransmitters, which are thought to malfunction in such children (Dalldorf, 1995).

Dietary intervention. Some individuals with PDDNOS have been found to have food sensitivities or food allergies. Some parents choose to have their children evaluated by allergists and, based on the testing results, may eliminate or decrease foods to which their child shows the most sensitivity. For example, some foods seem to increase hyperactivity and autistic-like behavior. Eliminating these from the child's diet has been found to help decrease negative behaviors.

Anti-yeast therapy. Often the progression of autism and PDDNOS involves unusual behaviors and communication problems arising around the toddler stage, when many children are treated with antibiotics for problems such as middle ear infections. Antibiotics can upset the intestinal flora and possibly cause "yeast overgrowth." However, the existence of higher yeast levels in children with autism and PDDNOS could very well be coincidence (Dalldorf, 1995). Some parents have found that giving their child an anti-yeast medication decreases some negative behaviors. Some preliminary study findings support this type of treatment; however, the results are not conclusive.

Summary. Since well-designed studies of these therapies have not been conducted, their effectiveness in treating PDDNOS is unclear.

Helping Children at Home

Parents can use many techniques and treatments to help their young child with PDDNOS at home. These techniques should be discussed with other family members and the professionals who are working with the child, so that the individuals close to the child may employ the same methods. This will help the child generalize skills learned at home to other settings, such as at school and in the community. Parents can work at improving communication skills and social skills.

Finding a Parent Support Group

Children with PDDNOS are not the only ones who need extra help and support. Parenting a child with special needs is a demanding task. Learning and accepting that a child has a disability is a very emotional process. Initially, parents may feel alone and not know where to begin their search for information, assistance, and support. Parent groups offer parents and families a place to share information, give and receive emotional and practical support, and work as a team to address common goals.

Autism parent support groups are located throughout the country. Families whose child has PDDNOS can benefit from joining these support groups.

Conclusion

Children with PDDNOS happen to have a unique disorder that will make certain parts of life more challenging. Many articles, booklets, and books contain useful information; however, these resources will probably not be found at the local library or bookstore. To get these materials, contact the organizations and publishers listed in chapters 47 and 48 of this *Sourcebook*.

Learning more about the special needs of children with PDDNOS can be of enormous emotional and practical help to those who are involved with, and who care about, these special children.

References

American Psychiatric Association. (1994). *Diagnostic and statistical manual of mental disorders (4th ed.)*. Washington, DC: Author.

Autism Society of America. (1995). Asperger's Syndrome information package. Bethesda, MD: Author.

Boyle, T. (1995). Diagnosing autism and other pervasive development disorders [excerpt from *Autism: Basic information* (3rd ed., pp. 6-7)]. Ewing, NJ: The New Jersey Center for Outreach & Services for the Autism Community, Inc. (COSAC).

Dalldorf, J. (1995). *A pediatric view of the treatment options for the autistic syndrome*. Chapel Hill, NC: Division TEACCH (Treatment and Education of Autistic and Related Communication Handicapped Children).

Mailloux, Z., & Lacroix, J. (1992). *Sensory integration and autism.* Torrance, CA: AYERS Clinic.

Moeschler, J., Gibbs, E., & Graham, J., Jr. (1990). *A summary of medical and psychoeducation aspects of Rett Syndrome.* Lebanon, NH: Clinical Genetics and Child Development Center.

Prizant, B. M., & Rydell, P. J. (1993). Assessment and intervention considerations for unconventional verbal behavior. In J. Reichle & D. Wacker (Eds.), *Communicative alternatives to challenging behaviors* (pp. 263-297). Baltimore, MD: Paul H. Brookes.

ZERO TO THREE: National Center for Infants, Toddlers, and Families. (1994).

Diagnostic Classification of Mental Health and Developmental Disorders of Infancy and Early Childhood. Washington, DC: Author.

Section 12.2

Autism

This section includes "Autism, Fact Sheet," National Institute of Neurological Disorders and Stroke (NINDS), NIH Publication No. 96-1877, August 1996; and the following documents reprinted with the permission of the Center for the Study of Autism, Salem, Oregon; "Learning Styles and Autism" by Stephen M. Edelson, Ph.D., © undated; "Teaching Tips for Children and Adults with Autism" by Temple Grandin, Ph.D., © 1998, and "Basic Information about Auditory Integration Training (AIT)," by Stephen M. Edelson, Ph.D., © 1995.

What Is Autism?

Autism is not a disease, but a developmental disorder of brain function. People with classical autism show three types of symptoms: impaired social interaction, problems with verbal and nonverbal communication and imagination, and unusual or severely limited activities and interests. Symptoms of autism usually appear during the first three years of childhood and continue throughout life. Although there is no cure, appropriate management may foster relatively normal development and reduce undesirable behaviors. People with autism have a normal life expectancy.

Autism affects an estimated two to ten of every 10,000 people, depending on the diagnostic criteria used. Most estimates that include people with similar disorders are two to three times greater. Autism strikes males about four times as often as females, and has been found throughout the world in people of all racial and social backgrounds.

Autism varies a great deal in severity. The most severe cases are marked by extremely repetitive, unusual, self-injurious, and aggressive behavior. This behavior may persist over time and prove very difficult to change, posing a tremendous challenge to those who must live with, treat, and teach these individuals. The mildest forms of autism resemble a personality disorder associated with a perceived learning disability.

What Are Some Common Signs of Autism?

The hallmark feature of autism is impaired social interaction. Children with autism may fail to respond to their names and often avoid looking at other people. Such children often have difficulty interpreting tone of voice or facial expressions and do not respond to others' emotions or watch other people's faces for cues about appropriate behavior. They appear unaware of others' feelings toward them and of the negative impact of their behavior on other people.

Many children with autism engage in repetitive movements such as rocking and hair twirling, or in self-injurious behavior such as biting or head-banging. They also tend to start speaking later than other children and may refer to themselves by name instead of "I" or "me." Some speak in a sing-song voice about a narrow range of favorite topics, with little regard for the interests of the person to whom they are speaking.

People with autism often have abnormal responses to sounds, touch, or other sensory stimulation. Many show reduced sensitivity to pain. They also may be extraordinarily sensitive to other sensations. These unusual sensitivities may contribute to behavioral symptoms such as resistance to being cuddled.

How Is Autism Diagnosed?

Autism is classified as one of the pervasive developmental disorders. Some doctors also use terms such as "emotionally disturbed" to describe people with autism. Because it varies widely in its severity and symptoms, autism may go unrecognized, especially in mildly affected individuals or in those with multiple handicaps. Researchers and therapists have developed several sets of diagnostic criteria for autism. Some frequently used criteria include:[1]

- Absence or impairment of imaginative and social play

- Impaired ability to make friends with peers

- Impaired ability to initiate or sustain a conversation with others

- Stereotyped, repetitive, or unusual use of language

- Restricted patterns of interests that are abnormal in intensity or focus

- Apparently inflexible adherence to specific routines or rituals

- Preoccupation with parts of objects

[1]Adapted from the *Diagnostic and Statistical Manual of Mental Disorders IV* and the *International Classification of Diseases-10*.

Children with some symptoms of autism, but not enough to be diagnosed with the classical form of the disorder, are often diagnosed with pervasive developmental disorder—not otherwise specified (PDD-NOS). The term Asperger syndrome is sometimes used to describe people with autistic behavior but well-developed language skills. Children who appear normal in their first several years, then lose skills and begin showing autistic behavior, may be diagnosed with childhood disintegrative disorder (CDD). Girls with Rett's syndrome, a sex-linked genetic disorder characterized by inadequate brain growth, seizures, and other neurological problems, also may show autistic behavior. PDD-NOS, Asperger syndrome, CDD, and Rett's syndrome are sometimes referred to as autism spectrum disorders.

Since hearing problems can be confused with autism, children with delayed speech development should always have their hearing checked. Children sometimes have impaired hearing in addition to autism. About half of people with autism score below 50 on IQ tests, 20 percent score between 50 and 70, and 30 percent score higher than 70. However, estimating IQ in young children with autism is often difficult because problems with language and behavior can interfere with testing. A small percentage of people with autism are savants.

These people have limited but extraordinary skills in areas like music, mathematics, drawing, or visualization.

What Causes Autism?

Autism has no single cause. Researchers believe several genes, as well as environmental factors such as viruses or chemicals, contribute to the disorder. Studies of people with autism have found abnormalities in several regions of the brain, including the cerebellum, amygdala, hippocampus, septum, and mamillary bodies. Neurons in these regions appear smaller than normal and have stunted nerve fibers, which may interfere with nerve signaling. These abnormalities suggest that autism results from disruption of normal brain development early in fetal development. Other studies suggest that people with autism have abnormalities of serotonin or other signaling molecules in the brain. While these findings are intriguing, they are preliminary and require further study. The early belief that parental practices are responsible for autism has now been disproved.

In a minority of cases, disorders such as fragile X syndrome, tuberous sclerosis, untreated phenylketonuria (PKU), and congenital rubella cause autistic behavior. Other disorders, including Tourette syndrome, learning disabilities, and attention deficit disorder, often occur with autism but do not cause it. For reasons that are still unclear, about 20 to 30 percent of people with autism also develop epilepsy by the time they reach adulthood. While people with schizophrenia may show some autistic-like behavior, their symptoms usually do not appear until the late teens or early adulthood. Most people with schizophrenia also have hallucinations and delusions, which are not found in autism.

What Role Does Genetics Play?

Recent studies strongly suggest that some people have a genetic predisposition to autism. Scientists estimate that, in families with one autistic child, the risk of having a second child with the disorder is approximately five percent, or one in 20, which is greater than the risk for the general population. Researchers are looking for clues about which genes contribute to this increased susceptibility. In some cases, parents and other relatives of an autistic person show mild social, communicative, or repetitive behaviors that allow them to function normally but appear linked to autism. Evidence also suggests that some affective, or emotional, disorders, such as manic depression, occur more frequently than average in families of people with autism.

Do Symptoms of Autism Change Over Time?

Symptoms in many children with autism improve with intervention or as the children mature. Some people with autism eventually lead normal or near-normal lives. However, reports from parents of children with autism indicate that some children's language skills regress early in life, usually before age three. This regression often seems linked to epilepsy or seizure-like brain activity. Adolescence also worsens behavior problems in some children with autism who may become depressed or increasingly unmanageable. Parents should be ready to adjust treatment for their child's changing needs.

How Can Autism Be Treated?

There is no cure for autism at present. Therapies, or interventions, are designed to remedy specific symptoms in each individual. The best-studied therapies include educational/behavioral and medical interventions. Although these interventions do not cure autism, they often bring about substantial improvement.

- *Educational/behavioral interventions*: These strategies emphasize highly structured and often intensive skill-oriented training that is tailored to the individual child. Therapists work with children to help them develop social and language skills. Because children learn most effectively and rapidly when very young, this type of therapy should begin as early as possible. Recent evidence suggests that early intervention has a good chance of favorably influencing brain development.

- *Medication:* Doctors may prescribe a variety of drugs to reduce self-injurious behavior or other troublesome symptoms of autism, as well as associated conditions such as epilepsy and attention disorders. Most of these drugs affect levels of serotonin or other signaling chemicals in the brain.

Many other interventions are available, but few, if any, scientific studies support their use. These therapies remain controversial and may or may not reduce a specific person's symptoms. Parents should use caution before subscribing to any particular treatment. Counseling for the families of people with autism also may assist them in coping with the disorder.

Learning Styles and Autism

'Learning styles' is a concept which attempts to describe the methods by which people gain information about their environment. People can learn through seeing (visually), hearing (auditorily), and/or through touching or manipulating an object (kinesthetically or 'hands-on' learning). For example, looking at a picture book or reading a textbook involves learning through vision; listening to a lecture live or on tape involves learning through hearing; and pressing buttons to determine how to operate a VCR involves learning kinesthetically.

Generally, most people learn using two to three learning styles. Interestingly, people can assess their own interests and lifestyle to determine the ways in which they obtain much of their information about their environment. In my case, when I read a book, I can easily understand the text. In contrast, it is difficult for me to listen to an audiotape recording of that book—I just cannot follow the story line. Thus, I am a strong visual learner, and a moderate, possibly poor, auditory learner. As far as kinesthetic learning, I am very good at taking apart objects to learn how an object works, such as a vacuum cleaner or a computer.

One's learning style may affect how well a person performs in an educational setting, especially from junior high through college. Schools usually require both auditory learning (i.e., listening to a teacher) and visual learning (i.e., reading a textbook). If one is poor at one of these two ways of learning, he/she will likely depend mostly on his/her strength (e.g., a visual learner may study the textbook rather than rely on the lecture content). Using this logic, if one is poor at both visual and auditory learning, he/she may have difficulty in school. Furthermore, one's learning style may be associated with one's occupation. For example, those individuals who are kinesthetic learners may tend to have occupations involving their hands, such as shelf stockers, mechanics, surgeons, or sculptors. Visual learners may tend to have occupations that involve processing visual information, such as data processors, artists, architects, or manufacturing part sorters. Moreover, auditory learners may tend to have jobs which involve processing auditory information, such as sales people, judges, musicians, 9-1-1 operators, and waiters/waitresses.

Based on my experience as well as those of my colleagues, it appears that autistic individuals are more likely to rely on only one style of learning. By observing the person, one may be able to determine his/her primary style of learning. For example, if an autistic child enjoys looking at books (e.g., picture books), watching television (with or without sound), and tends to look carefully at people and objects, then he/she may be a visual learner. If an autistic child talks excessively, enjoys people talking to him/her, and prefers listening to the radio or music, then he/she may be an auditory learner. And if an autistic child is constantly taking things apart, opening and closing drawers, and pushing buttons, this may indicate that the child is a kinesthetic or 'hands-on' learner.

Once a person's learning style is determined, then relying on this modality to teach can greatly increase the likelihood that the person will learn. If one is not sure which learning style a child has or is teaching to a group with different learning styles, then the best way to teach could be to use all three styles together. For example, when teaching the concept 'jello,' one can display a package and bowl of jello (visual); describe its features such as its color, texture, and use (auditory); and then let the person touch and taste it (kinesthetic).

One common problem evidenced by autistic children is running around the classroom and not listening to the teacher. This child may not be an auditory learner; and thus, he/she is not attending to the teacher's words. If the child is a kinesthetic learner, the teacher may choose to place his/her hands on the child's shoulders and then guide the student back to his/her chair, or go to the chair and move it towards the student. If the child learns visually, the teacher may need to show the child his/her chair or hand them a picture of the chair and gesture for the child to sit down.

Teaching to the learning style of the student may make an impact on whether or not the child can attend to and process the information which is presented. This, in turn, can affect the child's performance in school as well as his/her behavior. Therefore, it is important that educators assess for learning style as soon as an autistic child enters the school system and that they adapt their teaching styles in rapport with the strengths of the student. This will ensure that the autistic child has the greatest chance for success in school.

Teaching Tips for Children and Adults with Autism

Editor's Note: Temple Grandin, Ph.D, is an Assistant Professor at Colorado State University. She has personally experienced autism and its challenges.

Good teachers helped me to achieve success. I was able to overcome autism because I had good teachers. At age 2 1/2 I was placed in a structured nursery school with experienced teachers. From an early age I was taught to have good manners and to behave at the dinner table. Children with autism need to have a structured day, and teachers who know how to be firm but gentle.

Between the ages of 2 1/4 and 5 my day was structured, and I was not allowed to tune out. I had 45 minutes of one-to-one speech therapy five days a week, and my mother hired a nanny who spent three to four hours a day playing games with me and my sister. She taught 'turn taking' during play activities. When we made a snowman, she had me roll the bottom ball, and then my sister had to make the next part. At mealtimes, everybody ate together; and I was not allowed to do any "stims." The only time I was allowed to revert back to autistic behavior was during a one-hour rest period after lunch. The combination of the nursery school, speech therapy, play activities, and "miss manners" meals added up to 40 hours a week, where my brain was kept connected to the world.

1. Many people with autism are visual thinkers. I think in pictures. I do not think in language. All my thoughts are like videotapes running in my imagination. Pictures are my first language, and words are my second language. Nouns were the easiest words to learn because I could make a picture in my mind of the word. To learn words like "up" or "down," the teacher should demonstrate them to the child. For example, take a toy airplane and say "up" as you make the airplane takeoff from a desk.

2. Avoid long strings of verbal instructions. People with autism have problems with remembering the sequence. If the child can read, write the instructions down on a piece of paper. I am unable to remember sequences. If I ask for directions at a gas station, I can only remember three steps. Directions with more than three steps have to be written down. I also have difficulty remembering phone numbers because I cannot make a picture in my mind.

3. Many children with autism are good at drawing, art, and computer programming. These talent areas should be encouraged. I think there needs to be much more emphasis on developing the child's talents.

4. Many autistic children get fixated on one subject such as trains or maps. The best way to deal with fixations is to use

them to motivate schoolwork. If the child likes trains, then use trains to teach reading and math. Read a book about a train and do math problems with trains. For example, calculate how long it takes for a train to go between New York and Washington.

5. Use concrete visual methods to teach number concepts. My parents gave me a math toy that helped me to learn numbers. It consisted of a set of blocks that had a different length and a different color for the numbers one through ten. With this I learned how to add and subtract. To learn fractions my teacher had a wooden apple that was cut up into four pieces and a wooden pear that was cut in half. From this I learned the concept of quarters and halves.

6. I had the worst handwriting in my class. Many autistic children have problems with motor control in their hands. Neat handwriting is sometimes very hard. This can totally frustrate the child. To reduce frustration and help the child to enjoy writing, let him type on the computer. Typing is often much easier.

7. Some autistic children will learn reading more easily with phonics, and others will learn best by memorizing whole words. I learned with phonics. My mother taught me the phonics rules and then had me sound out my words. Children with lots of echolalia will often learn best if flash cards and picture books are used so that the whole words are associated with pictures.

8. When I was a child, loud sounds like the school bell hurt my ears like a dentist drill hitting a nerve. Children with autism need to be protected from sounds that hurt their ears. The sounds that will cause the most problems are school bells, PA systems, buzzers on the score board in the gym, and the sound of chairs scraping on the floor. In many cases the child will be able to tolerate the bell or buzzer if it is muffled slightly by stuffing it with tissues or duct tape. Scraping chairs can be silenced by placing slit tennis balls on the ends of the legs or installing carpet. A child may fear a certain room because he is afraid he may be suddenly subjected to squealing microphone feedback from the PA system. The fear of a dreaded sound can cause bad behavior.

9. Some autistic people are bothered by visual distractions and fluorescent lights. They can see the flicker of the 60-cycle electricity. To avoid this problem, place the child's desk near the window or try to avoid using fluorescent lights. If the lights cannot be avoided, use the newest bulbs you can get. New bulbs flicker less.

10. Some hyperactive autistic children who fidget all the time will often be calmer if they are given a padded weighted vest to wear. Pressure from the garment helps to calm the nervous system. I was greatly calmed by pressure. For best results, the vest should be worn for twenty minutes and then taken off for a few minutes. This prevents the nervous system from adapting to it.

11. Some individuals with autism will respond better and have improved eye contact and speech if the teacher interacts with them while they are swinging on a swing or rolled up in a mat. Sensory input from swinging or pressure from the mat sometimes helps to improve speech. Swinging should always be done as a fun game. It must *never* be forced.

12. Some children and adults can sing better than they can speak. They may respond better if words and sentences are sung to them. Some children with extreme sound sensitivity will respond better if the teacher talks to them in a low whisper.

13. Some nonverbal children and adults cannot process visual and auditory input at the same time. They are mono-channel. They cannot see and hear at the same time. They should not be asked to look and listen at the same time. They should be given either a visual task or an auditory task. Their immature nervous system is not able to process simultaneous visual and auditory input.

14. In older nonverbal children and adults touch is often their most reliable sense. It is often easier for them to feel. Letters can be taught by letting them feel plastic letters. They can learn their daily schedule by feeling objects a few minutes before a scheduled activity. For example, fifteen minutes before lunch give the person a spoon to hold. Let them hold a toy car a few minutes before going in the car.

15. Some children and adults with autism will learn more easily if the computer keyboard is placed close to the screen. This enables the individual to simultaneously see the keyboard and screen. Some individuals have difficulty remembering if they have to look up after they have hit a key on the keyboard.

16. Nonverbal children and adults will find it easier to associate words with pictures if they see the printed word and a picture on a flashcard. Some individuals do not understand line drawings, so it is recommended that work with real objects and photos be done first.

17. Some autistic individuals do not know that speech is used for communication. Language learning can be facilitated if language exercises promote communication. If the child asks for a cup, then give him a cup. If the child asks for a plate, when he wants a cup, give him a plate. The individual needs to learn that when he says words, concrete things happen. It is easier for an individual with autism to learn that their words are wrong if the incorrect word resulted in the incorrect object.

18. Many individuals with autism have difficulty using a computer mouse. Try a roller ball (or tracking ball) pointing device that has a separate button for clicking. Autistics with motor control problems in their hands find it very difficult to hold the mouse still during clicking.

19. Children who have difficulty understanding speech have a hard time differentiating between hard consonant sounds such as 'D' in dog and 'L' in log. My speech teacher helped me to learn to hear these sounds by stretching out and enunciating hard consonant sounds.

20. Several parents have informed me that using the closed captions on the television helped their child to learn to read. The child was able to read the captions and match the printed works with spoken speech. Recording a favorite program with captions on a tape would be helpful because the tape can be played over and over again and stopped.

21. Some autistic individuals do not understand that a computer mouse moves the arrow on the screen. They may learn more easily if a paper arrow that looks *exactly* like the arrow on the screen is taped to the mouse.

Basic Information about Auditory Integration Training (AIT)

Clarifications about Auditory Integration Training and other issues that relate to autism.

1. A health care professional should examine the individual's ears prior to AIT to ensure there is no excessive wax and/or fluid. Excessive wax or fluid may reduce the volume of the AIT input. It is the responsibility of the practitioner to ensure that this has been done prior to AIT.

2. The listener receives 18 to 20 listening sessions, and each listening session lasts for 1/2 hour. In most cases, the listener has two sessions a day for 10 days. At some AIT clinics, the listening sessions are given for 10 consecutive days; however, it is also acceptable to have a 1 or 2 day break after 5 days of listening. The number of sessions and length of the sessions are not subject to change until formal research procedures determine that such changes are beneficial.

3. During the listening sessions, the person listens to processed music. That is, the AIT sound amplifier deletes low and high frequencies at random from the compact discs, and then sends this modified music through headphones to the listener. This random selection of frequencies is termed "modulation."

4. The intensity level (volume) during the AIT listening sessions should not exceed 85 dBA (slow scale) and may be set at much lower intensities depending on the individual's comfort level. Basically, the music is played at a moderately loud, but not uncomfortable, level. The 85 dBA level for a total of one-hour per day is well below the Occupational Safety and Health Act (OSHA) guidelines for non-hazardous noise levels. The OSHA Noise Standard permits exposure to an average noise exposure of 85 dBA for eight continuous hours. For reference, 85 dBA is approximately as loud as standing 5 feet from a vacuum cleaner, with 92-94 dBA as loud as wind noise in a car with the window down. It is also important to note that the perception of intensity varies considerably depending on the pitch of the sound. For example, a high-pitched song sung by Carly Simon may be perceived as louder than one sung by a male vocalist such

172

as Gordon Lightfoot even though both may have the same dBA measurement.

5. Audiograms are typically obtained prior to, at the midpoint, and at the completion of the AIT listening session. The first and the midpoint audiograms are used to set filters on the AIT machines. These filters are used to dampen (40 dBA or more) those frequencies which the person hears too well (peaks).

6. Dr. Guy Berard, developer of Berard method of AIT, and Bill Clark, developer of the BGC method of AIT, state that filtering peaks is optional for the developmentally disabled population. In addition, Dr. Bernard Rimland, Director of the Autism Research Institute in San Diego, and Dr. Stephen M. Edelson from the Center for the Study of Autism, Salem, Oregon, have conducted an empirical study on 650 individuals with various degrees of autism and have found that filtering peaks in one's hearing is not related to one's level of improvement using various post-assessment measures. The music is modulated throughout the 10 hours of listening, whether or not peaks are filtered.

7. AIT involves several components including some audiological work, behavior analysis and management, educational issues, and after care counseling for the client and family. The most satisfactory results can be obtained when a multi-disciplinary team approach is used for the administration of the AIT program. The Society for Auditory Integration Techniques (SAIT) recommends a multidisciplinary team which could include (but is not limited to) specialists in the fields of audiology, psychology, special education, and speech/language.

For More Information on Autism

National Institute of Mental Health
6001 Executive Boulevard, Rm. 8184
MSC 9663
Bethesda, Maryland 20892-9663
Tel: 301-443-4513

National Institute of Child Health and Human Development
Building 31, Room 2A32
Bethesda, Maryland 20892-2350
Tel: 301-496-5133

Autism Society of America
7910 Woodmont Avenue, Suite #300
Bethesda, Maryland 20814-3015
Tel: 301-657-0881
Toll-free: 800-3AUTISM

Autism Research Institute
4182 Adams Avenue
San Diego, California 92116
Tel: 619-281-7165

The New Jersey Center for Outreach and Services for the Autism Community, Inc. (COSAC)
1450 Parkside Avenue, Suite 22
Ewing, New Jersey 08638
Tel: 609-883-8100
Toll-free: 800-4-AUTISM (-288476)

National Autism Hotline
C/O Autism Services Center
P.O. Box 507
Huntington, West Virginia 25710-0507
Tel: 304-525-8014

National Organization for Rare Disorders, Inc. (NORD)
P.O. Box 8923
New Fairfield, Connecticut 06812-8923
Tel: 203-746-6518
Toll-free: 800-999-6673

National Institute of Neurological Disorders and Stroke
Office of Communications and Public Liaison
P.O. Box 5801
Bethesda, Maryland 20824
Tel: 301-496-5751
Toll-free: 800-352-9424

Section 12.3

Cephalic Disorders

Excerpts from "Cephalic Disorders Fact Sheet," National Institute of Neurological Disorders and Stroke (NINDS), NIH Publication No. 98-4339, July 1998.

What Are Cephalic Disorders?

Cephalic disorders are congenital conditions that stem from damage to, or abnormal development of, the budding nervous system. Cephalic is a term that means "head" or "head end of the body." Congenital means the disorder is present at, and usually before, birth. Although there are many congenital developmental disorders, this section briefly describes only cephalic conditions.

Cephalic disorders are not necessarily caused by a single factor, but may be influenced by hereditary or genetic conditions, or by environmental exposures during pregnancy such as medication taken by the mother, maternal infection, or exposure to radiation. Some cephalic disorders occur when the cranial sutures (the fibrous joints that connect the bones of the skull) join prematurely. Most cephalic disorders are caused by a disturbance that occurs very early in the development of the fetal nervous system.

The human nervous system develops from a small, specialized plate of cells on the surface of the embryo. Early in development, this plate of cells forms the neural tube, a narrow sheath that closes between the third and fourth weeks of pregnancy to form the brain and spinal cord of the embryo. Four main processes are responsible for the development of the nervous system: cell proliferation, the process in which nerve cells divide to form new generations of cells; cell migration, the process in which nerve cells move from their place of origin to the place where they will remain for life; cell differentiation, the process during which cells acquire individual characteristics; and cell death, a natural process in which cells die.

Damage to the developing nervous system is a major cause of chronic, disabling disorders and, sometimes, death in infants, children, and even adults. The degree to which damage to the developing

175

nervous system harms the mind and body varies enormously. Many disabilities are mild enough to allow those afflicted to eventually function independently in society. Others are not. Some infants, children, and adults die, others remain totally disabled, and an even larger population is partially disabled, functioning well below normal capacity throughout life.

Different Kinds of Cephalic Disorders

Anencephaly is a neural tube defect that occurs when the cephalic (head) end of the neural tube fails to close, usually between the 23rd and 26th days of pregnancy, resulting in the absence of a major portion of the brain, skull, and scalp. Infants with this disorder are born without a forebrain—the largest part of the brain consisting mainly of the cerebrum, which is responsible for thinking and coordination. The remaining brain tissue is often exposed—not covered by bone or skin.

Infants born with anencephaly are usually blind, deaf, unconscious, and unable to feel pain. Although some individuals with anencephaly may be born with a rudimentary brainstem, the lack of a functioning cerebrum permanently rules out the possibility of ever gaining consciousness. Reflex actions such as respiration (breathing) and responses to sound or touch may occur.

The disorder is one of the most common disorders of the fetal central nervous system. Approximately 1,000 to 2,000 American babies are born with anencephaly each year. The disorder affects females more often than males.

The cause of anencephaly is unknown. Although it is believed that the mother's diet and vitamin intake may play a role, scientists agree that many other factors are also involved.

There is no cure or standard treatment for anencephaly and the prognosis for affected individuals is poor. Most infants do not survive infancy. If the infant is not stillborn, then he or she will usually die within a few hours or days after birth. Anencephaly can often be diagnosed before birth through an ultrasound examination.

Recent studies have shown that the addition of folic acid to the diet of women of child-bearing age may significantly reduce the incidence of neural tube defects. Therefore it is recommended that all women of childbearing age consume 0.4 mg of folic acid daily.

Colpocephaly is a disorder in which there is an abnormal enlargement of the occipital horns—the posterior or rear portion of the lateral ventricles (cavities or chambers) of the brain. This enlargement occurs when there is an underdevelopment or lack of thickening of the white matter in the posterior cerebrum. Colpocephaly is characterized by microcephaly (abnormally small head) and mental retardation. Other features may include motor abnormalities, muscle spasms, and seizures.

Although the cause is unknown, researchers believe that the disorder results from an intrauterine disturbance that occurs between the second and sixth months of pregnancy.

Colpocephaly may be diagnosed late in pregnancy, although it is often misdiagnosed as hydrocephalus (excessive accumulation of cerebrospinal fluid in the brain). It may be more accurately diagnosed after birth when signs of mental retardation, microcephaly, and seizures are present.

There is no definitive treatment for colpocephaly. Anticonvulsant medications can be given to prevent seizures, and doctors try to prevent contractures (shrinkage or shortening of muscles).

The prognosis for individuals with colpocephaly depends on the severity of the associated conditions and the degree of abnormal brain development. Some children benefit from special education.

Holoprosencephaly is a disorder characterized by the failure of the prosencephalon (the forebrain of the embryo) to develop. During normal development the forebrain is formed and the face begins to develop in the fifth and sixth weeks of pregnancy. Holoprosencephaly is caused by a failure of the embryo's forebrain to divide to form bilateral cerebral hemispheres (the left and right halves of the brain), causing defects in the development of the face and in brain structure and function.

There are three classifications of holoprosencephaly. **Alobar holoprosencephaly**, the most serious form in which the brain fails to separate, is usually associated with severe facial anomalies. **Semilobar holoprosencephaly**, in which the brain's hemispheres have a slight tendency to separate, is an intermediate form of the disease. **Lobar holoprosencephaly**, in which there is considerable evidence of separate brain hemispheres, is the least severe form. In some cases of lobar holoprosencephaly, the patient's brain may be nearly normal.

Holoprosencephaly, once called arhinencephaly, consists of a spectrum of defects or malformations of the brain and face. At the most severe end of this spectrum are cases involving serious malformations of the brain, malformations so severe that they are incompatible with life and often cause spontaneous intrauterine death. At the other end of the spectrum are individuals with facial defects—which may affect

177

the eyes, nose, and upper lip—and normal or near-normal brain development. Seizures and mental retardation may occur.

The most severe of the facial defects (or anomalies) is **cyclopia,** an abnormality characterized by the development of a single eye, located in the area normally occupied by the root of the nose, and a missing nose or a nose in the form of a proboscis (a tubular appendage) located above the eye.

Ethmocephaly is the least common facial anomaly. It consists of a proboscis separating narrow-set eyes with an absent nose and microphthalmia (abnormal smallness of one or both eyes).

Cebocephaly, another facial anomaly, is characterized by a small, flattened nose with a single nostril situated below incomplete or underdeveloped closely set eyes.

The least severe in the spectrum of facial anomalies is the median cleft lip, also called *premaxillary agenesis.*

Although the causes of most cases of holoprosencephaly remain unknown, researchers know that approximately one-half of all cases have a chromosomal cause. Such chromosomal anomalies as Patau's syndrome (trisomy 13) and Edward's syndrome (trisomy 18) have been found in association with holoprosencephaly.

There is an increased risk for the disorder in infants of diabetic mothers. There is no treatment for holoprosencephaly and the prognosis for individuals with the disorder is poor. Most of those who survive show no significant developmental gains. For children who survive, treatment is symptomatic. It is possible that improved management of diabetic pregnancies may help prevent holoprosencephaly; however, there is no means of primary prevention.

Hydranencephaly is a rare condition in which the cerebral hemispheres are absent and replaced by sacs filled with cerebrospinal fluid. Usually the cerebellum and brainstem are formed normally. An infant with hydranencephaly may appear normal at birth. The infant's head size and spontaneous reflexes such as sucking, swallowing, crying, and moving the arms and legs may all seem normal. However, after a few weeks the infant usually becomes irritable and has increased muscle tone (hypertonia).

After several months of life, seizures and hydrocephalus may develop. Other symptoms may include visual impairment, lack of growth, deafness, blindness, spastic quadriparesis (paralysis), and intellectual deficits.

Hydranencephaly is an extreme form of porencephaly (a rare disorder, characterized by a cyst or cavity in the cerebral hemispheres) and may be caused by vascular insult or injuries, infections, or traumatic disorders after the 12th week of pregnancy.

Diagnosis may be delayed for several months because the infant's early behavior appears to be relatively normal. Transillumination, an examination in which light is passed through body tissues, usually confirms the diagnosis. Some infants may have additional abnormalities at birth including seizures, myoclonus (involuntary sudden, rapid jerks), and respiratory problems.

There is no standard treatment for hydranencephaly. Treatment is symptomatic and supportive. Hydrocephalus may be treated with a shunt.

The outlook for children with hydranencephaly is poor. Death generally occurs before age 1.

Iniencephaly is a rare neural tube defect that combines extreme retroflexion (backward bending) of the head with severe defects of the spine. The affected infant tends to be short, with a disproportionately large head. Diagnosis can be made immediately after birth because the head is so severely retroflexed that the face looks upward. The skin of the face is connected directly to the skin of the chest and the scalp is directly connected to the skin of the back. Generally, the neck is absent.

Most individuals with iniencephaly have other associated anomalies such as anencephaly, cephalocele (a disorder in which part of the cranial contents protrudes from the skull), hydrocephalus, cyclopia, absence of the mandible (lower jaw bone), cleft lip and palate, cardiovascular disorders, diaphragmatic hernia, and gastrointestinal malformation. The disorder is more common among females.

The prognosis for those with iniencephaly is extremely poor. Newborns with iniencephaly seldom live more than a few hours. The distortion of the fetal body may also pose a danger to the mother's life.

Lissencephaly, which literally means "smooth brain," is a rare brain formation disorder characterized by microcephaly and the lack of normal convolutions (folds) in the brain. It is caused by defective neuronal migration, the process in which nerve cells move from their place of origin to their permanent location.

The surface of a normal brain is formed by a complex series of folds and grooves. The folds are called gyri or convolutions, and the grooves are called sulci. In children with lissencephaly, the normal convolutions

179

are absent or only partly formed, making the surface of the brain smooth.

Symptoms of the disorder may include unusual facial appearance, difficulty swallowing, failure to thrive, and severe psychomotor retardation. Anomalies of the hands, fingers, or toes, muscle spasms, and seizures may also occur. Lissencephaly may be diagnosed at or soon after birth. Diagnosis may be confirmed by ultrasound, computed tomography (CT), or magnetic resonance imaging (MRI).

Lissencephaly may be caused by intrauterine viral infections or viral infections in the fetus during the first trimester, insufficient blood supply to the baby's brain early in pregnancy, or a genetic disorder. There are two distinct genetic causes of lissencephaly—X-linked and chromosome 17-linked.

The spectrum of lissencephaly is only now becoming more defined as neuroimaging and genetics has provided more insights into migration disorders. Other causes which have not yet been identified are likely as well.

Lissencephaly may be associated with other diseases including isolated lissencephaly sequence, Miller-Dieker syndrome, and Walker-Warburg syndrome.

Treatment for those with lissencephaly is symptomatic and depends on the severity and locations of the brain malformations. Supportive care may be needed to help with comfort and nursing needs. Seizures may be controlled with medication and hydrocephalus may require shunting. If feeding becomes difficult, a gastrostomy tube may be considered.

The prognosis for children with lissencephaly varies depending on the degree of brain malformation. Many individuals show no significant development beyond a 3 to 5 month old level. Some may have near normal development and intelligence. Many will die before the age of 2. Respiratory problems are the most common causes of death.

Megalencephaly, also called *macrencephaly*, is a condition in which there is an abnormally large, heavy, and usually malfunctioning brain. By definition, the brain weight is greater than average for the age and gender of the infant or child. Head enlargement may be evident at birth or the head may become abnormally large in the early years of life.

Megalencephaly is thought to be related to a disturbance in the regulation of cell reproduction or proliferation. In normal development, neuron proliferation—the process in which nerve cells divide to form new generations of cells—is regulated so that the correct number of cells is formed in the proper place at the appropriate time.

Symptoms of megalencephaly may include delayed development, convulsive disorders, corticospinal (brain cortex and spinal cord) dysfunction, and seizures. Megalencephaly affects males more often than females. The prognosis for individuals with megalencephaly largely depends on the underlying cause and the associated neurological disorders. Treatment is symptomatic. Megalencephaly may lead to a condition called macrocephaly.

Unilateral megalencephaly or hemimegalencephaly is a rare condition characterized by the enlargement of one-half of the brain. Children with this disorder may have a large, sometimes asymmetrical head. Often they suffer from intractable seizures and mental retardation. The prognosis for those with hemimegalencephaly is poor.

Microcephaly is a neurological disorder in which the circumference of the head is smaller than average for the age and gender of the infant or child. Microcephaly may be congenital or it may develop in the first few years of life. The disorder may stem from a wide variety of conditions that cause abnormal growth of the brain, or from syndromes associated with chromosomal abnormalities.

Infants with microcephaly are born with either a normal or reduced head size. Subsequently the head fails to grow while the face continues to develop at a normal rate, producing a child with a small head, a large face, a receding forehead, and a loose, often wrinkled scalp. As the child grows older, the smallness of the skull becomes more obvious, although the entire body also is often underweight and dwarfed. Development of motor functions and speech may be delayed. Hyperactivity and mental retardation are common occurrences, although the degree of each varies. Convulsions may also occur. Motor ability varies, ranging from clumsiness in some to spastic quadriplegia in others.

Generally there is no specific treatment for microcephaly. Treatment is symptomatic and supportive.

In general, life expectancy for individuals with microcephaly is reduced and the prognosis for normal brain function is poor. The prognosis varies depending on the presence of associated abnormalities.

Porencephaly is an extremely rare disorder of the central nervous system involving a cyst or cavity in a cerebral hemisphere. The cysts or cavities are usually the remnants of destructive lesions, but are sometimes the result of abnormal development. The disorder can occur before or after birth.

Porencephaly most likely has a number of different, often unknown causes, including absence of brain development and destruction of brain tissue. The presence of porencephalic cysts can sometimes be detected by transillumination of the skull in infancy. The diagnosis may be confirmed by CT, MRI, or ultrasonography.

More severely affected infants show symptoms of the disorder shortly after birth, and the diagnosis is usually made before age 1. Signs may include delayed growth and development, spastic paresis (slight or incomplete paralysis), hypotonia (decreased muscle tone), seizures (often infantile spasms), and macrocephaly or microcephaly.

Individuals with porencephaly may have poor or absent speech development, epilepsy, hydrocephalus, spastic contractures (shrinkage or shortening of muscles), and mental retardation. Treatment may include physical therapy, medication for seizure disorders, and a shunt for hydrocephalus. The prognosis for individuals with porencephaly varies according to the location and extent of the lesion. Some patients with this disorder may develop only minor neurological problems and have normal intelligence, while others may be severely disabled. Others may die before the second decade of life.

Schizencephaly is a rare developmental disorder characterized by abnormal slits, or clefts, in the cerebral hemispheres. Schizencephaly is a form of porencephaly. Individuals with clefts in both hemispheres, or bilateral clefts, are often developmentally delayed and have delayed speech and language skills and corticospinal dysfunction. Individuals with smaller, unilateral clefts (clefts in one hemisphere) may be weak on one side of the body and may have average or near-average intelligence. Patients with schizencephaly may also have varying degrees of microcephaly, mental retardation, hemiparesis (weakness or paralysis affecting one side of the body), or quadriparesis (weakness or paralysis affecting all four extremities), and may have reduced muscle tone (hypotonia). Most patients have seizures and some may have hydrocephalus. In schizencephaly, the neurons border the edge of the cleft implying a very early disruption in development.

There is now a genetic origin for one type of schizencephaly. Causes of this type may include environmental exposures during pregnancy such as medication taken by the mother, exposure to toxins, or a vascular insult. Often there are associated heterotopias (isolated islands of neurons) which indicate a failure of migration of the neurons to their final position in the brain.

Treatment for individuals with schizencephaly generally consists of physical therapy, treatment for seizures, and, in cases that are complicated by hydrocephalus, a shunt.

The prognosis for individuals with schizencephaly varies depending on the size of the clefts and the degree of neurological deficit.

Other Less Common Cephalic Disorders

Macrocephaly is a condition in which the head circumference is larger than average for the age and gender of the infant or child. It is a descriptive rather than a diagnostic term, and is a characteristic of a variety of disorders. Macrocephaly also may be inherited. Although one form of macrocephaly may be associated with mental retardation, in approximately one-half of cases mental development is normal. Macrocephaly may be caused by an enlarged brain or hydrocephalus. It may be associated with other disorders such as dwarfism, neurofibromatosis, and tuberous sclerosis.

Micrencephaly is a disorder characterized by a small brain and may be caused by a disturbance in the proliferation of nerve cells. Micrencephaly may also be associated with maternal problems such as alcoholism, diabetes, or rubella (German measles). A genetic factor may play a role in causing some cases of micrencephaly. Affected newborns generally have striking neurological defects and seizures. Severely impaired intellectual development is common, but disturbances in motor functions may not appear until later in life.

For More Information

For more information about disorders of the developing nervous system, cephalic disorders, or birth defects in general, you may wish to contact:

National Organization for Rare Disorders (NORD)
P.O. Box 8923
New Fairfield, Connecticut 06812-8923
Tel: 203-746-6518
Toll-free: 800-999-6673

The Lissencephaly Network, Inc.
716 Autumn Ridge Lane
Fort Wayne, Indiana 46804-6402
Tel: 219-432-4310

The March of Dimes Birth Defects Foundation
1275 Mamaroneck Avenue
White Plains, New York 10605
Toll-free: 888-663-4637

Association of Birth Defects Children
930 Woodcock Rd., Suite 225
Orlando, FL 32803
Tel: 407-245-7035
Toll-free: 800-313-ABDC (2232)

NIH Neurological Institute
Office of Communications and Public Liaison
P.O. Box 5801
Bethesda, Maryland 20824
Tel: 301-496-5751
Toll-free: 800-352-9424

Section 12.4

Cerebral Palsy

Fact Sheet Number 2 (FS2), National Information Center for Children and
Youth with Disabilities (NICHCY), 1999.

Definition of Cerebral Palsy

Cerebral palsy is a condition caused by damage to the brain, usually occurring before, during, or shortly following birth. "Cerebral"
refers to the brain and "palsy" to a disorder of movement or posture.
It is neither progressive nor communicable. It is also not "curable" in
the accepted sense, although education, therapy, and applied technology can help persons with cerebral palsy lead productive lives. It is
not a disease and should never be referred to as such. It can range
from mild to severe.

The causes of cerebral palsy include illness during pregnancy, premature delivery, or lack of oxygen supply to the baby; or it may occur

early in life as a result of an accident, lead poisoning, viral infection, child abuse, or other factors. Chief among the causes is an insufficient amount of oxygen or poor flow of blood reaching the fetal or newborn brain. This can be caused by premature separation of the placenta, an awkward birth position, labor that goes on too long or is too abrupt, or interference with the umbilical cord. Other causes may be associated with premature birth, RH or A-B-O blood type incompatibility between parents, infection of the mother with German measles or other viral diseases in early pregnancy, and microorganisms that attack the newborn s central nervous system. Lack of good prenatal care may also be a factor. A less common type is acquired cerebral palsy: head injury is the most frequent cause, usually the result of motor vehicle accidents, falls, or child abuse.

Incidence

Between 500,000–700,000 Americans have some degree of cerebral palsy. About 3,000 babies are born with the disorder each year, and another 500 or so acquire it in the early years of life.

Characteristics

There are three main types of cerebral palsy: spastic—stiff and difficult movement; athetoid—involuntary and uncontrolled movement; and ataxic—disturbed sense of balance and depth perception. There may be a combination of these types for any one individual. Other types do occur, although infrequently.

Cerebral palsy is characterized by an inability to fully control motor function. Depending on which part of the brain has been damaged and the degree of involvement of the central nervous system, one or more of the following may occur: spasms; tonal problems; involuntary movement; disturbance in gait and mobility; seizures; abnormal sensation and perception; impairment of sight, hearing or speech; and mental retardation.

Developmental, Educational, and Employment Implications

Early identification of cerebral palsy can lessen developmental problems and lead to appropriate intervention when it helps the most. Early intervention programs are family-centered in which professionals and families work together with the child in specific activities.

Educators, physical and occupational therapists, social workers, speech- language pathologists, psychologists, and physicians can assist families by providing information and education. Activities for children with cerebral palsy may include:

- speech and language therapy;
- occupational therapy;
- physical therapy;
- medical intervention;
- family support services;
- early education; and
- assistive technology.

As a child gets older and begins formal schooling, the intensity of services will vary from individual to individual. Persons with cerebral palsy are usually able to attain a substantial degree of independence but, in some cases, may need considerable assistance. Services for the school age child may include continuing therapy, regular or special education, counseling, technical support, community integration opportunities, recreation and possible personal attendants. A key factor seems to be a supportive family. People extensively affected by cerebral palsy can still be highly functional and independent. The HEATH Resource Center, the clearinghouse on postsecondary education for individuals with disabilities, states that a significant number of students with cerebral palsy are enrolled in colleges and universities.

Important advances have taken place in the last 15 years which have had a great effect on the long-term well-being of children born with cerebral palsy. Advanced technology, including computers and engineering devices, has been applied to the needs of persons with cerebral palsy. Technological innovations have been developed in the areas of speech and communication, self-care, and adapting living arrangements and work sites. The future may bring even more significant applications.

Another important development has been the increased ability of persons with disabilities, including those who have cerebral palsy and other severe disabilities, to live independently in the community. Adults with cerebral palsy are now living, with or without assistance, in their own apartments or townhouses. Independent Living Centers have also proven to be important resources for persons with disabilities.

Resources

Geralis, E. (1991). *Children with Cerebral Palsy, A Parent's Guide.* Rockville, MD: Woodbine House. (Telephone: 1-800-843-732.)

Metzger, L. (1993). *Barry's Sister.* New York: Puffin. A book for children ages 10 and up. The story line is about a child with cerebral palsy and his sister.(Telephone: 1-800-253-6476.)

Weiss, S. (1993). *Each of Us Remembers: Parents of Children with Cerebral Palsy Answer Your Questions.* Washington, DC: United Cerebral Palsy Associations, Inc. (See address and telephone number below.)

Organizations

United Cerebral Palsy
1660 L Street N.W., Suite 700
Washington, D.C. 20036
Toll-free (V/TT): 800-872-5827
Fax: 202-776-0414
E-mail: ucpanatl@ucpa.org
URL: http://www.ucp.org

Independent Living Research Utilization Project (ILRU)
The Institute for Rehabilitation and Research
2323 South Sheppard
Suite 1000
Houston, TX 77019
Tel: 713-520-0232
TT: 713-520-5136
E-mail: ilru@ilru.org
URL: http://www.ilru.org

Easter Seals—National Office
230 West Monroe Street
Suite 1800
Chicago, IL 60606
Tel: 312-726-6200
TT: 312-726-4258
Toll-free: 800-221-6827
E-mail: info@easter-seals.org
URL: http://www.easter-seals.org

National Rehabilitation Information Center (NARIC)
1010 Wayne Avenue, Suite 800
Silver Spring, MD 20910-5633
TT/Voice in MD: 301-562-2400
Toll-free: 800-346-2742
E-mail: naricinfo@kra.com
URL: http://www.naric.com/naric

National Information Center for Children and Youth with Disabilities
P.O. Box 1492
Washington, DC 20013-1492
Tel: 800-695-0285 (V/TTY)
E-mail: nichcy@aed..org
URL: http://www.nichcy.org

Section 12.5

Rett Syndrome

National Institute of Neurological Disorders and Stroke Information Sheet, NIH April 1996, updated August 31, 1999; and "Rett Syndrome Studies Funded by the NICHD," National Institute of Child Health and Development (NICHD).

Description

Rett syndrome was previously described as a neurodegenerative disorder, with very poor prognosis and little potential for learning. NICHD supported studies have now identified Rett Syndrome as a disorder of developmental arrest, which begins shortly after birth at a critical time of brain and synapse formation. Individuals exhibit reduced muscle tone, autistic-like behavior, hand movements consisting mainly of wringing and waving, loss of purposeful use of the hands, diminished ability to express feelings, avoidance of eye contact, a lag in brain and head growth, gait abnormalities, and seizures. Hypotonia (loss of muscle tone) is usually the first symptom. The syndrome

188

affects approximately 1 in every 10,000-15,000 live female births, with symptoms usually appearing in early childhood—between ages 6 and 18 months. The cause of Rett syndrome is unknown.

Developmental Arrest

Supportive Clinical Evidence

- Early onset
- Normal OFC at birth
- Hypotonia
- Weak cry and poor suck
- Abnormal 4th toe
- Improved learning and gaining new skills

Supportive Neurobiological Evidence

- Small brain (12-33% reduction)
- No malformations, storage, demyelinization, infection, or gliosis
- Dendritic arborizations, cell differentiation, and neuronal growth affected
- Small neurons with increased neuronal packing, migration not affected
- Thinning of hippocampus
- Significant involvement of caudate nucleus
- Decreased melanin in substantia nigra
- Lack of mature olfactory neurons

Autonomic Findings

- Agitation
- Dyspraxia
- Slow responsiveness
- Poor sensory-motor integration
- Dysrhythmic breathing
- Vasomotor changes
- Vacant spells

- Constipation 90%
- Abdominal distention 50%

Cardiovascular Findings

- Sudden unexplained death, 25% of all deaths
- Immaturity of the atrio-venticular conduction system

Nutritional Findings

- Growth failure is multifactorial, but has a strong basis in nutritional deficit.
- Progressive weight and height failure unless aggressive nutritional rehabilitation is instituted.
- Repetitive involuntary motor movements are not associated with increased energy expenditure.
- Sleeping metabolic rates are low and are consistent with features of malnutrition; these findings can be reversed with nutritional support.
- Deficits in lean body mass persist despite aggressive refeeding regiments.
- Deficits in lean body mass may be associated with increased rates of amino acid oxidation and urea recycling.
- Preliminary data suggest that the intestinal absorption of calcium and vitamin D status are normal in Rett syndrome, despite the presence of reduced bone mineral density.
- Oropharynegeal dysfunction and gastroesophageal dysmotility are found in 100% and 69% of Rett syndrome girls, respectively.
- Abnormalities of oropharyngeal dysfunction include poor tongue mobility, reduced oropharyngeal clearance, and laryngeal penetration of liquid & solid food during swallowing.
- Esophageal dysmotility included abnormal wave patterns, delayed emptying, atony, gastroesophageal reflux; gastric dysmotility included diminished gastric peristalsis or atony.

Neurophysiological Findings

- Seizures are reportedly a common problem

- Prolonged video/EEG/polygraphic studies confirm that the occurrence of epileptic seizures is over estimated in Rett syndrome

- Many events were frequently reported as typical "seizures" but were not associated with EEG severe discharge; these events include twitching, head turning, staring, laughing, pupil dilatation, breath holding, and hyperventilation

- Actual seizures may be under recognized

- No one characteristic seizure type has been identified in Rett syndrome; both focal and generalized electrographic seizures are recorded

- Video/EEG monitoring may be necessary to provide definitive information regarding the need for anticonvulsant therapy

Neuropathological Findings

- Morphologic features are unique, with only decreased brain weight being consistently present. The brain is preferentially involved in this altered growth; other organ weights are appropriate for the individual's height

- No consistent evidence of a degenerative, inflammatory or ischemic process.

- No evidence of a progressive change in brain morphology over time. MRI and EEG studies support this observation

- Best hypothesis to fit the fact that there is no recognizable disease process is that RS seems to be the result of a maturational arrest of brain development.

- Golgi studies suggest that arrested brain development affects dendritic size in selected brain regions, namely the frontal, motor, and limbic regions. This change is not seen in Trisomy 21.

- Alterations in numerous neurotransmitters have been observed, but there does not yet appear to be consistent data suggesting that the primary defect is in any of them

- Mitochondrial disease—secondary effect?

- Morphologic research is directed towards identifying possible deficiencies in neurotrophic factors which could initiate the changes which appear to be an arrest of brain development

Epidemiology and Survival

- The prevalence of Rett syndrome is 1 per 22800 (0.44/1000) females aged 2-18 years of age

- Rett syndrome has been reported in all races/ethnicities

- Rett individuals have an estimated 70% survival at age 35 years; this contrasts sharply with an estimated 27% survival at 35 years for other groups of severely retarded individuals

- The majority of deaths in Rett syndrome are either sudden and unexpected or secondary to pneumonia

Treatment

There is no cure for Rett syndrome; however, there are several treatments options. These include treatments for the orthopedic and learning disabilities and seizures that may occur in individuals with Rett syndrome. Some children may require special nutritional programs to maintain adequate weight.

Prognosis

In spite of the severe impairments that characterize this disorder, the majority of individuals with Rett can be expected to reach adulthood, surviving at least into their 40s. However, the risk of death is increased. Sudden, unexplained death—possibly from brainstem dysfunction with respiratory arrest—often occurs.

Additional Information

International Rett Syndrome Association
9121 Piscataway, Suite 2B
Clinton, MD 20735
Tel: 301-856-3334
Toll-free: 800-818-7388

National Easter Seal Society Inc
230 W. Monroe Street, Suite 1800
Chicago, IL 60606
(312) 762-6200
(312) 762-4258
Toll-free: 800-221-6827

National Institute of Child Health and Human Development
Building 31, Room 2A34
Bethesda, MD 20892-2425
Tel: 301-496-5133

Research for Rett Foundation
PO Box 50347
Mobile, AL 36605
Toll-free: 800-422-7388

Section 12.6

Spina Bifida

"General Information about Spina Bifida," Fact Sheet 12, National Information Center for Children and Youth with Disabilities (NICHCY), 1999.

Definition of Spina Bifida

Spina Bifida means cleft spine, which is an incomplete closure in the spinal column. In general, the three types of spina bifida (from mild to severe) are:

1. **Spina Bifida Occulta:** There is an opening in one or more of the vertebrae (bones) of the spinal column without apparent damage to the spinal cord.

2. **Meningocele:** The meninges, or protective covering around the spinal cord, has pushed out through the opening in the vertebrae in a sac called the "meningocele." However, the spinal cord remains intact. This form can be repaired with little or no damage to the nerve pathways.

3. **Myelomeningocele:** This is the most severe form of spina bifida, in which a portion of the spinal cord itself protrudes through the back. In some cases, sacs are covered with skin; in others, tissue and nerves are exposed. Generally, people use the terms "spina bifida" and "myelomeningocele" interchangeably.

Incidence

Approximately 40% of all Americans may have spina bifida occulta, but because they experience little or no symptoms, very few of them ever know that they have it. The other two types of spina bifida, meningocele and myelomeningocele, are known collectively as "spina bifida manifesta," and occur in approximately one out of every thousand births. Of these infants born with "spina bifida manifesta," about 4% have the meningocele form, while about 96% have myelomeningocele form.

Characteristics

The effects of myelomeningocele, the most serious form of spina bifida, may include muscle weakness or paralysis below the area of the spine where the incomplete closure (or cleft) occurs, loss of sensation below the cleft, and loss of bowel and bladder control. In addition, fluid may build up and cause an accumulation of fluid in the brain (a condition known as hydrocephalus). A large percentage (70%-90%) of children born with myelomeningocele have hydrocephalus. Hydrocephalus is controlled by a surgical procedure called "shunting," which relieves the fluid buildup in the brain. If a drain (shunt) is not implanted, the pressure buildup can cause brain damage, seizures, or blindness. Hydrocephalus may occur without spina bifida, but the two conditions often occur together.

Educational Implications

Although spina bifida is relatively common, until recently most children born with a myelomeningocele died shortly after birth. Now that surgery to drain spinal fluid and protect children against hydrocephalus can be performed in the first 48 hours of life, children with myelomeningocele are much more likely to live. Quite often, however, they must have a series of operations throughout their childhood. School programs should be flexible to accommodate these special needs.

Many children with myelomeningocele need training to learn to manage their bowel and bladder functions. Some require catheterization, or the insertion of a tube to permit passage of urine.

The courts have held that clean, intermittent catheterization is necessary to help the child benefit from and have access to special education and related services. Many children learn to catheterize themselves at a very early age.

A successful bladder management program can be incorporated into the regular school day.

In some cases, children with spina bifida who also have a history of hydrocephalus experience learning problems. They may have difficulty with paying attention, expressing or understanding language, and grasping reading and math. Early intervention with children who experience learning problems can help considerably to prepare them for school.

Mainstreaming, or successful integration of a child with spina bifida into a school attended by nondisabled young people, sometimes requires changes in school equipment or the curriculum. Although student placement should be in the least restrictive environment the day-to-day school pattern also should be as "normal" as possible. In adapting the school setting for the child with spina bifida, architectural factors should be considered. Section 504 of the Rehabilitation Act of 1973 requires that programs receiving federal funds make their facilities accessible. This can occur through structural changes (for example, adding elevators or ramps) or through schedule or location changes (for example, offering a course on the ground floor).

Children with myelomeningocele need to learn mobility skills, and often require the aid of crutches, braces, or wheelchairs. It is important that all members of the school team and the parents understand the child's physical capabilities and limitations. Physical disabilities like spina bifida can have profound effects on a child's emotional and social development. To promote personal growth, families and teachers should encourage children, within the limits of safety and health, to be independent and to participate in activities with their non-disabled classmates.

Resources

Lutkenhoff M. & Oppenheimer, S. (1996). *SPINAbilities: A young person's guide to spina bifida*. Bethesda, MD: Woodbine. (Telephone: 1-800-843-7323.)

McLone, D. (1994). *An introduction to spina bifida*. Washington, DC: Spina Bifida Association of America. (See address below.)

Rowley-Kelly, F.L., & Reigel, D.H. (Eds.). (1993). *Teaching the student with spina bifida*. Baltimore, MD: Paul H. Brookes. (Telephone: 1-800-638-3775.)

Spina Bifida Association of America. (1996). Publications list. Washington, DC: Spina Bifida Assoc. (See address below.)

Organizations

Spina Bifida Association of America
4590 MacArthur Boulevard, Suite 250
Washington, D.C. 20007
Tel: 202-944-3285
Toll Free: 800-621-3141
E-mail: sbaa@sbaa.org
URL: http://www.sbaa.org

Easter Seals—National Office
230 West Monroe Street, Suite 1800
Chicago, IL 60606
Tel: 312-726-6200;
Toll-free: 800-221-6827
E-mail: info@easter-seals.org
URL: http://www.easter-seals.org

March of Dimes Birth Defects Foundation
1275 Mamaroneck Avenue
White Plains, NY 10605
Toll-free: 888-663-4637
E-Mail: resourcecenter@modimes.org
URL: http://www.modimes.org

National Rehabilitation Information Center (NARIC)
1010 Wayne Aveue, Suite 800
Silver Spring, MD 20910-5633
Tel (TTY): 301-495-5626
Toll-free: 800-227-0216
URL: http://www.naric.com/naric

National Information Center for Children and Youth with Disabilities (NICHCY)
P.O. Box 1492
Washington, DC 20013-1492
Toll-free: 800-695-0285 (Voice/TTY)
E-Mail: nichcy@aed.org
URL: http://www.nichcy.org

Chapter 13

Environment and Injury

Contents

Section 13.1

Traumatic Brain Injury

National Information Center for Children and Youth with Disabilities
(NICHCY), Fact Sheet Number 18 (FS18), 1999.

Susan's Story

Susan was 7 years old when she was hit by a car while riding her
bike. She broke her arm and leg. She also hit her head very hard. The
doctors say she sustained a traumatic brain injury. When she came
home from the hospital, she needed lots of help, but now she looks fine.

In fact, that's part of the problem, especially at school. Her friends
and teachers think her brain has healed because her broken bones
have. But there are changes in Susan that are hard to understand.
It takes Susan longer to do things. She has trouble remembering
things. She can't always find the words she wants to use. Reading is
hard for her now. It's going to take time before people really understand the changes they see in her.

What Is Traumatic Brain Injury (TBI)?

A traumatic brain injury (TBI) is an injury to the brain caused by
the head being hit by something or shaken violently. (The exact definition of TBI, according to special education law, is given below.) This
injury can change how the person acts, moves, and thinks. A traumatic
brain injury can also change how a student learns and acts in school.
The term TBI is used for head injuries that can cause changes in one
or more areas, such as:

- thinking and reasoning
- understanding words
- remembering things
- paying attention
- solving problems
- thinking abstractly

198

- talking
- behaving
- walking and other physical activities
- seeing and/or hearing
- learning

The term TBI is not used for a person who is born with a brain injury. It also is not used for brain injuries that happen during birth.

The definition of TBI below comes from the Individuals with Disabilities Education Act (IDEA). The IDEA is the federal law that guides how schools provide special education and related services to children and youth with disabilities.

IDEA's Definition of TBI

Our nation's special education law, the Individuals with Disabilities Education Act (IDEA) defines traumatic brain injury as...

an acquired injury to the brain caused by an external physical force, resulting in total or partial functional disability or psychosocial impairment, or both, that adversely affects a child's educational performance. The term applies to open or closed head injuries resulting in impairments in one or more areas, such as cognition; language; memory; attention; reasoning; abstract thinking; judgment; problem-solving; sensory, perceptual, and motor abilities; psycho-social behavior; physical functions; information processing; and speech. The term does not apply to brain injuries that are congenital or degenerative, or to brain injuries induced by birth trauma. 34 Code of Federal Regulations §300.7(12)

How Common Is TBI?

More than one million children receive brain injuries each year. More than 30,000 of these children have lifelong disabilities as a result of the brain injury.

What Are the Signs of TBI?

The signs of brain injury can be very different depending on where the brain is injured and how severely. Children with TBI may have one or more difficulties, including:

- **Physical disabilities**: Individuals with TBI may have problems speaking, seeing, hearing, and using their other senses. They may have headaches and feel tired a lot. They may also have trouble with skills such as writing or drawing. Their muscles may suddenly contract or tighten (this is called spasticity). They may also have seizures. Their balance and walking may also be affected. They may be partly or completely paralyzed on one side of the body, or both sides.

- **Difficulties with thinking**: Because the brain has been injured, it is common that the person's ability to use the brain changes. For example, children with TBI may have trouble with short-term memory (being able to remember something from one minute to the next, like what the teacher just said). They may also have trouble with their long-term memory (being able to remember information from a while ago, like facts learned last month). People with TBI may have trouble concentrating and only be able to focus their attention for a short time. They may think slowly. They may have trouble talking and listening to others. They may also have difficulty with reading and writing, planning, understanding the order in which events happen (called sequencing), and judgment.

- **Social, behavioral, or emotional problems**: These difficulties may include sudden changes in mood, anxiety, and depression. Children with TBI may have trouble relating to others. They may be restless and may laugh or cry a lot. They may not have much motivation or much control over their emotions.

A child with TBI may not have all of the above difficulties. Brain injuries can range from mild to severe, and so can the changes that result from the injury. This means that it's hard to predict how an individual will recover from the injury. Early and ongoing help can make a big difference in how the child recovers. This help can include physical or occupational therapy, counseling, and special education.

It's also important to know that, as the child grows and develops, parents and teachers may notice new problems. This is because, as students grow, they are expected to use their brain in new and different ways. The damage to the brain from the earlier injury can make it hard for the student to learn new skills that come with getting older. Sometimes parents and educators may not even realize that the student's difficulty comes from the earlier injury.

What about School?

Although TBI is very common, many medical and education professionals may not realize that some difficulties can be caused by a childhood brain injury. Often, students with TBI are thought to have a learning disability, emotional disturbance, or mental retardation. As a result, they don't receive the type of educational help and support they really need.

When children with TBI return to school, their educational and emotional needs are often very different than before the injury. Their disability has happened suddenly and traumatically. They can often remember how they were before the brain injury. This can bring on many emotional and social changes. The child's family, friends, and teachers also recall what the child was like before the injury. These other people in the child's life may have trouble changing or adjusting their expectations of the child.

Therefore, it is extremely important to plan carefully for the child's return to school. Parents will want to find out ahead of time about special education services at the school. This information is usually available from the school's principal or special education teacher. The school will need to evaluate the child thoroughly. This evaluation will let the school and parents know what the student's educational needs are. The school and parents will then develop an Individualized Education Program (IEP) that addresses those educational needs.

It's important to remember that the IEP is a flexible plan. It can be changed as the parents, the school, and the student learn more about what the student needs at school.

Tips for Parents

- Learn about TBI. The more you know, the more you can help yourself and your child. See the list of resources and organizations at the end of this section.

- Work with the medical team to understand your child's injury and treatment plan. Don't be shy about asking questions. Tell them what you know or think. Make suggestions.

- Keep track of your child's treatment. A 3-ring binder or a box can help you store this history. As your child recovers, you may meet with many doctors, nurses, and others. Write down what they say. Put any paperwork they give you in the notebook or

201

throw it in the box. You can't remember all this! Also, if you need to share any of this paperwork with someone else, make a copy. Don't give away your original!

- Talk to other parents whose children have TBI. There are parent groups all over the U.S. Parents can share practical advice and emotional support. Call NICHCY (1-800-695-0285) to find out how to find parent groups near you.

- If your child was in school before the injury, plan for his or her return to school. Get in touch with the school. Ask the principal about special education services. Have the medical team share information with the school.

- When your child returns to school, ask the school to test your child as soon as possible to identify his or her special education needs. Meet with the school and help develop a plan for your child called an Individualized Education Program (IEP).

- Keep in touch with your child's teacher. Tell the teacher about how your child is doing at home. Ask how your child is doing in school.

Tips for Teachers

- Find out as much as you can about the child's injury and his or her present needs. Find out more about TBI. See the list of resources and organizations at the end of this section.

- Give the student more time to finish schoolwork and tests.

- Give directions one step at a time. For tasks with many steps, it helps to give the student written directions.

- Show the student how to perform new tasks. Give examples to go with new ideas and concepts.

- Have consistent routines. This helps the student know what to expect. If the routine is going to change, let the student know ahead of time.

- Check to make sure that the student has actually learned the new skill. Give the student lots of opportunities to practice the new skill.

- Show the student how to use an assignment book and a daily schedule. This helps the student get organized.

- Realize that the student may get tired quickly. Let the student rest as needed.

- Reduce distractions.

- Keep in touch with the student's parents. Share information about how the student is doing at home and at school.

- Be flexible about expectations. Be patient. Maximize the student's chances for success.

Resources

DeBoskey, D.S. (Ed.). (1996). *Coming home: A discharge manual for families of persons with a brain injury*. Houston, TX: HDI. (Telephone: 800-321-7037; 713-526-6900.)

DePompei, R., Blosser, J., Savage, R., & Lash, M. (1998). *Special education: IEP checklist for a student with a brain injury*. Wolfeboro, NH: L&A Publishing/Training. (Telephone: 603-569-3826. Web: http://www.lapublishing.com)

DePompei, R., & Cluett, B. (1998). *All about me!* Wolfeboro, NH: L&A Publishing/Training. (For use by elementary school children with TBI. Available from L&A, at the phone number above.)

Glang, A., Singer, G.H.S., & Todis, B. (1997). *Students with acquired brain injury: The school's response*. Baltimore, MD: Paul H. Brookes. (Telephone: 1-800-638-3775.)

Lash, M. (1998). Resource guide: Children and adolescents with brain injuries. Wolfeboro, NH: L&A Publishing/Training. (See phone number above.)

Lash, M., Wolcott, G., & Pearson, S. (1995). *Signs and strategies for educating students with brain injuries: A practical guide for teachers and schools*. Houston, TX: HDI. (Telephone: (800) 321-7037; (713) 526-6900.)

Savage, R. (1995). *An educator's manual: What educators need to know about students with TBI (3rd ed.)*. Houston, TX: HDI. (See phone number above.)

Snyder, H. (1998). *Elvin the elephant who forgets*. Wolfeboro, NH: L&A Publishing/Training. (A 16-page picture book for children. Available from L&A at the phone number above.)

Ylvisaker, M. (1998). *Collaborative brain injury intervention: Positive everyday routines. San Diego*, CA: Singular Publishers. (Telephone: 800-521-8545.)

Organizations

Brain Injury Association (formerly the National Head Injury Foundation)
105 North Alfred Street
Alexandria, VA 22314
Telephone: 800-444-6443
Family Helpline: 703-236-6000
E-mail: FamilyHelpline@biausa.org
Web site: http://www.biausa.org

Emergency Medical Services for Children—National Resource Center
111 Michigan Avenue N.W.
Washington, DC 20010-2979
Telephone: 202-884-4927

Epilepsy Foundation—National Office
4351 Garden City Drive, Suite 500
Landover, MD 20785
Telephone: 301-459-3700
Toll-free: 800-332-1000
TTY: 800-332-2070
E-Mail: postmaster@efa.org
Web site: http://www.efa.org

Family Caregiver Alliance
690 Market Street, Suite 601
San Francisco, CA 94104
Telephone: 415-434-3388
Toll-free: 800-245-6686 (CA only)
Web site: http://www.caregiver.org

Family Voices
P.O. Box 769
Algodones, NM 87001
Telephone: 505-867-2368
E-mail: kidshealth@familyvoices.org
Web site: http://www.familyvoices.org

Head Injury Hotline
212 Pioneer Building
Seattle, WA 98104
Telephone: 206-621-8558
E-mail: brain@headinjury.com
Web site: http://www.headinjury.com

National Information Center for Children and Youth with Disabilities
P.O. Box 1492
Washington, DC 20013
E-Mail: nichcy@aed,org
Web site: http://www.nichcy.org
Toll-free: 800-695-0285 (Voice/TTY)

Section 13.2

Shaken Baby Syndrome

Reprinted with permission © 1998, The Arc, Susan Palmer, Ph.D., Project Director, Department of Research and Program Services.

What Is Shaken Baby Syndrome?

Shaken baby syndrome is caused by vigorous shaking of an infant or young child by the arms, legs, chest, or shoulders. Forceful shaking can result in brain damage leading to mental retardation, speech and learning disabilities, paralysis, seizures, hearing loss, and even death. It may cause bleeding around the brain and eyes, resulting in blindness. A baby's head and neck are especially vulnerable to injury because the head is so large and the neck muscles are still weak. In addition, the baby's brain and blood vessels are very fragile and easily damaged by whiplash motions, such as shaking, jerking, and jolting.

Shaken baby syndrome has been identified by other names such as abusive head trauma, shaken brain trauma, pediatric traumatic brain injury, whiplash shaken infant syndrome, and shaken impact syndrome.

How Is Shaken Baby Syndrome Diagnosed?

Shaken baby syndrome is difficult to diagnose, unless someone accurately describes what happens. Physicians often report that a child with possible shaken baby syndrome is brought for medical attention due to falls, difficulty breathing, seizures, vomiting, altered consciousness, or choking. The caregiver may report that the child was shaken to try to resuscitate it. Babies with severe or lethal shaken baby syndrome are typically brought to the hospital unconscious with a closed head injury.

To diagnose shaken baby syndrome, physicians look for retinal hemorrhages (bleeding in the retina of the eyes), subdural hematoma (blood in the brain,) and increased head size indicating excessive accumulation of fluid in the tissues of the brain. Damage to the spinal cord and broken ribs from grasping the baby too hard are other signs of shaken baby syndrome. Computed tomography (CT) and magnetic resonance imaging (MRI) scans can assist in showing injuries in the brain, but are not regularly used because of their expense.

A milder form of this syndrome can also be observed and may be missed or misdiagnosed. Subtle symptoms which may be the result of shaken baby syndrome are often attributed to mild viral illnesses, feeding dysfunction, or infant colic. These include a history of poor feeding, vomiting, or flu-like symptoms with no accompanying fever or diarrhea, lethargy, and irritability over a period of time. Often the visit to the medical facility does not occur immediately after the initial injury. Without early medical intervention, the child may be at risk for further damage or even death, depending on the continued occurrences of shaking.

How Many Children Are Affected by Shaken Baby Syndrome?

An estimated 50,000 cases occur each year in the United States (Ramirez, 1996). One shaken baby in four dies as a result of this abuse (Poissaint & Linn, 1997). Head trauma is the most frequent cause of permanent damage or death among abused infants and children, and shaking accounts for a significant number of those cases (Showers, 1992). Some studies estimate that 15 percent of children's deaths are due to battering or shaking and an additional 15 percent are possible cases of shaking. The victims of shaken baby syndrome range in age from a few days to five years, with an average age of six to eight months (Showers, 1997).

Who Is Responsible for Shaking Babies?

While shaken baby abuse is not limited to any special group of people, males tend to predominate as perpetrators in 65 to 90 percent of cases. In the United States, adult males in their early 20s who are the baby's father or the mother's boyfriend are typically the shaker. Females who injure babies by shaking them are more likely to be babysitters or childcare providers than mothers (Showers, 1997).

Frustration from a baby's incessant crying and toileting problems have been described as events leading to severe shaking. The adult shaker also may be jealous of the attention which the child receives from his or her partner.

What Happens to a Child Who Has Been Severely Shaken?

Immediate medical attention can help reduce the impact of shaking, but many children are left with permanent damage from the shaking. While data on outcomes are limited, fewer than 10 to 15 percent of shaken babies are believed to recover completely. The remaining victims exhibit a variety of disabilities, including partial or complete loss of vision, hearing impairments, seizure disorders, cerebral palsy, sucking and swallowing disorders, developmental disabilities, autism, cognitive impairments, behavior problems, and permanent vegetative state.

The treatment of survivors falls into three major categories—medical, behavioral, and educational. In addition to medical care, children may need speech and language therapy, vision therapy, physical therapy, occupational therapy, and special education services. Some may need the assistance of feeding experts and behavioral consultants (Showers, 1997).

What Will It Take to Solve the Problem of Shaken Baby Syndrome?

Dr. John Caffey who first described shaken baby syndrome in 1972 called for a massive public education program to describe the dangers of shaking infants. Experts views vary on the effectiveness of education. Some experts believe that shaking is primarily the result of anger felt by an adult, combined with a loss of impulse control, and that the perpetrator is aware of the potential harm to the child. They say that shaken baby syndrome requires a great deal of force by the shaker, such that the ordinary person would recognize the action as harmful to a child (Showers, 1997).

Other experts believe lack of knowledge about the dangers of shaking is a contributing factor and that most people don't intend to harm or kill children by shaking them. Thus, they believe physicians, social workers, educators, attorneys, families, and others should collaborate to educate the public about preventing shaken baby syndrome. In addition to public education, other proposed strategies to reduce the problem include identifying families at high risk for abuse and providing supports to reduce stress and funding and monitoring high quality child care, so that parents leave their children with safe caregivers.

How Can People Be Educated about the Dangers of Shaking Babies?

Parents should receive information about shaken baby syndrome prevention in the hospital and/or at their child's two-month immunization appointment. Pediatricians and nurses should talk to parents about their level of stress and how they respond to a crying infant who cannot be readily calmed. They can discuss adequate care for infants and how the family is adjusting to the new family member. Guidance can be given to let parents know that a crying infant should never be shaken and what to do when their frustration is overwhelming. Any professional or experienced caregiver who interacts with parents of newborns and young children can assist in this effort.

Child caregivers, teenage babysitters, and respite workers should be warned by parents and others of the dangers of shaking a child. Day care centers should train staff and display shaken baby information in their facilities to inform both workers and parents. All childcare providers should be screened by the parent to determine the potential caregiver's ability to understand infant behavior and how he or she might handle stressful situations, such as incessant crying. Social service agencies, state and national agencies, and hospitals need to educate the public as well. Several agencies which assist parents or caregivers who may have a strong or recurrent impulse to shake their children include CHILDHELP (800-4-ACHILD) or the National Child Abuse Hotline (800-422-4453).

Message to Caregivers
Prevent Shaken Baby Syndrome

Don't Shake a Baby! Do not handle a baby if you are angry.

- Shaking can cause brain damage, vision loss, and other injuries.
- If you are afraid you might hurt your child, follow these three simple steps:

Stop*****Calm Down*****Try Again

1. Stop

   - Place the baby in a safe place such as a playpen or a crib.

2. Calm Down

   - Sit down or walk out of the room—but not too far away that you can't hear the child.

   - Listen to music for a short time. Call a friend or relative for support and advice.

   - Run the vacuum cleaner to drown out crying noise. This noise also calms some babies.

   - Remember that crying may indicate hunger, pain or illness, discomfort, teething, ear ache, or other problems. If you can't calm the baby and the crying continues for a long time, call the doctor.

3. Try Again

   - When you have calmed down, resume trying to help the baby.

References:

American Academy of Pediatrics: Committee on Child Abuse and Neglect (1993). Shaken Baby Syndrome: Inflicted Cerebral Trauma. *Pediatrics,* 92 (6), 872-875.

Poissaint, A. & Linn, S. (1997). Fragile: Handle with Care. *Newsweek,* Special Edition, Spring/Summer, 33.

Phillips, Mary Beth (1996, November). Ten things parents of children with SBS want you to know. Information presented at the

National Conference on Shaken Baby Syndrome, Salt Lake City, UT.

Ramirez, Domingo (1996, November 19). Beware of the dangers of shaking infants. Fort Worth, Texas: Star-Telegram, B2. Showers, J. (1992). "Don't Shake the Baby": The effectiveness of a prevention program. *Child Abuse & Neglect*, 16, 11-18.

Showers, J. (1997). Executive Summary: The National Conference on Shaken Baby Syndrome. Alexandria, VA: National Association of Children's Hospitals and Related Institutions.

When a baby cries: What should you know, what can you do. (Online, WWW). New Jersey Chapter of the National Committee to Prevent Child Abuse. Newark, NJ.

The Arc
National Organization on Mental Retardation
1010 Wayne Ave, Suite 650
Silver Spring, MD 20910
Tel: 301-565-3842
Fax: 301-565-3843
E-mail: thearc@metronet.com
URL: http://www.thearc.org

Section 13.3

Diet, Toxins, Disease, and Drugs

This section contains excerpts from "Decreasing the Chance of Birth Defects," by Rebecca Williams, *FDA Consumer*, November 1996, Updated September 1997, and "Prenatal Exposure to Drugs of Abuse May Affect Later Behavior and Learning," by Robert Mathias, *NIDA Notes Research Findings*, Volume 13, Number 4, 1997.

When Tammy Troutman of Knoxville, Tenn., was planning her first pregnancy, she had a good reason to be concerned about birth defects.

Born with a mild form of spina bifida, Troutman worried her child would also have the condition. So she did what health-care experts say is the best first step toward preventing birth defects: She visited her physician for an exam well before she and her husband tried to conceive. "Before I decided to have children, I went to the doctor to make sure everything would be OK," Troutman remembers.

He advised her to take a daily multivitamin supplement containing folic acid, a B vitamin that would decrease her chances of having a baby with spina bifida. Troutman took the vitamins for five months before conceiving her son, Evan, who was born in August 1993 with a normal, healthy spine.

"Even if he had been born with spina bifida," Troutman says, "I felt secure knowing that I had done everything I could to prevent it."

Of the 4 million infants born annually in the United States, about 3 to 5 percent are born with birth defects, according to the March of Dimes. Birth defects account for 20 percent of all infant deaths in the United States, more than from any other single cause.

"For the majority of birth defects, the cause is unknown," says Franz Rosa, M.D., a pediatrician, formerly with the Food and Drug Administration, who monitored reports of prescription drugs causing birth defects. Rosa cites a list of drugs that are known to be birth defect causing, but he says they only account for a small percentage of all malformations.

"There's a lot we just don't know," Rosa says. "Most birth defects are not preventable and mothers should not feel guilty about causing defects that they really didn't. Worrying too much is not good for pregnancies."

What experts do know is that most birth defects occur in the first three months of pregnancy, when the organs are forming. It is in these crucial first few weeks—often before a woman even knows she's pregnant—that an embryo is most susceptible to teratogens, substances that can cause defects. However, some birth defects do occur later in pregnancy as well.

"The key is what your life is like at the time you become pregnant," says Deborah Smith, M.D., an obstetrician and gynecologist in FDA's Office of Women's Health. "Are you getting enough folic acid, are you immune to rubella, are you avoiding alcohol and smoking? These are some of the things we know are important."

Despite the benefits of seeing a doctor before conceiving, only 26 percent of women planning a pregnancy do so, according to the March of Dimes. Furthermore, health experts estimate more than 50 percent of pregnancies are unplanned. That's why a healthy lifestyle for all women who could become pregnant—even if they don't intend to— is the best way to minimize the risk of birth defects.

211

Healthy Diet

The maxim "You are what you eat" is sterling advice during the first three months of pregnancy.

Studies of women who had endured starvation during World War II illustrate the importance of diet early in pregnancy. Contrary to what researchers expected, it was not the babies *born* during food deprivation that had the most malformations, but those *conceived* during food deprivation.

One nutrient known to prevent birth defects is folic acid, the B vitamin Tammy Troutman took before her pregnancy. Folic acid is the chemical form of folate, which is found in green leafy vegetables, citrus fruits, and legumes. Folate aids in cell division, and taking extra folic acid reduces a woman's chance of having a child with spina bifida and other abnormalities of the spine and brain.

Spina bifida occurs when the vertebrae do not close completely. It is one of several conditions known as neural tube defects, because the neural tube is the portion of the embryo that develops into the brain and spinal column. In very mild cases, spina bifida causes few or minor problems, but in more severe cases, the spinal cord protrudes through the vertebrae into a sac outside the child's body. This impairs the child's mobility and other neurological functions and requires surgery to repair the opening.

To help prevent neural tube defects, the U.S. Public Health Service has recommended that all women of childbearing age who are capable of becoming pregnant consume 0.4 milligrams (mg) of folic acid per day. (For pregnant or lactating women, the daily value increases to 0.8 mg per day.) It is especially important that women take in sufficient folate before they become pregnant.

FDA recently published regulations requiring manufacturers to add folic acid to enriched grain products such as flour, noodles, bread, rolls, buns, farina, cornmeal, grits, and rice by January 1998.

Although the main challenge in pregnancy is getting enough nutrients, too much of a good thing is not good for a developing baby, either. Vitamins A and D are the most notable examples. Both can be toxic at levels higher than the recommended daily allowance. Such levels are rarely reached through food intake; however, women taking dietary supplements need to be aware of this risk and the amount of these vitamins they are taking. Women who take vitamin and mineral supplements should discuss with a health care professional what vitamins are safe to continue taking during pregnancy.

Only a few foods are completely off-limits during pregnancy. These include raw or undercooked meat, such as "pink-in-the-middle" burgers, and raw or undercooked seafood. Bacteria from these can cause severe food poisoning, which is dangerous to a fetus and very unpleasant for the mother.

Soft drinks, coffee, tea, and other caffeinated drinks can be used in moderation. Although large doses of caffeine have caused skeletal defects in rats, one or two cups of coffee daily are not considered dangerous for developing fetuses.

Alcohol should be avoided at all times during pregnancy because it leads to low birth weight and can cause deformities as well.

According to the March of Dimes, alcohol is the most common known cause of fetal damage in the country and the leading cause of preventable mental retardation. Pregnant women who drink alcohol, especially in large amounts, put their babies at risk for fetal alcohol syndrome, which causes growth retardation, facial deformities such as a small head, thin upper lip, and small jaw bone, an underdeveloped thymus gland, and mental deficiencies or developmental delays.

If a woman has had a glass or two of wine before finding out she was pregnant, she probably has not harmed her child. But since no one knows the exact amount of alcohol that is dangerous, it's best to avoid alcohol when pregnancy is possible.

Healthy Mothers, Healthy Babies

A pregnant woman who has a serious medical condition may face a greater than normal risk that her child will have a birth defect.

Diabetes, for example, can complicate a pregnancy in many ways. Women who must take insulin daily to control their blood sugar are three or four times more likely to have a baby with major birth defects than are other mothers. That's not to say they should abandon insulin, however. Without it, many diabetic women and their babies wouldn't survive pregnancy at all.

Birth defects among diabetics can be greatly reduced if women get their blood sugar levels under control before becoming pregnant and strictly manage their diets throughout pregnancy. Gestational diabetes, which develops during pregnancy, can also be harmful to mother and child, but it can be controlled through diet or medication.

Epilepsy also increases a woman's chance of having a baby with a birth defect. It's not clear whether the disease itself or the drugs used to control it cause malformations, but in either case, the woman's neurologist and obstetrician should work together to find the safest course of treatment for the epilepsy and pregnancy.

Rubella, toxoplasmosis, cytomegalovirus, and syphilis can cause birth defects in the infants of women who have these infectious diseases. Rubella infection during early pregnancy can cause abnormalities of the heart, eyes, and ears. Any woman planning a pregnancy should be tested for rubella immunity and vaccinated if necessary. She must wait three months after vaccination before becoming pregnant, however, because the vaccine itself can endanger a developing fetus.

Toxoplasmosis is transmitted only through raw meat and cat feces, both of which pregnant women should try to avoid. The disease causes malformations of the brain, liver, and spleen if a fetus becomes infected in the first trimester.

If a woman has syphilis, she should be treated with antibiotics before pregnancy. If not treated by at least the fourth month, syphilis can cause bone and tooth deformities in the baby, as well as nervous system and brain damage.

Cytomegalovirus (CMV) is a herpes virus that causes no real problem—and sometimes not even symptoms—for adults and children. In pregnancy, however, it can damage the fetus' brain, eyes, or ears. Because most people contract the infection, whose symptoms are very much like a cold, when they are children, most adults are immune to it. Pregnant women who do not know if they've had CMV and who work with large groups of young children should discuss the situation with their health care providers.

Drugs and Birth Defects

Sometimes it is not a disease that causes birth defects, but the medication used to treat it. Unfortunately, no one knows for certain how most drugs will affect a developing fetus. Historically, most women of childbearing age have been excluded from clinical trials of new drugs, and, although that is changing, drug manufacturers are understandably reluctant to involve pregnant women in clinical trials for new drugs. Therefore, the effects of many drugs are not known until they are in wider use after market approval.

To be on the safe side, a pregnant woman shouldn't take any drug unless it is absolutely necessary and not until she's checked with her health care provider. However, even physicians have little information when prescribing medication for pregnant women. What is known about most drugs in pregnancy is based either on animal studies or on reports of problems after the drug is on the market. To give guidance about pregnancy safety, FDA requires that manufacturers include in the professional labeling for each drug which one of several categories, reflecting information from studies available at the time the label was developed.

Taxol (paclitaxel), used to treat ovarian and breast cancer, may in some instances be appropriate in pregnancy even though it causes birth defects in animals and is therefore believed to cause fetal harm in humans. The benefits of its use to fight life-threatening cancers may outweigh the potential harm to a fetus.

Accutane (isotretinoin), a relative of vitamin A, is approved to treat severe cystic acne that doesn't respond to other drugs. It has some serious side effects, though, especially if a woman taking it becomes pregnant. There are other drugs available to treat acne, and the disease is not life threatening to the mother.

The drug's manufacturer has included strong warnings in the package labeling to inform doctors and patients about the birth defects this drug can cause.

Pregnant women who take Accutane even for a short time are at great risk of having a baby with severe facial birth defects, malformed thymus glands, and mental retardation.

The risk is so great that any woman of childbearing age who is taking Accutane—even if she's not sexually active—must also use effective contraception at least one month before beginning Accutane, while using the drug, and for one month after stopping.

Who Should Paint the Nursery?

Chemicals—whether it's paint in the nursery or exhaust fumes in a parking garage—have long been suspected of causing birth defects. It's important for pregnant women to realize that most birth defects are not caused by a single factor, nor are they usually caused by faint traces of toxins. Scientists believe it takes a combination of factors to trigger a congenital malformation.

"Most birth defects have one or more genetic factors and one or more environmental factors," explains Richard Leavitt, director of science information at the March of Dimes.

Most of the chemicals a pregnant woman encounters pose little threat compared with the harm in smoking, drinking alcohol, or eating a poor diet.

"Most environmental exposure is at a low level compared to things you put in your mouth or inhale purposefully into your lungs," Leavitt says. "Public health warnings are aimed at the many to help the relatively few avoid a problem."

Daily, heavy exposure to chemicals may be dangerous, however. If a pregnant woman must work around fumes or chemicals, such as in a dry-cleaning business, art studio, or factory, she should use gloves, masks, and adequate ventilation. But if she just gets a whiff of dry-cleaning fluid while picking up her laundry from the cleaners, there's little need to worry, Leavitt says.

Some environmental toxins such as lead are best avoided at any time, but especially during pregnancy. Scraping leaded paint off an old house window, drinking water from a pipe soldered with lead, or drinking out of decorative pottery containing lead can all potentially cause lead poisoning—and mental retardation—in a fetus.

Radiation is also dangerous to developing babies. A pregnant woman who works in an x-ray department of a hospital must take precautions to avoid exposure. Elective dental x-rays should be postponed until delivery, and any woman, whether or not she is pregnant, should have her reproductive organs shielded with a lead apron when she has an x-ray.

Taking hot baths, using saunas, or exercising in hot, humid weather can raise a woman's core temperature and have the potential to cause birth defects, especially in the first trimester. Lukewarm baths and moderate exercise are fine, however.

And what about computers or video display terminals? Although they have at times been accused of causing harm, there's probably no need to worry. Recent studies have not found any relationship between computer terminals and miscarriages.

And as for who should paint the nursery—today's paints don't contain lead and therefore probably aren't dangerous. But there are other reasons to find someone else to do this task. The repetitive motion of painting can be a strain on back muscles already under pressure from the extra weight of pregnancy, and standing on your feet for hours can make advanced pregnancy miserable. If someone else can do it, pass this chore along.

Of all the environmental harms, undoubtedly the most harmful is one women can control—smoking. Although there is no evidence smoking causes birth defects, it deprives the fetus of oxygen and leads to a number of problems. If all pregnant women avoided smoking, the United States would see a 5 percent reduction in miscarriages, a 20 percent reduction in low-birth-weight births, and an

8 percent reduction in premature deliveries in this country, according to the March of Dimes.

Prenatal Exposure to Drugs of Abuse May Affect Later Behavior and Learning

NIDA-funded studies are beginning to show that children who have been prenatally exposed to illicit drugs may be at risk of later behavioral and learning difficulties. Long-term studies using sophisticated assessment techniques indicate that prenatally exposed children may have subtle but significant impairments in their ability to regulate emotions and focus and sustain attention on a task. These neurobehavioral deficits may place these children on a developmental pathway that leads to poor school performance and other adverse consequences over time, researchers say.

"The evidence that prenatal exposure to drugs may contribute to later behavioral and learning problems has important public health implications," says NIDA Director Dr. Alan I. Leshner. "Although these effects are subtle and may not be universal, the rising tide of data from ongoing studies indicates that we need to be alert to the fact that children who have been exposed to drugs before birth may need special attention." However, because the long-term effects of prenatal drug exposure are still unclear, "we need more answers from research about the full extent of drug-induced impairments in children and what we ought to be doing to best address this problem," he says.

NIDA's 1992 National Pregnancy and Health Survey indicated that more than 5 percent of women use an illicit drug, most often marijuana or cocaine, during pregnancy. NIDA-supported researchers have been studying the effects of this prenatal drug exposure on infant and child development for a number of years. Most of these long-term studies have been assessing the clinical status of cocaine-exposed children since birth. Other long-term studies have been focusing on the status of children who have been prenatally exposed to opiates or marijuana and cocaine.

With some groups of cocaine-exposed children entering school and children in the marijuana-and-opiate-exposure studies well into their school years, the time was right to assess the status of developmental follow-up research with school-age, drug-exposed children. Therefore, NIDA convened more than 30 researchers conducting long-term studies with these children at a meeting in Bethesda, Maryland, in April 1997. Representatives from the National Institute of Child Health and Human Development, the Substance Abuse and Mental

Health Services Administration, and the Administration on Children, Youth, and Families also participated in the meeting. Meeting participants assessed current knowledge about the effects of prenatal drug exposure on school-age children, examined the biological and environmental mechanisms underlying these consequences, and discussed the "nuts and bolts" of conducting research to determine what happens to drug-exposed children as they progress through school and enter adolescence.

Generally, most studies of physical and neurobehavioral outcomes in newborn infants have shown that prenatal exposure to marijuana, cocaine, and/or opiates increases the risk that exposed infants will be born prematurely, weigh less, have smaller heads, and be shorter than unexposed infants. However, assessing the full consequences of prenatal drug exposure for these children as they get older is a more complex task. The timing and amount of prenatal exposure, the mother's abuse of multiple drugs, poverty, poor nutrition, and inadequate prenatal and postnatal care are just some of the factors that can cloud the effects of prenatal maternal drug abuse on infants and children.

Because animal studies can exclude complicating variables, such research has provided valuable clues for researchers studying the consequences of prenatal drug exposure in children. Some important findings from animal research were presented at a conference in Washington, D.C., in September 1997, sponsored by the New York Academy of Sciences with support from NIDA. The conference brought together a number of leading basic scientists and clinical investigators to discuss what both lines of research were showing about the effects of cocaine on the developing brain. Several researchers presented data indicating that rabbits and mice prenatally exposed to cocaine develop specific and permanent brain changes. Dr. Pat Levitt, a NIDA-funded scientist from the University of Pittsburgh School of Medicine in Pennsylvania, reported finding abnormalities among rabbits prenatally exposed to cocaine in areas of the brain that are involved in attention and learning. Dr. Levitt's work buttresses other findings from animal research. For example, a NIDA-funded study at the University of Massachusetts in Amherst, Massachusetts, has shown that cocaine can enter the fetal brain of prenatally exposed rats and directly modify neurotransmitter activity in areas that play a role in learning, memory, motivation, motor control, and sensory processing.

The brain alterations found in prenatally exposed animals may provide a biological explanation for subtle impairments in emotional control and behavior that clinical researchers are uncovering in drug-exposed children whom they have been studying since the children were born. Although they remain cautious about drawing conclusions, researchers at the NIDA developmental follow-up meeting revealed a common thread of findings indicating that children who have been prenatally exposed to drugs may have early and persistent difficulties in regulating arousal appropriately, delaying gratification, tolerating frustration, and handling stress.

Dr. Margaret Bendersky of the Institute for the Study of Child Development at the University of Medicine and Dentistry of New Jersey in New Brunswick noted that her NIDA-funded study with Dr. Michael Lewis showed that a significantly greater number of 4-month-old cocaine-exposed infants had negative emotional reactions than nonexposed infants when play with their mothers was interrupted. These infants also responded more strongly to the stress of inoculation and took longer to calm down than nonexposed infants, she said.

Further analyses of the children at 2 years of age showed that, compared to nonexposed children, they were less able to control impulses and delay gratification and showed more frustration by kicking and screaming when restrained momentarily by their mothers. These findings were particularly true for children who were heavily exposed to cocaine. While the interaction of biological effects of early drug exposure on the brain and many other environmental factors is difficult to work out, "prenatal exposure may predict later difficulties in emotional regulation and social interactions and behaviors in the classroom," Dr. Bendersky noted.

The difficulty that some drug-exposed infants have in achieving a quiet, alert state may also affect their intellectual development because it can affect their ability to respond to new stimuli, focus and sustain attention, and process information. These abilities are critical components of learning. Cocaine-exposed children appear to be more impulsive than nonexposed children and have more difficulty screening out distractions and focusing their attention appropriately, reported Dr. Linda Mayes of the Yale University Child Study Center in New Haven, Connecticut.

Dr. Mayes' NIDA-funded study has been looking at emotional arousal and attention in a group of 475 children since they were born. Slightly more than half of these children were exposed to cocaine before birth. Follow-up assessments at 24 months showed cocaine-exposed children were more impulsive and language-delayed than noncocaine-exposed children, Dr. Mayes said. When both groups were tested again between ages 4 and 5, the cocaine-exposed children continued to be more impulsive, responding more quickly than nonexposed children when asked to press a button whenever they saw a picture that was repeatedly flashed on a computer screen. When the researchers added more pictures and asked the children to respond only when the designated picture appeared, the cocaine-exposed children still responded more quickly. However, they were unable to screen out the distracting pictures and made more errors than the nonexposed children did, Dr. Mayes said. "Their motor response is there, and it is fast, but it is separated from their processing of the difficulty of the task," she explained.

As children enter their school years, assessing the long-term consequences of drug exposure becomes even more difficult as school, teacher, peer, and neighborhood factors are added to the maternal, family, caregiver, and other home influences that continue to shape children's development. However, after sorting through the effects of these burgeoning variables, some studies are discovering differences in school performance between exposed and nonexposed children. For example, a NIDA-supported study with one of the oldest groups of cocaine-exposed children has completed an initial analysis of data on the first 22 cocaine-exposed and 24 nonexposed children in the study to complete the first grade. "The analysis showed that cocaine-exposed children were much more likely to be held back a grade and require special education classes than their peers in the control group," said Dr. Hallam Hurt of the Albert Einstein Medical Center in Philadelphia, Pennsylvania, who is conducting the study. Dr. Hurt cautions that these early findings are based on a relatively small number of children in the initial group. However, "if they are true, they are extremely important," she says. Dr. Hurt is continuing follow-up analyses with a second group of 55 children in the study who have just completed the first grade.

The subtle neurobehavioral impairments in arousal, emotional regulation, and the ability to focus and maintain attention shown in these studies may constitute a biological vulnerability that interacts with other developmental influences, such as a chaotic home environment or poor maternal care, says Dr. Vincent Smeriglio of NIDA's Center on AIDS and Other Medical Consequences of Drug Abuse. The interaction of these influences may produce a snowball effect on development and learning over time, he says. For this reason, researchers now are focusing more on understanding how the early neurobehavioral effects of prenatal drug exposure interact with environmental factors that change over time to produce different outcomes for different drug-exposed children, Dr. Smeriglio says. "Such analyses are necessary to understand more clearly what is going on with drug-exposed children," he concludes.

Section 13.4

Poverty and Cultural Deprivation

"Findings about Early Childhood Development, Poverty, and Child Care Environments," by Dr. Sandra L. Hofferth, University of Michigan, Office of Behavioral and Social Sciences Research, NIH June 30, 1997, and reprinted with permisssion, "Members of Minority Groups and Mental Retardation," © The Arc.

Early Childhood Development, Poverty, and Inequality

* Children who are born into poverty are more likely to be small at birth; they are more likely than middle-income children to be low height-for-age and low weight-for height; and they score lower on cognitive development tests. The effects of low birth weight and early nutritional deficits have been shown to be cumulative (Miller and Korenman 1994; Korenman, Miller and Sjaastad 1994).

* Fifty-two percent of white adults who were born in the United States during the late 1960s and early 1970s experienced at least one major economic loss during their childhood. The reason for this economic hardship was either a loss of income (28 percent) or unemployment (39 percent). For blacks, the proportions were higher (61 percent overall), 47 percent resulting from income loss and 48 percent due to loss of work hours (Yeung and Hofferth 1997).

* One-third of children have experienced poverty (i.e., economic deprivation resulting in a lack of money for food, housing, clothing, and transportation) for at least one year during their lives before they reach age 17 (Smith and Yeung 1997).

* There appears to be a strong association between family income in childhood and ability and achievement measures. Children with families whose income is less than half the poverty line scored 6-13 points lower on tests than children in families with incomes between 1.5 and twice the poverty line (Smith, Brooks-Gunn and Klebanov 1997). For children in families with incomes

slightly below the poverty line, differences in these assessment measures are smaller, controlling for a variety of other factors. The achievements of children in families with income around the poverty line were more strongly affected than children in families with income falling above the poverty line.

- One study found that poor children were less likely to complete their schooling than those who were not poor or those who were poor later in life (Duncan, Harris and Boisjoly 1997).

- Low-family income during childhood was shown be to linked to aggression and delinquency during adolescence and young adulthood (Yoshikawa 1994).

Young Children and Their Social Settings: In- and Out-of-Home Environments

- The proportion of young children in out-of-home care while parents are working has risen. In 1993, half of infants and toddlers aged 1-2 years were in nonparental care settings. By the time they entered kindergarten, four out of five had some preschool experience (West, Wright and Hausken 1995).

- The home environment is crucial. Children from two-parent families who were not in poverty were shown to be more accomplished in literacy/numeracy and in school readiness than their impoverished counterparts (Zill et al. 1995).

- Given the large proportion of young children in out-of-home settings, there is reason for concern about quality. In 1993, 40 percent of infant/toddler classrooms were found to be below the minimal standard of quality (Helburn et al. 1995). Another study, using observational methods, found that 35 percent of family daycare homes were below minimal quality (Galinsky et al. 1994).

- Childcare programs play a crucial role in childhood development.

- High quality childcare programs appeared to be associated with better cognitive development and more secure attachment to provider (Galinsky et al. 1994). Children in high quality preschool classrooms displayed greater receptive language ability and pre-math skills; they also demonstrated more advanced social skills than those in lower quality classrooms (Helburn et al. 1995).

• Childcare centers that served children of low- and high-income parents scored higher on developmentally appropriate caregiving and interaction than centers that cared for children from middle-income families (Phillips, Voran and Kisher 1994).

• The availability of quality child care has a direct impact on the employment of mothers.

• Poor quality child care was associated with the attrition of single mothers from the California GAIN program—a welfare reform demonstration program (Meyers 1993).

• Job stability for moderate-income mothers was associated with lower cost and more stable child care. Availability of care is significantly related to job stability for all mothers (Hofferth and Collins 1997).

• The amount of federal investment in early education and care for children doubled for all children, but tripled for low-income children over the past decade (Hofferth and Chaplin 1994; Hofferth 1993)

• Increased federal spending on children yields a positive return on investments. Federal funds have been linked to higher quality care (Helburn et al. 1995). Children from families with both low and high income benefit from this funding.

• One key study of high quality preschool programs showed a $7.16 return on a dollar invested in early childhood education (Schweinhart, Barnes and Weikert 1993). This occurred through reduced arrests, higher earnings, lower public assistance receipt, higher schooling completed, longer marriages, and fewer out-of-wedlock births.

References

Duncan, G., K. Harris, and J. Boisjoly. 1997. "Time Limits and Welfare Reform: New Estimates of the Number and Characteristics of Affected Families." Northwestern University, Evanston, IL: Unpublished manuscript.

Galinsky, E., Carollee Howes, S. Kontos, and M. Shinn. 1994. *The Study of Children in Family Child Care and Relative Care*. New York, NY: Families and Work Institute.

Helburn, S., C. Howes, M. Cryher and K. Peisner-Feinberg. Cost, Quality and Child Outcomes in Child Care Centers. Denver, Colorado: University of Colorado.

Hofferth, S. 1993. "The 101st Congress: An Emerging Agenda for Children in Poverty." Pp. 203-43 in *Child Poverty and Public Policy*. Washington, DC: The Urban Institute.

Hofferth, S. and D. Chaplin. 1994. *Child Care Quality versus Availability: Do We Have to Trade One for the other?* Washington, DC: The Urban Institute.

Hofferth, S. and N. Collins. 1997. "Child Care and Employment Turnover." Presented at the Biennial Meeting of the Society for Research in Child Development, April, Washington, DC.

Korenman, S., J. Miller, and J. Sjaastad. 1994. "Long-Term Poverty and Child Development in the United States." University of Minnesota, St. Paul, MN. Unpublished manuscript.

Meyers, M. 1993. "Child Care in JOBS Employment and Training Programs: What Difference Does Quality Make?" *Journal of Marriage and the Family* 55:767-83.

Miller, J. and S. Korenman. 1994. "Poverty and Children's Nutritional Status in the United States." *American Journal of Epidemiology* 140:233-43.

Phillips, D., M. Voran, and E. Kisher. 1994. "Child Care for Children in Poverty: Opportunity or Inequality." *Child Development* 65:472-92.

Schweinhart, L, H. Barnes and D. Weikert. 1993. *Significant Benefits: The High / Scope Perry Preschool Study Through Age 27.* Ypsilanti, MI: High/Scope Press.

Smith, J., J. Brooks-Gunn, and P. Klebanov. 1997. "Consequences of Growing up Poor for Young Children." In *Consequences of Growing up Poor*. New York: Russell Sage.

Smith, P., and W. J. Yeung. 1997. "Childhood Welfare Receipt and the Implications of Welfare Reform." University of Michigan-Dearborn: Dearborn, MI. Unpublished manuscript.

West, J., D Wright, and E. Hausken. 1995. *Child Care and Early Education Program Participation of Infants, Toddlers, and*

Preschoolers, NCES 95-824. Washington, DC: U.S. Department of Education.

Yeung, W. J., and S. Hofferth. 1997. "Family Adaptation to Economic Loss." Ann Arbor, MI. Unpublished manuscript.

Yoshikawa, H. 1994. "Prevention as Cumulative Protection: Effects of Early Family Support and Education on Chronic Delinquency and Its Risks." *Psychological Bulletin* 115:27-54.

Zill, N., M. Collins, J. West, and E. Hausken. 1995. *Approaching Kindergarten: A Look at Preschoolers in the United States,* NCES 95-280. Washington, DC: U.S. Department of Education.

Members of Minority Groups and Mental Retardation

According to the 1990 United States census, there are more than 71 million people who are minorities. The definitions by the United States Equal Employment Opportunity Commission and their numbers follow:

- African-American or Black. All persons having origins in any of the Black racial groups of Africa—30 million.

- Hispanic. All persons of Mexican, Puerto Rican, Cuban, Central or South American, or other Spanish culture of origin, regardless of race—22.8 million.

- Asian or Pacific Islander. All persons having origins in any other original peoples of the Far East, Southeast Asia, the Indian Subcontinent or the Pacific Islands—7.3 million.

- American Indian or Alaskan Native. All persons having origins in any of the original peoples of North America and who maintain cultural identification through tribal affiliation or community recognition—1.9 million.

- Minorities not included in above groups—9.8 million.

The United States is in the midst of a shift in the minority composition of its population which has important implications of its population which has important implications for The Arc. Demographic projections indicate that shortly after the turn of the century, one out of every three Americans will be a member of a minority group.

The Hispanic population has been growing at an exceptionally high rate since 1970. If this growth rate continues, Hispanics will outnumber blacks by the year 2000 and become the largest segment of the minority population. According to the 1990 census, minority groups have already become the majority in 51 U.S. cities with populations over 100,000. Most of the cities affected are in the South and West. This new populations pattern is due mainly to immigration of Hispanics and Asians from abroad and the movement of whites from the cities into the suburbs.

How Many Minorities Have Mental Retardation and Related Developmental Disabilities?

At this time, very little information is available. However, the U.S. Census Bureau is preparing a report on people with disabilities from data collected in the 1990 census.

There is information available on minority school age children who are in special education. The 1986-87 U.S. Office for Civil Rights survey of schools reported that 219,169 minority students had mental retardation. The figure for white children was 308,393. These numbers indicate that 41.5 percent of the total children with mental retardation in special education belong to a minority group, an apparent disproportionately high number. Thirty percent of all students in special education are members of minority groups, a number that closely reflects the composition of the general population.

Is There a Disproportionate Prevalence of Mental Retardation/Developmental Disabilities within Minority Groups?

Evidence has been collected indicating a disproportionate number of black children have mental retardation. The information is not readily available for other minority groups. The Centers for Disease Control conducted a study to determine the prevalence of mental retardation in 10 year old children in Metropolitan Atlanta. This study found that black children were four times as likely as white children to be classified as having mental retardation based on school or medical records (Yeargin-Allsopp, 1990).

Racial differences in prevalence of mild mental retardation, in particular, may be explained by differential referral patterns for IQ testing, cultural biases in IQ tests, and differences in the prevalence of medical or environmental risk factors in blacks and whites. The CDC researchers found the low maternal education is an important and independent risk factor for mild mental retardation in both black and white children. Continued research is needed to examine behavioral, environmental, and medical factors explaining differences in prevalence between the two groups.

Are There Special Problems for Minority Children That May Explain Their Chance of Being Developmentally Disabled?

The poverty rate for minorities tends to be higher than for white families. Even though the majority of poor children are white, a greater proportion of children who belong to minority groups live in poor families. About 44 percent of all black children and more than 36 percent of Hispanic children are poor, compared to fewer than 15 percent of white children. (National Commission on Children, 1991, p. 24).

Poverty can lead to health problems and influence social environments in ways that can interfere substantially with a child's ability to learn. Children from poor families are more likely to have low birth weights, higher rates of infant mortality, and a higher risk of developing disabilities and health problems early in life. This is caused by many conditions such as poor maternal diet; inadequate education about the need for prenatal care; lack of access to proper care; and smoking, alcohol, and drug abuse.

Are There Special Problems Facing Some Groups of Minorities?

HIV infection. Through July 1991, the Centers for Disease Control reported 186,895 cases of AIDS. Forty-six percent or 85,677 were minorities. Of the minorities reported to have AIDS, blacks represented 63 percent and Hispanics 35 percent. Only two percent were members of other minority groups. Pediatric AIDS takes a particularly severe toll on minority children. Black children constitute 15 percent of the nation's children, yet account for 60 percent of all childhood AIDS cases. Hispanic children, who represent 10 percent of children in the United States, account for 22 percent of all childhood AIDS cases. More than half of the adolescents with AIDS are of minority origin. An estimated 93 percent of children with HIV infection acquire developmental disabilities that result in some degree of mental and/ or physical impairment.

Infant mortality. A U.S. Department of Health and Human Services Task Force has been examining infant mortality and low birth weight among minorities. The task force found much diversity and wide disparities among the different groups. The death rate for black babies is more than twice that for white babies. Their rate of infant mortality is 17.6 per 1,000 compared to 8.5 for white infants.

Among Hispanics, the rate of infant mortality is highest for Puerto Rican babies. Among other Hispanic groups, the rate is not much higher than that for Anglo babies. While the infant mortality rate has dropped for Native Americans, it still remains high compared to white babies. The rate of infant mortality for Asian and Pacific Islander groups was only slightly higher than for whites (Office of Minority Health Resource Center, 1990).

Disproportionate Placement in Special Education. Records from the federal Office for Civil Rights show that black students are enrolled in special education in disproportionately high numbers in more than half the nation's school districts (Eig, 1991).

On the other hand, many Asian-American students may be excluded from special education. They are underrepresented in every disability category. Asian parents often refuse to allow schools to test their children for a disability because the Asian culture disdains failure (Education of Handicapped, April 10, 1991.)

Drug-Exposed Babies. A tremendous number of babies are being exposed to drugs in the womb, perhaps as many as 10 percent of all live births, or 375,000 babies per year. In some inner city hospitals, as many as 60 percent of the babies are born to drug abusers (Education of the Handicapped, August 19, 1992). While many of these babies are born to minority mothers, it should be noted that drug abuse also affects babies born to white mothers.

In addition to illicit drugs, such as cocaine and heroin, the use of alcohol is a problem for some minorities. Certain Native American tribes are particularly affected, and many of their children have Fetal Alcohol Syndrome.

Public Policy Designed to Prevent Discrimination of People with Mental Retardation Who Are Minorities

Rehabilitation Act of 1973, as amended, Section 504 of the Act protects people with disabilities against discrimination in all federally assisted programs and activities.

Public Law 94-142: The Individuals with Disabilities Education Act. This law mandates that all children receive a free, appropriate public education regardless of the level or severity of their disability.

Civil Rights of Institutionalized Persons Act. The U.S. Department of Justice is granted the right to sue states for alleged violations of the rights of people who live in institutions for people with mental retardation.

Child Abuse Prevention and Treatment and Adoption Reform Act of 1978. This law prevents the withholding of medical treatment for infants born with mental or physical impairments.

The Civil Rights Commission Act Amendments of 1978. The jurisdiction of the Civil Rights Commission was expanded to include protection against discrimination on the basis of handicap.

Fair Housing Act Amendments of 1988. The Act was amended to prohibit discrimination against individuals with disabilities in renting and buying housing and to broaden the government's enforcement powers.

The Americans with Disabilities Act of 1990. The ADA bans discrimination based on disability in employment, public accommodations, transportation, state and local government services and telecommunication relay services.

Additional Information

Office of Minority Health Resource Center/DHHS
Rockwall Bldg. 2, 5515 Security Lane, 1st Floor
Washington, DC.
Rockville, MD 20852

National Coalition of Hispanic Health and Human Services Organizations
Washington, DC.
Tel: 202-387-5000

Native American Research and Training Center
162 E. Helen
Tucson, AZ. 85719
Tel: 520-621-5075

References

Yeargin-Allsopp, M. (1990, June 14). "Prevalence and sociodemographic risk factors for mental retardation in ten-year-old children in Metropolitan Atlanta." Unpublished presentation. Centers for Disease Control.

Education of the Handicapped. (1991, April 10). "Culture gap may inhibit Asian participation in special ed." Alexandria, VA: Capitol Publications, Inc.

Education of the Handicapped. (1991, August 28). "New faces at school: How changing demographics reshape American education." Alexandria, VA: Capitol Publications, Inc.

Eig, Jonathan. (1991, September 29). "Black students likelier to be placed in special ed than whites, data show." *The Dallas Morning News*, p. 1.

National Commission on Children. (1991). *Beyond Rhetoric: A New American Agenda for Children and Families.* Washington, DC: U.S. Government Printing Office.

Office of Minority Health Resource Center. (1990). "Closing the gap: Infant mortality, low birthweight, and minorities." Washington, DC: Department of Health.

Part Four

Preventing Mental Retardation

Chapter 14

Genetics and Testing

An Introduction to Genetics and Genetic Testing

What do you know about your family tree? Have any of your relatives suffered from health problems that tend to "run in families?" Which of these problems affected your parents or grandparents? Which ones affect you now, or your brothers or sisters? Which problems might you pass on to your children?

Thanks to advances in genetics, doctors now have the tools to understand how certain illnesses, or increased risks for certain illnesses, pass from generation to generation. According to some health experts, the definition of an inherited or "genetic" illness should be expanded beyond the classic inherited disorders (like hemophilia and sickle cell anemia) to include many types of cancer, Alzheimer's disease, and other illnesses. They look toward a future where genetic test results are an important part of every healthy person's medical file. Let's see what this new biotechnology can mean to you and your family.

Genes and Chromosomes: The Basics

Each of us has a unique set of chemical "blueprints" that determines how our body looks and functions. These blueprints are contained in a complex chemical called DNA, a long, spiral-shaped molecule that is found inside each body cell. Specific segments of DNA

Reprinted with permission, "An Introduction to Genetics and Genetic Testing," from KidsHealth (http://KidsHealth.org), © 1999 The Nemours Foundation.

that contain the instructions for making specific body proteins are called genes. Right now, scientists believe that human DNA carries up to 100,000 genes. Some genes direct the formation of structural proteins that eventually determine how our bodies look (blue eyes or brown, curly hair or straight), while others code for important body chemicals called enzymes. Sometimes, depending on what a specific gene code is for, even a small genetic error can mean serious problems for the entire body. Sometimes, an error in just one gene can mean the difference between a normal life and one that is shortened or physically difficult.

Genes line up along the length of human DNA, neatly packaged in structures called chromosomes. Human cells have 46 chromosomes, arranged in 23 pairs, with one member of each pair inherited from each parent at the time of conception. After conception, these original 46 chromosomes duplicate again and again to pass on the same genetic information to each new cell in the developing child. Human chromosomes are large enough to be seen with a light microscope, and the 23 pairs can be identified according to differences in their size, shape, and the way they pick up special laboratory dyes.

Genetic Problems: What Doctors Look For

Genetic problems can happen for many different reasons. Sometimes a mistake occurs during cell division, causing an error in chromosome number either before or shortly after conception. The developing embryo grows from cells that have either too many chromosomes or too few. In "trisomy," for example, there are three copies of one particular chromosome instead of the normal two (one from each parent). Down syndrome, trisomy 18 (Edwards) syndrome, and trisomy 13 (Patau) syndrome are all important examples of this type of genetic problem. In "monosomy," another form of number error, one member of a chromosome pair is missing. There are too few chromosomes rather than too many.

Sometimes it's not the number of chromosomes that's the problem. Instead, one or more chromosomes is incomplete or abnormally shaped. In both deletions and microdeletions, for example, some small part of a chromosome is missing. In a microdeletion, the missing part of a chromosome is usually so small that it amounts to only a single gene. Some important genetic disorders caused by deletions and microdeletions include: Wolf-Hirschhorn syndrome (affects chromosome 4); Cri-du-chat syndrome (chromosome 5); DiGeorge syndrome (chromosome 22); and Williams syndrome (chromosome 7).

In translocations, bits of chromosomes shift from one chromosome to another, while in inversions, small parts of the DNA code seem to be snipped out and reinserted backwards.

Very special types of genetic problems also occur when abnormalities affect the sex chromosomes. Normally, a child will be a male if he inherits one X chromosome from his mother and one Y chromosome from his father. A child will be a female if she inherits a double dose of X (one from each parent), and no Y. Sometimes, however, children are born with only one sex chromosome (usually a single X), or with an XXY or XYY inheritance. Sometimes, too, a genetic problem is sex-linked, meaning that it is carried by either the X or Y chromosome.

Some genetic problems are caused by a single gene that is present but abnormal. When this is the case, chromosome number and appearance are often entirely normal. To pinpoint the defective gene, scientists use sophisticated DNA screening techniques. Some examples of genetic illnesses caused by a single problem gene include: cystic fibrosis, sickle cell anemia, Tay-Sachs disease, and achondroplasia (a type of dwarfism).

Although experts originally believed that no more than three percent of all human diseases were caused by errors in a single gene, new research suggests that this may be an underestimate. Within the last two years, scientists have discovered genetic links to many different diseases that were not originally thought of as "genetic," including several different types of cancer. They have identified 20 to 30 "cancer susceptibility genes" that greatly increase a person's odds of getting some form of malignancy. For example, a gene has been identified on chromosome number 9 that may be linked to a common skin cancer called basal cell carcinoma. This gene, labeled PTC or "patched," may someday be important in screening for the cancer. Another gene, called HNPCC, is carried by one out of every 300 Americans and may greatly increase an individual's chance of getting colon cancer. And the doubly dangerous gene called BRCA-1 seems to give women an 85% chance of developing breast cancer, as well as a 50% chance of ovarian tumors.

Altered genes may also play a role in the development of many other devastating illnesses besides cancer. Parkinson's disease, for example, may be linked to a gene on chromosome number 4, and multiple sclerosis may be linked to alterations in a gene on chromosome number 6. Alzheimer's disease, linked to the ApoE4 gene on chromosome 19, can already be diagnosed (in some cases) by screening for that altered gene.

Although heart disease and diabetes appear to be related to simultaneous changes in many different genes, the first of these, called LpL PvuII, may already have been identified. According to American Heart Association reports, this gene may be an "artery-clogging gene" that almost doubles the risk of fatty deposits blocking the coronary arteries. Having the LpL PvuII gene may also triple someone's changes of getting adult-onset diabetes. Like heart disease, depression and other mental illnesses may be the result of alterations in several genes at once. Although no specific genes have yet been found, doctors estimate that 48-75% of depression is inherited, and they believe that they will find the exact genetic mechanism very soon.

It is important to note that much of the newest information from genetic research has not yet been translated into useful screening tests for your doctor's office. However, experts predict that this will soon change, and they estimate that the number of available genetic tests will increase tenfold in the next decade.

Genetic Tests

At one time doctors could only diagnose genetic problems by karyotyping—checking the number, shape, and dye stains in chromosomes. Now genetic testing has developed far enough to allow doctors to pinpoint missing or defective genes. The type of genetic test needed to make a specific diagnosis depends on the particular genetic illness that your doctor suspects. If he or she suspects a trisomy, for example, a simple chromosome check will probably be enough. If the problem is a single problem gene, however, more high-tech DNA screening will usually be necessary. For genetic testing in children before birth, chorionic villus sampling or amniocentesis is usually performed.

Many different types of body fluids and tissues can be used in genetic testing. For DNA screening, only a very tiny bit of blood, skin, bone, or other tissue is needed. Even the small amount of tissue at the bottom end of a human hair is usually enough.

When Do Doctors Recommend Genetic Testing?

A doctor may recommend genetic testing for any of the following reasons:

- **A couple is planning to start a family and one of them or a close relative has an inherited illness.** Some people are carriers of genetic illnesses, even though they do not suffer from the illness themselves. This happens because some genetic illnesses are recessive—they are only expressed if a person inherits two doses of the problem gene, one from each parent. Someone who inherits one problem gene from one parent but a normal gene from the other parent will not have symptoms of a recessive illness but will have a 50-50 chance of someday passing the problem gene to their own children.

- **An individual already has one child with a severe birth defect.** Not all children who suffer from birth defects have genetic problems. Sometimes birth defects are caused by exposure to a toxin (poison), infection, or physical trauma before birth. Even if a child does have a genetic problem, there is always a chance that it was not inherited, that it happened because of some spontaneous error in the child's cells, not the parents'.

- **A woman has had two or more miscarriages.** Severe chromosome problems in the fetus can sometimes lead to a spontaneous miscarriage. Several miscarriages may point to a genetic problem.

- **A woman has delivered a stillborn child with physical signs of a genetic illness.** Many serious genetic illnesses cause specific physical abnormalities that give an affected child a very distinctive appearance.

- **A woman is pregnant and over age 34.** Chances of having a child with Down syndrome increase dramatically when a pregnant woman is older.

- **A child has medical problems that might be genetic.** When a child has medical problems involving more than one body system, genetic testing may be recommended to identify the cause and make a diagnosis.

- **A child has medical problems that are recognized as a specific genetic syndrome.** Genetic testing is performed to confirm the diagnosis. In some cases it also may aid in identifying the specific type or severity of a genetic illness, which can help identify the most appropriate treatment.

A Word of Caution

Although advances in genetic testing have created a revolution in the way that doctors diagnose and treat certain illnesses, there are

237

still some limits that parents need to recognize. First, although genetic tests can identify a particular problem gene, they cannot always predict how severely that gene will affect the person who carries it. In cystic fibrosis, for example, finding a problem gene on chromosome number 7 cannot necessarily predict whether a child will have serious lung problems or only mild respiratory symptoms.

Second, since many illnesses develop from a deadly mix of high-risk genes and unhealthy lifestyle (for example, a smoker with a family history of heart disease), simply having problem genes is only half the story. Knowing that you carry high-risk genes may actually be an advantage, if it gives you the chance to modify your lifestyle to avoid becoming sick.

A Great Potential for Good

Every day researchers are finding new evidence that people who have specific genes are at a greater risk for illnesses like cancer, heart disease, psychiatric disorders, and many other medical problems. The next step is to discover just how these problem genes work. Once we learn this, it may be possible to develop specific types of gene therapy to prevent some of humanity's major killer diseases.

Right now, gene therapy is already being used successfully to treat cystic fibrosis and ADA deficiency (an immune deficiency). Sickle cell anemia, the thalassemias, and other blood disorders may be the next targets for a genetic cure. Although genetic treatments for major killers, like cancer, may be a long way off, there is still great hope that many more genetic cures will be found. In less than ten years, scientists working on the Human Genome Project will have finished identifying and mapping out all of the genes (up to 100,000) carried in our human chromosomes. The map will be just a beginning, but it's a very hopeful beginning.

Chapter 15

Prenatal Care

When I was pregnant with my third child, I had two friends who were also expecting. We would get together once a week and, over milkshakes, compare our growing bellies and laugh about our big maternity pants.

We would also share our fears. Together we obsessed about nearly everything that could go wrong in the 40 weeks of pregnancy. What are these pains? Why am I so tired? How much will labor hurt? Can I handle another child? And the big one: Will my baby be healthy?

Worries and pregnancy seem to go hand in hand. Fortunately, however, most women of childbearing age are healthy and most pregnancies are considered "low-risk." For most women, the surest way to have a healthy baby is to live a healthy lifestyle. The March of Dimes suggests the following precautions:

- Get early prenatal care, even before you're pregnant.

- Eat a well-balanced diet, including a vitamin supplement that contains folic acid.

- Exercise regularly with your doctor's permission.

- Avoid alcohol, cigarettes, and illicit drugs, and limit caffeine.

- Avoid x-rays, hot tubs, and saunas.

- Avoid infections.

"Healthy Pregnancy, Healthy Baby," *FDA Consumer*, March-April 1999.

Getting Good Care

When it comes to medical care and pregnancy, you can never start too early.

"The best start to having a healthy baby is to see your health-care provider before you conceive," says Richard Schwarz, M.D., an obstetrician and national consultant for the March of Dimes.

"There are lots of things you can do ahead of time," Schwarz adds. "You can make sure you're immune to rubella (German measles), you can know your blood type, you can stop smoking and make sure your diet is healthy, and you can get any illnesses you might have under control."

Once you're pregnant, your health professional—either an obstetrician, family practitioner, nurse-practitioner, or nurse-midwife—will have you begin with monthly visits that increase to once a week or more at the end.

At each visit, the physician or nurse will perform a series of examinations and tests to determine the health of the mother and baby. These include measuring the growth of the uterus, listening to the baby's heartbeat, taking the mother's blood pressure and weight, and checking her urine for evidence of protein or sugar, which could be symptoms of complications. The care provider will ask the mother if she has any concerns or problems such as blurred vision, leg cramps, abdominal cramps, or unusual headaches. The mother may also undergo ultrasound and genetic tests during the pregnancy.

Although prenatal visits may seem simple and even mundane, their importance can't be overestimated. Years of research have shown that pregnant women who get adequate prenatal care are more likely to have healthy babies and fewer complications during labor and recovery. Says Schwarz, "We know that pregnancy outcomes are better in women with early prenatal care."

Eating for Two

Good nutrition is another crucial step in having a healthy baby. A pregnancy takes about 300 extra calories a day to maintain, and an average-sized woman can expect to gain between 25 and 35 pounds overall.

Those extra calories should be nutritious ones, however. A pregnant woman needs a balanced diet complete with protein, fruits, vegetables, whole grains, and a minimum of sweets and fats.

"Good nutrition is extremely important even before a pregnancy," says Shirley Blakely, Ph.D., a registered dietitian with the Food and

Drug Administration's Center for Food Safety and Applied Nutrition. "If nature favors the growing fetus, the mother will suffer if she hasn't had a good diet."

According to the March of Dimes, a pregnant woman should increase her daily food portions to include:

- 6 to 11 servings of breads and other whole grains

- 3 to 5 servings of vegetables

- 2 to 4 servings of fruits

- 4 to 6 servings of milk and milk products

- 3 to 4 servings of meat and protein foods

- 6 to 8 glasses of water, and no more than one soft drink or cup of coffee per day to limit caffeine.

Some nutrients have been found to provide specific benefit to mother or child. For example, the B vitamins have been found to be especially important. One of them, folate, or its synthetic form, folic acid, can reduce the risk of birth defects of the brain and spinal cord, called the "neural tube."

Each year, an estimated 2,500 babies are born with neural tube defects. The most common of these is spina bifida, in which the spine is not closed. The exposed nerves are damaged, leaving the child with varying degrees of paralysis, incontinence, and sometimes mental retardation.

Because neural tube defects develop in the first 28 days after conception, "Once you know you're pregnant it's too late to do anything about (them)," says Blakely.

Because half of all pregnancies are unplanned, the U.S. Public Health Service recommends that all women of childbearing age get 400 micrograms of folic acid each day. If all women received that amount daily, the incidence of neural tube defects might be reduced by an estimated 45 percent, studies suggest. To help reach this goal, FDA now requires that all flour products, such as breads, buns and bagels, be fortified with extra folic acid.

Natural sources of folic acid include green leafy vegetables, nuts, beans, and citrus fruits. It's also in many fortified breakfast cereals and some vitamin supplements.

Calcium and iron are also especially important during pregnancy. Getting enough calcium will help prevent a new mother from losing her own bone density as the fetus uses the mineral for bone growth.

Iron helps both the mother and baby's blood carry oxygen. Most women need supplements to maintain adequate levels of these minerals. A daily vitamin supplement, while not an adequate substitute for a healthy diet, helps fill in the gaps on days when a woman's diet is less than perfect.

Avoid Infections

Many infections during pregnancy can be dangerous to an unborn child. Urinary tract infections and any sexually transmitted diseases need to be treated immediately.

Cat litter and raw meat may contain the parasite Toxoplasma gondii, which can cause toxoplasmosis infection. It's rare for a pregnant woman to get the infection, but if she does, her baby could be at risk for serious illness or death. Get someone else to change the kitty litter if possible, or wear a face mask and rubber gloves for protection.

Problems also may arise when a pregnant woman eats undercooked or raw foods, or cooked foods that have been cross-contaminated with bacteria from raw food nearby. Food poisoning can cause meningitis, pneumonia, or even death to an unborn child, plus the vomiting and diarrhea involved leave the mother exhausted and dehydrated.

The 'Naughty' Stuff

Nearly everyone knows pregnant women shouldn't take illicit drugs, but it's the legal ones—alcohol and tobacco—that are more commonly the source of pregnancy problems.

"I think if women truly understood the adverse impact smoking and drinking have on their babies, they would quit," says Jeffrey King, M.D., the director of the division of maternal and fetal medicine at Wright State University School of Medicine, and the author of a recent study on substance abuse in pregnancy.

Smokers put their babies at a significantly higher risk of preterm birth, low birth weight, and stillbirth compared with nonsmokers. After birth, the babies of mothers who smoked during pregnancy are more likely to have poor lung development, asthma and respiratory infections, and to die of sudden infant death syndrome (SIDS).

If a woman quits smoking early in pregnancy, however, she can still improve her chances of having a healthy baby. Expectant fathers or other members of the family should quit, too, because studies suggest breathing second-hand smoke may be dangerous as well.

Alcohol, too, can damage a developing fetus. Alcohol travels rapidly to the bloodstream, so when an expectant mother drinks, her baby drinks also.

Alcohol is known to cause mental retardation and facial abnormalities in babies, a condition called fetal alcohol syndrome. The Institute of Medicine estimates some 12,000 children with fetal alcohol syndrome are born in the United States each year. No one knows what amount of alcohol is safe during pregnancy; therefore, the U.S. Surgeon General recommends pregnant women avoid alcohol altogether.

A few other activities are known to be dangerous during pregnancy. X-rays can expose the fetus to radiation and potentially cause birth defects. Hot tubs and saunas can raise the core temperature of a pregnant woman's body and could potentially harm the fetus. Warm baths, however, are fine if the water is kept at body temperature.

Medications

Many drugs are appropriate for use in pregnancy, if really needed. But a pregnant woman shouldn't take any medication, even an over-the-counter one, unless she checks with her doctor first. If possible, she should avoid taking drugs in the first trimester or taking more than one medication at a time. She can also ask for the lowest dose possible to treat her condition.

Some medications have a long history of being used in pregnancy without problems. A pregnant woman shouldn't be deprived of drug therapy she really needs, says Sandra Kweder, M.D., the co-chair of FDA's task force on pregnancy labeling. She adds that women with pre-existing medical conditions such as epilepsy, lupus, asthma, or high blood pressure shouldn't quit their drugs because of pregnancy. Safer drugs can be used if necessary, but those medical conditions still need to be treated.

Kweder explains, "A common thing with patients is that they'll say, 'I know I'm supposed to take medication, but I'm worried about my baby, so I'll take less of it instead.' They'll take it every other day, or half as much. That's not wise. "The risks of a drug have to be weighed against its benefits. For example, some epilepsy drugs are known to cause birth defects, but an epileptic seizure can cause brain damage to the fetus. Most experts agree that the benefits of medication in such cases outweigh the risks.

Other drugs, however, are not so clear-cut. "It's really hard because there aren't easy answers," says Kweder. "For a baby to be healthy, it needs a mother who's healthy." However, most drugs have not been tested scientifically in pregnant women. Reliable scientific information about medication use in pregnancy is often incomplete or nonexistent. FDA is trying to change that.

The agency has begun a comprehensive review about how it regulates drugs for pregnant women and how safety information is communicated on the label. The present system is not as helpful as the agency would like. "The system has been criticized, and rightly so," says Kweder. "It is complicated to interpret data for medications used in pregnancy. We're making progress, but it's slow."

A new system is needed, she says, but it will be difficult to create. Drugs can't be tested in pregnant women the same as in other groups of people. Animal studies, while helpful, don't necessarily show what a drug will do to a woman and developing fetus.

In the meantime, a woman who has taken a drug and discovers she is pregnant should consult her doctor and avoid making decisions about her pregnancy in panic. While about 80 percent of approved drugs lack adequate scientific evidence about use in pregnancy, that doesn't necessarily mean they can harm the fetus or are harmful in the doses prescribed.

Only a very few drugs definitely known to be extremely bad for a human fetus are clearly labeled or, in one case, have special requirements attached to their approval. The drug thalidomide, which was recently approved by FDA to treat leprosy and is being explored for other uses, is devastating to developing fetuses and causes severe deformities of the arms and legs. FDA is requiring that patients who take the drug enroll in a national registry that will track their progress monthly and record the occurrence of any pregnancy. The hope is that this process will discourage physicians from prescribing the drug to women who might become pregnant and keep patients from "sharing" the drug with a woman of childbearing age.

Exercise

There's increasing medical evidence to show that exercise, even a vigorous workout, is healthy during pregnancy. An October 1998 study published in the American Journal of Public Health found that exercise is usually safe during pregnancy, and that women who exercised vigorously were more likely to carry their babies to full term compared with women who exercised less or not at all.

A pregnant woman should check with her doctor before exercising, however. If she gets the OK to work out, she should do so at least three times a week for 20 minutes each time, recommends the American College of Obstetrics and Gynecology.

Walking, swimming, riding a stationary bicycle, and joining a prenatal aerobics class are all excellent exercise choices for a pregnant woman. Exercises that require jerky, bouncy movements and being outside in hot weather are not good choices. Don't try deep knee bends, sit-ups (or any exercise that requires you to lie on your back after the first trimester), and toe touches. Other sports to avoid include downhill skiing, rock climbing, and horseback riding.

Wear a supportive bra and properly fitting athletic shoes while exercising. Stop if you feel dizzy, faint, overheated, or in pain. Drink plenty of water.

Staying in shape will help you keep up your stamina during your own impending marathon—labor! And, afterward, the more muscle mass you have, the quicker you'll regain your pre-pregnancy shape and be able to pack away those maternity pants.

—Rebecca D. Williams

Rebecca D. Williams is a writer in Oak Ridge, Tenn.

Additional Information

March of Dimes
(Organization devoted to healthy pregnancies and preventing birth defects.)
1275 Mamaroneck Ave.
White Plains, NY 10605
Tel: 914-428-7100
URL: http://www.modimes.org

Chapter 16

Newborn Screening

There is much public attention surrounding the use of DNA for genetic testing. What the lay public fails to realize is that genetic testing in the form of newborn screening has been in use for two to three decades. While newborn screening is not considered as fancy as the polymerase chain reaction amplification or allelic-specific oligonucleotide hybridization, the testing of protein products of genes or metabolites of metabolic pathways is an indirect genetic test.

Newborn screening has clearly proved quite effective for selected disorders. For example, cretinism from untreated hypothyroidism is now a medical rarity, and patients with late or untreated phenylketonuria no longer populate residential treatment programs. While early identification of patients with hypothyroidism or phenylketonuria has not eliminated all of the problems associated with these disorders, there is no argument that newborn screening is particularly effective for these two disorders and has been implemented in all fifty states. Thus, hypothyroidism and phenylketonuria are good examples of the success of newborn screening as a public health measure.

Reprinted with permission © *The Genetic Drift Newsletter*, Vol. 15. Winter 1998. Published by the Mountain States Regional Genetic Services Network for associates and those interested in Human Genetics. Contributions by C. Holly Nyerges, MSN, CPNP (NM), Benjamin Wilfond, MD (AZ), Peter A. Lane, MD (CO), and Carol Green, MD (CO).

Issues Relating to Early Hospital Discharge and the Impact on Newborn Genetic Screening Programs

For more than three decades, newborn screening has been a successful example of a population-based screening program to detect and treat disorders which cause preventable mental retardation and morbidity. However, some trends in managed care and demand for cost containment are raising concerns for state newborn screening programs across the country. The greatest impact thus far relates to increasing frequency in early hospital discharge (i.e., hospital stays of 24 hours or less) of healthy infants after birth.

When newborn screening started in 1962, hospital stays allowed for the ideal timing of specimen collection between 48 and 96 hours following birth and for the infants to be monitored. Early newborn screening specimen collection (i.e. before 48 hours of age) is primarily a result of early discharge. This practice affects newborn genetic screening programs in two ways: (1) by decreasing the ability to detect infants with inborn errors of metabolism who have not had adequate nutritional intake, and (2) by not being able to minimize the impact on families that is generated by a high number of false positive test results requiring further testing and follow-up to reach a confirmed diagnosis.

The results of a 1994 study of the impact of early discharge on newborn screening in California showed the following:

- Two-thirds of specimens were collected before 24 hours.

- 10% of specimens were collected before 12 hours.

- 50% of low birth weight (LBW) specimens were collected before 24 hours (7% before transfusions).

- Larger hospitals had more early discharges than smaller hospitals.

Issues Related to Specific Screening Tests

Phenylketonuria

Screening tests for phenylketonuria (PKU) are affected by "too early" specimen collection because there is a physiological rise in phenylalanine levels for the first 10 hours following birth gradually falling back to the level one hour post birth at approximately 24 hours of age. At a cut-off level of 4 mg/dl, a significant number of normal results will be falsely positive if collected during the first 24 hours.

California found a false positive rate as high as 11/1000 before 24 hours compared to 1.1/1000 between 24-48 hours. Lowering the cut-off level for specimens collected before 24 hours resulted in more false positives without an increase in confirmed cases.

Early discharge can also result in false negative newborn screening results. For example, discharge of an infant with PKU may occur before blood phenylalanine levels have increased to sufficient levels to be detected by the newborn screen. Hence, the early screen would miss an infant with PKU. This scenario is particularly likely for infants with hyperphenylalaninemia, who do not have classical PKU, but still have an error of phenylalanine metabolism.

Hypothyroidism

The detection of primary hypothyroidism presents a similar problem because of a thyroid stimulating hormone (TSH) surge at birth which peaks at around six hours and then gradually declines to reach normal cut-off values by the fifth day of life. Since the majority of screening programs in the U.S. take the lowest 10% of T4 results and run TSH analysis to determine a positive screening result for primary hypothyroidism, specimens collected during the first 24 hours will have a high false positive rate.

Maple Syrup Urine Disease

Screening for maple syrup urine disease (MSUD), by detection of elevation of leucine, is optimal at 24-48 hours of age. This elevation is subject to the same considerations as PKU but the medical issues are more complex in that life-threatening symptoms may become evident before screening results are available.

Homocystinuria

Early specimen collection affects screening for homocystinuria (HCU) by increasing the number of false negative results, since the measured metabolite methionine is often not elevated above normal levels during the first week of life. The optimal time to screen for homocystinuria is actually at 3 to 4 weeks of age.

Congenital Adrenal Hyperplasias

There are four different forms of congenital adrenal hyperplasia (CAH) that can be detected through newborn screening: salt-wasting, simple virilizing, non-classical late onset, and cryptic. The analyte tested is 17-hydroxyprogesterone (17-OHP). At birth, 17-OHP is normally elevated and undergoes a rapid decline to adult normal levels by one to three weeks of age. During the first week of life, the levels of 17-OHP show marked variation. Thus, early specimen collection is expected to result in an unacceptably high number of false positives.

Sickle Cell Disease, Biotinidase Deficiency, and Galactosemia

Other conditions screened for, but not dependent on the time of specimen collection, include tests for sickle cell disease, biotinidase deficiency, and galactosemia. The screening tests for these conditions rely on red cell components. These test results are affected by blood transfusions and specimens must be collected before transfusion for valid results.

Potential Strategies and Solutions

It is evident from the above information that early discharge has the potential to adversely affect the accuracy of newborn screening for the majority of conditions included in the panels of most newborn screening programs. Several strategies are being implemented to remedy this problem. The most important of these may be the legislation signed in the fall of 1997 by President Clinton whereby health insurers must cover 48 hour hospital stays for mothers and babies for a normal delivery and 96 hours for Cesarean sections. This will hopefully decrease the number of specimens collected at less than 24 hours. This legislation went into effect January 1998.

The 1992 AAP and ACOG Guidelines state that all newborns must be screened prior to discharge regardless of age or feeding status of the infant and that the optimal time to collect a sample is at 3 days of age. Most state programs have initiated a routine second screen if the newborn was screened before 24 hours of age. These second screens are collected between 1-2 weeks of age for some programs and 1-4 weeks for others. Some states are narrowing the period of time for the second screen to no later than two weeks of age because of the concern of delayed detection and treatment.

There are seven states that have implemented a routine second screen on the entire screening panel as a safeguard. They include Delaware, Oregon, New Mexico, Nevada, Texas, Colorado, and Utah.

All these states consider a routine second screen to be an effective means (both medically and economically) of detecting clinically significant disorders not detected on the original screen.

In the state of Oregon, the routine second screen has resulted in 38 confirmed cases in whom diagnosis would either have been missed or delayed. Since 1991, five PKU cases have been picked up on the second screen. Oregon has also found that the routine second screening enhances practitioners' involvement in the screening process since second screening specimens are collected in their offices. They receive copies of both screening results for all the infants in their care and hopefully discuss these with the parents. Despite this apparent success in Oregon, there is much controversy in the newborn screening community concerning the effectiveness of the routine second screen. The following questions need to be considered in any discussion:

- Is it effective in detecting treatable cases?

- Is the comparative cost/benefit positive? (In comparison to improved testing sensitivity, liability costs, etc.)

- What is the appropriate time of collection for a second screen? (1-2 weeks, 2-4 weeks, etc.)

- What other factors may play a role in whether a second screening test is performed? (Are race and socioeconomic factors significant?)

- Should the second screen be recommended or required? (Is there discrimination if not required?)

Screening for Cystic Fibrosis

While newborn screening for cystic fibrosis (CF) has been feasible since 1979 using the IRT (immunoreactive trypsinogen test), and there have been slowly accumulating observational data regarding the potential benefits of such testing, it is not routinely performed in most states. In part, this is because CF is different from the classic model of PKU newborn screening in which a relatively simple intervention must be initiated within a short time frame (weeks) in order to avoid a significant complication (severe mental retardation). In contrast, cystic fibrosis is a chronic and gradually progressive disease and the potential benefit of newborn screening may be harder to discern.

Issues Regarding Identification of Hemoglobinopathy Carriers by Neonatal Screening

The primary purpose of neonatal screening for hemoglobinopathies is to identify infants with sickle cell disease, for whom early diagnosis, parental education, prophylactic penicillin, and comprehensive medical care markedly reduce morbidity and mortality.

In 1987, an NIH consensus development panel concluded that "the benefits of screening (for sickle cell disease) are so compelling that universal screening should be provided. State law should mandate the availability of these services while permitting parental refusal." During the subsequent 10 years, the number of states that conduct newborn screening for hemoglobinopathies has increased dramatically. Currently, 43 states and the District of Columbia screen newborns for sickle cell disease. In the Mountain States Region, 4 of 6 states (Arizona, Colorado, New Mexico, and Wyoming) screen all newborns for sickle cell disease.

Logistically, the provision of appropriate education and counseling services to families of hemoglobinopathy carriers identified by newborn screening is a formidable and potentially costly task. Approximately 50 infants who are carriers for hemoglobin variants are identified for each individual with sickle cell disease. Thus, thousands of carrier infants are identified each year by neonatal screening programs in the United States.

In many states, the large number of such cases far exceeds the capacity of clinical genetics programs and genetic counselors. Many states have long-standing contracts with community-based sickle cell organizations or with academic sickle cell centers to provide follow-up services. Frequently, but not always, education and counseling are provided by health care professionals (nurses, social workers, etc.) who have extensive knowledge of and experience with hemoglobinopathies. To help ensure the highest quality for the services, many have advocated that a national program be established to set minimum standards of education and training for hemoglobinopathy educators/counselors and to provide for a certification process.

In September 1995, a national symposium was held to address the legal, ethical, technical and logistical issues concerning the follow-up of hemoglobinopathy carriers identified through neonatal screening. Participants included representatives from newborn screening programs and sickle cell organizations, geneticists, ethicists, hematologists, and consumers. There was a clear consensus that families of hemoglobinopathy carriers should be notified of the results and that

252

appropriate education and counseling should be available. As a direct outgrowth of that conference, the CORN Sickle Cell, Thalassemia and Other Hemoglobin Variants Committee (with advice and support from the CORN Newborn Screening Committee) developed guidelines for the follow up of hemoglobinopathy carriers detected by newborn screening.

These guidelines (available through the Mountain States Regional Genetic Services Network coordinator) were recently endorsed by the Steering Committee of CORN and are summarized below:

- Ideally, education about newborn screening, which usually includes testing for sickle cell disease, should be provided to families during prenatal care well in advance of the time of delivery. A mechanism should be in place in State Newborn Screening Programs so that all results of sickle cell newborn screening can be made available to parents of all infants who are tested.

- Parents of all infants who are detected to be carriers of hemoglobin variants should be offered appropriate education, counseling, and testing.

- Individuals who counsel should have appropriate training and credentials in order to insure the highest quality of services for families of carriers detected by newborn screening.

- Newborn screening programs should have a mechanism for monitoring and assessing the approaches to, responses to, and costs of providing carrier education and counseling services.

Meanwhile, the Sickle Cell Disease Association of America has initiated the lengthy process of developing a national certification program for hemoglobinopathy counselors.

Top Ten Pitfalls in Newborn Screening

Assuming That the Result of the Newborn Screening Test Is Negative (or Normal) Because You Have Not Heard Otherwise.

There are many reasons why the primary care provider may not be notified about an abnormal newborn screening result: difficulty finding and notifying a provider, a test might have never been sent, or an error in delivery of the result to the primary health care provider. The primary care provider of record at the birth of an infant assumes the responsibility to assure that a screen was obtained and that the results are duly recorded in the medical records. In light of the increasing complexity of the health care system, many newborn screening programs are working to facilitate proper dissemination of newborn screening results.

Assuming That a Negative (or Normal) Result of Newborn Screening Definitively Excludes the Conditions Screened For.

"False negative" test results may occur for a wide variety of reasons including human error such as sample transposition and the statistically "built in" false negative tests. For example, approximately 30% of hypothyroidism is missed in babies who were tested before the second week of life. If the primary care provider observes symptoms, which could be the result of one of the disorders on the newborn screening panel in your state, it is appropriate to confirm the results. Any baby with symptoms which might be caused by PKU, hypothyroidism, sickle cell disease, galactosemia, cystic fibrosis or any other disorder for which newborn screening was negative should have specific diagnostic testing performed by an appropriate diagnostic laboratory.

Submitting a Newborn Screening Sample with Incomplete or Illegible Information.

All states design the newborn screening forms to suit the specific panel of tests they perform and each piece of requested information is essential. Nevertheless, all newborn screening programs receive samples with inaccurate or incomplete information. The submitter of the sample cannot, of course, be responsible when families deliberately provide misinformation. The submitter is, however, responsible for providing legible information that is correct so far as she/he is aware. When the screening lab requires multiple copies, all copies must be legible (often a problem with hospital card stamps). When a newborn screening form asks for information about the use of antibiotics, history of transfusion or prematurity, that information is necessary for accurate interpretation of test results. Date of birth is always necessary for proper identification of the newborn, and date of sample for test interpretations. Precise information on age in hours may be necessary for the increasingly complex interpretation of results for early screening.

Ordering a Solubility Test (Sickledex, Sickleprep) as the Follow Up in an Infant with Positive Newborn Screen for Hemoglobinopathy.

Diagnostic follow-up testing is required after a positive newborn screen to exclude a false positive result and to define the specific diagnosis. The false positive rate and the differential diagnosis varies with the disease for which screening is performed and with the nature of the test. Confirmation testing for infants with abnormal hemoglobinopathy screening tests (hemoglobin Barts excepted) should always include hemoglobin electrophoresis. The solubility test (Sickledex, Sickle-prep) should never be performed in this setting because it is often falsely negative in infants with sickle cell disease, does not define the specific hemoglobinopathy present, and fails to differentiate individuals with disease from those with hemoglobin traits.

Similarly, for other conditions on a newborn screen, specific protocols and policies for confirmatory testing have been developed by each newborn screening program. For example, in Colorado, a result of 4 mg/dl on the screen for PKU should be followed by a repeat screen; while a baby with one level of more than 4 mg/dl or two levels of 4 mg/dl each should have diagnostic testing sent to a specific laboratory for phenylalanine and tyrosine levels.

Consultants are available for each disorder and can assist with routine follow-up and with unusual circumstances in which follow-up might need to be tailored to a particular newborn's situation.

Prescribing a PKU Treatment Formula Before Confirming the Diagnosis of PKU.

A significant number of babies with a positive screening test for PKU ultimately prove to be unaffected. After a positive screen, diagnostic test results can be completed in hours to days and treatment begun in a timely fashion, once the diagnosis is confirmed. If treatment is started after the screen only, this may interfere with subsequent diagnostic testing. Also, the PKU diet may be harmful to a child without PKU.

The diet for PKU needs to be carefully calculated by a trained registered dietitian to give a precise amount of essential amino acids by combination of the metabolic formula with human milk or infant formula. In contrast, if a state screens for galactosemia using a test with a low rate of false-positive results, an immediate diet change might be required while diagnostic tests are pending.

Each state has recommendations that take into consideration the specific tests performed in the screening laboratory and the nature of the population served. Guidance regarding any necessary treatment while follow-up screening or diagnostic testing is pursued will be provided.

Not Collecting a Newborn Screening Sample Prior to Blood Transfusion Because the Baby Is "Too Young" or Has Not Yet Been Fed.

Transfusion will alter the results of certain newborn screening tests. If a baby is transfused and then screened using an assay affected by transfusion of red cells, the transfusion will affect the test results. For example, when red cells are transfused prior to screening for hemoglobinopathy, the newborn screening laboratory will be testing donor hemoglobins. One test for galactosemia uses the Beutler Assay to measure in red blood cells the activity of galactose-1-phosphate uridyltransferase, the enzyme deficient in galactosemia. The enzyme is present in red cells and thus the transfused red cells will affect the test results. The appropriate strategy always is to collect a newborn screening sample immediately before transfusion in the very young newborn.

Not Collecting a Newborn Screening Sample Prior to Transfer of the Infant to Another Institution.

Sick and premature babies, some of whom require transfer for more intensive/specialized care, are at no lower risk than healthy newborns for disorders detected by newborn screening. States may have explicit regulations about responsibility for screening when a baby is transferred from or to a nursery. Regardless of specific regulations, it is appropriate for a newborn screen to be sent by the hospital or institution from which the baby is transferred and for the receiving hospital or institution to verify that screen was sent and subsequently to repeat the screen if appropriate.

Not Collecting an Adequate Newborn Screening Sample.

In each state, a variable percentage of healthy babies are never screened. Reasons for failing to screen a healthy baby vary. A sample may have been collected but failed to reach the laboratory, or the newborn screening laboratory may receive a sample that is inadequate for testing because of insufficient sample, unacceptable collection, or sample contamination. Despite the fact that records will show a sample was collected, that baby was never screened. In other cases, no sample is ever collected. This may be a result of human or system error, and is one reason that the primary care provider must ascertain that each baby has been screened.

Home births present special issues, as the lay midwife or delivering family member who would be responsible to collect and send the screening sample may be uninformed about the purpose and process of newborn screening.

Assuming That an Abnormal Newborn Screen Is a False Positive Because the Baby Is Well and/or Because One or More Factors Known To Be Associated with False Positive Results Are Present.

The screening process is successful when affected babies are identified before onset of symptoms. The corollary is that the appearance of good health is not evidence against the presence of the disorder. Even in the presence of special clinical circumstances known to be associated with an increased frequency of physiologic false positive screening tests, a baby who tests positive may be truly affected. For example, the baby who is premature or tested very early, and who has a positive test for thyroid disease, may have real disease and needs prompt confirmation testing.

Referring to the Newborn Screening Test as a "PKU Test".

This is a very common practice among hospital staff and practicing physicians. It is misleading to refer to the newborn screen as "a PKU test," because tests for other diseases are included. Parent confusion about the full scope of testing may impact compliance with follow-up should the newborn screen be abnormal. It is good practice to use the term "newborn screen" and to inform the family of the breadth of the newborn screen.

For Further Information

Carol Clericuzio, MD
Department of Pediatrics
The University of New Mexico
Albuquerque, NM 87131

Chapter 17

Immunizations

Immunizations Are Important for All Children

Prior to widespread immunization in the United States, infectious diseases killed or disabled thousands of children each year. Immunization is one of the most effective ways to prevent disease. Vaccine preventable disease levels have been reduced by over 99 percent since the introduction of vaccines.

Children need to receive almost all of their vaccinations in the first two years of life. All states and the District of Columbia have immunization requirements for children entering day care and school, but there are no such laws assuring that children are up-to-date on their shots by age two. Approximately one in four children under the age of two in the U.S. are not properly immunized against infectious and potentially deadly diseases.

Necessary Vaccinations

Vaccines and recommended schedule:

- Hepatitis B: Three vaccinations—at 0-2 months, 1-4 months, and 6-18 months.

- Diphtheria/tetanus/acellular pertussis (DTaP) or diphtheria/ tetanus/pertussis (DTP): Four vaccinations—at 2, 4, 6, and 12-15 months.

Reprinted with permission, "Facts About Childhood Immunizations," © 1997, The Arc.

- H. influenzae type b (Hib): Four vaccinations—at 2, 4, 6, and 12-15 months. One type of the Hib vaccine requires only three doses at 2, 4, and 12-15 months.

- Polio: Three options—two shots of inactivated polio vaccine (IPV) at 2 and 4 months, followed by a dose (drops) of oral polio vaccine (OPV) at 12-18 months; or 3 shots of IPV at 2 and 4 months and 12-18 months; or 3 doses of OPV at 2 and 4 months and 12-18 months.

- Measles/mumps/rubella (MMR): One vaccination—at 12-15 months.

- Varicella (Chickenpox): One vaccination—at 12-18 months.

If a child is behind in his or her immunization series, he or she does not have to start over again.

Most children with mental retardation and other developmental disabilities are immunized on the same schedule as all other children. However, parents should always discuss immunization concerns with their child's doctor.

What Diseases Are Prevented by These Vaccinations?

Diphtheria. Diphtheria is spread when germs pass from an infected persons or carrier to the nose or throat of others. It is a very serious disease that can block the airway, making it impossible to breathe. It can also cause heart problems. Five to ten out of 100 people who get diphtheria die.

Tetanus (Lockjaw). Tetanus is caused by a toxin produced by a germ that enters the body through a cut or wound. Tetanus causes serious, painful spasms of all muscles, and can lead to "locking" of the jaw so a person cannot open his or her mouth, swallow, or breathe. Three out of ten people who get tetanus die.

Pertussis (Whooping Cough). Pertussis is easily spread when germs pass from an infected person to the nose or throat of others. Pertussis can cause spells of violent coughing and choking, making it hard to breathe, drink, or eat. The cough can last for weeks. This disease is most serious for infants, particularly those who are younger than 6 months of age. Babies can get pneumonia, have seizures, become brain damaged, or even die. About half of the babies who get pertussis have to go to the hospital. There are pertussis outbreaks every year because children are not immunized.

Polio. Polio is caused by a virus that is spread by contact with the feces (bowel movements) of an infected person. Symptoms can include a sudden fever, sore throat, headache, muscle weakness and pain. Polio can cause paralysis and death.

Measles. Measles is caused by a virus that is very easily spread. Even being in the same room with an infected person is enough to catch the disease. Symptoms include a rash, fever, cough, and watery eyes. Measles can also cause pneumonia, brain damage, seizures, or death. Of every 1,000 children who get measles, one to two will die.

Mumps. Mumps is spread when germs pass from an infected person to the nose or throat of others. Mumps causes fever, headaches, and swollen glands under the jaw. One out of every ten children who get mumps may develop a mild meningitis, sometimes causing encephalitis, which can cause brain damage, particularly in infants and young children. Mumps can also result in permanent loss of hearing.

Rubella (German measles). Rubella is caused by a virus that is spread when germs pass from an infected person to the nose or throat of others. It is usually a mild sickness with fever, swollen glands, and a rash which lasts for about three days. If a pregnant woman contracts rubella, she can have a miscarriage, or the baby can be born with birth defects, be blind and/or deaf, have mental retardation, heart defects, or other serious problems.

Hib disease. Haemophilus influenzae type b (Hib) germs are spread from an infected person to the nose or throat of others. Hib causes meningitis (brain damage), pneumonia, and infection of the blood, joints, bone, throat, and heart covering. This disease is very serious for children under five, especially infants.

Hepatitis B. Hepatitis B in an infection of the liver caused by a virus. This virus causes a flu-like illness with loss of appetite, nausea, vomiting, rashes, joint pain, and jaundice (yellowing of the eyes and skin). An infected pregnant woman can expose her newborn to this virus during birth. The virus stays in the liver of some people for the rest of their lives. Later, they can develop severe liver diseases, or cancer. Hepatitis B spreads through contact with blood or other body fluids. This can happen through sexual contact, or sharing a razor, toothbrush, or needles used to inject drugs.

Varicella (Chickenpox). Chickenpox is caused by a virus that spreads when germs pass from an infected person to the nose or throat of others. It usually causes a rash, itching, tiredness, and fever. It can lead to pneumonia, brain infection, or death. Complications occur most often in very young children, adults, or people with damaged immune systems.

What about Vaccines for Older Children?

Most children who have not completed the recommended series of vaccinations by age two will be required to receive them to enter school. However, some children already in school may have missed the hepatitis B vaccine. Children and adolescents who have not been vaccinated against hepatitis B in infancy may begin the three dose series during any childhood visit.

The Varicella (chickenpox) vaccine, added to the list of recommended vaccinations in 1996, is another one many children may have missed. They may receive Varicella vaccine during any visit after their first birthday. Children who lack a reliable history of chickenpox should be vaccinated during the recommended 11-12 year old visit. Susceptible persons older than 13 should receive two doses of the vaccine one month apart.

Other vaccines which older children may receive include the second dose of MMR at 4-6 or 11-12 years. Td (tetanus and diphtheria toxoids for adults) vaccine is recommended at 11-12 years. Subsequent routine Td boosters are recommended every 10 years.

Do These Vaccines Have Side Effects?

Vaccines are actually very safe. Reactions to the vaccines may occur, but they are rarely serious. They are usually mild and brief, such as low fever, sore arm, or tiredness after taking the shot. Health care providers should inform parents about the benefits and risks of a specific vaccine before immunizing their child.

Health officials agree that the benefits of vaccination are greater than the small risk of possible side effects from the vaccine. A child is far more likely to be seriously injured by one of these diseases than by any vaccine.

How Do Vaccine Recommendations Change Through Progress?

The members of the Advisory Committee on Immunization Practices (ACIP), experts on vaccines, vaccine research, and vaccine policy are constantly reviewing developments and recommending new immunization procedures to the Centers for Disease Control and Prevention. For example, the ACIP developed recommendations for the chickenpox vaccine in 1996. In 1997, they revised the recommendations for the polio vaccination, approving the three options described above. Recently, the committee also approved the use of acellular pertussis vaccines which contain inactivated pertussis toxin as opposed to whole-cell pertussis vaccines. The acellular vaccine causes fewer side effects, such as redness, fever, and swelling at the vaccination site.

Resources

Most of the information presented above was obtained from fact sheets prepared by the U.S. Centers for Disease Control and Prevention (CDC). Additional information is available from:

National Immunization Program
Centers for Disease Control and Prevention
1600 Clifton Rd., NE
Mailstop E-52
Atlanta, GA 30333
Hotline: 800-232-2522 (English), 800-232-0233 (Spanish)

Immunization Education and Action Committee
A Program of the Healthy Mothers Healthy Babies Coalition
409 12th St., SW
Washington, DC 20024-2188
Tel: 202-863-2458

Chapter 18

Dangers of Lead Still Linger

The hazardous substance lead was banned from house paint in 1978. U.S. food canners quit using lead solder in 1991. And a 25-year phase-out of lead in gasoline reached its goal in 1995.

As a result of such efforts, the number of young children with potentially harmful blood lead levels has dropped 85 percent in the last 20 years, as shown in National Health and Nutrition Examination Surveys conducted by the National Center for Health Statistics. Interested in measuring the impact of lead solder's removal from food cans, the Food and Drug Administration funded collection of the data during the 1976-1980 period and has continued to support the survey efforts.

Similarly, FDA's 1994-1996 Total Diet Studies showed that, since 1982-1984, daily intakes of lead from food dropped 96 percent in 2- to 5-year-olds (from 30 micrograms a day to 1.3) and nearly 93 percent in adults (from 38 micrograms a day to 2.5).

Yet in 1997, FDA approved a new, portable blood lead screening test kit for health professionals to use. In the face of so much success, why is another screening tool even necessary?

The answer: Lead is still around.

Lead paint abounds in older housing. The deteriorating paint exposes youngsters indoors to lead-laden dust and paint chips and outdoors to exterior paint lead residues in nearby soil—residues which

FDA Consumer, January-February 1998.

remain unless removed. Lead particles emitted by the past use of leaded gasoline are also in the soil, especially near major highways. Lead persists at some work sites and, occasionally, in drinking water, ceramic ware, and a number of other products.

"The risk of lead exposure remains disproportionately high for some groups, including children who are poor, non-Hispanic black, Mexican American, living in large metropolitan areas, or living in older housing," the national Centers for Disease Control and Prevention noted in its Feb. 21, 1997, *Morbidity and Mortality Weekly Report.* Indeed, CDC reports that nearly a million children under 6 still have blood lead levels high enough to damage their health. While CDC considers the blood lead level of concern in adults to be 25 micrograms per deciliter (mcg/dL) of blood, this level in young children is only 10 mcg/dL.

Based on CDC's levels, FDA's "tolerable" daily diet lead intakes are 6 mcg for children under age 6, 25 mcg for pregnant women, and 75 mcg for other adults. However, some risk exists with any level of lead exposure, says toxicologist Michael Bolger, Ph.D., chief of FDA's contaminants branch in the Office of Plant and Dairy Foods and Beverages.

And harmful levels need never occur, according to Sheryl Rosenthal, M.S.P.H., R.D., a lead educator at FDA's Center for Food Safety and Applied Nutrition. "Lead poisoning is preventable and just should not happen today," she says.

Lead Absorption

While adults absorb about 11 percent of lead reaching the digestive tract, children may absorb 30 to 75 percent. When lead is inhaled, up to 50 percent is absorbed, but less than 1 percent of lead is absorbed when it comes in contact with the skin. The body stores lead mainly in bone, where it can accumulate for decades.

"Anyone in poor nutritional status absorbs lead more easily," adds Cecilia Davoli, M.D., a pediatrician with Kennedy Krieger Institute's Lead Poisoning Prevention Program, in Baltimore. Calcium deficiency especially increases lead absorption, as does iron deficiency, which can also increase lead damage to blood cells. A high-fat diet increases lead absorption, and so does an empty stomach.

The Risks of Lead

Lead disrupts the functioning of almost every brain neurotransmitter, says David Bellinger, Ph.D., a psychologist and epidemiologist at Children's Hospital in Boston. Neurotransmitters are chemical messengers between the body's nerve cells. The messenger calcium, for example, is essential to nerve impulse transmission, heart activity, and blood clotting, but if it doesn't work right, affected systems may also be askew.

"Lead fits into binding sites that calcium should," Bellinger says, "so it can disturb cellular processes that depend on calcium. But there's no unifying theory that explains in detail what lead does to the central nervous system, which is where lead typically affects children."

Bellinger estimates that each 10 mcg/dL increase in blood lead lowers a child's IQ about 1 to 3 points.

"Evidence is less clear," he says, "on whether mild blood lead elevations in pregnancy cause permanent effects on the fetus. Studies have tended not to find that early developmental delays related to minor fetal exposure carry through to school age, when IQ is measured." Studying middle- and upper-middle-class children exposed before birth to mild lead levels, Bellinger and colleagues found delays in early sensory-motor development, such as grasping objects, but did not find such effects by school age.

However, he adds, "When lead exposure in the uterus is quite high, the impact can be devastating on the fetus, causing serious neurological problems." High lead exposures can cause a baby to have low birth weight or be born prematurely, or can result in miscarriage or stillbirth.

"Symptoms of lead poisoning can be highly variable depending, in part, on the age of the child, the amount of lead to which the child is exposed, and how long the exposure goes on," says pediatrician Randolph Wykoff, M.D., FDA associate commissioner for operations. Children exposed to lead may have no symptoms, he says, or may report sometimes vague symptoms, including headache, irritability, or abdominal pain.

While a child's chronic exposure to relatively low lead levels may result in learning or behavioral problems, Wykoff says that "higher levels of exposure can be associated with anemia and changes in kidney function, as well as significant changes in the nervous system that may, at extreme exposures, include seizures, coma, and death."

In adults, lead poisoning can contribute to high blood pressure and damage to the reproductive organs. Severe lead poisoning can cause subtle loss of recently acquired skills, listlessness, bizarre behavior, incoordination, vomiting, altered consciousness, and—as with children—seizures, coma, and death. Poisoning without severe brain effects can cause lethargy, appetite loss, sporadic vomiting, abdominal pain, and constipation.

By the time symptoms appear, damage is often already irreversible.

The most important thing for families to do, says Baltimore's Davoli, is to learn what steps they can take to prevent lead poisoning. We don't want to get to treatment. And they should take their children to the doctor regularly for checkups and, if the children are at risk, get blood lead tests done.

Critical to prevention is focusing on the important lead sources. FDA's Rosenthal says, "Dealing with sources of lead means recognizing them in your family's environment, knowing which ones contribute significant exposures, and eliminating or avoiding those exposures."

Top Contaminator: Lead Paint

America's No. 1 source of lead exposure in children is deteriorating lead paint in older housing. Because young children frequently put their thumbs and fingers and objects they handle in their mouths, they are easily poisoned from chronic ingestion of lead paint chips and house dust or soil that may have lead particles in it.

The Consumer Product Safety Commission (CPSC) banned house paint having more than 0.06 percent lead in 1978. But housing built before then, particularly before 1950, may contain lead paint. The Environmental Protection Agency and Department of Housing and Urban Development require owners of pre-1978 housing to give prospective buyers or renters federally approved information on the risk. Buyers must have 10 days to inspect for lead-based paint before being obligated by a contract.

Improper housing renovation increases exposure. The riskiest practices are sanding, scraping, or removing lead paint with a heat gun, which taint the air with lead paint dust. CPSC warns: There is no completely safe method for do-it-yourself removal of lead paint. Only experts should remove lead paint.

Occupational Hazards

Clark Carrington, Ph.D., of FDA's dairy foods and beverages contaminants branch, names workplace exposure as the next major potential source of lead. Besides their own exposures, workers may bring lead dust home on clothes, hands, or hair, exposing children in the household.

Occupations that may expose workers to lead include painting, smelters, firearms instruction, automotive repair, brass or copper foundries, and bridge, tunnel, and elevated highway construction.

To help protect workers from such exposure, the Occupational Safety and Health Administration calls for removal of workers from the workplace if their blood lead levels reach 50 mcg/dL. EPA limits lead emissions from certain industries.

Keeping Drinking Water Safe

Certain drinking water systems can also pose a lead risk. Under EPA rules, if lead exceeds 15 parts per billion (ppb) in more than 10 percent of public water taps sampled, the system must undergo a series of corrosion control treatments. The main culprits are corroded lead plumbing, lead solder on copper plumbing, and brass faucets. Lead is highest in water left in pipes for a long time—for example, when the faucet isn't used overnight.

FDA's quality standard for bottled water requires that lead not be present at 5 ppb, the lowest concentration that generally available methods for water analysis can reliably measure. If bottled water contains lead above this level, it is subject to regulatory action, including removal from the marketplace.

Lead in Ceramicware

Some ceramicware has lead in the glaze and may introduce small amounts of lead in the diet, which the body can tolerate, says Carrington. "The major problem with ceramicware is the rare poorly made piece with very high levels of leaching lead."

Bolger adds that even with these pieces, risk varies. "A plate coming in brief contact with food is not an issue," he says, "but storage of food in such a bowl or pitcher is a risk." It's especially wise to avoid storing acidic foods like juice and vinegar in ceramicware, as acids promote lead leaching.

FDA has established maximum levels for leachable lead in ceramicware, and pieces that exceed these levels are subject to recall or other agency enforcement action. The levels are based on how frequently a piece of ceramicware is used, the type and temperature of the food it holds, and how long the food stays in contact with the piece. For example, cups, mugs, and pitchers have the most stringent action level, 0.5 parts per million, because they can be expected to hold food longer, allowing more time for lead to leach. Also, a pitcher may be used to hold fruit juice. And a coffee mug is generally used every day to hold a hot acidic beverage, often several times a day.

Michael Kashtock, Ph.D., chief of FDA's Office of Plant and Dairy Foods and Beverages enforcement branch, says, "FDA allows use of lead glazes because they're the most durable. But we regulate them tightly to ensure their safety. Commercial manufacturers ... employ extremely strict and effective manufacturing controls that keep the lead from leaching during use." Small potters often can't control the firing of lead glazes as well, he warns, so their ceramics are more likely to leach illegal lead levels, although many do use lead-free glazes. "The best advice is to stick to commercially made products. If you are going to buy something hand-made or hand-painted, get assurance that lead-free glazes were used," he says.

Antique ceramicware may leach high levels of lead. Consumers can use a lead test kit from a hardware store on such pieces and on other hand-painted ceramicware they may already own. Avoid using such items—particularly cups, mugs, or pitchers—if the glaze develops a chalky gray residue after washing.

"And you want to make sure," says Rosenthal, "that you know whether an item is for food use, or if it's for decorative use only." FDA requires high-lead-leaching decorative ceramicware to be permanently labeled that it's not for food use and may poison food. Such items bought outside the United States may not be so labeled, potentially posing serious risk if used for food.

Other Lead Sources

Tin-coated lead foil capsules on wine bottles: FDA banned these capsules in 1996 after a study by the Bureau of Alcohol, Tobacco and Firearms found that 3 to 4 percent of wines examined could become contaminated during pouring from lead residues deposited on the mouth of the bottle by the foil capsule.

U.S. winemakers stopped using lead foils before the ban, but older bottles with the foils may still be around. "Remove the entire foil before using such wines," says attorney Martin Stutsman, a consumer safety officer in FDA's dairy foods and beverages enforcement branch. "Then before uncorking the bottle, wipe its neck and rim and the top of the cork with a clean wet cloth."

Lead-soldered food cans: Despite U.S. food canners' voluntary elimination of lead solder and a 1995 FDA ban on lead-soldered cans, requiring their removal from shelves by June 1996, this source of lead in the diet hasn't been fully eliminated. Some countries still use lead-soldered cans for food, and these food items may still occasionally be imported, albeit illegally, into the United States. Also, some small vendors may still stock old inventories of food in lead-soldered cans. In fact, a 1997 FDA investigation found more than 100 such cans in ethnic grocery stores in California alone.

Glassware: Lead crystal glassware may leach lead. "The crystalware industry has established voluntary lead-leaching limits for crystalware," says Kashtock, "that most foreign and domestic manufacturers follow." As a precaution, children and pregnant women should avoid frequent use of crystal glassware. Lead crystal baby bottles should never be used.

Also, FDA intends to issue industry guidance to prohibit use of lead-based (and cadmium-based) pigments for decorating the lip rim area of glassware, says Kashtock. "Use of the pigments may pose only a negligible risk, but it is avoidable."

Calcium products: Some people have expressed concern about lead in calcium supplements. Lead is a common contaminant in calcium from such natural sources as dolomitic limestone and oyster shells, but levels vary considerably from trace amounts to higher levels. However, FDA's Carrington says, "Since calcium intakes decrease lead absorption, supplements that correct low calcium intakes may reduce lead absorption, even though they contain small amounts of lead."

Lead is also found in other calcium sources. For example, lead in milk is usually too low to measure, but FDA's yearly Total Diet Study of foods in grocery stores sometimes detects lead in milk, says Carrington.

FDA has been petitioned to establish a tolerance level for lead in calcium sources used in dietary supplements. According to Robert Moore, Ph.D., of the agency's Office of Special Nutritionals regulatory branch, two petitions propose different tolerance levels—one similar to current industry standards and one considerably lower. FDA is reviewing the issues raised in the two documents.

Progressive hair dyes: Applied over time to gradually color the hair, these dyes contain lead acetate. After studying information on their safety, FDA found that lead exposure from these dyes was insignificant and that the dyes could be used safely, says John Bailey, Ph.D., director of FDA's Office of Cosmetics and Colors. "But we restricted how much could be in the product, and we required specific labeling instructions, including a warning to keep it out of the reach of children."

Kajal and surma, or kohl: These unapproved dyes in certain eye cosmetics from the Middle East contain potentially harmful amounts of lead. A 7-month-old in 1992 had a 39 mcg/dL blood lead level due to surma applied to the lower inner eyelid. Bailey says, "They are sold in stores specializing in Middle East products or brought into the country in personal luggage." He stresses that people using these cosmetics "need to understand the potentially serious health risk."

Foreign digestive remedies: Certain unapproved foreign digestive remedies containing lead include Alarcon, Azarcon, Coral, Greta, Liga, Maria Luisa, or Rueda. Greta, for example, is 99 percent lead oxide.

FDA orders the detention at U.S. borders of items known to possibly contain potential harmful levels of lead, including the Middle East eye cosmetics, the foreign digestive remedies, lead crystal baby bottles, and many other prohibited items. Lead sources outside FDA's purview include lead-based artists' paints, lead solder used in electronics work and stained glass, fishing weights, lead toy soldiers, and old painted toys and furniture.

Reflecting that these many lead sources are not all in every family's environment, new CDC screening guidance calls for state lead-poisoning prevention programs to identify communities at risk of high exposure and recommend appropriate screening. To this end, CDC funded 30 state and 10 local programs in 1996.

When announcing the new guidance, Health and Human Services Secretary Donna E. Shalala said, "Lower lead levels for America's children constitute a public health achievement of the first importance. But a significant number of children are still at risk for high lead exposure, and we have to finish the job on their behalf."

Screening and Treatment

Decisions about who needs lead screening should be made by individual doctors as well as state health departments, who can examine local lead hazards and conditions to determine which children are at risk of lead exposure, according to 1997 guidance issued by the national Centers for Disease Control and Prevention.

A screening test is especially suited for use in isolated U.S. rural areas and in developing countries. In September 1997, FDA approved the LEADCARE In Office Test System, a portable blood lead screening kit for health professionals' use in areas lacking refrigeration and other complex equipment needed with previously approved tests. Manufacturers developed the quick, easy, and reliable kit in conjunction with CDC.

FDA has approved three drugs that bind to, or chelate, lead molecules so the body can remove them in urine and stool. Calcium Disodium Versenate (edetate calcium disodium) requires injections or intravenous infusion in the hospital. Along with this drug, BAL (dimercaprol), also injected, may be used. The pediatric oral drug Chemet (succimer) may be taken at home, but it's important to eliminate the lead sources. Like other chelator drugs, Chemet should not substitute for effective environmental assessment and removal of the source of lead exposure. These drugs may have side effects, however, so doctors closely monitor their patients during treatment.

Additional Information

Centers for Disease Control and Prevention
Tel: 404-639-3534
Toll-free: 800-311-3435
URL: http://www.cdc.gov/nceh/programs/lead/lead.htm

Consumer Product Safety Commission
4330 East-West Highway
Bethesda, Maryland
Tel: 800-638-CPSC
TDD: 800-638-8270
URL: http://www.cpsc.gov/

Environmental Protection Agency's Safe Drinking Water
Hotline: 800-426-4791
URL: http://www.epa.gov/opptintr/lead/index.html

National Lead Information Center
Tel: 800-424-LEAD
TDD: 800-526-5456
URL: http://www.nsc.org/ehc/lead.htm

—Dixie Farley

Dixie Farley is a staff writer for *FDA Consumer*.

Chapter 19

Safety Counts: Bike Helmets and Child Car Safety

Bicycle Helmet Use Laws

The United States Department of Transportation's National Highway Traffic Safety Administration (NHTSA) supports the enactment of bicycle helmet usage laws. Bicycle helmets offer bicyclists the best protection from head injuries resulting from bicycle crashes, and bicycle helmet laws have been proven effective in increasing bicycle helmet use.

Key Facts

- Almost 44,000 bicyclists have died in traffic crashes in the United States since 1932—the first year that bicycle fatality estimates were recorded.

- In 1996, 761 bicyclists were killed, and approximately 59,000 were injured in traffic-related crashes. Children ages 14 and under accounted for 223 (29%) of these fatalities, making this one of the most frequent causes of injury-related death for young children.

This chapter includes text from "State Legislative Fact Sheets: Bicycle Helmet Use Laws," National Highway Traffic Safety Administration (NHTSA), January 1998; "Preventing Mental Retardation Through Use of Bicycle Helmets," © 1996, The Arc, reprinted with permission; and "Protect Your Kids in the Car," National Highway Traffic Safety Administration (NHTSA), August 1997.

- Each year almost 400,000 children ages 14 and under are treated in emergency rooms for bicycle-related injuries.

- Universal bicycle helmet use by children ages 4 to 15 would prevent 39,000 to 45,000 head injuries, and 18,000 to 55,000 scalp and face injuries annually.

- Bicycle helmets are 85-88 percent effective in mitigating head and brain injuries, making the use of helmets the single most effective way to reduce head injuries and fatalities resulting from bicycle crashes.

- Despite the fact that 70 to 80 percent of all fatal bicycle crashes involve head injuries, only 18 percent of all bicyclists wear bicycle helmets.

- Nationally, bicyclists ages 14 and under are at five times greater risk for injury than older cyclists.

- As with safety belts, child safety seats, and motorcycle helmets, the enactment of laws requiring the use of bicycle helmets, along with education and visible enforcement, is likely to be the most promising way to increase bicycle helmet usage.

Legislative Status

- The first bicycle helmet law was passed in California in 1986. This law was amended in 1993 to cover all children under age 18.

- By September 1997, 15 states had enacted age-specific bicycle helmet laws. Most of these laws cover bicyclists under age 16.

- On June 16, 1994 H.R. 965, the Child Safety Protection Act of 1994, was passed. It requires the Consumer Product Safety Commission (CPSC) to develop a mandatory bicycle helmet standard.

- An interim mandatory bicycle helmet standard became effective March 17, 1995. Helmets are required to meet one of the following voluntary standards: ANSI, ASTM, Snell, or Canadian (CSA).

- On March 10, 1998, the CPSC published 16 CFR Part 1203, Safety Standard for Bicycle Helmets. This rule applies to bicycle helmets manufactured after March 10, 1999. In addition, helmets meeting the new standard will have a label indicating that they meet CPSCAE's new safety standard. The standard mandates several performance requirements including:

- Impact protection in a crash: The standard establishes a performance test to ensure that helmets will adequately protect the head in a collision of fall.

- Children's helmets and head coverage: The standard specifies an increased area head coverage for children ages 1 to 5.

- Chin strap strength and stability: The performance tests measure chin strap strength to prevent breakage or excessive elongation, and the helmet's resistance to rolling off the head during a collision or fall.

Mandatory Bicycle Helmet Laws: A Summary

Table 19.1. Mandatory Helmet Laws: A Summary.*

Jurisdiction	Ages/Conditions
New Jersey	Under 14
Georgia	Under 16
Connecticut	Under 15
Oregon	Under 16
Tennessee	Under 12
New York	Under 14
California	Under 18
Massachusetts	Under 13
Pennsylvania	Under 12
Alabama	Under 16
Maryland	Under 16
Delaware	Under 16
West Virginia	Under 15
Rhode Island	Under 16
Florida	Under 16
Maine	Under 16

Source: Bicycle Helmet Safety Institute, BHSI home page web: www.helmets.org, 2000

*Check with your state bicycle and pedestrian coordinators for county, city, and local bicycle helmet laws.

Cost Savings

- The estimated cost of bicycle-related injuries and deaths (for all ages) is $8 billion.

- It is expensive to treat bicycle-related head injuries because these injuries can endure throughout a lifetime.

- Every $10 bike helmet saves this country $30 in direct health costs, and an additional $365 in societal costs. In fact, if 85 percent of all child bicyclists wore helmets every time they rode a bicycle for a year, the lifetime medical cost savings would total $109 to $142 million.

Who Supports Bicycle Helmet Use Laws?

- American Academy of Pediatrics
- American Automobile Association
- Brain Injury Association
- Centers for Disease Control
- Consumer Product Safety Commission
- Health Resources and Services Administration
- Little League Baseball
- Major League Baseball
- National Football League
- National Safe Kids Campaign
- National Safety Council
- Snell Memorial Foundation

Bicycling has served as a means of transportation and a popular recreational activity throughout this century. During the last decade alone, Americans have purchased more than 100 million bicycles. An expansion of bicycle usage and an ever-growing, complicated traffic system have resulted in an increasing number of injuries to cyclists. Research has shown that the most effective method of preventing serious injury to bike riders is bicycle helmet use.

A bicycle helmet cannot keep a cyclist from crashing, but it can significantly reduce the chance of serious brain injury by absorbing the impact that would hit the skull and brain in a crash. The helmet's protective inner liner absorbs the blow and cushions the rider's head.

Because the brain is so important, controlling thought processes, motor activities, memory, and emotion, even a mild injury can cause serious problems. Bicycle helmet use can reduce disability and save many lives each year.

Yearly Injuries and Fatalities in Bicycle Crashes

Scientists from the U.S. Centers for Disease Control and Prevention (CDC) reviewed bicycle deaths and injury data from 1984 through 1988 and found that some 1,000 people died each year from bicycle crashes. Head injury was involved in 62 percent of those deaths. Some 558,000 people sustained bicycle-associated injuries each year, and of those, 32.5 percent or 181,000 suffered head injuries. The CDC estimated that if all bicyclists had worn helmets during the five-year study period, one death could have been prevented every day and one head injury could have been prevented every four minutes (Sacks et al., 1991).

Data about Children and Bicycle Head Injuries

The same study found that each year more than 138,000 children age 14 and under suffered head injuries from bicycle crashes. About 245 died from their head injuries. Males in the 10-14 age group had the highest death rate due to head injuries, and males age 5-9 had the highest rate of head injuries. At all ages, males were much more involved in bicycle crashes than females (Sacks et al., 1991). A third of the head injuries due to bike crashes are traumatic and can result in physical or mental impairment (The National SAFE KIDS Campaign, undated).

Young children are at special risk because their stages of development limit their understanding and, therefore, influence how they behave in traffic situations. For instance, children may not understand stopping distance, believing a car can stop as fast as a person. They typically do not develop a sense of danger until much before age 8 and may not understand the threat cars pose. Young riders may also think that if they can see the driver, the driver can see them. Traffic is only part of the problem, for the majority of bike crashes occur in parks, bike paths, or driveways and not on roads (Harborview Injury Prevention and Research Center).

Rate of Bicycle Riders Helmet Usage

In the study cited above, fewer than 10 percent of all cyclists wore helmets, and fewer than 2 percent of riders under age 15 wore them

(Sacks et al., 1991). A study in the *New England Journal of Medicine* (Thompson et al., 1989) concluded that helmet use reduced head injuries by 85 percent and brain damage by 88 percent. People who ride without helmets are seven times more likely to suffer head injuries and eight times more likely to suffer brain damage than those who wear helmets.

Bike helmets are critical safety equipment because a child need only fall from a height of 2 feet and hit his head to suffer traumatic brain injury. A cyclist riding at only 20 miles per hour (an average speed for young cyclists) can be killed by hitting her head on a hard surface.

Traumatic brain injury impairs cognitive, physical, psychosocial, and emotional functioning temporarily or permanently, and can lead to death. A child could suffer memory loss, problems with reading comprehension, an inability to concentrate, severe mood swings, and impulsive, uncontrollable behavior (The National SAFE KIDS Campaign, undated).

Tips for Choosing and Fitting a Bike Helmet

A helmet should be snug, but not tight, and have an adjustable inner liner. Most have different sizes of foam pads that can be inserted to make the helmet fit better. It should sit level and not rock back and forth or from side to side. The helmet should meet approved safety standards which means it has been tested by the American National Standards Institute (the label will say "ANSI"), Snell Memorial Foundation ("Snell") or the American Society for Testing and Materials ("ASTM"). Any helmet worn in a crash should be replaced, as it may be damaged even though the damage is not visible.

Barriers to Children's Helmet Use

The main barriers are parents' lack of awareness of the need, cost of the helmet, and peer pressure. Because so few children are wearing helmets, nobody wants to start. The American Academy of Pediatrics (Undated) offers the following tips for parents to encourage their child to develop a helmet habit.

Establish the helmet habit early. Have your children wear helmets as soon as they start to ride bikes—even if they are passengers on the back of adults' bikes. If they learn to wear helmets whenever they ride bikes, it will become a habit for a lifetime. It's never too late, however, to get your children into helmets.

- Wear a helmet yourself. Kids learn best by observing you. Whenever you ride your bike, put on your helmet. Plan bicycle outings during which all family members wear their helmets to further reinforce the message. The most important factor influencing children to wear helmets is riding with an adult who wears a helmet.

- Talk to your kids about why you want them to protect their head. There are many things you can tell your children to convince them of the importance of helmet use: 1) Bikes are vehicles, not toys. 2) You love and value your children. 3) They can hurt their heads permanently or even die from head injuries.

- Reward your kids for wearing helmets. Praise them; give them special treats or privileges when they wear their helmets without having to be told to.

- Don't let children ride their bikes unless they wear their helmets. Be consistent. If you allow your children to ride occasionally without their helmets, they won't believe that helmet use really is important. Tell your kids they have to find another way to play, or must walk, or take a bus to get somewhere, if they don't want to use their helmets.

- Encourage your children's friends to wear helmets. Peer pressure can be used in a positive way if several families in the neighborhood start making helmet use a regular habit at the same time.

Remember: Accidents causing head injuries can occur on sidewalks, driveways, bike paths, and parks as well as streets. You and your children cannot predict when a fall from a bike will occur. It's important to wear a helmet on every ride, no matter how short.

How States and Communities Can Increase Use of Bicycle Helmets

States and local communities are implementing a variety of strategies to increase use of bicycle helmets, particularly by children. These range from educational programs for parents and children, to public media campaigns, to helmet distribution programs, to promoting helmet purchase through a hang tag on a new bicycle purchase. A study by Dannenberg et al., (1993) found that legislation combined with education increased helmet use substantially more than did education alone.

In 1992, New Jersey became the first state to make bike helmets mandatory for children as old as 13, and, thus, now has several years of experience with the law. At the end of the first year, the New Jersey State Highway Traffic Safety division conducted a survey to determine what actually was happening. Their research observed a helmet usage rate of 68.6 percent for children under age 14.

This rate is unprecedented for any region of the United States. In addition, the rate for adults (not covered under the law), had also risen dramatically—to 37.2 percent. At the end of year two, New Jersey had a 65 percent drop in bike injuries.

References

A Case Control Study of the Effectiveness of Bicycle Safety Helmets. Thompson, Robert S., Frederick P. Rivara and Diane C. Thompson, *New England Journal of Medicine*, 1989.

A Case Control Study of the Effectiveness of Bicycle Safety Helmets in Preventing Facial Injury. Thompson, Diane C., Robert S. Thompson, Frederick P. Rivara and Marsha E. Wolf, *American Journal of Public Health*, 1990.

Bicycle-Associated Head Injuries and Deaths in the United States from 1984 through 1988. Sacks, Jeffrey J., Patricia Holmgren, Suzanne Smith and Daniel M. Scai, *Journal of American Medical Association*, 1991.

Mandatory Bicycle Helmet Use: The Victorian Experience. Vulcan, AP., Cameron, MH., and Watson, MH. *World Journal of Surgery*, 1992.

Bicycle Helmet Laws and Educational Campaigns: An Evaluation of Strategies to Increase Children's Helmet Use. Dannenberg, Andrew, et al, 1993.

Bicycle Use and Hazard Patterns in the United States. Rodgers, Gregory. Consumer Product Safety Commission, Washington, DC, 1994.

Mandatory Helmet Wearing for Bicycle Riders. Parliament of Western Australia, 1994.

Injury Control Recommendations: Bicycle Helmets. *Morbidity and Mortality Weekly Report*, Centers for Disease Control, 1995.

American Academy of Pediatrics. (Undated). *Tips for getting your kids to wear bicycle helmets*. Elk Grove Village, Illinois. Author.

Dannenberg, A. L., Gielen, A. C., Beilenson, P. L., Wilson, M. H., & Joffe, A. (1993). Bicycle helmet laws and educational campaigns: An evaluation of strategies to increase children's helmet use. *American Journal of Public Health*, 83(5), 667-674.

Harborview Injury Prevention and Research Center. (Undated). *Children's Bicycle Safety. The Facts.* Seattle, WA: Harborview Injury Prevention and Research Center. Sacks, J. J., Holmgreen, P., Smith, S. M., & Sosin, D. M. (1991).

Bicycle-associated head injuries and death in the United States from 1984 through 1988. *Journal of the American Medical Association*, 266(21), 3016-3018.

The National SAFE KIDS Campaign, a program of Children's National Medical Center. (Undated). *Bicycle helmets for kids: The best protection against head injury*. Washington, D.C: The National SAFE KIDS Campaign.

Thompson, R.S., Rivera, F.P., & Thompson, D.C. (1989). A case-control study of the effectiveness of bicycle safety helmets. *New England Journal of Medicine*, 320, 1361-1367.

World Health Organization, 1995. *Bicycle Helmet Legislation*. World Health Organization.

Protect Your Kids in the Car

The safest place for any child 12 years old and under is in the back seat. Every child should be buckled in a child safety seat, a booster seat, or with a lap/shoulder belt, if it fits.

Riding with Babies

- Infants up to about 20 pounds and up to 1 year old should ride in a rear-facing child seat.

- The child seat must be in the BACK seat and face the rear of the car, van, or truck.

- Babies riding in a car must never face front. In a crash or sudden stop, the baby's neck can be hurt badly.

- Infants in car seats must never ride in the front seat of a car with air bags. In a crash, the air bag can hit the car seat and hurt or kill the baby.

- Never hold your baby in your lap when you are riding in the car. In a crash or sudden stop, your child can be hurt badly or killed.

Riding with Young Kids

- Kids over 20 pounds and at least 1 year old should ride in a car seat that faces the front of the car, van, or truck.

- It is best to keep kids in the forward facing car seat for as long as they fit comfortably in it.

- Older kids over 40 pounds should ride in a booster seat until the car's lap and shoulder belts fit right. The lap belt must fit low and snug on their hips. The shoulder belt must not cross their face or neck.

- Never put the shoulder belt behind their back or under their arm.

Remember—

- All kids are safest in the back seat, in a safety seat or seat belt.

- Always read the child seat instructions and the car owner's manual. Test the child seat to ensure a snug fit by pulling the base to either side or toward the front of the car.

More Information

The National SAFE KIDS Campaign
1301 Pennsylvania Ave., NW, Suite 1000
Washington, D.C. 20004-1707
Tel: 202-662-0600; Fax: 202-393-2072
URL: www.safekids.org

The Bicycle Federation of America
1506 21st Street, NW, Suite 200
Washington, D.C. 20036
Tel: 202-463-6622

American Academy of Pediatrics
AP Publications
141 Northwest Pont Blvd.,
Elk Grove Village, Illinois 60007
Tel: 800-433-9016

Harborview Injury Prevention Research Center
325 Ninth Avenue, Box 359960
Seattle, Washington 98104
Tel: 206-521-1520

Brain Injury Association
(formerly the National Head Injury Foundation)
105 North Alfred Street
Alexandria, VA 22314
Tel:703-236-6000, 800-444-NHIF
Fax: 703-236-6001

National Highway Traffic Safety Administration (NHTSA) Headquarters
Traffic Safety Programs, NTS-15,
400 Seventh Street, S.W.
Washington, D.C. 20590
Tel: 202-366-1739
Hotline: 888-327-4236

Part Five

Family Life

Chapter 20

Parenting a Child with Special Needs

When parents learn that their child has a disability or a chronic illness, they begin a journey that takes them into a life that is often filled with strong emotion, difficult choices, interactions with many different professionals and specialists, and an ongoing need for information and services. Initially, parents may feel isolated and alone, and not know where to begin their search for information, assistance, understanding, and support. This chapter has been developed expressly to respond to the information needs of parents—those who have just learned their child has special needs and those who have lived with this reality for some time but who have reached a transition point where they need new information or renewed support. This chapter provides a starting point for families in their search for information and resources.

You Are Not Alone: For Parents When They Learn That Their Child Has a Disability

If you have recently learned that your child is developmentally delayed or has a disability (which may or may not be completely defined), this message may be for you. It is written from the personal

Excerpts from "You Are Not Alone: For Parents When They Learn That Their Child Has a Disability," by Patricia McGill Smith, and "Unplanned Journey: When You Learn That Your Child Has a Disability," by Carole Brown, Samara Goodman, and Lisa Kupper, News Digest, Second Edition, #ND20, National Information Center for Children and Youth with Disabilities (NICHCY), February 1997.

perspective of a parent who has shared this experience and all that goes with it.

When parents learn about any difficulty or problem in their child's development, this information comes as a tremendous blow. The day my child was diagnosed as having a disability, I was devastated—and so confused that I recall little else about those first days other than the heartbreak. Another parent described this event as a "black sack" being pulled down over her head, blocking her ability to hear, see, and think in normal ways. Another parent described the trauma as "having a knife stuck" in her heart. Perhaps these descriptions seem a bit dramatic, yet it has been my experience that they may not sufficiently describe the many emotions that flood parents' minds and hearts when they receive any bad news about their child.

Many things can be done to help yourself through this period of trauma. That is what this paper is all about. In order to talk about some of the good things that can happen to alleviate the anxiety, let us first take a look at some of the reactions that occur.

Common Reactions

On learning that their child may have a disability, most parents react in ways that have been shared by all parents before them who have also been faced with this disappointment and with this enormous challenge. One of the first reactions is that of denial—"This cannot be happening to me, to my child, to our family." Denial rapidly merges with anger, which may be directed toward the medical personnel who were involved in providing the information about the child's problem. Anger can also color communication between husband and wife or with grandparents or significant others in the family. Early on, it seems that the anger is so intense that it touches almost anyone, because it is triggered by the feelings of grief and inexplicable loss that one does not know how to explain or deal with.

Fear is another immediate response. People often fear the unknown more than they fear the known. Having the complete diagnosis and some knowledge of the child's future prospects can be easier than uncertainty. In either case, however, fear of the future is a common emotion: "What is going to happen to this child when he is five years old, when he is twelve, when he is twenty-one? What is going to happen to this child when I am gone?" Then other questions arise: "Will he ever learn? Will he ever go to college? Will he or she have the capability of loving and living and laughing and doing all the things that we had planned?"

Other unknowns also inspire fear. Parents fear that the child's condition will be the very worst it possibly could be. Over the years, I have spoken with so many parents who said that their first thoughts were totally bleak. One expects the worst. Memories return of persons with disabilities one has known. Sometimes there is guilt over some slight committed years before toward a person with a disability. There is also fear of society's rejection, fears about how brothers and sisters will be affected, questions as to whether there will be any more brothers or sisters in this family, and concerns about whether the husband or wife will love this child. These fears can almost immobilize some parents.

Then there is guilt—guilt and concern about whether the parents themselves have caused the problem: "Did I do something to cause this? Am I being punished for something I have done? Did I take care of myself when I was pregnant? Did my wife take good enough care of herself when she was pregnant?" For myself, I remember thinking that surely my daughter had slipped from the bed when she was very young and hit her head, or that perhaps one of her brothers or sisters had inadvertently let her drop and didn't tell me. Much self-reproach and remorse can stem from questioning the causes of the disability.

Guilt feelings may also be manifested in spiritual and religious interpretations of blame and punishment. When they cry, "Why me?" or "Why my child?," many parents are also saying, "Why has God done this to me?" How often have we raised our eyes to heaven and asked: "What did I ever do to deserve this?" One young mother said, "I feel so guilty because all my life I had never had a hardship and now God has decided to give me a hardship."

Confusion also marks this traumatic period. As a result of not fully understanding what is happening and what will happen, confusion reveals itself in sleeplessness, inability to make decisions, and mental overload. In the midst of such trauma, information can seem garbled and distorted. You hear new words that you never heard before, terms that describe something that you cannot understand. You want to find out what it is all about, yet it seems that you cannot make sense of all the information you are receiving. Often parents are just not on the same wavelength as the person who is trying to communicate with them about their child's disability.

Powerlessness to change what is happening is very difficult to accept. You cannot change the fact that your child has a disability, yet parents want to feel competent and capable of handling their own life situations. It is extremely hard to be forced to rely on the judgments, opinions, and recommendations of others. Compounding the problem is that these others are often strangers with whom no bond of trust has yet been established.

Disappointment that a child is not perfect poses a threat to many parents' egos and a challenge to their value system. This jolt to previous expectations can create reluctance to accept one's child as a valuable, developing person.

Rejection is another reaction that parents experience. Rejection can be directed toward the child or toward the medical personnel or toward other family members. One of the more serious forms of rejection, and not that uncommon, is a "death wish" for the child—a feeling that many parents report at their deepest points of depression.

During this period of time when so many different feelings can flood the mind and heart, there is no way to measure how intensely a parent may experience this constellation of emotions. Not all parents go through these stages, but it is important for parents to identify with all of the potentially troublesome feelings that can arise, so that they will know that they are not alone. There are many constructive actions that you can take immediately, and there are many sources of help, communication, and reassurance.

Remember That This Is Your Child

This person is your child, first and foremost. Granted, your child's development may be different from that of other children, but this does not make your child less valuable, less human, less important, or in less need of your love and parenting. Love and enjoy your child. The child comes first; the disability comes second. If you can relax and take the positive steps just outlined, one at a time, you will do the best you can, your child will benefit, and you can look forward to the future with hope.

The Unplanned Journey: When You Learn That Your Child Has a Disability

Growth is endless and our lives change and change us beyond anticipation. I do not forget the pain—it aches in a particular way when I look at Jessy's friends (her paid companions), some of them just her age, and allow myself for a moment to think of all she cannot be. But we cannot sift experience and take only the part that does not hurt us. (Park, 1988, p. 320)

No parent wants his or her child to be sick, disabled, or harmed in any way. It is not an experience anyone expects to have; rather, it is a journey that is unplanned. The terrain families must travel is often rough in places. The stress families may experience because of their child's disability may be the most difficult of their lives and often affects important aspects of family functioning (Mahoney, O'Sullivan, & Robinson, 1992). And yet, the majority of families are able to find the strength within themselves and among their circles of support to adapt to and handle the stress and challenges that may accompany their child's illness or disability.

Many parents have described the progression—and pendulum—of feelings they experienced upon learning that their child has an illness or a disability. Patty McGill Smith touched upon many of these emotions in "You Are Not Alone"—shock, denial, grief, guilt, anger, confusion. Not all parents will experience all of these emotions (Blacher, 1989). Some families feel that they experience no more greater sorrow than any other person, while others feel a sense of sorrow that is never completely resolved (Coleman, 1990). Still others feel that these reactions are not necessarily experienced sequentially but may, in fact, occur repeatedly, precipitated by various life crises and turning points (Wikler, Wasow, & Hatfield, 1981). Usually the first crisis is when a child is initially identified as having a disability. Other crises may occur during times of transition, such as (1) at school-entry age, (2) during adolescence, (3) when leaving school, and (4) when parents grow older. (Seligman & Darling, 1989)

The type of emotions parents experience, as intense and overwhelming as they may be, are also normal and acceptable. Parent Rhonda Krahl writes that "these feelings and others are a necessary part of the adjustment process" (Krahl, 1989, p. 6). However, through whatever means of adjustment each parent finds—and these will vary from person to person—stability does return, both to the individual and to the family. Tobi Levin points out, "Most parents eventually go from asking 'why' to 'what do I do now?'" (Levin, 1992, p. 3). At this point, parents may begin to search for needed information. Many parents also report feelings of personal growth that are often, in retrospect, astounding to them.

One mother, describing the first two years of life after the birth of a child with spina bifida, said:

> I can now admit that having Laura is mostly a blessing...much of the experience has been positive, challenging, and rewarding, and I have grown as a person in ways I may not have without

her...In fact, the past two years have changed me for the better in just about every way. Nevertheless, I still don't want to be the mother of a handicapped child. But I am Laura's mother, I love her deeply, and that makes all the difference. (Sutton, 1982, p. 213)

Taken together, the many suggestions and insights offered by parents who have lived for years with the experience of disability in the family can provide parents who are new to the experience with much guidance and support. The remainder of this chapter will outline many of the ways that parents have helped themselves and those they love adjust to living with and caring for a child with special needs.

Accessing Information and Services

One of the first things you can do that may prove enormously helpful, now and in the future, is to collect information—information about your child's disability, about the services that are available, and about the specific things you can do to help your child develop to the fullest extent possible. Collecting and using the information available on disability issues is a critical part of being a parent of a special needs child. Fortunately, there is a great deal of information available on many disabilities and many disability issues. Parents often report, however, that at first they did not know where to begin searching for the information they needed.

Joining a Group

Much of the information that will be helpful to you is in the hands, heads, and hearts of other parents like yourselves. For this reason, it is worthwhile to join a parent's group, which can offer you the opportunity to meet other people with children who have disabilities. Some groups are organized around one particular disability (e.g., cerebral palsy, Tourette syndrome, Down syndrome), while other groups draw together parents who, irrespective of the disabilities of their children, have similar concerns, such as daycare, transportation, coping, or finding out about and supporting special education in their community. Within each of these groups, information, emotional and practical support, and common concerns can be shared. The power of this mutual sharing to combat feelings of isolation, confusion, and stress is a consistent thread running throughout the literature written by and for parents.

I belonged to a group of moms and from them came the reassurance that I was going to be okay...Here I could let it all hang out. We talked about resentment at mismanaged pregnancies and birthings; frustration with case managers that didn't manage, doctors who didn't listen, and spouses who didn't help. This was a safe place to express my feelings where the listener would really understand and wouldn't think I was "falling apart" or "still grieving" or "not handling it too well." We laughed together. We cried together. Even though our children had different disabilities, we were alike: Alike in our anger, alike in our fear, alike in our hope. (McAnaney, 1992, pp. 17-18)

There are many ways to identify a parent group in your area, including asking your family doctor, calling a local school, contacting the state or local parent training and information (PTI) center, and looking in the telephone directory. NICHCY's *A Parent's Guide to Accessing Parent Groups* describes a process for finding (or starting) a group suited to your particular interests and needs; NICHCY also makes available a State Resource Sheet for each state, which provides information about parent groups within the state.

Reading Books Written for and by Parents

You may also find it worthwhile to read many of the excellent books that are available on disability issues. A good starting point for identifying the book or books most suited to your family's needs is *A Reader's Guide for Parents of Children with Mental, Physical, or Emotional Disabilities* by Cory Moore (1990), which includes annotated descriptions of more than 1,000 books and articles on disabilities. Although this book is currently out of print, you may be able to find a copy in your local library, a parent resource room, or the lending library of a local chapter of many disability groups. A new version of the book—*The Special-Needs Reading List: An Annotated Guide to the Best Publications for Parents and Professionals* (Sweeney, in press)—was released in 1997. There are also many shorter bibliographies available. Worthwhile suggestions for reading can come as well from talking to a local librarian, your child's teacher, or other involved professional; contacting a national, state, or local disability group; talking to other parents of children with disabilities; or by contacting NICHCY.

You may also wish to obtain information about your child's disability and other medical issues, such as how to choose a doctor and obtain needed medical services. NICHCY's *Parent's Guide to Doctors, Disabilities, and the Family* is a useful beginning point, for it contains many suggestions for finding and interacting with doctors when there is a child with a disability involved.

Many children, however, have problems that are difficult to diagnose. Parents may be told, "It's nothing and will go away. You're overreacting. It's a stage" (Finston, 1990, p. 28). These parents "will need stamina, patience, and unusual resources to find out what is wrong with their child. That label may not come easily, but if parents don't pursue it, most likely no one else will" (p. 29).

If you are having trouble obtaining a diagnosis for your child, one mother who searched for years for a diagnosis of her son's condition recommends that you:

- keep accurate records that can provide a clue to the problem;

- talk to others (nurses, doctors, teachers, pharmacists, parent groups, local medical board) who may be able to offer valuable information, leads, or assistance;

- research the problem on your own, through reading books and articles, conducting computer searches, and utilizing interlibrary loan materials; and

- trust your own observations and evaluate new information based upon your own knowledge of the child. (Finston, 1990, p. 7-9)

For those who have an early, accurate diagnosis of their child's disability, the search for information is generally easier. There are many books available that look comprehensively and in-depth at one disability. Typically, these books describe the disability, discuss the family's adjustment, identify medical issues, provide guidance about dealing with medical practitioners and developing appropriate therapy programs, discuss daily life, describe how a child with that disability might be expected to develop, and address educational implications and legal issues.

Accessing Services

The search for available services is a challenge for families and one that continues as the child's needs change. Most of these services are made available because of legislation at the federal and state levels. Because a core of laws affects the services that are available, how and to whom those services are provided, and the process of obtaining the services, it becomes essential for families to be informed about their legal rights. For a quick read on the core of federal laws governing the educational rights of children and youth with disabilities, NICHCY offers *"The Education of Children and Youth with Special Needs: What do the Laws Say?"* and *"Questions and Answers about the IDEA."*

Typically, there are many services available within communities, districts, and states to assist you in meeting the needs of your child with disabilities and your family. For families with a young child—birth through the third birthday—with disabilities, it may be critically important to access early intervention services, which are designed to identify and treat developmental problems as early as possible. For school-aged children with disabilities, special education and related services can be important factors in addressing a child's educational needs.

Early intervention services. Early intervention services are designed to address the needs of infants and toddlers with disabilities as early as possible and, as such, can range from feeding support from a nutritionist in a hospital to developing a complete physical therapy program for an infant with cerebral palsy. However, these services are not just for the child with special needs.

When framing the law describing early intervention services, Congress recognized that families are central in a young child's life. Therefore, the family's priorities, concerns, and resources have become the foundation for planning services for infants and toddlers with disabilities. The plan that is developed through this process is called an Individualized Family Service Plan (IFSP).

Parents, too, can benefit from early intervention services; as full members of the team developing the program for their child, they can learn skills that may be useful for a long time—skills in decision-making, planning, being of support to others, and influencing the policy-making process in their communities. Giving testimony before the Senate on the value of early intervention services, one mother stated:

...Children, and the families that love and nurture them, have needs that cannot be easily compartmentalized. Especially in early childhood, a family's priorities may be rapidly changing and may cross over numerous "systems" boundaries. As I recall the hours of early intervention our daughter received, the most valuable lessons were based on recognizing her worth as an individual, taking into account our abilities, as her parents, to seek out ways to encourage her growth and development and, finally, reaching out to other families with children, with or without disabilities, to participate in mutually supportive relationships that meet the needs of each individual in the family as well as the community. (Behr, 1991)

The services themselves are offered through a public or private agency and are provided in different settings, such as your home, a clinic, a neighborhood daycare center, a hospital, or the local health department. Initial evaluation and assessment of your child will be provided free of charge. Services may also be provided at no cost, although this may vary from state to state; some states charge a "sliding-scale" fee based upon what you, as parents, earn.

It is important to know that some states are still in the process of developing these services. Therefore, depending upon the state in which you live, early intervention services may be fully available or may still be in the process of developing. Every state now has developed a central directory of early intervention services, and many states will provide service coordinators to help parents find services for their child. Your family physician, hospitals, or a specialist working with your child can also be important resources of information, as can the NICHCY State Resource Sheet, which identifies the name and telephone number of your state's contact person for programs for infants and toddlers with disabilities.

Special education and related services. Through the mandates of a number of federal laws—most notably, the Individuals with Disabililties Education Act, or IDEA (formerly known as the Education of the Handicapped Act, EHA, or Public Law 94-142) and Section 504 of the Rehabilitation Act of 1973—each eligible child with special needs is guaranteed a free, appropriate public education designed to address his or her unique needs. This education is planned by a multi-disciplinary team, including the parents of the child. In order to benefit from this special education, the child may also need to receive a variety of related services (e.g., transportation assistance, occupational and physical therapy, audiology, school health services, speech-language pathology, and psychological services). These, too, are to be provided by the school to eligible children at no cost to their families.

Thus, as parents, you are key participants in the team that determines what type of special education your child will receive, as well as what related services are necessary to help him or her maximize the benefits of that special education. Together, the members of your child's team develop an Individualized Education Program (IEP), which states in writing the educational program that is planned for your son or daughter, including learning goals and the educational services that the school system is to provide.

Supporting and Empowering the Family

There are a number of vital factors within each family which will influence its ultimate well-being. One is the emotional and physical health of each parent individually. Because it is generally the parents who confront the issues associated with their child's disability (e.g., dealing with medical practitioners, caring for the child), while simultaneously trying to maintain the household (e.g., holding down jobs, shopping, cooking, cleaning up, taking care of other children), it is not surprising that many parents of children with disabilities report times of feeling overwhelmed. It is, thus, very important for you, as parents, to take some time to care for yourselves as individuals: getting enough sleep, eating regular meals, trying to exercise every day, even if it is just taking a short walk (Callahan, 1990). As one mother relates:

> I would sometimes retreat to my "tower" and pretend that I had no responsibilities other than to amuse myself with a good book or a soothing tape. The respite usually didn't last more than a half hour, and it was never enough, but it helped me break the "martyr" pattern of thinking I was required to live and breathe only for my children. In those brief moments of quiet reflection I could renew my sense of self and remember that I was important, too; that I was Kate, a person, with lots of abilities and interests that did not all coincide with my role as Mommy. I came to realize that a little selfishness is not a bad thing. If I could enjoy myself more, I could enjoy my children more. (McAnaney, 1992, p. 22)

This sentiment is echoed throughout most of the literature written by parents. As Rhonda Krahl remarks, "What your child needs most is a healthy, loving parent. You can give him that by taking care of yourself" (Krahl, 1989, p. 7).

Many families will be single-parent families, but for those who are not, the relationship between the parents is a factor that can influence the family's well-being. When the parents' relationship is a strong and supportive one, it enriches family life for all members. Conversely, when there are problems in the relationship, the tension affects the rest of the family as well. This is stating what most of us already know, as is saying that marriages undergo change with the birth of a child—any child. But when a child in the family has special needs, "the changes (in the marriage relationship) will be greater and more demanding." (Krahl, 1989, p. 11) For a number of reasons, parenting a special needs child can create stress and conflict between the parents. For one, fathers and mothers may react differently to the fact of the disability. Mothers typically respond more emotionally than fathers, who are apt to focus more on the future and the long-term concerns of the child (Lamb, 1976). At times, one parent may be actively experiencing grief and may feel alone if the other parent is unable to express his or her grief and sorrow (Featherstone, 1980). At other times, decisions must be made about the child's care, and parents may not agree. And when all is said and done, the sheer demands of parenting can leave each partner exhausted and drained. "With all the time you must spend with and for your child, it's easy to forget to take time for your mate...You can easily lose track of what your mate is thinking, feeling, or doing as you concentrate on keeping up with family routines." (Krahl, 1989, p. 12)

Much of the literature written by parents discusses ways for parents to protect their relationship. One point emerges again and again, and that is the importance of making time for each other: meeting for lunch, getting away for a few hours together, sharing an activity. "This isn't neglecting your responsibilities. If the relationship crumbles you will face even more duties. Taking time to preserve your relationship makes good, practical sense, even if something else has to suffer temporarily." (Krahl, 1989, p. 14) Talking to each other and really listening are also important—and conversations do not always have to revolve around the children in the family. Finding other topics to discuss can do much to revitalize parents and preserve intimacy between them. It is also important to recognize that there are times when one partner needs to have space. As Peggy Finston (1990) puts it, "We need to accept how our mate distracts himself or herself" (p. 58). Sharing the duties of providing care is also necessary, although couples report that they often have to work hard at communicating in order to achieve the "we-ness" that goes behind teamwork. Many parents have found it is necessary and helpful to seek joint counseling. Through this process, they grew to understand each other's needs and concerns more fully and found ways of discussing and resolving their differences.

The Child with Special Needs

Much of how you raise your child with a disability will depend on your family's personal beliefs about childrearing, your child's age, and the nature of his or her disability. An important point to remember is that most of the regular child-raising issues will apply—children with disabilities will go through the usual childhood stages. They may not go through stages at the same age, at the same rate, or use the same words as children without disabilities, but they are children and kids are kids.

We, as parents, may believe that all children should be treated the same, but in practice that is usually not the case. Why? Because anyone who has been around children, even infants, knows they have different personalities and react differently to similar situations. We encourage and coax the shy child and set limits for the rambunctious one. We tell the loud ones to be quiet and the quiet ones to speak up. We offer different activities to the child who loves to paint than to the one who wants to play ball. Children just are not the same—but they should have the same opportunities.

Among their opportunities should be the chance to assume increasingly greater degrees of responsibility and independence. There may be many ways in which your child can help himself or herself or other members of the family, including doing chores around the house. You will need to consider what these activities might be, given your son or daughter's disabilities and capabilities. As you expect and encourage your child to assume responsibility, his or her sense of pride and competence will also increase. As Ivonne Mosquera remarks:

> Even though I'm blind, even though it may take me a bit longer to do certain things, I can still do them...Once you accomplish a goal, you'll be the person who feels good about it. Whether or not other people congratulate you for it, you'll feel better, and you'll know that you did it because of you—because you never gave up. (Krementz, 1992, p. 37)

Conversely, to not expect or encourage your child to contribute to self-care or household matters may send the message that he or she is not capable of helping. Dependence is fostered instead, as Teresa discovered with her daughter Betsy. "First, they were little things like turning on the bath water. Then she wanted me to carry her instead of using crutches. She refused to even try using them. I couldn't make myself say no, yet I knew that somehow this was going too far. (Finston, 1990, p. 72)

301

Of course, the nature and severity of your child's disability may affect how much he or she is able to participate in household duties and so on. Peggy Finston (1990) remarks:

The issue, then, for each of us is what is a "realistic" amount of normality to expect from our child? If we expect too much, we run the risk of rejecting him as he is. If we expect too little, we will fail to encourage him to do the most he can with himself. There is no one answer for all of us, or even for all of us dealing with the same condition. The best we can do is to realize that this is an ongoing question that we need to consider. (p. 81)

Perhaps some of the most encouraging words for parents come from children who have disabilities, whose experiences and feelings are described in numerous books. One consistent idea they express is that when parents expect a child with a disability to develop his or her capabilities—whatever these may be—this empowers and strengthens the child. This sense of empowerment can be found, for example, in the dedication Tom Bradford wrote for his book about hearing loss; he dedicated the book to his mother "who never let me know that my hearing loss could have been a limitation" (Bradford, 1991, p. iii). Eli, a twelve-year-old whose stroke resulted in several physical disabilities, writes, "My friends and family helped me overcome my fears. They encouraged me to try everything, even if I was determined that I couldn't" (Krementz, 1992, p. 16). Fourteen-year-old Sarah says that, despite her artificial leg, "my parents sent me to a regular nursery school, to swimming lessons, and camp—everything other kids did...I think my family's encouragement has a lot to do with the fact that I have such a positive attitude. They never sat me in front of the TV or stopped me from doing anything I wanted to try. They gave me a normal childhood" (Krementz, 1992, p. 83). Robert, who has cerebral palsy, remembers that his mother said to him one day, "Robert, why don't we focus on what you can do instead of what you can't do?" This was, he believes, "my biggest turning point—I took off like a rocket!" (Kriegsman, Zaslow, & D'Zmura-Rechsteiner, 1992, pp. 43-44)

Grandparents

Grandparents are often greatly affected by the birth of a child with a disability; the pain they feel may be two-fold—pain for their grandchild and pain for you, their own child. It is important to remember that they will need support and information, too, and that "the way you relate to them can create the setting for how they will help or not help you, or how they will deal with the child." (Routburg, 1986, p. 32) Some grandparents may have difficulty accepting their grandchild's disability, which is as normal as the stage of denial parents themselves may have experienced. Others will be a great source of help and support, and their involvement can benefit the nuclear family. (Seligman & Darling, 1989)

Therefore, your parents and other members of the extended family need to be given opportunities to get to know your child as a person and not just a person with disabilities. (Routburg, 1986, p. 32) Allowing them to become involved with your child may also allow you some much-needed time away from the responsibilities associated with caring for a child with special needs.

The Parent/Professional Relationship

Parent Cory Moore, speaking directly to professionals, writes, "We need respect, we need to have our contribution valued. We need to participate, not merely be involved. It is, after all, the parent who knew the child first and who knows the child best. Our relationship with our sons and daughters is personal and spans a lifetime." (Moore, 1993, p. 49)

Recognizing the central role of the family in a child's life, many service systems now provide assistance to parents and other family members using what is known as family-centered support principles. (Shelton, Jeppson, & Johnson, 1989) Within this philosophy, the family's influence is recognized as primary, both because of its direct impact on the child's development and because the family serves as the link between the child and the outside world. Thus, you have the right to be fully informed and involved in decisions affecting your child and family.

Many of the books listed throughout this chapter offer insight into how you might work together with professionals for the benefit of your child and family. The best relationships are characterized by mutual respect, trust, and openness, where both you and the professional exchange information and ideas about the best care, medical intervention, or educational program for your child. Information also must be exchanged about the needs of your family and about ways to take advantage of helping patterns that already exist within the family. (Fewell & Vadasy, 1986) Both you and the professional need to speak clearly about issues and listen carefully. Indeed, both of you have important expertise to share.

You, for example, have intimate knowledge of your child with special needs; you live with and observe your son or daughter on a daily basis and can contribute invaluable information about his or her routine, development, history, strengths, weaknesses, and so on. To make an accurate diagnosis, determine appropriate therapy or other interventions, and understand both your child and the needs and resources of your family, the professional needs your perspective and unique insight.

The professional, too, has specialized knowledge to contribute—that of his or her discipline. Often you must rely upon the judgment of the professional in matters that are critical to the well-being of your child, a position that may make you feel on unequal and uncertain footing. How comfortable you feel with the professional, how well you feel that individual relates to your child, and how openly he or she responds to your concerns and input will, in many cases, determine whether you continue to work with the professional or decide to seek the services of another.

Thus, there should be a mutuality in the parent/professional relationship. Both parents and professionals need to trust and feel trusted, both need to admit when they do not know or are wrong, and both need to negotiate with each other. (Finston, 1990) Trust, respect, and open communication between parent and professional are, therefore, essential to building a good, working relationship. This can take time to develop and may require effort from both parties. To that end, many parent writers suggest:

- If you are looking for a specialist with whom you can work well, ask other parents of children with disabilities. Often, they can suggest the name of a good speech or physical therapist, doctor, dentist, surgeon, and so on.

- If you don't understand the terminology a professional uses, ask questions. Say, "What do you mean by that? We don't understand."

- If necessary, write down the professional's answers. This is particularly useful in medical situations when a medication or therapy is to be administered.

- Learn as much as you can about your child's disability. This will assist you with your child, and it can help you participate most fully in the team process.

- Prepare for visits to the doctor, therapist, or school by writing down a list of the questions or concerns you would like to discuss with the professional.

- Keep a notebook in which you write down information concerning your special needs child. This can include your child's medical history, test results, observations about behavior or symptoms that will help the professional do his or her job, and so on. (A loose-leaf notebook is easy to maintain and add information to.)

- If you don't agree with a professional's recommendations, say so. Be as specific as you can about why you don't agree.

- Do whatever informed "shopping around" and "doctor-hopping" is necessary to feel certain you have explored every possibility and potential. As Irving Dickman (1989) says, "Shop. Hop. Hope." (p. 100)

- Measure a professional's recommendations for home treatment programs or other interventions against your own schedule, finances, and other commitments. You may not be able to follow all advice or take on one more thing, feeling as Helen Featherstone (1980) did when she wrote, "What am I supposed to give up?...There is no time in my life that hasn't been spoken for, and for every fifteen-minute activity that has been added, one has to be taken away" (p. 78). Peggy Finston (1990) points out that "most professionals won't be familiar with the sum total of our obligations and will not take it upon themselves to give us permission to quit. This is up to us. It's in our power to make the decision." (p. 188)

In conclusion, it is important that the parent/professional relationship empower the parent to be a full participant in information-gathering, information-sharing, and in decision- making. However, it is ultimately up to you to decide what role(s) you want to take in this process and what role(s) you need help with. It is helpful to know that families do, indeed, choose different roles in relationship to professionals. Some parents want to allow professionals to make most decisions about their child, others want to serve as an informant to the professional, some want veto power, and some parents want a shared role in the intervention with their child. (McBride, Brotherson, Joanning, Whiddon, & Demmit, 1992)

You are also free to change your mind about the role or level of involvement you may want or be able to assume regarding your child's services. You may find that you choose different roles at different times for different purposes. Be as direct as possible about what you want or don't want to take on in this regard.

Addressing Financial Concerns

The expenses associated with raising children can stretch a family's resources. When a child has a disability, particularly one that involves high-priced medical care, a family can quickly become overwhelmed financially. While it is often difficult to resolve financial concerns completely, there are a number of things parents can do that may help. Charlotte Thompson recommends that, as soon as parents find out that their child has a disability, two actions should be taken immediately. These are:

- Start a program to organize and manage your new financial demands. "This not only means management of everyday money, but it also means keeping very careful track of your medical bills and payments" (Thompson, 1986, pp. 101-102). There are a number of money management guides available that explain how to do this.

- Seek information about any and all financial assistance programs. "If the state agency caring for handicapped children is contacted immediately, it may be able to assume financial responsibility for your child's care right from the start." (Thompson, 1986, p. 102)

Often, so much attention is focused on the provision of health care that doctors and other medical staff may not mention available sources of financial aid. Many states have passed legislation intended to help families of children with a disability address their financial concerns, but parents will need to be "well focused and persistent" to get the answers they need.

Many children with disabilities are eligible to receive Supplemental Security Income (SSI) benefits, based upon their disability. A Supreme Court decision (Sullivan v. Zebley) has created changes in the eligibility requirements for these benefits. Because of these changes, many more children are now eligible than in the past. Some children who formerly were denied benefits (i.e., after January 1, 1980) may even be eligible for back benefits. Therefore, it is a good idea for all families with a child who is blind or who has a disability to apply for SSI. If a child is found eligible for SSI, he or she is automatically eligible for Medicaid benefits, even if the family income is higher than what is traditionally required for Medicaid in that state. This is very important for children with disabilities who may have many medical needs. (Clark & Manes, 1992)

If your child qualifies for Medicaid, most early intervention services can be paid for by Medicaid. If your child qualifies for Medicaid, it is important to have him or her assessed by a provider qualified to perform the Early Periodic Screening, Diagnostic, and Treatment (EPSDT) program. If an EPSDT program determines that your child has a condition that requires treatment because of "medical necessity," then it can be paid for by Medicaid. Furthermore, each state has a "Child Find" system, which is responsible for locating and assessing children with disabilities. This is required to be free by Federal law. But sometimes, even though there is not supposed to be a waiting list, it can take a long time to get your child assessed. Therefore, it is important to know about what other resources can be used to get help for your child.

Private insurance benefits are one such resource. Usually, nursing, physical therapy, psychological services, and nutrition services can be reimbursed by private insurance. In some cases, occupational therapy and speech therapy are also reimbursable. Educational expenses related to a child's disability are only rarely covered by insurance. However, it is useful to keep track of educational expenses, because these are deductible on your Federal income tax returns.

Some additional resources to contact in your search for financial assistance include:

- Hospital social workers;
- Public health department;
- Public health nurses;
- Volunteer agencies;
- Disability organizations; and
- State government agencies (usually listed under "State Government" in the telephone book), particularly those departments that oversee programs for children with disabilities.

Because searching for assistance may involve a lot of telephone calls, it is a good idea to have paper and pen at hand to record the names and telephone numbers of all those you contact, as well as any referrals they give you. Whether or not you believe your income is too high for your family to quality for financial aid:

...the key is to keep trying—to get more information, to follow up leads, and to continue applying for various types of financial assistance. This may seem like an endless paperwork maze to you,

307

but with luck some of the paper at the end will be the green kind that can help you pay your child's medical bills. Keep at it. (Thompson, 1986, p. 103)

References

Ambler, L. (Ed.). (1988). Children with disabilities: Understanding sibling issues. NICHCY *News Digest,* Number 11, 1-12.

Behr, J. (1991). [Testimony on early intervention.] In U.S. Senate, Senate report to accompany S. 1106. Washington, DC: GPO.

Blacher, J. (1989). Sequential stages of parental adjustment to the birth of a child with handicaps: Fact or artifact? In B.E. Hanft (Ed.), *Family centered care.* Rockville, MD: American Occupational Therapy Association.

Bradford, T.H. (1991). *Say that again, please! Insights in dealing with hearing loss.* Dallax, TX: Author.

Callahan, C.R. (1990). Since Owen: *A parent-to-parent guide to care of the disabled child.* Baltimore, MD: John Hopkins University Press.

Cernoch, J. (1989). Respite care: A gift of time. NICHCY *News Digest,* Number 12, 1-12.

Clark, J., & Manes, J. (1992). The advocate's guide to SSI for children. Washington, DC: Mental Health Law Project. (A second edition of this guide, published in 1995, is now available. A third edition, incorporating further changes in welfare law, was released in 1997.)

Coleman, R. (1990, April). [Unpublished remarks]. Washington, DC: The George Washington University.

Dickson, I.R. (1989). The parent-professional partnership: A parent's perspective. In J.M. Levy, P.H. Levy, & B. Nivin (Eds.), *Strengthening families: New directions in providing services to people with developmental diabilities and their families.* New York: Young Adult Institute and Workshop, Inc.

Dickman, I.R. (1993). *One miracle at a time: Getting help for a child with a disability* (rev. ed.). New York: Simon & Schuster. (This book has gone out of print but may be available through your public or university library.)

Featherstone, H. (1980). *A difference in the family: Life with a disabled child*. New York: Basic Books.

Fewell, R.R., & Vadasy, P.F. (1986). *Families of handicapped children: Needs and supports across the life span*. Austin, TX: Pro-Ed. (This book has gone out of print but may be available through your public or university library.)

Finston, P. (1990). *Parenting plus: Raising children with special health needs*. New York: Dutton. (This book has gone out of print but may be available through your public or university library.)

Krahl, R. (1989). Rebuilding your dream: Family life with a disabled child. Iowa City, IA: University of Iowa.

Krementz, J. (1992). *How it feels to live with a physical disability*. New York: Simon & Schuster. (This book has gone out of print but may be available through your public or university library.)

Kriegsman, K.H., Zaslow, E.L., & D'Zmura-Rechsteiner, J. (1992). *Taking charge: Teenagers talk about life and physical disabilities*. Rockville, MD: Woodbine House.

Lamb, M.E. (1976). Fathers and child development: An integrative overview. In M.E. Lamb (Ed.), *The role of the father in child development*. New York: John Wiley and Sons. (This book has gone out of print but may be available through your public or university library.)

Levin, T. (1992). *Rainbow of hope: A guide for the special needs child*. North Miami Beach, FL: Starlight. (This book has gone out of print but may be available through your public or university library.)

Lobato, D.J. (1990). Brothers, sisters, and special needs. Baltimore, MD: Paul H. Brookes. Mahoney, G., O'Sullivan, P., & Robinson, C. (1992). The family environment of children with disabilities: Diverse but not so different. *Topics in Early Childhood Special Education*, 12(3), 386-402.

McAnaney, K.D. (1992). *I wish: Dreams and realities of parenting a special needs child*. Sacramento, CA: United Cerebral Palsy Associations, Inc.

McBride, S., Brotherson, M.J., Joanning, H., Whiddon, D., & Demmit, A. (1992). Implementation of family centered services:

Perceptions of professionals and families. Unpublished manuscript, Human Development and Family Studies, Iowa State University, Iowa.

McLaughlin, M.J. (1993). Promising practices and future directions for special education. NICHCY *News Digest*, 2(2), 1-24.

Moore, C. (1990). *A reader's guide for parents of children with mental, physical, or emotional disabilities (3rd ed.)*. Rockville, MD: Woodbine. (This book has gone out of print but may be available through your local library. A new version is scheduled for release mid-year 1997. See reference for Sweeney.)

Moore, C. (1993). Maximizing family participation in the team process. In L. Kupper (Ed.), *Second National Symposium on Effective Communication for Children and Youth with Severe Disabilities*: Topic papers, reader's guide, and videotape (pp. 43-54). McLean, VA: Interstate Research Associates.

Park, C. (1988). *The siege: The first eight years of an autistic child with an epilogue, fifteen years later*. Boston, MA: Little, Brown.

Peck, C.A., Odom, S.L., & Bricker, D.D. (1993). *Integrating young children with disabilities into community programs: Ecological perspectives on research and implementation*. Baltimore, MD: Paul H. Brookes.

Powell, T., & Gallagher, P.A. (1993). *Brothers and sisters: A special part of exceptional families (2nd ed)*. Baltimore, MD: Paul H. Brookes.

Ramirez, C. (1993, April 19). [Unpublished panelist remarks]. In A. Turnbull (Leader), Forum on future directions: Visions and strategies for family-researcher collaboration. Forum conducted at the annual meeting of the Council for Exceptional Children, San Antonio, TX.

Routburg, M. (1986). *On becoming a special parent: A mini-support group in a book*. Chicago, IL: Parent/Professional Publications. (This book has gone out of print but may be available through your public or university library.)

Seligman, M., & Darling, R.B. (1989). *Ordinary families, special children: A systems approach to childhood disability*. New York: Guilford Press. (A second edition of this book, published in 1992, is available.)

Shelton, T., Jeppson, E., & Johnson, B. (1989, June). Family centered care for children with special health needs. Washington, DC: *Association for the Care of Children's Health*. (A third edition of this book, published in 1994, is available.)

Sutton, B. (1982). A mother's view. Clinical proceedings. Children's Hospital National Medical Center. *The Child with Spina Bifida: II Psychological, Educational, and Family Concerns*, 38(4), 213. [As cited in Pueschel, S., Bernier, J., & Weidenman, L. (1988).

The special child: A sourcebook for parents and children with developmental disabilities (pp. 16-17). Baltimore, MD: Paul H. Brookes.] (This book has gone out of print but may be available through your public or university library.)

Thompson, C.E. (1986). *Raising a handicapped child: A helpful guide for parents of the physically disabled*. New York: Ballantine Books. (This book has gone out of print but may be available through your public or university library.)

Wandry, D., & Repetto, J. (1993, March). Transition services in the IEP. NICHCY Transition Summary, 1-28.

Wickler, L., Wasow, M., & Hatfield, E. (1981). Chronic sorrow revisited: Parent vs. professional depiction of the adjustment of parents of mentally retarded children. *American Journal of Orthopsychiatry*, 51, 63-70.

Chapter 21

Supporting the Family

What Is Family Support?

Family support refers to services provided to help families keep a member with a disability at home. The home is typically the best environment to grow up in, no matter what a child's disabilities, so family support is often defined as "whatever it takes" to prevent a person from being placed outside the natural home.

The delivery of support should be "family-centered." Services should allow families to make informed decisions, be sensitive to the needs of the entire family, and be flexible enough to satisfy the unique needs of different families (Bradley, 1990).

What Services May Be Provided as Family Support?

Examples of services usually considered family support include, but are not limited to:

- Respite care
- Special clothing
- Crisis intervention
- Cash subsidies
- Information/referral
- Vehicle modification

Reprinted with permission © 1992, "The Arc's Q&A on Family Support," The Arc.

313

- Family training
- Diagnosis and evaluation
- Home modifications
- Transportation
- Counseling
- Behavior intervention
- Medical/dental services
- Recreation

Respite care is the most available family support service, but when surveyed, families reported that their greatest need was financial assistance accompanied with an assortment of services geared toward their individual needs (US/GAO, 1990).

Why Is Family Support Needed?

Family support services can help eliminate some of the stress that families experience in trying to meet the unique needs of a family member with mental retardation. Providing supports for children with disabilities in their natural homes helps maintain their quality of life. It also may cost society less to let the family supply the residence and supports that are normally provided by a family.

How Were Family Support Programs Developed?

In the seventies, a movement toward deinstitutionalization began. People started to recognize that individuals with disabilities have contributions to make and that "warehousing" them in institutions was a waste of life. Parents of children with disabilities began to raise their children at home instead of placing them in institutions. With these changes, the need for family support programs increased.

Grassroots movements across the country made policy makers recognize the need for changes in public policies. Although these movements continue to play an important role, many states still have not developed adequate family support policies.

How Is Family Support Funded?

In most states the family support budget is only one percent or less of the total budget available for people with mental retardation and other developmental disabilities (Wieck, 1985). Examples of sources of funds are:

Community-based programs: Most communities have local sources of family support which may include:

- Schools
- Organizations such as local chapters of The Arc
- Specialized family service agencies
- University programs
- Programs sponsored by employers
- Churches

Families also should not overlook the "natural resources" of family, friends, and their community. Often, when families make their needs known, programs and services can be created in the community to help meet those needs.

State programs: The primary source of funding for family support programs is state dollars. A 1990 report indicates that all states but Oklahoma offered some type of state funded family support program (Bradley, 1990).

In another study, eleven state programs provided cash subsidies to families; 33 provided respite care services, and 30 provided other types of family support programs. California led the states in terms of numbers of persons served as well as total expenditures (Braddock, 1990).

Private insurance: Private health insurance covers the health needs of only a fraction of children with disabilities and is not considered a primary source of funding for family support services. Still, families who do have health insurance coverage should examine their policy for services that may be covered.

Government Entitlements: Many people are eligible for income and health benefits under the Social Security Administration. Some people with mental retardation can receive either Supplemental Security Income (SSI) or Social Security Disability Insurance (SSDI) income, or both. Medicaid and Medicare health benefits are often a part of SSI and SSDI assistance.

Eligibility for these programs is based on disability and family income. A person over 18 must be considered disabled to the point that the individual is unable to participate in "substantial gainful activity," as defined by the Social Security Administration. Children under 18 are evaluated by their responses in terms of age-appropriateness in areas such as stimuli, cognition, communication, motor skills, social interaction, and concentration.

While it is possible that these benefits can be lost if the individual with a disability goes to work, all or a portion of income and health benefits may be kept if proper planning is done. More information is available from the local Social Security office (Social Security Administration, June 1991).

How Do Families Obtain Support?

Entering the system can be complicated because family support services and eligibility standards vary from community to community. Locating and getting information about eligibility for services might be obtained by contacting the state's planning council on developmental disabilities, department of social services, or local community mental retardation agency. If one agency can't help, the family should ask for the name of an appropriate agency.

Individual service coordination (case management) services are very important, especially for those families or individuals with many needs. Because all needed services are not usually provided by one agency, having the help of a professional who knows how to access the system is vital.

What about Direct Cash Subsidies to Families?

Families have different needs, so direct cash subsidies can be a good option. This gives them more control over the service they receive. It is also better if eligibility is based on need and not income. Some of the criteria used to determine family support eligiblility in states reporting cash subsidy programs are:

- The family's income and size
- The family receives no other public assistance
- The family has a great need for resources
- The family has insufficient income to cover costs of care
- The person with a disability is at risk of out-of-home placement
- The person is returning to the family from an out-of-home placement

A disadvantage to making all family support into direct cash subsidies is that even though the dollars are available, service providers may not be available for people with more specialized needs. When needed services are not available, it may be more practical to fund private service providers to create the necessary support.

What about Family Support for Adults with Mental Retardation Living at Home?

Many questions surround the issue of family support when the person with mental retardation is an adult. For example, should family support be provided for adults as well as children? Is it appropriate for adults to live with their parents?

In the United States approximately 25 percent of adult children who are not disabled live at home. Adults living with their parents is common in many cultures throughout history. In fact, children leaving the home upon reaching adulthood is a relatively recent development in society. Therefore, having society supply some type of family support for adults with mental retardation who live with their parents can be a desirable alternative.

Where Can I Find Out More about Family Support?

The Arc
National Organization on Mental Retardation
1010 Wayne Ave, Suite 650
Silver Spring, MD 20910
Tel: 301-565-3842
Fax: 301-565-3843
E-mail: thearc@metronet.com
URL: http://www.thearc.org

The Arc maintains an updated library of family support materials and has current listings of national, state, and local resources.

Beach Center on Families and Disability
The University of Kansas
3111 Haworth Hall
Lawrence, KS 66045
Tel: 785-864-7600

Civitan International Research Center
University of Alabama at Birmingham
1719 6th Avenue, South
Birmingham, AL 35294
Tel: 205-934-8900

Human Services Research Institute
2336 Massachusetts Ave.
Cambridge, MA 02140
Tel: 617-876-0426

The Center on Human Policy
Syracuse University
805 S. Crouse
Syracuse, NY 13244
Tel: 315-443-3851

References

Bradley, V.J. et al. (1990). *Family Support Services in the United States: An End of Decade* Status Report. Boston, MA: Human Services Research Institute.

Braddock, D. et al. (1990). *The State of the States in Developmental Disabilities*. Baltimore, MD: Paul H. Brookes Publishing Co., Inc.

Respite Care: An Overview of Federal, Selected State, and Private Programs. Report number GAO/HRD-90-125, (1990). Washington, D.C.: United States General Accounting Office, (US/GAO).

Social Security Administration. (June 1991). *Red Book on Work Incentives*. Department of Health and Human Services.

Wieck, C. (1985). The development of family support programs. In: Agosta, J.M. & Bradley, V.J. (Eds.). Family care for persons with developmental disabilities: A growing commitment. Boston, MA: Human Services Research Institute.

—by Debby Storey

Debby Storey is a research associate with the Family Support Project, *"Strengthening American Families Through National and Grassroots Support."*

Chapter 22

Siblings

Developmental Considerations

What Do You Tell—

1. Preschoolers (before age 5)

   Children in this age group are unable to articulate their feelings about things, so they will likely show their feelings through behaviors. They will be unable to understand the special needs of their sibling, but they will notice differences and try to teach their brother or sister. Children of this age are likely to enjoy their sibling because they have not learned to be judgmental, and their feelings toward their siblings will likely be linked to "normal" sibling interactions.

2. Elementary School Age (6–12)

   These children start venturing out into the world and become acutely aware of the differences between people. They have the ability to understand a definition and explanation of their sibling's special need as long as it is explained to them in terms they can understand. They may worry that the disability is contagious or wonder if something is wrong with them, too. They may also experience guilt for having negative thoughts or feelings about their sibling as well as, guilt for being the child who is not disabled.

Reprinted with permission, "Sibling Needs—Helpful Information for Parents," by Derenda Timmons Schubert, Ph.D., © Center for the Study of Autism, and "The Arc's Q&A on Siblings," © 1993 The Arc, reprinted with permission.

Some typical responses of children this age are to become over-helpful and well-behaved or to become non-compliant in order to obtain a parent's attention. Throughout this age span, the children will have conflicting feelings about their sibling. This happens in sibling relationships that do not include a disability, too.

3. Adolescents (13–17)

Adolescents have the capability of understanding more elaborate explanations of the particular disability. They may ask detailed and provocative questions. The developmental task of adolescence is to begin discovering oneself outside of the family. At the same time, conformity with a peer group is important. Therefore, for children this age having a sibling who is different may be embarrassing in front of friends and dates. They may feel torn between their desire for independence from the family and maintaining a special relationship with their sibling. They may resent the amount of responsibility, and they may begin worrying about their sibling's future.

Educate Your Children

Provide Information to the Child about How the Condition Is Evaluated, Diagnosed, and Treated.

*   The children need to know what the disability is and what to expect
*   Explain strengths and weaknesses of the child with the disability
*   Explain ways to interact with sibling
*   Explain ways to help with sibling

Balance Time Spent with Children

*   Encourage child to have activities unique to him/her
*   Parental participation in activities outside the disability world/community
*   Parental recognition of child's strengths and accomplishments

Open Discussion

*   Open discussion in the family should exist where members' positive and negative feelings are expressed

- Discussion of ways to cope with stressful events such as peers and public reaction, as well as unexpected changes in family plans and extra home responsibility

Sibling Groups

- Participation in a group for siblings allows the children to meet others who are in the same circumstance

- Provides children with the chance to discuss feelings which may be difficult to express to the family

Warning Signs

Depression

- Change in child's sleeping habits
- Change in the child's eating habits
- Sense of helplessness/hopelessness
- Continued sense of irritability
- Mentions hurting self (i.e. "I wish I was dead")
- Difficulty making decisions or concentrating
- Lack of pleasure in activities
- Social Withdrawal
- Low self-esteem

Anxiety

- Excessive worry
- Increasesd energy level without a purpose
- Tearful at slightest frustration
- Has difficulty separating from parents
- Sleeping problems or change in sleeping habits
- Changes in eating habits
- School phobia
- Worry about health or well-being of family members
- Somatic symptoms (i.e. stomachaches and headaches) perfectionism

If your child displays a number of these symptoms for a prolonged period of time (2 weeks or more), it may be advisable to discuss the situation with the child's pediatrician or a local mental health professional.

Brothers and Sisters of People Who Have Mental Retardation

Is Having a Sibling with a Disability Different Than Having a Sibling Who Does Not Have a Disability?

Yes and no. The relationship between siblings can be a very important part of any person's life. Siblings often share the same family experiences and form a special relationship that can last throughout their lives.

Children who grow up together in the same family can form a unique bond, regardless of a brother or sister having a disability. In fact, the relationship between siblings and their brother or sister with a disability can be identical to the relationship between any brother or sister. They may be close and remain so into adulthood, or they may never develop a close relationship or grow apart as they get older. Family situations and circumstances, such as divorce or even cultural differences, can also affect the way a sibling relationship develops.

It's important to remember that a lot of factors affect how siblings relate to each other, and not just the fact that one of them has a disability. However, sometimes having a brother or sister with a disability in the family creates challenges that other families may not experience. Some of these challenges can directly affect the siblings.

What Are Some of the Concerns of Siblings of People with Disabilities?

In any family, good or unfavorable feelings may develop between siblings or because of siblings. This is true in both families with and without a family member with a disability. But many siblings who have a brother or sister with a disability have reported concerns surrounding having a brother or sister with a disability. Valdivieso, Ripley and Ambler (1988) discuss these concerns which include:

- Guilt about not having a disability, while the brother or sister does have one. Some siblings may even feel they are to blame for their brother's or sister's disability.

- Embarrassment of the sibling's behavior or appearance. The sibling who does not have a disability may avoid contact with the brother or sister, not invite friends to the home, etc.

- Fear that they might develop the disability. Children (and sometimes adults) think that disabilities such as mental retardation are contagious.

- Anger or jealousy over the amount of attention the brother or sister with a disability receives, especially if the child's disability requires additional care.

- Isolation or feeling like no one else has the same feelings or experiences about having a sibling with a disability.

- Pressure to achieve in order to "make up for" a brother or sister's inabilities. The sibling who does not have a disability may feel that excelling in school, sports, or other ways will compensate for the fact that a brother or sister with a disability is not able to do as well.

- Caregiving, especially if it conflicts with plans with friends or the responsibility becomes overly burdensome.

- Information needed about a brother or sister's disability. Siblings often are not given thorough information about why a sibling has a disability, how it affects him or her, and what the family can do to help this family member.

Many of these feelings affect children as they are growing up, but siblings often continue to have concerns even as adults. For example, siblings who do not have a disability may be concerned about the future of their sibling with a disability after the parents die, especially if this brother or sister still lives at home.

Are There Any Benefits to Being the Brother or Sister of a Person with a Disability?

Yes. Research on siblings indicates that there are positive aspects in being the sibling of a brother or sister with a disability. Researchers have found that children in families where a sibling has a disability can become more mature, responsible, self-confident, independent, and patient. These siblings can also become more altruistic (charitable), more sensitive to humanitarian efforts, and have a greater sense of closeness to family (Lobato, 1990; Powell, 1993).

Growing up with a sibling who has a disability may instill a greater level of understanding and development in the siblings who are not disabled. They may develop greater leadership skills, especially in areas where understanding and sensitivity to human awareness issues are important. Many leaders in The Arc and other contributors to the field of mental retardation, as well as other notable people, grew up in families with a brother or sister with a disability.

What Are Some Positive Actions Parents Can Take with Their Children When There Is a Sibling with a Disability?

Itzkowitz (1991) discusses some positive actions parents can take with their children, including:

* Treat the child who does not have a disability as a child, not just as another adult caretaker. Do not demand or expect a child to take on responsibilities for which he or she is unprepared.

* Remember that children have feelings too. Take time to ask them how they feel about having a sibling with a disability. Encourage them to express their feelings openly.

* Provide siblings with choices and include them in decision-making. Discuss family matters with your children, especially if it affects them personally. Ask for and value their opinions.

* Give them information about their brother or sister's disability. Answer their questions and respond to their concerns in a simple but precise manner.

How Does Family Structure Affect Siblings?

Some studies have looked at gender and birth order to see if either one has an affect. In most situations, these factors may make only a slight difference, except in the case of increased caregiving responsibility. Research has shown that older daughters who do not have a disability are typically expected to provide more caregiving to a brother or sister with a disability. (Lobato, 1990).

What Is Being Done to Address Concerns That Siblings May Have about Having a Brother or Sister with a Disability?

Many chapters of The Arc and other organizations are focusing services and sibling support groups aimed at meeting the needs and concerns of young children, teen-agers, and adult siblings of people with disabilities. Sibling groups provide a forum where siblings can discuss their experiences, share ideas, and give each other support. Other sibling services include seminars and meetings that address topics of interest to siblings such as futures planning (guardianship, alternative living arrangements, etc.). Programs which provide family supports, such as respite care, are also including the siblings in the planning process or by providing services in integrated settings where all siblings can participate.

For Further Information

The Arc
National Organization on Mental Retardation
1010 Wayne Ave, Suite 650
Silver Spring, MD 20910
Tel: 301-565-3842
Fax: 301-565-3843
E-mail: thearc@metronet.com
URL: http://www.thearc.org

Sibling Support Project
Children's Hospital and Medical Center
4800 Sand Point Way NE
Seattle, WA 98105
Tel: 206-368-4911

Sibling Information Network
The A.J. Pappanikou Center
University of Connecticut
249 Glenbrook Road, U64
Storrs, CT 06269-2064
Tel: 860-486-5035

References

Author, *Family Support Bulletin.* "Tips for Dealing with 'Siblings' of Persons with Disabilities." Spring/Summer 1988. Washington, D.C.: United Cerebral Palsy Associations.

Itzkowitz, J., *Springboard.* "Fostering Supportive Relationships: Remember the Siblings." Vol. 1, No. 2, Fall 1991. Minneapolis: The Center for Children with Chronic Illness and Disability.

Lobato, D.J. (1990). *"Brothers, Sisters, and Special Needs: Information and Activities for Helping Young Siblings of Children with Chronic Illnesses and Developmental Disabilities."* Baltimore: Paul H. Brookes Publishing Co., Inc.

Powell, T.H. & Gallagher, P.A. (1993). *"Brothers and Sisters: A Special Part of Exceptional Families."* Baltimore: Paul H. Brookes Publishing Co., Inc.

Valdivieso, C., Ripley, S., & Ambler L., NICHCY *News Digest.* "Children with Disabilities: Understanding Sibling Issues." Number 11, 1988. Washington, D.C.: Interstate Research Associates.

Special thanks to Donald J. Meyer, Director of the Sibling Support Project, Children's Hospital and Medical Center, Seattle, Washington, for his assistance in preparing of this information.

Chapter 23

Friendships between People With and Without Mental Retardation

Why Are Friendships between People With and Without Disabilities Important?

Friends are important for several reasons. They support each other emotionally, are willing to see things from the other's point of view, and provide assistance and feedback when needed. Friends choose each other and remain close through good times and times of crisis. They provide companionship for community and school activities and help each other enjoy new experiences and appreciate life more fully. Friendships between people with and without disabilities usually enrich the lives of both.

When Should Friendships Begin?

If people with mental retardation are to form friendships and be a part of society as adults, these relationships must develop during childhood. Classmates and neighbors will grow into adult coworkers and friends later in life.

Therefore, integrated classrooms and recreational activities are important. In these settings children with and without disabilities get to meet each other and form relationships. Unfortunately, many parents have found that even though their children are integrated in school, they have few nondisabled friends.

Reprinted with permission © 1997, "The Arc's Q&A on Friendships," The Arc.

What Makes the Development of Relationships Difficult?

Many individuals with disabilities interact primarily with their family, the people who take care of or provide services to them, and others in the programs in which they participate. These relationships can clearly be significant and should be encouraged. However, outside of family members, people may have no freely given and chosen relationships. Generally, many people with disabilities face certain disadvantages in meeting and getting to know others.

Opportunity. Many people with disabilities have limited opportunities to take part in activities where they can meet peers. This may be due to physical segregation or being placed in a role as "client" or "special education student." Services may restrict people's chances to get together, through program or funding rules, curfews, transportation restrictions, and other limitations. Whatever the reason, people with disabilities frequently become cut off and isolated from others.

Support. Relationships between people with and without disabilities are not formed by simply grouping people together. Some individuals need assistance with fitting into certain settings and activities. Others may need someone to facilitate their involvement or to interpret for them. Without supports, some people with and without disabilities may never have the opportunity to know each other.

Continuity. While most people enjoy meeting new people, they are sustained by those they have known over time. The continuity of relationships over the years is an important source of security, comfort, and self-worth. Many people with disabilities do not have continuous relationships. Instead, they may leave their families, be moved from one program to another and have to adjust to staff people who come and go.

What Are Some of the Ways to Facilitate Personal Relationships between People With and Without Disabilities?

It takes effort to help people establish connections. Described below are some of the ways this has been tried:

"Bridge-Building." Facilitators who initiate, support, and maintain new relationships are called bridge-builders, as they "...build bridges and guide people into new relationships, new places, and new opportunities in life" (Mount, et al., 1988). Bridge-builders involve people with disabilities in existing groups or with specific individuals.

Circles of Friends or Circles of Support. Groups of people who "meet on a regular basis to help a person with a disability accomplish certain personal visions or goals" (Perske, 1988). Circle members try to open doors to new opportunities, including establishing new relationships.

Citizen Advocacy. Recruited and supported by an independent citizen advocacy office, a citizen advocate voluntarily represents the interests of a person with a disability as if the interests were the advocate's own. Citizen advocates may take on one or several roles (e.g., friend, ally, mentor, protector), and some of these may last for life.

There are different ways that personal relationships between people with and without disabilities may be encouraged. Perhaps more important than the specific method is the supporting, connecting role of one or more people (family members, staff members, friends, neighbors, etc.) who can spend time and energy for this purpose.

What Are Some Important Dimensions of Friendship?

Genuine friendships between people with and without disabilities do exist. While each friendship is unique, there are some shared ideas and expectations about what friendship means. According to a recent study of pairs of friends (Lutfiyya, 1990), these meanings include:

Mutuality. The people defined their relationship as a friendship and themselves as friends. Although they acknowledge differences between themselves, they clearly found a sense of mutuality in the friendship. Mutuality was expressed in the giving and receiving of practical assistance and emotional support, and enjoyment of each other's company.

Rights, Responsibilities, and Obligations. Once a friendship is established, it is assumed that friends can make certain demands of each other and be assured of a response. Nondisabled friends talked about the obligations that they had assumed for their friend with a disability, such as teacher, mentor, caretaker, or protector. The friends with disabilities assumed certain responsibilities in maintaining the relationship such as keeping in touch or suggesting possible activities.

Feelings, from Companionship to Intimacy. All of the friends held feelings of affection for each other, expressed through their interactions with each other.

Freely Chosen and Given. Friends choose each other. It is this voluntary aspect of friendship that is regarded as the "amazing and wonderful" part of the relationship.

Private and Exclusive Nature. Within the boundaries of each friendship is a private relationship that is inaccessible to others. The friends have a history and an understanding of their connection to each other that separates this from all of their other relationships.

What Can Families and Service Providers Do to Enhance Opportunities for Friendships?

People can establish friendships with each other, but it is not possible to force friendships upon others. It is possible to create opportunities for people with and without disabilities to meet and share time with each other in ways that encourage friendships to take root and flourish. Families and service providers can do different things to make such opportunities available.

Families Can:

Work for the total inclusion of their son or daughter into the regular school system. In addition to being physically present, students with disabilities need adequate supports to enable them to fully participate in classroom and school activities. Parents can also ensure that their child with a disability takes part in a variety of integrated recreation and leisure activities after school hours. A consistent physical presence in each others' lives helps lead to friendships between children with and without disabilities.

Ensure social participation. How people with disabilities are supported within integrated settings is important. Students need to be enabled to participate as much as possible, and to do so in ways acceptable to other people. People without disabilities need the opportunity to meet their counterparts with disabilities as peers, not as objects of tutoring or volunteer service.

Involve and trust others. All parents feel protective toward their children. While there may be differences in how independent people

330

can become, parents can come to believe that there are people in the community who would, if given the opportunity, enjoy and welcome a friendship with their son or daughter.

Service Providers Can

Reduce barriers to friendship. The way in which support services are provided to people with disabilities and their families can enhance or reduce the opportunities for friendships to develop. Segregated programs dramatically lessen the chances for contact between people with and without disabilities.

Even in integrated settings, students with disabilities may not be able to take part in extracurricular activities (e.g., choir, clubs, sports) because of lack of transportation from school. When efforts are made to bring people with and without disabilities together, the people without disabilities are often treated as volunteers responsible to the teacher or program coordinator rather than as peers.

Encourage people who seem to like one another to pursue friendships. Service providers can review practices, such as curfews, lack of privacy and so on, which limit opportunities for people to meet and form friendships with each other.

With an awareness of and commitment to facilitating friendships between people with and without disabilities, all people can have the opportunity to form relationships which allow them to live life more fully.

Additional Information

Amado, A.N. (Ed.) (1993). *Friendships and community connections between people with and without developmental disabilities*. Baltimore: Paul H. Brookes Publishing Co.

Heyne, L.A., Schleien, S.J. & McAvoy, L.H. (n.d.). *Making friends: Using recreation activities to promote friendship between children with and without disabilities*. Minneapolis: College of Education, University of Minnesota.

Human Services Research and Development Center (1989-90). *Friends: A manual for connecting persons with disabilities and community members*. Minneapolis: Human Services Research and Development Center and the Governor's Planning Council on Developmental Disabilities.

Lutfiyya, Z.M. (1990). *Affectionate bonds: What we can learn by listening to friends*. Syracuse, NY: Center on Human Policy.

Lutfiyya, Z.M. (1991). *Personal relationships and social networks: Facilitating the participation of individuals with disabilities in community life*. Syracuse, NY: Center on Human Policy.

Mount, B., Beeman, P., and Ducharme, G. (1988). *What are we learning about circles of support?* Manchester, CT: Communitas, Inc.

Mount, B., Beeman, P., and Ducharme, G. (1988). *What are we learning about bridge-building?* Manchester, CT: Communitas, Inc.

O'Brien, J., & Lyle O'Brien, C. (1993). Unlikely alliances: Friendships and people with developmental disabilities. In A.N. Amado (Ed.). *Friendships and community connections between people with and without disabilities* (pp. 9-40). Baltimore: Paul H. Brookes Publishing Co.

O'Connell, M. (1988). *The gift of hospitality: Opening the doors of community life to people with disabilities*. Evanston, IL: Community Life Project.

Perske, R. (1988). *Circles of friends*. Nashville, TN: Abingdon Press.

Wolfensberger, W. (1975). Citizen advocacy for the impaired. In D. A. Primrose (Ed.), Proceedings of the Third Congress of the International Association for the Scientific Study of Mental Deficiency (pp. 14-19). Lorbert, Scotland: IASSMD, Royal Scottish National Hospital.

The Arc
National Organization on Mental Retardation
1010 Wayne Ave, Suite 650
Silver Spring, MD 20910
Tel: 301-565-3842
Fax: 301-565-3843
E-mail: thearc@metronet.com
URL: http://www.thearc.org

—Zana Marie Lutfiyya, Center on Human Policy

Chapter 24

Respite Care

What Is Respite?

"Respite" refers to short term, temporary care provided to people with disabilities in order that their families can take a break from the daily routine of caregiving. Unlike childcare, respite services may sometimes involve overnight care for an extended period of time.

One of the important purposes of respite is to give family members time and temporarily relieve the stress they may experience while providing extra care for a son or daughter with mental retardation or other disability. This, in turn, can help prevent abuse and neglect, and support family unity (US/GAO, September 1990). Respite care enables families to take vacations, or just a few hours of time off. Respite is often referred to as a gift of time.

Who Needs Respite Services?

Parents may be reluctant to use a respite program. They may even question the need for this type of service. Valdivieso (1989) recommends families of children with mental retardation and other disabilities ask themselves these questions to determine if respite services are necessary:

- Is it difficult to find temporary care for my child?

- Does caring for my child interfere with scheduling appointments or with personal projects?

Reprinted with permission, © The Arc.

- Is it important that my spouse and I enjoy an evening alone together, without the children?

- If I had appropriate care for my child with a disability, would I use the time for a special activity with my other children?

- Am I concerned that in the event of a family emergency there is no one with whom I would feel secure with to leave my child?

- Would I feel comfortable having a trained, caring respite provider care for my child?

- Do I avoid going out because I feel I would be imposing on the family and friends who care for my child?

If family members answer "yes" to any of these questions, the family may very well benefit from respite care services.

Who Provides Respite Services?

Most programs are managed by affiliates or chapters of national organizations such as The Arc, Easter Seal Society, and United Cerebral Palsy Associations in cooperation with local hotels (US/GAO). Many other programs are provided by local organizations such as churches, schools, and other non-profit groups. Sometimes families arrange for care with neighbors or other people they know.

What Kinds of Services Are Provided?

Services are provided in many ways depending on the provider, the needs of the family, and available funds. Some respite programs send a caregiver to the family's home. Others require that the individual come to a day care center or respite group home.

In some programs the care is provided by a host family which also has a family member with a disability. They usually provide respite services in exchange for the same services from another family. These programs are called "host family" or exchange programs.

Emergency respite services are also important. Parents need to be able to access services on short notice in the event that an unexpected family emergency occurs.

How Are Respite Services Funded?

Many programs receive public funding for their services. Some charge fees on a sliding scale based on the family's income. Other programs may be operated by non-profit organizations which receive funding from donations or other sources. Many programs must use a combination of funding sources in order to meet their financial needs.

Are There Eligibility Requirements for Respite Services?

In almost all state-funded programs, eligibility is based on the child's age and disabilities. Family income is also usually considered. In a 1990 survey of 111 respite care programs, 97 programs provided services for children as young as newborns. 71 programs provided services until age 22, 11 programs provided services only for young children and 29 programs provided care throughout the child's life (US/GAO).

How Do Families Benefit from Respite Services?

The benefits are numerous, but not always obvious. Providing a break in the daily routine may help parents avoid burnout, stress, and fatigue. Periodic respite care can help parents relax for a while and come back revitalized and better able to care for their son or daughter.

Respite care not only provides caregivers a break, but also gives the child a change in his or her daily routine. It can provide the child opportunities to build new relationships and move toward independence (Valdivieso, 1989).

How Do Families Obtain Services?

Accessing the system can be difficult, but not impossible. Contact your state's planning council on developmental disabilities, community mental health/mental retardation center, or a local chapter of The Arc and ask them to refer you to a program. Many programs have been developed when families made their needs known to community mental retardation advocates and service providers.

Many respite programs have been developed by parents to fulfill their own needs. For example, Jody and His Friends, Inc. is a respite program started in California by a couple who were unable to find respite services. These parents joined with the Vallejo-Benica chapter of The Arc and developed an in-home respite program. Jody and His Friends, Inc. was such a success that it is now an agency of the

State of California Department of Developmental Services (Valdevieso, 1989).

What Can I Do to Get a Respite Program Started in my Community?

A good way to get started is to first determine what kinds of services are needed.

- Ask other parents in the community about their needs for respite services: Do they need or want in-home care, or could care be provided at a community center? Determine if overnight or weekend care is needed.

- Find a respite provider in another community that already provides these types of services and ask them how they started their program.

- Contact state licensing agencies to find out licensing requirements for operating a respite program.

- Find an organization in your community that might be interested in helping you start a program. Churches, schools, local Red Cross chapters, and disability organizations may provide the personnel, experience, and/or financial resources necessary to start or operate a new program.

Are Respite Care Providers Required to Be Licensed?

Of the 111 programs surveyed, 91 had eligibility or licensing requirements that addressed the areas of age, training, education, and licensing or certification by a profession or specialty. To ensure that quality services are being provided, 91 programs were required to 1) maintain records of services, 2) provide follow-up to families that have been served, and 3) pass site inspections where services are provided (US/GAO).

Parents should make the final determination about respite providers. They should examine various aspects of the program such as staff training, monitoring by outside agencies, safety and health measures, parental involvement in decision-making, and other related areas. The state or local licensing office should be able to answer questions about complaints against a specific program and whether that program has consistently met all licensing requirements.

Some questions to ask about a respite care program are:

- How are care providers screened?

- What is the training and level of experience of the care providers?

- Will care providers need additional training to meet specific family needs?

- How, and by whom, are the care providers supervised?

- What happens during the time the children are receiving services? Are there organized activities? How are meals handled?

- Does the program maintain current information about each child's medical and other needs? Is there a written care plan?

- What procedures does the program have for emergencies?

- Can parents meet and interview the people who care for the children?

- How far ahead of time do parents need to call to arrange for services?

- Are families limited to a certain number of hours of services?

- Does the program provide transportation?

- Can the provider take care of brothers and sisters as well?

- What is the cost of services? How is payment arranged? (Karp, undated).

Can I Use a Regular Child Care Program for Respite?

Many day care centers in the community offer "drop in" services for a day or sometimes for an extended period. To use drop in services, parents must often give some advance notice and complete the required paperwork, such as the child's medical history and emergency contact persons.

With the passage of the Americans with Disabilities Act (ADA), these programs must now make every reasonable attempt to provide the same services for a child with a disability. The ADA mandates that public accommodations, including child care centers, make reasonable modifications in policies, practices and procedures in order to accommodate individuals with disabilities. However, child care centers and other entities covered under the ADA are not required to modify their policies and practices if it would "fundamentally alter" the nature of their services.

If a child care center restricts its services to minor children, parents who have an adult child with mental retardation may have to consider other respite options. In addition, centers may not have to provide certain services, for example, those involving skilled medical procedures or on site nursing, because the provision of these services could be considered a "fundamental alteration" or a service outside a child care centers' area of specialization (DOJ, July 1991).

Additional Information

The Arc
National Organization on Mental Retardation
1010 Wayne Ave, Suite 650
Silver Spring, MD 20910
Tel: 301-565-3842
Fax: 301-565-3843
E-mail: thearc@metronet.com
URL: http://www.thearc.org

Texas Respite Resource Network
P.O. Box 7330, Station A
San Antonio, TX 78207-3198
Tel: 512-228-2794

Maine Respite Project
159 Hogan Road
Bangor, ME 04401
Tel: 207-941-4400

Georgia Respite Network
878 Peachtree St., NE
Room 620
Atlanta, Georgia
Tel: 404-894-5700

References

Federal Register: 28 CFR Part 35, "Nondiscrimination on the Basis of Disability in State and Local Government Services, Final Rule. Number 1512-91.", (July, 1991). Washington, D.C.: Department of Justice, Office of the Attorney General, (DOJ).

Karp, Naomi, et al., "Respite Care: A Guide for Parents" (undated). Washington, D.C.: CSR, Incorporated and Association for the Care of Children's Health.

Respite Care: An Overview of Federal, Selected State and Private Programs. *Report number GAO/HRD-90-125*, (September, 1990). Washington, D.C.: United States General Accounting Office, (US/GAO).

Valdivieso, Carol, et al., NICHY *News Digest*, "Respite Care: A Gift of Time", Number 12, 1989. Washington, D.C.: Interstate Research Associates.

—Debby Ingram

Debby Ingram is a research associate with the Family Support Project, "Strengthening American Families Through National and Grassroots Support".

Chapter 25

Decision Making

Contents

Section 25.1

Person and Family Centered Planning

Person-Centered Planning (PCP)

This phrase refers to an entire family of approaches to organizing and guiding individual and community change in collaboration with individuals with disabilities, their families, and their friends. PCP requires important investments in order to build both personal and community support.

Some of the Approaches That Use Person-Centered Planning

- Whole Life Planning;
- Personal Futures Planning;
- Making Action Plans (MAPS);
- Planning Alternative Tomorrows with Hope (PATH); and
- Essential Lifestyles Planning.

Key Characteristics of Person-Centered Planning

1. The person who is at the focus of the planning, and those who love the person, are the primary authorities on the person's life direction.

2. The primary purpose of PCP is to learn through shared action (i.e., the process is more than producing paperwork, it is about taking action to reach goals) and reflection/evaluation of that action.

3. PCP aims to change common patterns of community life (e.g., segregation and congregation of people with disabilities,

devaluing stereotypes, inappropriately low expectations, denial of opportunity).

4. PCP requires collaborative action and fundamentally challenges practices that separate people and perpetuate controlling relationships.

5. Respect for the dignity and completeness of the focus person.

6. PCP calls for sustained search for the effective ways to deal with difficult barriers and conflicting demands.

7. Promotes and values accurate individual services and supports, and clarifies individual interests and needs.

8. Shaping services to support a person's vision of a valued lifestyle.

9. Facilitates change in services to be more responsive to, the interests of people.

10. Search for capacities.

11. Organize efforts in the community to include the person, family, and direct support professionals.

12. Focus on quality of life and emphasize dreams, desired outcomes, and meaningful experiences.

Family-Centered Planning (FCP)

This phrase refers to principles which if followed lead to partnership and collaboration between parents and professionals to ensure the best possible supports and services for a child with a disability and for the child's entire family.

Key Characteristics of Family-Centered Planning

1. Incorporate into policy and practice the recognition that the family is the constant in a child's life, while the service system and support persons fluctuate.

2. Strive for family and professional collaboration in all settings (home, community, hospital, school), especially in the areas of care giving, program development, program implementation,

program evaluation, program evolution, and policy formulation.

3. Exchange complete and unbiased information between families and professionals in supportive manner at all times.

4. Incorporate into policy and practice the recognition and honoring of cultural diversity, strengths, and individuality within and across all families: including, ethnic, racial, spiritual, social, economic, educational, and geographic diversity.

5. Recognize and respect different methods of coping.

6. Implement comprehensive policies and programs that provide developmental, educational, emotional, environmental, and financial supports that meet the diverse needs of families.

7. Encourage family-to-family support and networking.

8. Ensure that all service and support systems for children with disabilities and their families are flexible, accessible, and comprehensive in responding to diverse family identified needs.

9. Appreciate families as families and children as children, recognizing that they possess a wide range of strengths, concerns, emotions, and aspirations beyond their need for specialized services and supports.

Limitations of Person and Family-Centered Planning

- Belief that only certain families or individuals can use or will benefit from PCP/FCP,

- Lack of training in understanding and honoring cultural diversity,

- Tendency for professionals to be seen in the role of expert,

- Lack of open and effective communication,

- Traditional model of service delivery is entrenched,

- Moves slowly if the focus person's vision is not clear,

- Requires a lot of learning to develop the supports and create the opportunities the person needs,

- Family members and professionals can define people in clinical terms,
- Often done in isolation from other complementary systems change efforts,
- Requires a large expenditure of time, and
- Not a quick fix or a cure all for people's difficulties.

References

1. Mount. B. (1992). *Person centered planning finding directions for change using personal futures planning.* New York, NY: Graphic Futures.

2. Mount, B. (1992). *Personal futures planning: promises and precautions.* New York, NY: Graphic Futures.

3. Mount, B., Darcharme, G., & Beeman, P. (1991). *Person centered development: A journey learning to listen to people with disabilities.* New York, NY: Graphic Futures.

4. O'Brien, J., & Lovett, H. (1992). *Finding a way toward everyday lives: The contribution of person centered planning.* Harrisburg, PA: Pennsylvania Office of Mental Retardation.

5. Shelton, T.L., &; Stepanek, J.S. (1994). *Family centered care for children needing specialized health and developmental services.* Bethesda, MD: Association for the Care of Children's Health.

6. Smull, M. (1991). *Supporting people with severe reputations in the community: A handbook for trainers.* Baltimore, MD: University of Maryland.

Resources

1. Virginia Institute for Developmental Disabilities, Virginia Commonwealth University, 301 West Franklin Street, #1514, P.O. Box 843020, Richmond, VA, 23284-3020. Point of contact: Anne Malatchi, (804) 828-8593, (804) 828-0042.

2. Inclusion Press, 24 Thome Cresant, Toronto, Ontario, Canada, M6H 2S5, 416-658-5363 (T& F). Points of contact: Jack

Pearpoint & Dr. Marsha Forest, creators of PATH and MAPS. Inclusion Press publishes a great deal of material on PATH, MAPS, and Circles of Friends.

3. Dr. Beth Mount, Graphic Futures Inc., 25 West 81st Street, 16-B, New York, NY 10024, (212) 362-9492.

4. Rehabilitation Research and Training Center on Supported Employment, Virginia Commonwealth University, 1314 West Main Street, Richmond, VA, 23220. (804) 828-1851. Fax: (804) 828-2193.

5. Communitas, Inc., P.O. Box 374, Manchester, CT, 06040. (202) 645-6976.

6. Alicia A. Cone, VCU-RRTC on Supported Employment, 1314 West Main Street, Richmond, VA, 23220. (804) 828-1851. Fax: (804) 828-2193.

—Alicia A. Cone

Section 25.2

Self Advocacy

This section is reprinted with the permission of the American Association on Mental Retardation including text from the following articles: "Self Advocacy Movement" by Esther Lee Pederson and Tia Nelis, © 1999; "FAQ about Self Advocacy, Leadership & People with Developmental Disabilities" by Esther Lee Pederson and Tia Nelis, © 1999; and "Self Advocacy and People with Mental Retardation" by Mitchell Levitz, © 1999.

Never doubt that a small group of thoughtful, committed citizens can change the world; indeed, it's the only thing that ever does.

Margaret Mead

"Self-advocacy means that individually or in groups (preferably both), people with mental retardation speak or act on behalf of themselves or others on behalf of issues that affect people with disabilities." (Adapted from Williams & Shoultz, 1982). It is frequently referred to as people with disabilities joining together to learn how to speak out for themselves.

In What Ways Is Self-Advocacy a Movement?

When we speak of "the civil rights movement," "the parents movement," or the "independent living movement," we are referring to something like a crusade, powered by people who have been directly affected by unfair attitudes and practices, which has fostered change in our society. Similarly, the self-advocacy movement has redefined the "disability problem" as being less about rehabilitation and more about equality. People involved in the movement are very clear about not wanting to be called retarded, handicapped, disabled, or to be treated like children. They are clear that self-advocacy represents "rights" not "dependence"—the right to speak out, the right to be a person with dignity, the right to make decisions for themselves and others.

History of the Self-Advocacy Movement

The self-advocacy movement probably began in Sweden during the 1960's. There, people with mental retardation were supported to form and lead their own leisure clubs. National conferences for the members of these clubs were held in 1968 and 1970, and the participants developed statements about how they wanted to be treated.

In 1972, the idea spread to Great Britain and Canada, and in 1973 a group from Oregon attended a conference in Canada that was intended to be for people with mental retardation. However, this group was unhappy with the Canadian conference, which they felt was dominated by professionals, and went home and formed a self-advocacy group. They called themselves "People First." The name "People First" was chosen to reflect members' dislike of being called "retarded." They felt that their disabilities were secondary to their personhood.

Along the way, they have held international, national, and statewide conferences and have formed their own national organization, Self-Advocates Becoming Empowered, which is governed by a board made up of 18 representatives from across the United States. It was formed in September 1991 at a national conference in Nashville, TN, where participants voted to have a national coalition of state and local organizations. In 1993, there were at least 37 statewide self-advocacy organizations, some having as many as 75 local chapters and some with as few as two or three. Because the movement is growing so rapidly it is difficult to get accurate numbers of groups. Many of these are supported by local or state chapters of The Arc. Many others are independent or are supported by other organizations that provide assistance to the group members.

Importance of Self-Advocacy Groups

Self-advocacy has brought out wisdom and qualities of leadership from some unexpected sources. Membership is not contingent upon any skills but simply on the desire and willingness of individuals to speak out with and for oneself and/or others. Within the group, members can learn about their rights and responsibilities, develop confidence about their abilities, practice the skills of speaking in public and studying an issue, learn about voting and group decision-making, exercise problem-solving techniques, and develop assertiveness skills. They can also give and receive personal support from people who have had experiences like their own. Even group members who do not communicate verbally can and do participate in the group and learn ways of advocating for themselves and others.

Just as parents' groups gave parents the opportunities and skills they needed to make effective changes on behalf of their family members with disabilities, so too do self-advocacy groups give people with mental retardation these opportunities. Involvement in a self-advocacy group is, for many people, the best way of participating in the self-advocacy movement.

Some of the Barriers That Self-Advocates Face

Progress has been made by people with mental retardation in letting others know what they can do and what their vision for the future holds. The challenge that self-advocates struggle with is the low expectations of professionals, parents, and the public of their abilities. Mostly, people with mental retardation continue to have limited access to policy makers at local, state, national, and international levels and to be excluded from collaborative efforts of disability related organizations that make public policy that directly affects their lives.

Self-Advocacy Is Important for Mentally Retarded People

Decisions are being made that directly affect our lives and we want to tell you what self-advocacy means to all of us. We are registered voters from across the country and we make our own choices and decisions. If you remember back in the 1970's, most of our decisions were made for us. Even doctors told our parents that we would not live a normal life, and we would not be able to read or write and that we should be sent away to institutions.

We, as self-advocates, believe that we should be treated with dignity and respect. It is important for us to have the same opportunities as any other person. We feel that we should be given chances to take risks because we know what is important to us. That is why the Americans with Disabilities Act (ADA) became a law. The ADA helps us by letting people around the country become more aware of supports we might need to live in our communities and to have access to all places in this country.

Who Is a Self-Advocate?

It is a person who speaks out for him or herself.

Who Is an Advocate?

An advocate is someone who speaks for others or helps others speak for themselves. Advocates are different than self-advocates because self-advocates speak for themselves.

What Is Self-Advocacy?

Advocacy gives a person with a disability a chance speak up for themselves and others. By letting individuals tell others how they feel about issues that affect their lives, they can educate the public about persons with disabilities and how they can be included in all aspects of community life.

How Can We Teach Self-Advocacy?

- By joining a self-advocacy support group, e.g. People First
- Through education by taking courses in school
- By being involved in a training session

- By writing for the different national newsletters
- By using new technology like the Internet

Some Issues That Self-Advocates Feel Are Important to Them

- **SSI:** With help from SSI we have been able to live our lives with our families, in our communities, and become independent. Placing people in institutions costs more money than just helping us through SSI.

- **Families:** Listen to families.

- **Budget:** Be cost effective. Help us to help ourselves. Continue to fund programs that have made us more independent, productive, and part of our communities.

- **Education:** Keep inclusive education. We have the right to go to school with everyone else.

- **Health Insurance:** Do not let insurance companies discriminate against us. It is not fair that these companies refuse to allow us to have health insurance.

- **Discrimination:** Do not discriminate against us. We want anti-discrimination laws to work just as well for us as they do for other groups.

- **Labels:** Do not label us. See us for what we can do, not for what we cannot do.

- **Legislation:** Learn more about how current legislation has improved our lives.

- **Sensitivity:** Help professionals to be more sensitive to people's needs.

- **Housing:** Housing programs that help us have a home of our own are important. These programs help make it possible for us to live independently.

- **Transitions:** Programs that help us to make the transition from school to work are important. With the guidance of job coaches, we can become employed and stay employed.

- **Choices:** Do not get in our way. Let us do what we can do. We do well on our own, please do not create obstacles for us.

- **Respect:** Listen. We are self-advocates. We deserve the same attention and respect for our views as any other group before Congress—So count us in!

Leadership

Leadership is when a person learns the skills they need to run a group or be a part of a board or committee. It is also speaking up for yourself and helping each other learn how you can work together as a TEAM (Together Everyone Achieves More). It is learning new things and sharing what you have learned with others.

Leaders also know how to listen to people when they are talking and know when a person might need support. Leadership sometimes is letting other people take over a discussion and have a chance to practice being a leader while they are learning new skills. Being a leader is being a part of the community and knowing what is going on and getting involved. Leadership means a lot of different things to a lot of people so it is important for people to figure out what is best for them. Being a leader is not always easy but it should be fun.

Qualities of a Good Leader

- Assertiveness.

- Self-determination.

- Decision-making skills.

- Being a good listener.

- A desire to share and believe in the common vision of the group.

- A willingness to take the time to learn leadership skills.

- Ability to include all members and not exclude anyone.

Learning Leadership Skills

There are many ways a person can learn leadership skills. They can take a class, learn from other people in the group, read materials from other people written about leadership, go to workshops on leadership, or go to conferences. Another approach is "supported leadership." That is an option that encourages the person to select a partner from the group to help them. The partner then offers tutorials or pre-meetings on issues to be discussed during the meetings, and provides the opportunity to practice parliamentary procedures and other formal and informal rules. People with disabilities can then both assist and serve as role models for other people "in training" or "considering" leadership roles. Another alternative is to establish co-leadership positions where two people assume the responsibilities normally done by a single position. This helps lessen the fear of a new role or responsibility.

What Kinds of Supports Might a Self-Advocate Need?

There are many kinds of supports a person might need. What is most important is to let that person choose his/her own supports and to figure out what will work best for him/her. Some people may need help before a meeting, for example, going over the written materials so they will understand the information to be discussed at the meeting. Others may need help during the meeting so that they will understand what is happening throughout the meeting.

It is important for people to know the date and time of the meeting so they can make an informed decision if they will need to take time off from work. Many groups who hold meetings during a person's work schedule pay an honorarium for the time they will not be at work. People need to know directions on how to get to the meeting and if they will need any money once they get there. It is sometimes necessary for people to receive money in advance because it is hard for them to wait a long time to be reimbursed. If this is not an option, some people may not be able to afford to be a leader. Before the person joins the group it is often helpful to explain how the meetings are run or to invite them to come to a meeting before they decide to join the group. Most important is for all members to feel welcome.

Decision-Makers Might Assist Self-Advocates during Meetings

Members of decision making groups need to listen to each other and really try to understand each other's points of view. It is important to treat people with respect and dignity even if it is necessary to wait a long time for the person to answer a question. Patience might be required of all members for each other. Materials that are passed out should be written so that all members can understand it, being careful to use simple, understandable words. Frequently asking people if they understand what is being discussed or asking them if they have any questions is helpful. The expectations of a new member should be the same whether they have a disability or not. Ask members at the end of each meeting how they felt the meeting went and if they need any other kinds of supports.

Resources

To Learn More about Self-Advocacy

A Call To Action: The Roles of People with Mental Retardation in Leadership. (1992). Texas: The Arc, P.O. Box 1947, Arlington TX 76004. Retardation in Leadership. (1992).

Dybwad, G. & Bersani, H. (1995). *New Voices: Self-Advocacy by Persons with Disabilities.* Boston: Brookline Books.

Enough is Enough! The story of People First of Illinois. (1993) Illinois: Illinois Developmental Disabilities Planning Council, 830 South Spring Street, Springfield, Illinois 62704

O'Brien, J. (Ed.) (1990) *Effective Self-Advocacy: Empowering People with Disabilities to Speak for Themselves.* Minneapolis, MN: Institute on Community Integration.

The National Reform Agenda and People with Mental Retardation: Putting People First, (1994). Washington, D.C.: U.S. Department of Health and Human Services, Administration for Children and Families. President's Committee on Mental Retardation.

Shapiro, J. (1993). *No Pity: People with Disabilities Forging a New Civil Rights Movement.* New York: Times Books, Random House.

Taking Place: Standing Up and Speaking Out About Living in Our Communities. (1994). Tennessee: Self-Advocates Becoming Empowered. Tulsa ARC, 1601 South Main Street, Suite 300, Tulsa, OK 74119. Voice: (918)592-8272 Fax: (918)582-6328

Williams, P. & Schultz, B. (1982). *We Can Speak for Ourselves.* Boston: Brookline Books.

How To Start A People First Chapter. People First International, Inc., P.O. Box 1642, Salem, Oregon 97309 Ph. 503-362-0336 Fax 503-585-0287.

People First Chapter Handbook: A reference guide for self-advocacy chapters. People First of Illinois, P.O. Box 2153, Loves Park, Illinois 61130

Community Advocacy Press. Newsletter. People with Developmental Disabilities Speaking Out For What They Believe (Quarterly, Free). Capabilities Unlimited Inc., 2495 Erie Avenue, Cincinnati, OH 45203 Ph. 1-800-871-2181 Fax 513-871-5893

Self-Advocates Becoming Empowered. National Self Advocacy Organization. Tia Nelis, Chair, University of Illinois at Chicago, 1640 West Roosevelt Road, Chicago, IL 60608-6904 Ph 312-413-1284 Fax 312-996-6942

To Learn about Leadership

Bales, J. (1992). *Do you really know what is best for me? OR how to help your board of directors become whole: a guide for including people with disabilities on boards.* Illinois: Illinois

Planning Council on Developmental Disabilities. Dybwad, G & Bersani, H. (1995)

New Voices: self-advocacy by persons with disabilities. Boston: Brookline Books.

Gobel, S. *Not Another Board Meeting! guides to building inclusive decision-making groups.* Oregon: Oregon Developmental Disabilities Planning Council.

Hoffman, M. (1992) *Leadership Plus.* Oklahoma: Oklahoma Planning Council on Developmental Disabilities.

Levitz, M., Nelis, T., & Peterson, M, (1996). Community Advocacy Press: People speaking out for what they believe. *Leadership:* Vol. 1, Issue 4. Cincinnati: Capabilities Unlimited, Inc., 2495 Erie Ave., Cincinnati, OH 45208

Pederson, E.L. & Chaikin, M.L. (1993) *Voices That Count. Making It Happen: a presenter's guide.* Rehabilitation Research and Training Center Consortium on Aging and Developmental Disabilities, Cincinnati, OH

Taking Place: Standing Up and Speaking Out About Living in Our Communities. (1994). *Self-Advocates Becoming Empowered.* Tulsa, ARC, 1601 South Main Street, Suite 300, Tulsa, OK 74119 Voice: (918) 592-8272 Fax: (918) 582-6328.

Chapter 26

Leisure and Therapy

Definition of Leisure

Leisure can be defined as available free choice time and those individually selected activities that characteristically are not related to work or other obligatory forms of activity, and which are expected to promote feelings of pleasure, affiliation, happiness, spontaneity, fantasy or imagination, fulfillment, creativity, self-expression, and self-development. Leisure is a major domain of life activity and is essential for lifelong development and personal well-being.

Typical Leisure Experiences Include

Typical leisure experiences include play behavior, recreation activities, diversion and amusement, art and creative activities, adventure challenges activities, sports and games, travel and vacations, holiday celebrations, to name just a few examples.

This chapter contains text from "Leisure" by Dr. Barbara A. Hawkins, © 1999 American Association on Mental Retardation, reprinted with permission; "Music Therapy and Language for the Autistic Child" by Myra J. Staum, Ph.D., © Center for the Study of Autism, reprinted with permission; "NIH Technology Assessment—Pets," Office of Medical Applications of Research, NIH 1987; "About Special Olympics," © Special Olympics, Inc. at http://www.specialolympics.org/; and "Directories of Summer Camps for Children with Disabilities, National Information Center for Children and Youth with Disabilities (NICYD), May 1999.

Typical Leisure Skills

Leisure skills include choosing and self-initiating interests, using and enjoying home and community leisure and recreational activities alone and with others, playing socially with others, taking turns, terminating or refusing leisure or recreational activities, extending one's duration of participation and expanding one's repertoire of interests, awareness, and skills.

How Is a Leisure Repertoire Constructed?

A personal leisure repertoire is constructed from the following: (a) a range of activity experiences sufficient enough to develop personal preferences and interests; (b) opportunities to engage in personal choice-making behavior; and (c) the depth of experience necessary to have perceived feelings of pleasure, fulfillment, creativity, happiness, and other feelings commonly associated with having an optimal leisure experience.

People with mental retardation will develop leisure skills and a leisure repertoire if provided with meaningful and structured leisure education opportunities, as well as a supportive environment (social and physical).

People with mental retardation have the right to pursue self-determined recreation activities and to experience a leisure-oriented lifestyle. Some people with mental retardation may need supports and services to assist in developing independence skills that support their leisure and recreation. AAMR calls for active consideration by local, state, national, and international organizations in recognizing that leisure and recreation are fundamental attributes of a healthy lifestyle and are associated with a high quality of life for people with mental retardation.

References and Resources

AAMR Leisure and Recreation Division Newsletter. Volume V, No. 2, *Leisure as an adaptive skill area,* p. 2-4. Washington, DC: American Association on Mental Retardation.

AAMR (1992). *Mental retardation: Definition. classification. and systems of supports.* Washington, DC: American Association on Mental Retardation.

Music Therapy

Editor's Note: This article focuses on the use of music therapy for autistic children; however, the information is applicable for many individuals with mental retardation.

Music therapy is the unique application of music to enhance personal lives by creating positive changes in human behavior. It is an allied health profession utilizing music as a tool to encourage development in social/ emotional, cognitive/learning, and perceptual-motor areas. Music therapy has a wide variety of functions with the exceptional child, adolescent, and adult in medical, institutional, and educational settings. Music is effective because it is a nonverbal form of communication, it is a natural reinforcer, it is immediate in time and provides motivation for practicing nonmusical skills. Most importantly, it is a successful medium because almost everyone responds positively to at least some kind of music.

The training of a music therapist involves a full curriculum of music classes, along with selected courses in psychology, special education, and anatomy with specific core courses and field experiences in music therapy. Following course work, students complete a six-month full time clinical internship and a written board certification exam. Registered, board certified professionals must then maintain continuing education credits or retake the exam to remain current in their practice.

Music therapy is particularly useful with autistic children owing in part to the nonverbal, nonthreatening nature of the medium. Parallel music activities are designed to support the objectives of the child as observed by the therapist or as indicated by a parent, teacher or other professional. A music therapist might observe, for instance, the child's need to socially interact with others. Musical games like passing a ball back and forth to music or playing sticks and cymbals with another person might be used to foster this interaction. Eye contact might be encouraged with imitative clapping games near the eyes or with activities which focus attention on an instrument played near the face. Preferred music may be used contingently for a wide variety of cooperative social behaviors like sitting in a chair or staying with a group of other children in a circle.

Music therapy is particularly effective in the development and remediation of speech. The severe deficit in communication observed among autistic children includes expressive speech which may be nonexistent or impersonal. Speech can range from complete mutism to grunts, cries, explosive shrieks, guttural sounds, and humming. There may be musically intoned vocalizations with some consonant-vowel combinations, a sophisticated babbling interspersed with vaguely recognizable word-like sounds, or a seemingly foreign sounding jargon. Higher level autistic speech may involve echolalia, delayed echolalia or pronominal reversal, while some children may progress to appropriate phrases, sentences, and longer sentences with non expressive or monotonic speech. Since autistic children are often mainstreamed into music classes in the public schools, a music teacher may experience the rewards of having an autistic child involved in music activities while assisting with language.

It has been noted time and again that autistic children evidence unusual sensitivities to music. Some have perfect pitch, while many have been noted to play instruments with exceptional musicality. Music therapists traditionally work with autistic children because of this unusual responsiveness which is adaptable to non-music goals. Some children have unusual sensitivities only to certain sounds. One boy, after playing a xylophone bar, would spontaneously sing up the harmonic series from the fundamental pitch. Through careful structuring, syllable sounds were paired with his singing of the harmonics and the boy began incorporating consonant-vowel sounds into his vocal play. Soon simple 2-3 note tunes were played on the xylophone by the therapist who modeled more complex verbalizations, and the child gradually began imitating them.

Since autistic children sometimes sing when they may not speak, music therapists and music educators can work systematically on speech through vocal music activities. In the music classroom, songs with simple words, repetitive phrases, and even repetitive nonsense syllables can assist the autistic child's language. Meaningful word phrases and songs presented with visual and tactile cues can facilitate this process even further. One six-year old echolalic child was taught speech by having the therapist/teacher sing simple question/answer phrases set to a familiar melody with full rhythmic and harmonic accompaniment. The child held the objects while singing:

Do you eat an apple? Yes, **yes.**
Do you eat an apple? Yes, **yes.**
Do you eat an apple? Yes, **yes.**
Yes, yes, **yes.**

and

Do you eat a pencil? No, **no.**
Do you eat a pencil? No, **no.**

Do you eat a pencil? No, **no.**
No, no, **no.**

Another autistic child learned noun and action verb phrases. A large doll was manipulated by the therapist/teacher and a song presented:

This is a doll.
This **is a doll.**
The doll is jumping.
The doll **is jumping.**
This is a doll.
This **is a doll.**

Later, words were substituted for walking, sitting, sleeping, etc. In these songs, the bold words were faded out gradually by the therapist/teacher. Since each phrase was repeated, the child could use his echolalic imitation to respond accurately. When the music was eliminated completely, the child was able to verbalize the entire sentence in response to the questions, "What is this?" and "What is the doll doing?"

Other autistic children have learned entire meaningful responses when both questions and answers were incorporated into a song. The following phrases were sung with one child to the approximate tune of *Twinkle, Twinkle, Little Star* and words were faded out gradually in backward progression. While attention to environmental sounds was the primary focus for this child, the song structure assisted her in responding in a full, grammatically correct sentence:

Listen, listen, what do you hear? (sound played on tape)
I hear an ambulance.

(I hear a baby cry.)
(I hear my mother calling, etc.)

Autistic children have also made enormous strides in eliminating their monotonic speech by singing songs composed to match the rhythm, stress, flow and inflection of the sentence followed by a gradual fading of the musical cues. Parents and teachers alike can assist the child in remembering these prosodic features of speech by prompting the child with the song.

While composing specialized songs is time consuming for the teacher with a classroom full of other children, it should be remembered that the repertoire of elementary songs are generally repetitive in nature. Even in higher level elementary vocal method books, repetition of simple phrases is common. While the words in such books may not seem critical for the autistic child's survival at the moment, simply increasing the capacity to put words together is a vitally important beginning for these children.

For those teachers whose time is limited to large groups, almost all singing experiences are invaluable to the autistic child when songs are presented slowly, clearly, and with careful focusing of the child's attention to the ongoing activity. To hear an autistic child leave a class quietly singing a song with all the words is a pleasant occurrence. To hear the same child attempt to use these words in conversation outside of the music class is to have made a very special contribution to the language potential of this child.

Additional Information about Music Therapy

National Association for Music Therapy
8455 Colesville Road, Suite 930
Silver Spring, MD 20910, U.S.A.
Tel: 301-589-3300
Fax: 301-589-5175

Therapeutic Riding

Throughout history animals have played a significant role in human customs, legends, and religions. Primitive people found that human-animal relationships were important to their very survival, and pet keeping was common in hunter-gatherer societies. In our own time, the great increase in pet ownership may reflect a largely urban population's often unsatisfied need for intimacy, nurturance, and contact with nature. However it is impossible to determine when animals first were used specifically to promote physical and psychological health. The use of horseback riding for people with serious disabilities has been reported for centuries. In 1792, animals were incorporated into the treatment for mental patients at the York Retreat, England, as part of an enlightened approach attempting to reduce the use of harsh drugs and restraints. The first suggested use of animals in a therapeutic setting in the United States was in 1919 at St. Elizabeths Hospital in Washington, D.C. The earliest extensive use of companion animals in the United States occurred from 1944-1945 at an Army Air Corps Convalescent Hospital at Pawling, New York.

During the 1970's numerous case studies of animals facilitating therapy with children and senior citizens were reported.

"Therapeutic riding" is an umbrella term to describe a variety of ways in which the horse may be used to influence the physical and psychological well-being of individuals. It incorporates riding skills and gymnastic exercises for emotional, cognitive, and sensorimotor benefits. For patients with movement disorders, specially trained physical and occupational therapists use therapeutic riding in which the horse influences the patient rather than the patient controlling the horse. The goal is to improve the patient's posture, balance, mobility, and function.

The Special Olympics

Special Olympics is an international program of year-round sports training and athletic competition for more than one million children and adults with mental retardation.

The Special Olympics oath is:

> Let me win. But if I cannot win,
> let me be brave in the attempt.

Special Olympics leaders are Eunice Kennedy Shriver, Founder and Honorary Chairman, and Sargent Shriver, Chairman of the Board.

The mission of Special Olympics is to provide year-round sports training and athletic competition in a variety of Olympic-type sports for individuals with mental retardation by giving them continuing opportunities to develop physical fitness, demonstrate courage, experience joy, and participate in a sharing of gifts, skills, and friendship with their families, other Special Olympics athletes, and the community.

The benefits of participating in Special Olympics for people with mental retardation include improved physical fitness and motor skills, greater self-confidence, a more positive self-image, friendships, and increased family support. Special Olympics athletes carry these benefits with them into their daily lives at home, in the classroom, on the job, and in the community. Families who participate become stronger as they learn a greater appreciation of their athlete's talents. Community volunteers find out what good friends the athletes can be. And everyone learns more about the capabilities of people with mental retardation.

Special Olympics believes that competition among those of equal abilities is the best way to test its athletes' skills, measure their progress, and inspire them to grow. Special Olympics believes that its program of sports training and competition helps people with mental retardation become physically fit and grow mentally, socially, and spiritually. Special Olympics believes that consistent training is required to develop sports skills.

Special Olympics began in 1968 when Eunice Kennedy Shriver organized the First International Special Olympics Games at Soldier Field, Chicago, Illinois, USA. The concept was born in the early 1960's when Mrs. Shriver started a day camp for people with mental retardation. She saw that people with mental retardation were far more capable in sports and physical activities than many experts thought. Since 1968, millions of children and adults with mental retardation have participated in Special Olympics.

There are accredited Special Olympics programs in nearly 150 countries. In the United States Special Olympics Chapters are established in all 50 states, the District of Columbia, Guam, the Virgin Islands, and American Samoa. About 25,000 communities in the United States have Special Olympics programs.

Through the Special Olympics Model School District programs, public school districts include Special Olympics in their physical education curriculum and provide extracurricular and interscholastic sports to elementary and secondary students with mental retardation. The Special Olympics Mega-Cities program coordinates Special Olympics training and competition in schools, community recreation programs, group homes, and institution in 11 large metropolitan areas.

To be eligible to participate in the Special Olympics, you must be at least eight years old and identified by an agency or professional as having one of the following conditions: mental retardation, cognitive delays as measured by formal assessment, or significant learning or vocational problems due to cognitive delay that require or have required specially-designed instruction.

The Unified Sports ® program brings persons without mental retardation together on the same team with persons with mental retardation of comparable age and athletic ability. Founded in 1987, Unified Sports fosters the integration of persons with mental retardation into school and community sports programs.

For More Information

Special Olympics International (SOI)
1325 G Street, NW, Suite 500
Washington DC 20005

Tel: 202-628-3630
Fax: 202-824-0200
URL: http://www.specialolympics.org/

Directories of Summer Camps for Children with Disabilities (May 1999)

General

Annual Special Camp Guide
Resources for Children with Special Needs
200 Park Avenue, South, Suite 816
New York, NY 10003
Tel: 212-677-4650
$24.50 including shipping and handling (available in English & Spanish)

Easter Seals Camping and Recreation List
Easter Seals—National Office
230 West Monroe Street, Suite 1800
Chicago, IL 60606
Toll-free: 800-221-6827
Tel: 312-726-6200
TTY: 312-726-4258
E-mail: nessinfo@seals.com
URL: http://www.easter-seals.org
Free (some "camperships" are available)

Guide to Summer Camps and Summer Schools 1995-1996 Edition
Porter Sargent Publishers, Inc.
11 Beacon Street, Suite 1400
Boston, MA 02108
Tel: 617-523-1670
$35.00 hard-cover; $25.00 soft-cover ($5.00 s/h)

1999 Guide to ACA Accredited Camps
American Camping Association (ACA), Inc.
5000 State Road 67, North
Martinsville, IN 46151-7902
Toll-free: 800-428-2267
Tel: 765-342-8456 (continued on next page)

363

URL: http://www.acacamps.org (The 1999 guide is free on the ACA web site)
$19.95 (includes shipping and handling)

Disability-Specific

Camps for Children with Spina Bifida
Spina Bifida Association of America
4590 MacArthur Boulevard, N.W., Suite 250
Washington, D.C. 20007-4226
Toll-free: 800-621-3141
Tel: 202-944-3285
E-mail: sbaa@sbaa.org
URL: http://www.sbaa.org
Call for a state-by-state listing

Directory of Summer Camps for Children with Learning Disabilities
Learning Disabilities Association of America (LDA)
4156 Library Road
Pittsburgh, PA 15234
Toll-free: 888-300-6710
Tel: 412-341-1515; 412-341-8077
E-mail: vldanatl@usaor.ne
URL: http://www.ldanatl.org/store/LD_Directories.html
$5.00

Web Sites

Camp Channel
Bringing Summer Camps to the Internet
URL: http://www.campchannel.com/docs/campsearch.html

The CampPage Guide to Summer Camps
URL: http://www.camppage.com/frame2.htm

Grown-Up Camp
URL: http://www.grownupcamps.com

InterCamp: Summer Camp Directory & Resource
URL: http://www.intercamp.com/directory/search.html

Kids' Camps
URL: http://www.kidscamps.com

Chapter 27

Managing Grief

Part of life is dealing with one's losses and grieving. We have social structures, support systems, teachings, and rituals that help us understand and recover from significant loss. It is not uncommon for adults to feel they must protect others from these difficulties, including children, elderly, and persons with disabilities. In fact, strenuous efforts are often made to protect people with developmental disabilities from life's losses and disappointments. The harsh reality of their own and their parent's mortality is a secret they will have been judged too vulnerable to be told. Their death education has often been nonexistent, so their bewilderment at the disappearance of a loved one should be no surprise. It is imperative that all people be able to access the supports given to understand death and loss. Protecting someone usually results in more problems in that grief and mourning will not be properly experienced, leading to more significant future difficulties.

In trying to understand how the needs of someone with a developmental disability might be similar or different to yours and mine, the context in which they have lived their lives must be considered. A very typical situation, for example, is that of a middle-aged person with a developmental disability living in a dependent relationship with aging parents. The family is often isolated with few friends and little practical support at home. Their adult son or daughter may have a

Reprinted with permission of The Arc, © "Managing Grief Better: People with Developmental Disabilities," *The Habilitative Mental Healthcare Newsletter*, May/June 1995, Vol. 14, No. 3.

regular daytime occupation, and be accustomed to staying in a respite care home or hostel from time to time. Many adult sons and daughters with a developmental disability play an important role in domestic affairs at home with dependency being very much a two-way matter. When their first parent dies, they may not be told directly of the death. Nevertheless, they will be aware of their parent's absence, of sadness in the family, and of whispered conversations and concern about themselves.

While the rest of the family grieves, emergency admission to respite care or an unexpected holiday with distant relatives may be arranged for the person with a developmental disability. Thus, the person is excluded and kept ignorant of facts that he or she needs to know. Their confusion and fear persists when other family members are coming to terms with their loss. Families comfort themselves with the hope that the person with developmental disability has not noticed or say, "we could not take her to the funeral—she'd be too upset," as if being upset at a funeral was inappropriate.

"Denial" of the loss by the person with a disability at the time is not surprising in these circumstances. The individual's ordinary routines and certainties will have been turned upside down. Prolonged searching behavior and an increase in separation anxiety can be expected. However, angry and aggressive reactions may be delayed to such a degree that, when such behavior does occur, no relationship to the loss is recognized.

A second scenario is seen when the surviving parent dies. The bereaved, dependent person is admitted to emergency care but never returns home. At one stroke, he or she has lost parent and confidante, home and possessions, a familiar neighborhood and routines, and perhaps a pet. Searching for the lost parent and home is difficult unless one is able to explain one's needs and unless a new caregiver is willing to help. In my experience, most caregivers do not recognize emotional needs such as these. A loss of skills, and decreased joi de vivre may lead to inappropriate and difficult to reverse decisions about future living arrangements and opportunities.

There are other loss situations which might be experienced by a resident of a long-term institutional placement. Staff turnover, the discharge of roommates to community care, the end of weekly visits by a devoted parent—now dead—and the death of people one has lived with for many years all go unremarked.

Developmental disabilities is a broad category which encompasses mild developmental difficulties to profound mental retardation with multiple disabilities. The greater the handicap, the less likely the individual's grief will be recognized. Caregivers tend to ignore or mis-understand the effects of such losses. Research has shown that some people with developmental disabilities will have a delayed under-standing of the aging process. It seems likely that the irreversibility, universality, and the inevitability of death will all be difficult concepts to understand, despite many years of experience as an adult. The capacity to integrate their experiences and to learn from them will be limited unless sensitive help is available.

It is unlikely that the attitudes of a family or of professional caregivers will change in the period between a death and the funeral. There is an important advocacy role for doctors, care managers, and social workers who must not be afraid to challenge caregivers and support providers who make decisions to exclude the person with a disability from the full grieving process.

The following recommendations are made to assist persons with disabilities in dealing with death and loss.

- Be honest, include and involve—Many caregivers find them-selves quite unable to be honest or to include and involve the person with a developmental disability. The person should be offered the choice of whether to attend the funeral or memorial service. If he or she is unable to choose directly because of cog-nitive limitations, it is usually advisable to involve the person as fully as possible in all the rituals being arranged.

- Listen—be there. Being available to listen and provide support is essential. This must occur immediately after the death, and, most importantly, also in the weeks and months following. Under-standing the permanence of death comes slowly, thus the person with a developmental disability may experience delayed grief.

- Actively seek out nonverbal rituals—The nonverbal rituals with which most cultures surround death are helpful to many of us. They are particularly helpful to people with developmental dis-abilities who cannot find solace in the written or spoken word. Counseling picture books may be helpful in explaining what happens when someone dies.

- Respect photos and other mementos—In the early stages of a bereavement it is quite common to avoid pictures and posses-sions and places which are associated with the person who died. As time passes, such mementos may come to be treasured. In-deed the reduction in avoidance of such cues can provide a useful measure toward resolution of grief. People with a developmental disability should be helped to choose some mementoes, and this choice should be offered again at a later date when some of their emotional pain has subsided. Sometimes people make unexpected choices, but these should be respected.

- Minimize change—It is advisable to minimize changes in routine and changes in accommodation or of caregivers at a time of grief. As a rule of thumb, we suggest major changes should be avoided for at least one year.

- Avoid assessment of skills—If a caregiver has died, it may seem sensible to assess an individual in order to "fit" him/her into the best service or support system. However, this can be the worst time to assess someone whose behavior and skills may have regressed because of the emotional energy being expended on grieving.

- Assist searching behavior—By revisiting old haunts and going to the cemetery, caregivers can assist appropriate searching behavior to support emotional recovery. Hoarding behavior may suggest that more help of this kind is required. For example, the person who absconds or is found wandering may be trying to find their lost home and family. Mark was asked to leave his "group home" of eight years standing some time after the death of his grandfather from cancer, and his dog in an accident. Despite not being told of the deaths officially, he became slow and uncooperative with ordinary routines and was missing for hours on end. On the second occasion he was found in a distressed state in a wooded park. His caretakers asked his parents to take him away. Anne moved to a group home after her mother's death. She went to great lengths to conceal the small possessions she took from the jackets, purses and bags of visitors to her group home. Staff knew things would have been hidden in her room and tried to make light about her behavior. It seemed she felt cheated about something as though she was trying to make up for her own loss. This behavior stopped after some individual bereavement counseling.

- Support the observance of anniversaries—Anniversaries must be formally observed. Many religions have formal services a year after someone has died. This is especially true at the time of the anniversary of an important loss.

- Seek specialists for consultation if behavioral changes persist— Referrals for consultation with specialists are typically made very late. It is important to make referrals, especially mental health referrals, as soon as any serious grief reactions are noted such as aggressive behavior, persistent irritability, mutism, loss of skills, inappropriate speech (i.e., asking "where is Dad?" all the time), self-injury, tearfulness, and absconding.

Conclusion

People with disabilities have a right to participate fully in the grief and mourning process and in all of society's support systems and rituals associated with these losses. Concerted effort is needed to offer death education to professionals and to parent organizations so that they may become familiar with normal grief reactions and provide proper supports. Death education can be introduced into the school and adult education curriculum for people with developmental disabilities. Advice is needed to construct guidelines for special agencies to follow when a death does occur. This might include helping professional caregivers rehearse breaking the news of a death. Practical plans to avoid immediate admission to residential care are required. The importance of ensuring that the bereaved person has some mementos of their deceased relative must be remembered and advice on the importance of nonverbal rituals at the funeral may be helpful. Bereavement counseling for persons with a developmental disability should be made available routinely and not just when a maladaptive reaction has been recognized as grief. Both individual and group work with bereaved individuals may be helpful, particularly if nonverbal approaches, such as the use of counseling picture books, are available.

References

1. Hollins S, Sireling L (eds). *When Dad Died*, 2nd Edition. London: St. George's Hospital Medical School, St. George's Mental Health Library, 1994.

2. Hollins S, Sireling L. (eds). *When Mum Died*, 2nd Edition. London: St. George's Hospital Medical School, St. George's Mental Health Library, 1989.

3. Hollins S, Sireling L (eds). *Working Through Loss with People Who Have Learning Disabilities*. Windsor: NFER-Nelson, 1990.

4. Kloeppel DA, Hollins S. *Double handicap: Mental retardation and death in the family*. Death Studies 1989;13:31-38.

5. Oswin M. *Am I Allowed to Cry?*. London: Souvenir Press (E & A) Ltd, 1991.

6. Stroebe MS, Storebe W, Hansson RO. *Handbook of Bereavement*. Cambridge, England: Cambridge University Press, 1993.

Dr. Sheila Hollins

Dr. Hollins is Professor of Psychiatry of Disability at St. George's Hospital Medical School, University of London, Consultant Psychiatrist in the Wandsworth Community Health Trust and Chairperson of the Section for the Psychiatry of Mental Retardation at the Royal College of Psychiatrists.

Part Six

Education

Chapter 28

Education of Students with Mental Retardation

The purpose of education is to prepare all children and adolescents for success in adulthood. Success must be measured in reference to the individual student, not exclusively by academic levels attained or economic productivity standards. Students with mental retardation need to have experiences with and instruction in skills which enable them to work, live, and enjoy life in their community. To accomplish this schools must adopt certain basic principles:

- All schools should value all students and include them in all aspects of school life;

- Preparation for life, respect for student's background and abilities, as they learn and socialize together in classrooms and other school settings;

- Each student with a disability belongs in an age-appropriate classroom with peers who are not disabled;

- Each student has the right to receive an individualized education which provides choices, meets his or her needs, and offers necessary support, and;

- Quality education should value and address the concerns of the student and the student's family.

Reprinted with permission "The Education of Students with Mental Retardation: Preparation for Life in the Community," © 1992, The Arc.

What School Experiences Best Prepare Students for Life in the Community?

All students need to acquire the skills necessary to live in their communities. They need to know how to shop, use the post office, and go to the doctor or clinic. Students need to learn such skills as how to participate in social and religious activities or how to drive or use public transportation. Schools can provide these opportunities to students with mental retardation, at least in part, by providing the opportunity to:

* receive an individualized educational program based on their unique characteristics and preferences;

* receive instruction based on curricular material, which is functional (based on community-oriented needs), and chronologically age-appropriate;

* follow the same daily schedule as that followed by all students in their neighborhood school;

* participate in recreational and extracurricular programs with sufficient support if necessary;

* develop meaningful social interactions with other students;

* receive related services, such as speech, physical, or occupational therapy, in accordance with individual needs, and;

* receive transportation services allowing participation in school activities on the same basis as other students.

How Are Views of the Role of Education for Students with Mental Retardation Changing?

The implementation of Public Law 94-142 in 1977 marked the beginning of a new era for learners with mental retardation and all students with unique learning needs. It ensured that these students were not excluded from educational services and that services provided were free and appropriate. Since then, however, continued advances in knowledge concerning how to better prepare these students for adult life have led to the continuing evolution of service-delivery approaches. These changes affect the way schools design the educational environment and interpret "least restrictive environment" regarding student placement.

In the years immediately following the implementation of the law, "least restrictive environment" was generally viewed as, in some manner, constituting segregated classrooms for students with mental retardation. However, this interpretation has increasingly been challenged by parents and educators based at least partially on a re-examination of P.L. 94-142. Of particular scrutiny are regulations which state that: "to the maximum extent appropriate, children with disabilities, including children in public or private institutions or other care facilities, are educated with children who do not have disabilities [Section 121a.550(1)]" and "removal of children with disabilities from the regular educational environment occurs only when the nature or severity of the disability is such that education in regular classes with the use of supplementary aides and services (our italics) cannot be achieved satisfactorily [Section 121a.550(2)]."

At the present time there is room for improvement. Nationwide, schools serve about 6 percent of students with mental retardation primarily in regular classrooms, with an additional 22 percent receiving services in a resource classroom (where the student spends part of his/her day in regular classrooms and part in a separate classroom). Seventy-two percent of students with mental retardation are still served in more restrictive settings. The majority of these students are served in separate classrooms, but 10 percent still receive services in separate schools (13th Annual Report to Congress on the Implementation of The Education of the Handicapped Act, 1991).

Views about the curriculum for students with mental retardation are also changing. Research has indicated that students with mental retardation learn more effectively and retain more skills if the education is provided in "functional" settings, (e.g., learning to shop in a grocery store of a simulated setting), or if the skills are presented in functional activities such as acquiring math skills in the context of learning to balance a checkbook (Brown, et al., 1983; Patton, et al., 1989). Schools must base the education of students with mental retardation upon individual, not system, needs and discard stereotypes and assumptions which limit learning opportunities to students with mental retardation.

Should All Students Spend All of Their Time in Regular Classrooms?

Education programs for students with mental retardation must be individualized to meet the unique characteristics and needs of each individual. Some students with mental retardation will benefit from instruction outside school environments, such as the aforementioned community based settings. As such, an appropriate learning environment will not be exclusively in the regular classroom. Other students with mental retardation may require related services which necessitate time out of the regular classroom. The IEP process should identify the appropriate program for each student and determine what arrangement best meets the student's needs.

Nonetheless, all students should be integrated in some way into regular education buildings, classrooms, and activities with same-age peers, who are not disabled. This does not mean that every student in the regular classroom must learn the same material nor does it mean that students with disabilities enter regular classrooms only for social benefits. It means that with adequate support, adaptation, and respect for individual differences, all students with mental retardation can benefit educationally and socially from integration.

How Do Integration and Inclusion Differ from Mainstreaming?

Historically, the term "mainstreaming" has been associated with the part-time placement of students with disabilities in classrooms for several purposes, including academic instruction and social interaction. Integration and inclusion, on the other hand, refer to the opportunity for all students to participate in the totality of the school experience. This includes integration into regular classrooms for educational and social opportunities. More than this, however, it means that students with mental retardation need to be provided the chance to participate in all aspects of the school experience, from extracurricular activities such as football games to eating and socializing with peers in the school lunchroom. Many people prefer to use the term inclusion because it implies involvement by individuals with disabilities in all aspects of school and the community.

Why Are Integration and Inclusion Important?

For students with mental retardation interaction with same age classmates provides role models for educational and social success. Interaction with students who have disabilities can affect the attitudes and expectations of teachers and classmates and help shed stereotypes which limit the student with a disability (York, et al., 1989). This, in turn, increases the opportunities available to students with mental retardation as they enter adulthood. When students with and without disabilities grow and learn together, the barriers created by stereotypes and stigmatization are more easily toppled.

The decision whether or not to integrate students reflects societal attitudes or values (Stainback & Stainback, 1988). Including students with mental retardation in all aspects of the school experience is one indicator of the acceptance of people with disabilities within our society. As such, the questions that need to be asked should not be, "Can inclusion work?" or "Is integration a good idea?" Instead, we need to ask how we can make integration work and focus our energies answering this query.

Why Is Placement in an Age-Appropriate Setting Important?

When students with mental retardation are seen only in terms of their "mental age" as reported by a test and not in relation to their actual chronological age, it is difficult to perceive them as adolescents or adults. Instead they tend to be seen as children, with the mental age estimates used to excuse the absence of effective education or integration into activities in which same-age peers are participating. Viewing people with mental retardation as perpetual children is inaccurate and colors the expectations of the public and employers, thus limiting the individual's opportunity for meaningful engagement in post-school life.

Alternatively, when children with mental retardation grow up in schools and classrooms with same-age peers—attend the same football games, form friendships with non-disabled children, and eat in the same lunchroom—they can learn age-appropriate skills, values, and attitudes. When provided experiences with age-appropriate activities, they can and do learn adolescent and adult roles. Teachers, peers, colleagues, and employers perceive them as adults and, consequently, as potential employees and friends.

The Family's Role in Determining Appropriate Education Programming and Placement

The parents' role is critical. They will be the one consistent factor across their child's educational experience. The most effective tool parents have in assuring an appropriate education for their child is the Individualized Education Program (IEP). The IEP is a legal document which establishes the services necessary for a student's education. Parents and professionals are equal partners in the IEP process.

This may not mean equal knowledge of educational terms or procedures, but it does mean equal status in decision-making. Parents have valuable information concerning their son, daughter, or family member. The focus upon functional, life-centered education for learners with disabilities requires information pertaining to the student's home, community experiences, and skills. Parents and family members have a wealth of information in this regard and should actively participate in IEP decisions.

Preparation for Employment

Like all other aspects of education, preparation for employment must be individually determined. Amendments to P.L. 94-142 require that a written transition plan be included in the IEP by grade ten to detail how this is to happen. Some students will need more time to learn specific occupational skills, and instruction may need to begin earlier. However, all students' skills and attitudes relating to work need to be addressed throughout their education. Students should have vocational experiences which enable them to make informed choices and decisions concerning where they want to work as an adult.

References

The Arc (1990), Position Statement on Education. Adopted by Delegate Body, 40th Annual Convention.

Brown, L., Nisbet, J., Ford, A., Sweet, M., Shiraga, B., York, J. & Loomis, R. (1983). The critical need for nonschool instruction in educational programs for severely handicapped students. *Journal of the Association for Persons w/ Severe Handicaps*, 71-77.

Stainback, W. & Stainback, S., (1988), The role of research in integration. *Minnesota UAP Impact: Feature issue on integrated education, 1, 5-6*. Minneapolis, MN: Minnesota University Affiliated Program on Developmental Disabilities.

York, J., Vandercook, T., MacDonald, D., Heise-Neff, C. & Caughey, E. (1989). *Regular class integration: Feedback from teachers and classmates*. Minneapolis, MN: University of Minnesota, Institute on Community Integration.

Chapter 29

Individuals with Disabilities Education Act

What Is P.L. 94-142?

The Individuals with Disabilities Education Act, a federal law passed in 1975 and reauthorized in 1990, mandates that all children receive a free, appropriate public education regardless of the level or severity of their disability. It provides funds to assist states in the education of students with disabilities and requires that states make sure that these students receive an individualized education program based on their unique needs in the least restrictive environment possible. P.L. 94-142 also provides guidelines for determining what related services are necessary and outlines a "due process" procedure to make sure these needs are adequately met.

Who Is Eligible for Services under P.L. 94-142?

Children ages 3 through 21 who need special education and related services because of a disabling condition are eligible. Eligibility for services is determined through "nondiscriminatory evaluation." This requires that school districts use testing materials free from racial or cultural discrimination and presented in the child's native language or means of communicating. Tests must be chosen which assess the

Reprinted with permission "Public Law 94-142: The Individuals with Disabilities Education Act," © 1992, The Arc, excerpts from "Due Process: Procedural Safeguards in P.L. 94-142," © 1992, The Arc, reprinted with permission; and "Major Issues," IDEA '97 Final Regulations, Department of Education.

child's actual abilities if sensory, motor, or language impairments are present. Evaluations cannot be based solely on one general test, such as an intelligence test, and the child is to be assessed across all areas related to the disability by a "multidisciplinary team."

A multidisciplinary team includes members from a number of education related professions, which may include educators, speech, occupational or physical therapists, and psychologists. An evaluation is to be performed by representatives from those disciplines in which the student may require special services.

Parents who are dissatisfied with an evaluation may have an outside evaluation performed. This evaluation must be considered by the school in decisions made with respect to the student's program. This independent evaluation may be at public expense if the school district is unable to show that its evaluation is appropriate, or it may be at the expense of the parent.

What Is Meant by "Free, Appropriate Public Education?"

"Free" means that education is provided without cost to the parent. Several court cases have tested the limits placed on public expenses. These courts have ruled that schools must fund an appropriate education despite limited local, state, or federal funds. Courts have also ruled that "free" includes needed related services. Related services may include, but are not limited to, transportation, speech therapy, audiological or hearing services, psychological services for diagnosis and evaluation, augmentative or assistive devices considered necessary, and counseling and/or medical services.

An appropriate education may include an out-of-district or private school placement if the school district cannot provide appropriate services in the district. The courts have also ruled, however, that an "appropriate" education is not always the same as the "best" education as long as the education services adequately meet the child's needs.

What Is an IEP?

An IEP refers to the Individualized Education Program. This is a written, legal document which describes the special education and related services to be provided to the student. It is developed in a team meeting in which all members of the IEP team decide what is an appropriate education for the child who needs services. The main goal of the IEP meeting is to discuss the educational needs of the student and write a program that identifies goals and objectives and needed related services for the year.

What Is the School's Responsibility in Developing an IEP?

The local education agency is responsible for:

- contacting parents about the need for an IEP;

- setting a date, time, and location to meet which is convenient for everyone on the team, including the parent(s) or family member(s);

- designating an official from the school district to be involved in and conduct the hearing;

- inviting all members of the IEP team;

- making sure that the meeting is held, the IEP written, and placement decisions made;

- making sure that the IEP is reviewed at least annually and revised if necessary.

What Is the Parents' Role in Developing the IEP?

In P.L. 94-142, the term "parent" refers to the child's biological parent, a guardian, a person acting as the parent of a child, (such as the grandparents), or a surrogate parent appointed if the child is a ward of the state.

P.L. 94-142 makes it clear that parents are equal partners in the IEP process. School personnel and parents must work toward the common goal of developing an effective education program for the child.

Parents should prepare for the meeting by reviewing their child's past education records. P.L. 94-192 ensures that parents are permitted to inspect and review records in a timely manner. Parents should also have in mind goals or objectives based on what they see as needed and may want to talk with their child's teacher before the meeting. The IEP should describe the student's educational goals and objectives, related services needed and the placement decision. If parents are dissatisfied with any aspect of the IEP and are unable to resolve the problem, they can refuse to sign the IEP and, if necessary, pursue due process options guaranteed by the law. Parents may obtain assistance in preparing for and/or attending IEP meetings from the local chapter of The Arc.

Who Should Be Involved in IEP Meetings?

P.L. 94-142 requires that every IEP meeting, whether it is the initial meeting or a review, include:

- a person from the school district, other than the student's teacher, who is qualified in special education or special education supervision;

- the student's teacher;

- one or both of the student's parents, family members or guardians;

- the student, when appropriate;

- other people who are involved in the education of the student as identified by the school or the parent.

A meeting may be held without a parent attending if the parent is unable or unwilling to do so. The district must, however, invite the parent(s) and document its attempts to set a time and place where all persons can attend. Parental absence from the meeting is not necessarily construed as reflecting dissatisfaction or disagreement; and IEP decisions, including placement, will be made by the school in their absence.

What Is Included in an IEP?

P.L. 94-142 required that the following items be included in the IEP:

- a statement of the student's present levels of educational performance;

- a statement of the yearly goals and the instructional objectives which need to be met to achieve these goals;

- a statement of the special education and related services which will be provided to the student as well as how much the student will participate in regular educational programs;

- the dates these services will begin and how long they will last;

- for each student age 16 and over, transition services which will be provided;

- what the school must do to enable the student to meet the objectives, how this is to be measured and, annually, whether the objectives from the previous year's IEP have been met.

When Is It Appropriate for the Student to Participate?

Students with mental retardation need to participate in the IEP process as much as they can. Their opinions, preferences, and choices need to be a part of the decision-making process. The chance to choose areas of instruction, based on their preferences, will help them develop skills which lead to independence and self-determination. Of course, there are several factors that limit how much students participate, including their age and their ability to make adequate decisions. However, almost all students can participate in some way in their IEP process.

What Is to Be Reviewed at IEP Meetings?

Each student's progress related to his or her individualized education program must be reviewed yearly to determine current progress and future needs. The review needs to consider the general progress of the student, staff, and parental concerns about the student's progress, whether objectives are reached according to the measures described in the IEP, and what changes need to be made to meet the student's needs.

Any changes in the student's program after the initial or annual IEP meeting necessitates another IEP meeting. P.L. 94-142 requires that parents receive written notice a reasonable time before the proposed meeting to consider the change.

Additionally, parents and educators should ensure that goals are functional, chronologically age appropriate, and prepare students for adulthood.

What Is Meant by Placement in the Least Restrictive Environment?

The decision to place a student with a disability in a particular education program must be based on the factors specified during the IEP process. This decision must be reviewed at least annually, and placement may change if the child's education program or needs change.

P.L. 94-142 requires that students with disabilities be educated with students who do not have disabilities to the greatest extent possible.

The law states that "unless a child's individualized education program requires some other arrangement, the child is (to be) educated in the school which he or she would attend if not disabled [Section 121a.522(c)]." It requires that removal of the child from the regular classroom occur only when education in regular classes "with the use of supplementary aids and services cannot be achieved satisfactorily [Section 121a.550(2)]."

The Arc and other organizations interpret "least restrictive" as representing instruction in the regular classroom to the greatest extent possible or appropriate. Families need, through the IEP process, to ensure that adequate accommodation and support is provided before alternative placement is considered and that time spent out of the regular classroom is based upon functional considerations such as community integration and instruction. The Arc is opposed to student's placement in segregated facilities, as they do not provide opportunities for learning from nondisabled role models.

What Can Parents Do if They Disagree with Their Child's IEP or Placement Decision?

Sometimes, despite the good intentions of parents and school officials, the IEP process or the resulting program become sources of dispute. However, if there are decisions which either the parent and student or the school district feel are inappropriate or if the family is dissatisfied with any other aspect of the educational program, P.L. 94-142 guarantees access to due process. Due process of law is a way of making sure that the law is fairly applied. P.L. 94-142 provides procedural safeguards for evaluation, assurances of parental consent and notification for actions, and the right to a due process hearing with an impartial hearing officer. This can be followed with an administrative appeal and, if the party is still dissatisfied, civil action. All due process procedures have time frames to ensure prompt action. A federal law provides for the reimbursement of attorneys' fees to families whose administrative and civil action is upheld.

What Is the Purpose of Due Process?

Due process of law is a way of making sure the provisions of P.L. 94-142 are fairly applied. If the family disagrees with any of the school's processes or decisions regarding their child's individualized education program, the law specifies procedures for resolving these disagreements.

What Due Process Procedures Does P.L. 94-142 allow?

If the parents and school officials disagree on aspects of the child's identification, evaluation, individualized education program, or placement, parents and school officials have the right to a due process hearing with an impartial hearing officer.

If either party is dissatisfied with the hearing officer's decision, they may appeal the decision to the state education agency. This is referred to as an administrative appeal.

If either party is still dissatisfied, they may initiate civil action. Federal law provides for the reimbursement of attorney's fees to families whose administrative and civil action is upheld.

What Procedural Safeguards Are Contained in P.L. 94-142 to Help Deal with Potential Disputes?

The law provides very specific guidelines for student evaluation, parental consent and involvement, access to records, individualized education program development and implementation, student placement, and due process procedures. These are referred to as "procedural safeguards." They provide standards for accountability, consistency across classrooms, districts, and states, and detail a process for settling disputes in a fair and equitable manner.

What Procedural Safeguards Do Parents Have Regarding the Educational Records of Their Child?

Parents of a child with mental retardation can inspect and review all records about the identification, evaluation, and educational placement of their son or daughter. Schools must make the records available without unneccessary delay (no longer than 45 days after making the request). Parents have the right to request that the school provide copies of these records. Schools may charge a fee for the copies unless this fee prevents parents from exercising their right to review the records. Schools may not charge for searching and retrieving the records.

In addition to the parent, schools must allow a representative of the parent access to records. However, schools must obtain the parents' permission before disclosing information to anyone else. Schools must instruct personnel about confidentiality requirements.

If parents believe that information in the record is inaccurate or misleading, they may request that these records be changed or amended. The education agency must decide whether to amend the records as requested or refuse to do so and in turn inform the parents of their right to a due process hearing.

How Does Due Process Work?

Parents have the right to request a due process hearing if they are dissatisfied with:

- proposals or refusals to initiate or change the student's identification, evaluation, or educational program/placement, or;

- a refusal to amend educational records as requested.

School officials may request a hearing if parents refuse or fail to consent for preplacement evaluation or initial placement. Schools must provide information parents about available free or low-cost legal services when a due process hearing is initiated.

Any party initiating a hearing has the right to:

- be accompanied by legal representation or counsel. This may include any advocate, not only a lawyer;

- present evidence, cross examine, and call witnesses;

- prohibit evidence not available to the party at least five days before the hearing, and;

- obtain written records of the hearing and decisions.

Parents' have the right to have their child present at the hearing and to open the hearing to the public should they so desire. The final decision must be reached and a copy mailed to all parties within 45 days of the request. Hearings are to be conducted by an impartial hearing officer. This person cannot be an employee of the agency involved in the education of the child or someone who may have conflicting interests. Schools must keep a list of qualified people who serve as hearing officers. While hearing and appeal procedures are in process, the student should remain in his or her existing program. In the case of an initial placement the school must serve the student until a decision is reached.

Parties have the right to appeal decisions of due process hearings conducted by an agency other than the state education agency (e.g. the local education agency, the hearing officer). This appeal will go to the state education agency, which will review the hearing to determine that all procedures were consistent with due process requirements. A final decision must be reached and a copy mailed to all parties within 30 days of the request. For both the initial hearing and any appeal, hearing officers may extend the time limits at the request of either party.

How Are Due Process Hearings Initiated?

Hearings are typically initiated by filing a written request with the local education agency. A copy of this request may be filed with the state education agency. Within five days of this request, the local agency will convene a meeting, sometimes referred to as the pre-hearing conference, in an attempt to reach an agreement before the actual hearing. If this is unsuccessful, a hearing officer will be appointed and the hearing scheduled.

Requests should include the parents' and child's names, address, and phone number. Also include the name, address, and contact person at the local agency and a brief narrative about the nature of the problem. When filing with the local education agency, parents should write to the superintendent of schools. If the request is filed by someone representing the parents, an authorization form so stating must be included.

What Other Procedural Safeguards Exist?

If the state education agency does not overturn the original decision, all parties have the right to civil action through state or federal courts. Public Law 99-372 (The Handicapped Children's Protection Act of 1986) amends P.L. 94-142 to reimburse legal fees and other costs for parents who win due process hearings, appeals, or court cases.

While due process hearings are an important feature ensuring an appropriate education for students with mental retardation, the most important component is the IEP process. If all parties proceed in good faith according to these guidelines the majority of conflicts can be resolved.

IDEA '97 Final Regulations Major Issues

The final regulations accompanying the Individuals with Disabilities Education Act (IDEA) amendments of 1997 appear in the March 12th Federal Register. This section reviews some of the major issues addressed in this package of regulations:

IEP's and General Curriculum

Prior to 1997, the law did not specifically address general curriculum involvement of disabled students. The 1997 Amendments shifted the focus of the IDEA to one of improving teaching and learning, with a specific focus on the Individualized Education Program (IEP) as the primary tool for enhancing the child's involvement and progress in the general curriculum.

The final regulations reflect the new statutory language which requires that the Individualized Education Program for each child with a disability include:

- A statement of the child's present levels of educational performance including how the child's disability affects the child's involvement and progress in the general curriculum;

- A statement of measurable annual goals related to meeting the child's needs that result from the child's disability to enable the child to be involved in and progress in the general curriculum;

- A statement of the special education and related services and supplementary aids and services; and

- A statement of the program modifications or supports for school personnel that will be provided for the child to advance appropriately toward attaining the annual goals, be involved and progress in the general curriculum, and participate in extra curricular and other nonacademic activities, and to be educated and participate with other children with disabilities and nondisabled children.

General State and District-Wide Assessments

The 1997 amendments specifically require that, as a condition of State eligibility for funding under Part B of IDEA, children with disabilities are included in general State and district-wide assessment programs. The amendments also address timelines and reporting requirements.

The final regulations essentially incorporate these statutory provisions on general State and district-wide assessments verbatim. These provisions require that States and LEAs must:

- Provide for the participation of children with disabilities in general State and district-wide assessments—with appropriate accommodations and modifications in administration, if necessary;

- Provide for the conduct of alternate assessments not later than July 1, 2000 for children who cannot participate in the general assessment programs; and

- Make available, and report, to the public on the assessment results of disabled children, with the same frequency and in the same detail as reported on the assessment results of non-disabled children.

Regular Education Teacher Involvement

Prior to 1997, the law did not include a regular education teacher as a required member of the Individualized Education Program team. Under the 1997 IDEA amendments, the IEP team for each child with a disability now must include at least one of the child's regular education teachers, if the child is, or may be, participating in the regular education environment. The new law also indicates that the regular education teacher, to the extent appropriate, participates in the development, review, and revision of the IEP of the child.

The final regulations package clarifies that:

- If a child has more than one regular education teacher, the LEA may designate which teacher (or teachers) will be on the IEP team;

- Depending upon the child's needs and the purpose of the specific IEP team meeting, the regular education teacher need not be required to participate in all decisions made as part of the meeting or to be present throughout the entire meeting or attend every meeting;

- The extent to which it would be appropriate for the regular education teacher member of the IEP team to participate in IEP meetings must be decided on a case-by-case basis; and,

- Each of the child's teachers, including the regular education teacher(s) and provider(s) must be informed of his or her responsibilities related to implementing the child's IEP and the specific accommodations, modifications, and supports that must be provided for the child.

Graduation with a Regular Diploma

Neither the old or revised IDEA speaks directly to the issue of students with disabilities graduating with a regular high school diploma.

However, the 1997 Amendments placed greater emphasis on involvement of disabled students in the general curriculum and in State and district-wide assessment programs.

The final regulations incorporate the Department's longstanding policy position clarifying that:

- Graduation from high school with a regular diploma is considered a change in placement requiring written prior notice;

- A student's right to FAPE is terminated upon graduation with a regular high school diploma (The statutory requirement for re-evaluation before a change in a student's eligibility does not apply.); and,

- A student's right to FAPE is not terminated by any other kind of graduation certificate or diploma.

Discipline

Prior to 1997, the statute only specifically addressed the issue of discipline in a provision that allowed personnel to remove a child to an interim alternative educational placement for up to 45 days if the child brought a gun to school or to a school function. The IDEA '97 incorporated prior court decisions and Department policy that allows schools to remove a child for up to ten school days at a time for any violation of school rules as long as there is not a pattern, and children with disabilities cannot be long-term suspended or expelled from school for behavior that is a manifestation of his or her disability and services must continue for children with disabilities who are suspended or expelled from school. The IDEA '97 also expanded the authority of school personnel to remove to an interim alternative educational placement for up to 45 days to apply to all dangerous weapons and to knowing possession of illegal drugs and sale or solicitation of the sale of controlled substances and added a new ability of schools to request a hearing officer to remove a child for up to 45 days if keeping the child in his or her current placement is substantially likely to result in injury to the child or others. The amendments added provisions requiring schools to assess children's troubling behavior and develop positive behavioral interventions to address that behavior, and defining how to determine whether behavior is a manifestation of a child's disability.

The final regulations incorporate these statutory provisions and provide additional specificity on a number of key issues:

- **Services During Periods of Disciplinary Removal:** Schools do not need to provide services during the first ten school days in a school year that a child is removed.

  - During any subsequent removal that is for ten school days or less, schools provide services to the extent determined necessary to enable the child to appropriately progress in the general curriculum and appropriately advance toward achieving the goals of his or her IEP. In cases involving removals for ten school days or less, school personnel, in consultation with the child's special education teacher, make the service determination.

  - During any long-term removal for behavior that is not a manifestation of disability, schools provide services to the extent determined necessary to enable the child to appropriately progress in the general curriculum and appropriately advance toward achieving the goals of his or her IEP. In cases involving removals for behavior that is not a manifestation of the child's disability, the child's IEP team makes the service determination.

- **Conducting Behavioral Assessments & Developing Behavioral Interventions:** Meetings of the IEP team to develop behavioral assessment plans or if the child has one, review the behavioral intervention plan, are only required when the child has first been removed from his or her current placement for more than ten school days in a school year and when commencing a removal that constitutes a change in placement. If other subsequent removals occur, the IEP team members review the child's behavioral intervention plan and its implementation to determine if modifications are necessary, and only meet if one or more team members believe that modifications are necessary.

- **Manifestation Determinations:** Manifestation determinations are only required if a school is implementing a removal that constitutes a change of placement.

- **Change of Placement:** The final regulations clarify that a change of placement occurs if a child is removed for more than ten consecutive school days or is subjected to a series of removals that constitute a pattern because they cumulate to more than ten school days in a school year, and because of factors such as the length of each removal, the total amount of time the child is removed, and the proximity of the removals to one another.

• **Removals of Up to Ten School Days at a Time:** The final regulations clarify that school personnel may remove a child with a disability for up to ten school days and for additional removals of up to ten school days for separate acts of misconduct as long as the removals do not constitute a pattern.

Attention Deficit Disorder & Attention Deficit Hyperactivity Disorder

Neither the old nor revised IDEA included Attention Deficit Disorder or Attention Deficit Hyperactivity Disorder as a separate disability category.

Relying on the Department's long-standing policy, the final regulations clarify that:

• ADD and ADHD have been listed as conditions that **could** render a child eligible under the "other health impaired"(OHI) category of Part B of IDEA; and,

• The term "limited strength, vitality, or alertness" in the definition of "OHI," when applied to children with ADD and ADHD, includes a child's heightened alertness to environmental stimuli that results in limited alertness with respect to the educational environment.

Developmental Delay

Prior to the 1997 IDEA amendments, States could define and require Local Education Agencies to use the developmental delay category for children ages 3 through 5. The 1997 IDEA amendments allowed States to define developmental delay for children ages 3 through 9 and authorized LEAs to choose to use the category and, if they do, they are required to use the State's definition.

The final regulations clarify that:

• A State that adopts the term *developmental delay* determines whether it applies to children ages 3 through 9, or to a subset of that age range (e.g., ages 3 through 5);

- If an LEA uses the term *developmental delay*, the LEA must conform to both the State's definition of that term and to the age range that has been adopted by the State;

- If the State does not adopt the term *developmental delay*, an LEA may not independently use that term as a basis for establishing a child's eligibility under Part B of IDEA; and,

- Any State or LEA that elects to use the term *developmental delay* for children aged 3 through 9 may also use one or more of the disability categories for any child within that age range if it is determined, through the evaluation under Part B of IDEA, that the child has an impairment under Part B of IDEA, and because of that impairment needs special education and related services.

Definition of Day and School Day

Prior to 1997, the law included only the term "day" that was interpreted by the Department to mean "calendar day." Now, law uses the terms "day," "business day," and "school day."

The final regulations clarify that:

- **Day** means calendar day, unless otherwise indicated as business day or school day;

- **Business day** means Monday through Friday, except for Federal and State holidays, unless holidays are specifically included in the designation of business day;

- **School day** means any day (including a partial day) that children are in attendance at school for instructional purposes; and,

- The term "school day" has the same meaning for all children with and without disabilities.

Charter Schools

The IDEA Amendments of 1997 contain two specific provisions on public charter schools, including requiring that: (1) in situations in which charter schools are public schools of the LEA, the LEA must serve children with disabilities in those schools in the same manner that it serves children with disabilities in its other schools, and provide Part B funds to those schools in the same manner as it provides Part B funds to its other schools; and (2) An SEA may not require a charter school that is an LEA to jointly establish its eligibility with another LEA unless it is explicitly permitted to do so under the State's charter school statute.

The final regulations clarify that:

• Part B final regulations apply to all public agencies, including public charter schools that are not included as LEAs or education service agencies (ESAs), and are not a school of an LEA or ESA;

• The term LEA includes public charter schools that are established as an LEA under State law;

• The term "public agency" includes among the list of examples of a public agency, public charter schools that are not otherwise included as LEAs or ESAs and are not a school of an LEA or ESA;

• Children with disabilities who attend public charter schools and their parents retain all rights under Part B of IDEA; and,

• Compliance with Part B of IDEA is required regardless of whether a public charter school receives Part B funds.

Parentally-Placed Children with Disabilities in Private Schools

Prior to 1997, the law did not extensively address the education of children with disabilities placed in private schools by their parents. These children were served based on the limited provisions of the statutes and on the Education Department's General Administrative Regulations (EDGAR) and the Department's long-standing policy interpretation.

The 1997 amendments included some of the old language and incorporated the Department's long-standing policy interpretation.

Specifically, the final regulations clarify that:

• The term "service plan" has been adopted for use in lieu of "IEP" for parentally-placed children in private schools;

• Part B services must be provided in accordance with a "service plan" that, to the extent appropriate, meets specified IEP requirements;

• Child find activities for private school children with disabilities must be comparable to that in the public schools;

- Public agencies must consult with representatives of parentally-placed private school children with disabilities on how to conduct child find activities for those children in a manner that is comparable to that for public school children;

- Each LEA must consult with representatives of private school children with disabilities to decide how to conduct the annual count of the number of those children;

- The costs of child find activities for private school children with disabilities may not be considered in determining whether the LEA met the minimum expenditure requirements; and,

- The due process procedures under Part B apply to child find activities for private school children with disabilities, including evaluations, but do not apply to the other provisions regarding children with disabilities enrolled by their parents in private schools.

For Further Information

Department of Education
Tel: 202-205-5507
URL: http:/www.ed.gov/offices/OSERS

The National Association of Protection and Advocacy (P&A) Systems, (NAPAS)
220 I Street, N.E., Suite 150
Washington, D.C. 20002
Tel: 202-546-8202

The NAPAS can give you information about the Protection and Advocacy organization in your state.

The National Information Center for Children and Youth with Handicaps (NICHCY).
P.O. Box 1492
Washington, D.C. 20013-1492
Toll-free: 800-695-0285
Tel: 202-884-8200
E-mail: nichcy@aed.org
URL: http://www.nichcy.org

A publications list is available from the NICHCY.

Chapter 30

Early Interventions

Developmental Disabilities Programs

There are nearly four million Americans with developmental disabilities. Developmental disabilities are severe, chronic disabilities attributable to mental and/or physical impairment which manifest before age 22 and are likely to continue indefinitely. They result in substantial limitations in three or more areas: self-care, receptive and expressive language, learning, mobility, self-direction, capacity for independent living, and economic self-sufficiency, as well as the continuous need for individually planned and coordinated services.

The major goal of the programs is a partnership with state governments, local communities, and the private sector to assist people with developmental disabilities to reach maximum potential through increased independence, productivity, and community integration. They address all elements of the life cycle: prevention; diagnosis; early intervention; therapy; education; training; employment; and community living and leisure opportunities.

The Developmental Disabilities programs comprise three State-based programs that collaborate from different mandated activity

This chapter includes excerpts from "Developmental Disabilities Fact Sheet," Administration for Children and Families (ACF), January 1999; "A Parent's Guide to Accessing Programs for Infants, Toddlers, and Preschoolers with Disabilities," National Information Center for Children and Youth with Disabilities (NICHCY), August 1994; and "Head Start 1998 Fact Sheet," AFC Press Room, Administration for Children and Families (ACF), June 17, 1999.

areas. A fourth program addresses issues that are of concern to residents across the nation.

Developmental Disabilities Grant Programs

State Developmental Disabilities Councils

Formula grants support Councils in the States to promote capacity building and advocacy activities, the development of a consumer and family-centered comprehensive system, and a coordinated array of culturally competent services, supports, and other assistance designed to help people with developmental disabilities achieve independence, productivity, and integration and inclusion into the community. The Councils address employment issues, and may also address community living activities, child development activities, system coordination and community education activities, and other activities.

These state grants are allotted on the basis of population, financial need, and need for service. Fifty-five states and territories receive Council grants. For Fiscal Year (FY) 1999, $64.8 million is available. The same amount has been proposed for FY 2000.

Protection and Advocacy (P&A) Program

The Protection and Advocacy (P&A) Program provides for the protection and advocacy of legal and human rights through formula grants to States. The P&A systems advocate on behalf of, and provide advocacy services to, persons with developmental disabilities in areas related to their disabilities, including: education, abuse and neglect, institutional and habilitation services, guardianship, and housing issues. These systems have provided individual advocacy to about 40,000 clients per year, pursued class-action advocacy on behalf of hundreds of thousands per year, and also provided training and information and referral services to additional thousands.

These State grants are allotted on the basis of population, financial need, and need for service. Fifty-six States and territories receive P&A grants. For FY 1999, $26.7 million is available. The same amount has been proposed for FY 2000.

University Affiliated Programs (UAP)

UAP is a discretionary grant program for public and private, nonprofit agencies affiliated with a university. Annual grants provide for interdisciplinary training, exemplary services, technical assistance, and information/dissemination activities.

The program is designed to garner additional assistance for a national network of UAPs. UAPs support activities which address individual needs from birth to old age, a variety of service issues from prevention to early intervention to supported employment, and a broad range of disabilities.

The UAP now consists of 61 programs which have provided clinical and community-based service and technical assistance to community services personnel. In addition, 61 UAPs receive supplemental training grants for early intervention, community-based programs, and other activities.

For FY 1999, $17.5 million is available in grants for operational and administrative support as part of a national network. The same amount has been proposeed for FY 2000.

Projects of National Significance (PNS)

PNS funds are awarded to public or private, non-profit institutions to enhance the independence, productivity, integration and inclusion into the community of people with developmental disabilities. Monies also support the development of national and state policy.

These Projects focus on the most pressing issues affecting people with developmental disabilities and their families. Issues transcend the borders of states and territories, but must be addressed in a manner which allows for local implementation of practical solutions. Examples include:

- Data collection and analysis;

- Technical assistance to program components;

- Projects which enhance participation of people with developmental disabilities from minority and ethnic groups;

- Projects which explore the transition of youth with developmental disabilities from school to work;

- Projects which develop strategies for self-advocacy and leadership skills among people with developmental disabilities and their families;

- Projects which develop training and ongoing programs for inclusion of children with developmental disabilities in child care settings;

- Projects which address involvement of people with developmental disabilities in the criminal justice system.

In addition, PNS funds may be awarded for technical assistance and demonstration projects which expand or improve the advocacy functions of the State Planning Councils, the functions performed by UAPs and the P&A System. In FY 1999, a total of $10.2 is available The same amount has been proposeed for FY 2000.

Parent's Guide to Accessing Programs for Infants, Toddlers, and Preschoolers with Disabilities (Ages Birth–Five Years)

This section addresses the most asked questions about early intervention services for children ages birth through 2 years old and special education and related services for children ages 3 through 5 years old.

The rules or guidelines for special education in the United States and its territories are outlined in a federal law known as the Individuals with Disabilities Education Act (IDEA), formerly known as the Education of the Handicapped Act (EHA). Each state or territory develops its own policies for carrying out this Act.

Early Intervention Services for Infants and Toddlers Who Have a Developmental Delay or Who Are At Risk of a Developmental Delay (Ages Birth–2 Years Old)

The term "parent" is used to mean anyone who is in charge of the care and well-being of a child. These can be guardians, single parents, grand-parents, surrogate parents, foster parents, or other family members.

The federal law known as Public Law (P.L.) 102-119 guarantees certain rights to young children (ages birth to 5) with special needs. This law is the most recent amendment to IDEA.

Q: What Should I Do if I Think My Child Has Special Needs?

A: First, you'll need to find out if your infant or toddler is eligible for early intervention services. There are many people who can help you with this. These are services for infants and toddlers that are designed to identify and treat a problem or delay as early as possible. Early intervention services are offered through a public or private agency and are provided in different settings, such as the child's home, a clinic, a neighborhood daycare center, hospital, or the local health department.

Early intervention services can range from prescribing glasses for a two-year-old to developing a complete physical therapy program for an infant with cerebral palsy.

Q: Who Do I Contact First for Help?

A: Each state decides which of its agencies will be the lead agency in charge of early intervention services for infants and toddlers with special needs. In your state, the first contact person may be an early interventionist (an early childhood specialist working with infants and toddlers), someone with the lead agency, or someone in your state's Child Find office.

To find out who can help you in your area, contact NICHCY at 1-800-695-0285 (Voice/TT). Explain that you want to find out about early intervention services for your child and ask for a name in your area.

Important. Write down the names and phone numbers of everyone you talk to. (You can use the Sample Record-Keeping Worksheet in this chapter as a guide.) Having this information available may be helpful to you later on.

When you talk with a local contact person explain that you think your child may need early intervention services and you would like to arrange for an evaluation and assessment. Write down any information you are given.

Evaluation and Assessment

Evaluation refers to the procedures used to determine if a child is eligible for early intervention services. Assessment refers to the ongoing process of gathering and using information about how a child is developing and determining what kind of help he or she might need.

In regards to your child, this information may come from some or all of the following:

- Doctors' reports;

- Results from developmental tests given to your child;

- Your child's medical history;

- Observations and feedback from all members of the multidisciplinary team, including parents; and

- Any other important observations, records, and/or reports about your child.

401

Depending on your state's policies or rules, usually a team of professionals, which may include a psychologist, an early interventionist, and an occupational or physical therapist, will evaluate a child.

Under P.L.102-119, evaluations and assessments are provided at no cost to families. Check with your contact person for local guidelines.

If you child is found to be eligible, services are usually provided at no cost to the family, however, you may have to pay for some services, depending on your state's policies. Check with the contact person in your area or state. Some services may be covered by your health insurance, by Medicaid, or by Indian Health Services.

In some areas, you may be charged a "sliding-scale" fee that is based on what you earn. Every effort is made to provide services to all infants and toddlers who need help, regardless of family income.

Service Coordinator (Case Manager)

When a child's needs are assessed and the child is found eligible for services, a service coordinator will be assigned to the family. This person should have a background in early childhood development and methods for helping young children who may have developmental delays. The service coordinator should know the policies for early intervention programs and services in your state.

This person can help you locate other services in your community, such as recreation, child care, or family support groups. The service coordinator will work with your family as long as your baby is receiving early intervention services and, after your child is 2 years old, the service coordinator will help your family move on to programs for children ages 3 through 5.

Individualized Family Service Plan (IFSP)

The family and the service coordinator work with other professionals, as appropriate, to develop an Individualized Family Service Plan, or IFSP. The guiding principal of the IFSP is that the family is a child's greatest resource, that a baby's needs are closely tied to the needs of their family. The best way to support children and meet their needs is to support and build upon the individual strengths of their family. So the IFSP is a whole family plan with the parents as the most important part of the IFSP team. Involvement of other team members will depend on what the baby needs. These other team members could come from several agencies, and may include medical people, therapists, child development specialists, social workers, and others.

The IFSP will describe the following: the child's development levels; family information (with parents' concurrence); the major outcomes expected to be achieved for the child and family; the services the child will be receiving; when and where he or she will receive these services, and the steps to be taken to support his or her transition to another program. The IFSP will identify the service coordinator. The IFSP may also identify services the family may be interested in, such as financial information or information about raising a child with a disability.

Each state has developed specific guidelines for the IFSP. Your service coordinator can explain what the IFSP guidelines are in your state.

Parent Support Groups

There are several types of parent groups available, including:

- Support groups (such as Parent-to-Parent) for families of children with disabilities;

- Parent training and information programs funded by the federal government, such as the Technical Assistance for Parent Programs (TAPP) Project; and

- Groups concerned with a specific disability, such as United Cerebral Palsy Associations, Inc. (UCPA) or the Arc (formerly the Association for Retarded Citizens of the United States).

Parent groups can offer information, support, and/or training to families of children with disabilities to help parents take a more active role in helping their children. Through such groups, families meet other families with similar needs to discuss resources, day-to-day problems, and personal insights.

Your service coordinator or someone at your local school may be able to tell you about nearby groups. For more details on parent groups, contact NICHCY (1-800-695-0285) and ask for the "Parent's Guide to Accessing Parent Programs."

Special Education Programs and Services for Preschoolers with Disabilities (Ages 3–5 Years Old)

The federal law known as Public Law (P.L.) 102-119 guarantees certain rights to young children (ages birth to 5) with special needs. This law is the most recent amendment to Public Law (P.L.) 94-142,

The Education For All Handicapped Children's Act, now called the Individuals with Disabilities Act (IDEA). Chapter 29 of this *Sourcebook* provides further information about IDEA.

Preschoolers and Special Education

If you think your preschooler needs special education, you will first want to find out if he or she is eligible for a special education program. Special education programs are specially designed programs in public schools offered at no cost to families of children with disabilities. Today, under P.L.102-119, all schools must offer special education services to eligible 3-5 year olds with disabilities.

The best place to start your search for assistance is your local public elementary school. (In most cases, this would be the school that other children who live near you attend.) Call and ask to speak to the principal or to someone in charge of special education at the school.

If this doesn't work, call NICHCY (1-800-695-0285) and ask for the name and phone number of the person in your area in charge of these programs. Explain that you want to find out about special education services for your child. Ask what you need to do to arrange for an evaluation.

Write down the names and phone numbers of everyone you talk to. (As a guide, you can use the Sample Record-Keeping Worksheet at the end of this document.) Having this information available may be helpful to you later on.

Evaluation

Evaluation means the procedures used to determine whether a child has a disability and the extend of the special education and related services the child needs. In regards to your child, this information may come from:

- Doctors' reports;

- Results from developmental tests given to your child;

- Your child's medical history;

- Observations and feedback from all members of the assessment team, including parents; and

- Any other important observations, records, and/or reports about your child.

404

Evaluations are conducted by a multidisciplinary team or group of persons. Who is involved will depend on the rules in your state or school district. Ask your school contact person what the policy is for getting an evaluation for your child.

Special education services are offered for 3-5-year-olds at no cost to parents. The assessment and evaluation process is considered part of these services and is provided at no cost to families.

Support Groups

There are many support groups available for parents.

- Support groups (such as Parent-to-Parent) for families of children with disabilities;

- Parent training and information programs funded by the federal government, such as the Technical Assistance for Parent Programs (TAPP) Project; and

- Groups concerned with a specific disability, such as United Cerebral Palsy Associations, Inc. (UPCA), or the Arc (formerly the Association for Retarded Citizens of the United States).

Parent groups can offer information, support, and/or training to families of children with disabilities to help them take a more active role in their children's education. Through such groups, families meet other families with similar needs to discuss local resources, daily problems, and personal insights. For more details on these and other parent groups, contact NICHCY and ask for the "Parent's Guide to Accessing Parent Groups."

IDEA and Early Intervention

For the past 25 years, laws have been passed by Congress instructing states to provide education for children and youth with disabilities. Public Law 94-142, the Education For All Handicapped Children Act (EHA), was passed by Congress and signed into law by President Ford in 1975. This law is well known; it required states to fully educate all children with disabilities. It has been amended several times. In 1986, the EHA was amended through P.L. 99-457 to, among other things, lower the age at which children can receive special services to three years old. It also established the Handicapped Infants and Toddlers Program (Part H), which is for children who need help from birth to their third birthday. The amendments of 1990 and 1991 brought about more changes, among which was a change in the name. Now the EHA will be called IDEA, the Individuals with Disabilities Education Act.

IDEA requires that all states and territories provide a public school education to children with disabilities from ages 3 to 21, no matter how severe their disabilities are. There are several basic rights that this law promises to children with disabilities (ages 3 to 21) and their parents:

- The right to a "free appropriate public education" at public expense (in some cases, this may include placing a child in a private school);

- The right to an educational placement that is based on an assessment and evaluation of each child's own special needs;

- The right of children with disabilities to receive teaching or instruction that is designed to meet their needs; these needs are to be clearly written and included in an Individualized Education Program (IEP) for each child, with statements about what services the child will receive;

- The right to a full range of educational services that may include related services such as counseling, special transportation, speech/language pathology, or occupational or physical therapy;

- The right of parents (or guardians) to be included in making decisions about their child's educational needs and to approve the educational plans for their child; and

- The right of parents (or guardians) to appeal any decisions made about the identification, evaluation, and placement of the child through a due process procedure.

Finally, IDEA requires that children with disabilities be educated in the "Least Restrictive Environment" (LRE), that is, in a setting with children who have no disabilities, with special help provided to those who need it.

Programs for Very Young Children

Under the IDEA, early intervention services are to be made available to infants and toddlers with disabilities, ages birth through two years. Services are not the same in all areas. To find out what is available where you live, call the early childhood specialist in your school system or check under "Programs for Infants and Toddlers with Disabilities" on NICHCY's State Resource Sheet. You can also call NICHCY at 1-800-695-0285 (Voice/TT) ask for assistance.

Congress made funds available to help states and territories plan a comprehensive service system to provide the following services:

- Early intervention services to infants and toddlers (ages birth through 2 years) with disabilities. If a state chooses to, it can also serve infants and toddlers at risk of developing disabilities; and

- Special education programs and related services to preschoolers (ages 3 through 5 years) who have disabilities.

Services for children 3 years old and up are provided by the state department of education. However, programs for children under age 3 are provided by different agencies in different states. Sometimes the department of education will handle all these programs; in other states it may be the health department or another agency.

The term "infants and toddlers with disabilities" in the law refers to children (ages birth through 2 years) who need early intervention services in any of the following areas:

- Physical,

- Cognitive,

- Communication,

- Social or emotional, and/or

- Adaptive development.

Early intervention services must be provided by people who are qualified to work with infants and toddlers who have disabilities or who are at risk of developing disabilities. Any services provided must be written into an Individual Family Service Plan (IFSP) that is reviewed every 6 months.

Parent's Record-keeping Worksheet

The sample record-keeping worksheet below can help you start a file of information about your child. As you contact different people and places, it's a good idea to keep records of people you've talked with and what was said. As time goes by, you will want to add other information to your file, such as:

- Letters and notes (from doctors, therapists, etc.);
- Medical records and reports;
- Results of tests and evaluations;
- Notes from meetings about your child;
- Therapist(s') reports;
- IFSP and IEP records;
- Your child's developmental history, including personal notes or diaries on your child's development;
- Records of shots and vaccinations; and
- Family medical histories.

Make sure you get copies of all written information about your child (records, reports, etc.). This will help you become an important coordinator of services and a better advocate for your child. Remember, as time goes on, you'll probably have more information to keep track of, so it's a good idea to keep it together in one place.

Sample Record-Keeping Worksheet

Problem/Topic:

Name of person or agency you talked to:
Name of your contact person(may be same as above):
Date you called:
Telephone:

Results of discussion:

Action taken (if any):

Person not helpful on this topic, but may be helpful regarding (list topics/areas/issues):

Head Start Program 1998 Facts

A total of 16,892,000 children have been served by the program since it began in 1965.

The program is administered by Head Start Bureau, the Administration on Children, Youth and Families (ACYF), Administration for Children and Families (ACF), Department of Health and Human Services (DHHS).

Grants are awarded by the DHHS Regional Offices and the Head Start Bureau's American Indian and Migrant Programs Branches directly to local public agencies, private non-profit organizations and school systems for the purpose of operating Head Start programs at the community level.

During the 1996-1997 operating period, Head Start programs report that:

- 13 percent of the Head Start enrollment consisted of children with disabilities, (mental retardation, health impairments, visual handicaps, hearing impairments, emotional disturbance, speech and language impairments, orthopedic handicaps, and learning disabilities).

- 90 percent of the Head Start teachers had degrees in early childhood education or had obtained the Child Development Associate (CDA) credential or a state certificate to teach in a preschool classroom.

- 571 programs operated a home based program. Home based services were provided to 39,833 children by 4,562 home visitors.

- 30 percent of the staff were parents of current or former Head Start children. Over 808,147 parents volunteered in their local Head Start program.

- 61 percent of Head Start families have incomes of less than $9,000 per year and 77.7 percent have yearly incomes of less than $12,000.

Head Start programs are encouraged to use non-Head Start resources in their communities for Head Start children and their families. Recent data show that 67.8 percent of the Head Start children are enrolled in the Medicaid/Early and Periodic Screening, Diagnosis and Treatment (EPSDT) program which pays for their medical and dental services.

About half of all programs provide some full day services to families who need childcare services.

39 percent of families need childcare for children enrolled in Head Start. Of those, 25 percent received child-care through the Head Start program or its parent agency.

The 1994 reauthorization of the Head Start Act established a new Early Head Start program for low-income families with infants and toddlers. In Fiscal Year 1997, $159,000,000 was used to support 173 projects to provide, Early Head Start child development and family support services in all 50 states and in the District of Columbia and Puerto Rico. These projects, plus a number of Parent and Child Centers and Comprehensive Child Development Program's serve 22,000 children under age three. In Fiscal Year 1998, funding of $279,250,000 will be used to support Early Head Start programs.

Table 30.1: Enrollment

Ages	Percent of Enrollment
Number of 5 year-olds and older	6%
Number of 4 year-olds	60%
Number of 3 year-olds	30%
Number under 3 years of age	4%

Racial/Ethnic Composition	Percent of Enrollment
American Indian	3.5%
Hispanic	26.1%
Black	36.1%
White	31.2%
Asian	3.1%
Total Enrollment	793,809

Table 30.2: Staff

Paid Staff	55,300
Volunteers	1,315,000

Additional Information

Head Start Bureau
330 "C" Street, SW
Washington, D.C. 20447
URL: http://www2.acf.dhhs.gov/programs/hsb

National Information Center for Children and Youth with Disabilities (NICHCY)
P.O. Box 1492
Washington, DC 20013
Toll-free: 800-695-0285 (Voice/TTY)
Tel: 202-884-8200 (Voice/TTY)
E-mail: nichcy@aed.org
URL: http://www.nichcy.org

Chapter 31

Your Rights in the Special Education Process

Parents of children with disabilities have a vital role to play in the education of their children. This fact is guaranteed in federal legislation that specifies the right of parents to participate in the educational decision-making process. As your child progresses through educational systems, knowing and following through on your rights and responsibilities ensures that you are a contributing partner with professionals who will influence your child's future. This chapter provides you with an introduction to your rights and responsibilities in the special education process.

What Are Your Rights in the Special Education Process?

Public Law 101-476 (IDEA) clearly defines the rights of children with disabilities and their parents. A basic provision of the law is the right of parents to participate in the educational decision-making process. Your rights, more specifically, include the following:

Your child is entitled to a free, appropriate public education meaning it is at no cost to you as parents, and it meets the unique educational needs of your child.

Reprinted with permission "Rights and Responsibilities of Parents of Children with Disabilities," © 1994, ERIC Clearinghouse on Disabilities and Gifted Education.

You will be notified whenever the school wishes to evaluate your child, wants to change your child's educational placement, or refuses your request for an evaluation or a change in placement.

You may request an evaluation if you think your child needs special education or related services.

You should be asked by your school to provide "parent consent" meaning you understand and agree in writing to the evaluation and initial special education placement for your child. Your consent is voluntary and may be withdrawn at any time.

You may obtain an independent evaluation if you disagree with the outcome of the school's evaluation.

You may request a reevaluation if you suspect your child's current educational placement is no longer appropriate. The school must reevaluate your child at least every 3 years, but your child's educational program must be reviewed at least once during each calendar year.

You may have your child tested in the language he or she knows best. For example, if your child's primary language is Spanish, he or she must be tested in Spanish. Also, students who are hearing impaired have the right to an interpreter during the testing.

The school must communicate with you in your primary language. The school is required to take whatever action is necessary to ensure that you understand its oral and written communication, including arranging for an interpreter if you are hearing impaired or if your primary language is not English.

You may review all of your child's records and obtain copies of these records, but the school may charge you a reasonable fee for making copies. Only you, as parents, and those persons directly involved in the education of your child will be given access to personal records. If you feel any of the information in your child's records is inaccurate, misleading, or violates the privacy or other rights of your child, you may request that the information be changed. If the school refuses your request, you then have the right to request a hearing to challenge the questionable information in your child's records.

You must be fully informed by the school of all the rights provided to you and your child under the law.

You may participate in the development of your child's Individualized Education Program (IEP) or, in the case of a child under school age, the development of an Individualized Family Service Plan (IFSP). The IEP and IFSP are written statements of the educational program designed to meet your child's unique needs. The school must make every possible effort to notify you of the IEP or IFSP meeting and arrange it at a time and place agreeable to you. As an important member of the team, you may attend the IEP or IFSP meeting and share your ideas about your child's special needs, the type of program appropriate to meeting those needs, and the related services the school will provide to help your child benefit from his or her educational program.

You may have your child educated in the least restrictive school setting possible. Every effort should be made to develop an educational program that will provide the greatest amount of contact with children who are not disabled.

You may request a due process hearing to resolve differences with the school that could not be resolved informally.

What Are Your Responsibilities in the Special Education Process?

Parental responsibilities to ensure that a child's rights are being protected are less clearly defined than are parental rights. These responsibilities vary depending on the child's disabling condition and other factors. Some of the following suggestions may be helpful:

Develop a partnership with the school or agency. You are now an important member of the team. Share relevant information about your child's education and development. Your observations and suggestions can be a valuable resource to aid your child's progress.

Learn as much as you can about your rights and the rights of your child. Ask the school to explain these rights as well as the regulations in effect for your district and state before you agree to a special education program for your child. Contact disability organizations for their publications on special education rights.

Ask for clarification of any aspect of the program that is unclear to you. Educational and medical terms can be confusing, so do not hesitate to ask.

Make sure you understand the program specified on the IEP or IFSP before agreeing to it or signing it. Ask yourself if what is planned corresponds with your knowledge of your child's needs.

Consider how your child might be included in the regular school activities program. Do not forget areas such as lunch, recess, art, music, and physical education.

Monitor your child's progress. If your child is not progressing, discuss it with the teacher and determine whether the program should be modified. As a parent, you can initiate review of your child's educational program.

Discuss with the school or agency any problems that may occur with your child's assessment, placement, or educational program. It is best to try to resolve problems directly with the agency or school. In some situations, you may be uncertain as to how you should resolve a problem. All states have advocacy agencies that can usually provide you with the guidance you need to pursue your case.

Keep records. There may be many questions and comments about your child that you will want to discuss, as well as meetings and phone conversations you will want to remember. It is easy to forget information useful to your child's development and education if it is not written down.

Join a parent organization. In addition to the opportunity to share knowledge and support, a parent group can be an effective force on behalf of your child. Many times parents find that as a group they have the power to bring about needed changes that strengthen special services.

What Can You Offer the IEP or IFSP Process?

In the final analysis, parents of children with disabilities should be involved in the IEP or IFSP process as much as they want to be and as much as they can be. The following are suggestions for ways parents can become involved:

Before attending an IEP or IFSP meeting, make a list of things you want your child to learn.

Bring any information the school or agency may not already have to the IEP or IFSP meeting. Examples include copies of medical records, past school records, and test and medical evaluation results.

Discuss what related services your child may need. Your child may need to be involved with many other specialists and professionals besides his or her teacher, including occupational therapists, physical therapists, or speech-language pathologists.

Discuss what assistive technology devices or services your child may need and have these listed in your child's IEP or IFSP.

Ask what you can do at home to support the program.

Make sure the goals and objectives listed in the IEP or IFSP are specific and measurable.

Periodically, ask for a report on your child's progress.

Regard your child's education as a cooperative effort. If, at any point, you and the school cannot reach an agreement over your child's educational and developmental needs, ask to have another meeting. Remember, compromise on your part and the school or agency's part may be important in resolving conflicts and maintaining a good working relationship. If, after a second meeting, there is still a conflict over your child's program, you may wish to ask for a state mediator or a due process hearing.

What Resources Are Available?

Many organizations have information to help guide you through the special education process. Since the specific criteria and procedures used by school districts vary, it is important to familiarize yourself with the information provided by state and local agencies. You will find your local school district's director of special education and his or her staff helpful in accessing such information and guiding you through the process.

Additional resources are available from national disability organizations. Some of them have state and local chapters that can provide more locally based support. All states now have federally supported parent information and training centers. The contacts cited below may be able to help you locate such a center in your state:

ERIC Clearinghouse on Disabilities and Gifted Education
The Council for Exceptional Children (CEC)
1920 Association Drive
Reston, VA 22091-1589
Tel: 800-328-0272 or 703-264-9474
URL: http://www.cec.sped.org/er-menu.htm

National Information Center for Children and Youth with Disabilities (NICHCY)
PO Box 1492
Washington, DC 20013-1492
Tel: 800-695-0285

Chapter 32

Assistive Technology

What Is Assistive Technology?

Assistive technology is the term used to describe devices that are used by children and adults with mental retardation and other disabilities to compensate for functional limitations and to enhance and increase learning, independence, mobility, communication, environmental control, and choice. It also refers to direct services that assist individuals in selecting, acquiring, or using such devices (The Arc, 1991).

How Can Assistive Technology Benefit People with Mental Retardation?

Technology can help people with mental retardation overcome barriers towards independence and inclusion. Assistive technology compensates for the functional limitations of the user and serves as a liberating agent for the individual. Specifically the user may communicate with others, engage in recreational and social activities, learn, work, control the environment, and increase his or her independence in daily living skills with the assistance of technology (Copel, 1991).

Reprinted with permission "The Arc's Q&A on Assistive Technology," © The Arc.

People with mental retardation should be introduced to the benefits of assistive technology early in their lives. There should be consistency in the kind of technology available, how it is used, and methods for instructing the user on operating the device. The device should be available for use throughout the day and in all settings, including home, school, work, and leisure time environments. Transitions from one device to another should be made as smooth as possible by building on and integrating previously learned skills.

Assistive technology solutions should be flexible and customizable to accommodate the unique abilities of each person with mental retardation. There is a growing use of assistive technology with infants and young children, particularly with communication devices being introduced to facilitate early language development. Technology is also being developed to address the needs of people as they age in an effort to help them continue to live independently.

How Is Assistive Technology Used by People with Mental Retardation?

Communication. For a person who cannot communicate with his/her voice, for physical and/or cognitive reasons, technology can substitute as a voice for the user. Computerized communication devices with vocal output are called augmentative communication devices.

Environmental Control. Devices to control the environment are important to people with severe or multiple disabilities and/or cognitive disabilities, whose ability to move about in the environment and to turn electrical appliances on or off is limited. Assistive technology allows a person to control electrical appliances, audio/video equipment such as home entertainment systems, or to do something as basic as lock and unlock doors.

Mobility. For a person who does not walk, simple to sophisticated computer controlled wheelchairs and mobility aids are available.

Education. For a student with disabilities, the computer becomes a tool for improved literacy, language development, mathematical, organizational, and social skill development. Students with severe and multiple disabilities use technology in all aspects of the classroom learning environment from academic software to communication. Alternative ways to access computers are available for

420

students who cannot operate a keyboard. Software can be regulated so it runs at a slower pace if a student needs this type of modification for learning.

Activities of Daily Living. Technology is assisting people with disabilities to successfully complete everyday tasks of self-care. Examples include:

- Automated and computerized dining devices allow an individual who needs assistance at mealtime to eat more independently (Brown, et al., 1991).

- Devices may be used to assist a person with memory difficulties to complete a task or to follow a certain sequence of steps from start to finish in such activities as making a bed or taking medication.

- Homes can be designed which use technology to assist a person to become more independent. Various devices can regulate and control many aspects of the living environment. An environment can be computerized to give cues and auditory direction for successfully performing tasks or for navigating.

- Directional guidance systems with auditory cues can assist a person to travel from one location to another.

- Technology can assist a person to shop, write a check, pay the bills, or use the ATM machine.

Employment. With the advent of the Americans with Disabilities Act, employers are making the workplace more cognitively accessible. For some employees, this requires work site modifications where the employer adapts the environment, to permit the employee to perform a job. As an example, an audio tape is an accommodation which can be used to prompt a worker to complete each task in a job.

Sports and Recreation. Computerized games can be adapted for the user with physical limitations. Adaptations can be made to computer games which allows the game activity to be slowed down for the user who cannot react as quickly to game moves and decision-making. Specially adapted sports equipment is available to compensate for functional limitations and which allow an individual to participate more fully. For example, people with mental retardation can participate in bowling using specially designed ball ramps.

What Are Some Considerations before Using Assistive Technology with an Individual Who Has Mental Retardation?

Before determining whether or not an individual with mental retardation will benefit from assistive technology, the following questions should be considered:

- What functional limitation does the individual with mental retardation have that might be helped by assistive technology?

- Have professionals conducted a comprehensive assessment to determine what assistive technology might be beneficial?

- Will the technology be available for the person to use at all times in all environments where needed, and if not, what alternatives exist in other environments?

- Will the assistive technology be a tool and not inhibit typical development and skill acquisition?

- Does the professional support system exist for the successful application and use of the identified technology?

- Can parents, teacher, and/or the person with mental retardation obtain training in the use of technology?

What Are Some Barriers in Obtaining Assistive Technology for People with Mental Retardation?

Sometimes, finding appropriate assistive technology for a person with mental retardation is difficult because the technology may not exist which takes into account the unique needs of people with cognitive disabilities. Assistive technology professionals, like computer scientists and rehabilitation engineers, have limited experience applying technology assistance to users with cognitive disabilities. Consequently, they may be unfamiliar with appropriate system design, training, and skill development strategies which encourage successful technology use by people with mental retardation.

Individuals with physical or sensory limitations have challenges that can be addressed through specific and generic problem solving. That is, by modifying a computer for a person who is blind, it will be accessible by many people who are blind. Because most people with mental retardation or cognitive limitations have a range of learning and processing abilities, it is difficult to develop generic assistive technology solutions which are appropriate for all individuals. Assistive technology solutions must be flexible and easily customized.

Developers and manufacturers of assistive technology often do not consider issues of cognitive access and flexibility when designing their products. An exception is the developers who are pioneering efforts to design communication devices for cognitive access recognizing that many users needing communication devices have cognitive limitations.

Sufficient instructional strategies for device use have not been developed to assist practitioners. Thus, even though a device is designed for cognitive access and use, if the user does not receive adequate instruction, the device has limited utility.

The predictable barrier of the cost of assistive technology is also an ever present issue.

Additional Sources

Currently, 42 of the 50 states have funding from the federal government to coordinate and organize statewide assistive technology services. To identify resources within your state, contact:

The RESNA Technical Assistance Project
1700 North Moore Street, Suite 1540
Arlington, VA 22209-1903
Tel: 703-524-6686
Fax: 703-524-5530
TTY: 703-524-6639
E-Mail: nbailey@resna.org
URL: http://www.resna.org

Some communities also have assistive technology learning centers. For information contact:

The Alliance for Technology Access
2175 East Francisco Blvd, Suite L
San Rafael, CA 94901
Tel: 415-455-4575
Toll-free: 800-455-7970
Fax: 415-455-0654
E-Mail: atainfo@ATAcess.org
URL: http://www.ATAcess.org

The Arc also maintains an extensive library of information on assistive technology and can provide information on specific topics.

The Arc
National Organization on Mental Retardation
1010 Wayne Ave, Suite 650
Silver Spring, MD 20910
Tel: 301-565-3842
Fax: 301-565-3843
E-mail: thearc@metronet.com
URL: http://www.thearc.org

References

The Arc. (1991). *Assistive Technology* Position Statement.

Copel, H. (1991). *Tech Use Guide: Students with moderate cognitive abilities* (Technical Report). Reston, VA: Center for Special Education Technology.

Brown, C., Sauer, M., Cavalier, A., Frische, E., & Wyatt, C. (1991). *The assistive dining device: A tool for mealtime independence.* Proceedings of the RESNA 14th Annual Conference (pp. 341-343). Kansas City, MO: RESNA.

Chapter 33

Transition from School to Work and Community Life

What Is the Transition Mandate?

The 1990 amendments to Public Law 94-142 (P.L. 101-476, The Individuals with Disabilities Education Act or IDEA) mandate that each student have transition services included in his or her Individualized Education Program no later than age 16. The act requires a systematic plan of action for vocational and other community activities.

The Individuals with Disabilities Education Act (IDEA) Definition of Transition Services

The Individuals with Disabilities Education Act defines transition services as "a coordinated set of activities for a student, designed within an outcome-oriented process, which promotes movement from school to post-school activities." Post-school activities include "post-secondary education, vocational training, integrated employment (including supported employment), continuing and adult education, adult services, independent living, or community participation."

IDEA also states that "the coordinated set of activities shall be based upon the individual student's needs, taking into account the student's preferences and interests." These activities include "instruction, community experiences, the development of employment and other post-school adult living objectives, and when appropriate, acquisition of daily living skills and functional vocational evaluation."

Reprinted with permission, © 1991, The Arc.

Why Is Preparation for Transition so Important?

Young people leaving the school system frequently find there is no coordinated adult service system to help them find work and participate in community life. A recent study found that only 28 percent of young adults with mental retardation who had been out of school for one year were currently competitively employed. An additional 9 percent were working in a sheltered workshop (SRI International, 1991).

What Can the School Do to Promote a Student's Successful Transition?

A school should provide for the following:

- Transition goals in the Individualized Education Program for students with disabilities. Public schools should provide education programs that teach practical daily living and socialization skills, as well as academic skills. As students grow older, they should have annual goals and objectives related to career education, vocational preparation, and community living included in their Individualized Education Programs.

- Students and parents should be involved in goal setting and the development of activities or strategies to reach those goals. Families often possess a perspective that teachers and professionals do not, and may be able to offer knowledge of unique resources to aid in successful transition.

- Integrated settings. Students with mental retardation greatly benefit from working and learning beside peers without disabilities. These students need to be involved in regular vocational and academic classrooms, as well as in actual work in community settings. Researchers have noted that integrated settings promote the acquisition of skills the student will need to succeed in a job and in other aspects of community living (Hasazi, Collins & Cobb, 1988).

- Opportunity to participate in vocational education programs. Vocational education programs in the public schools can provide training in a variety of skilled occupations, thereby helping some students graduate directly into employment. Students with mental retardation should be provided access to these options.

Their choices should not be limited to a small selection of segregated programs or courses leading to low-skill jobs.

- Training at employment sites. Students develop skills for real jobs and learn appropriate work and social behaviors through interactions with co-workers that occur naturally in a work setting. While students are still in school is a good time to arrange for work experiences in several kinds of jobs. This exploration will help students make decisions about the kinds of work they would like to seek upon graduation.

- Paid work experience. Studies have shown that students competitively employed while still in school are more likely to remain employed after graduation. Government sponsored employment programs, supervised part- or full-time work after school or in the summer and similar experiences can help prepare the student for eventual employment (Hasazi, Collins & Cobb, 1988).

- Job-seeking skills curriculum. A key element in transition to employment is the ability to seek and obtain employment. Schools can offer instruction and practice in the skills necessary to obtain one's own job. This means students do not have to depend on specialized employment programs that may or may not exist in that community.

What Can Parents Do to Prepare Their Younger Child for Transition?

While IDEA requires the school to address planning for transition by age 16, parents should begin planning for this transition as early as kindergarten. They can consider the skills the child needs for a meaningful and purposeful adult life and can be sure these are included in the child's IEP at the appropriate school level.

Parents can also be effective educators in communicating to their child the value of work and by teaching behaviors that develop their child's employment potential. Parents can provide opportunities for enjoyable community activities which allow the child to see people at work in different settings. Parents can allow as much independence as possible, assign the child responsibility for certain chores to help instill a positive work ethic, promote appropriate behavior at home and in social situations, assist the child in practicing good grooming skills, and emphasize the importance of physical fitness.

What Can Schools Do to Help Students as They Prepare to Leave School?

Schools can develop cooperative relationships with employers and adult human service agencies, so that students leaving school receive support in making the transition to their new life in the community. Vocational rehabilitation agencies, employment and training programs, local mental retardation services, residential programs, transportation systems, and other agencies should be included in the transition process. As the student's needs for services and supports are identified, services from each agency can be arranged and included in the student's transition plan.

Are Students Eligible for Income Support?

Yes. Many students will be eligible for income and health programs under the Social Security Administration. The two programs are Supplemental Security Income (SSI) and Social Security Disability Insurance (SSDI). Some people with mental retardation can receive one or the other, or even both. Eligibility for either program is based on disability and income. An adult must have a disability which affects his or her ability to work or participate in "substantial, gainful activity."

Social Security regulations note that a person under age 18 is considered disabled if the disability so limits his or her ability to function independently, appropriately, and effectively in an age-appropriate manner. Furthermore, the impairment and the limitations resulting from it must be of comparable severity to that which would disable an adult. People under age 18 are evaluated in terms of their age-appropriateness in the areas of response to stimuli, cognition, communication, motor skill, social interaction, personal/behavioral skill and concentration, persistence and pace.

Income is also an eligibility factor for these programs. For a person over 18, personal income is considered. For those under age 18, a portion of the parent's income is considered.

SSI and SSDI income, plus the Medicaid and Medicare health benefits which are often a part of these benefits, makes it important for parents to be aware of their child's eligibility for these programs prior to the child going to work. While it is possible that these benefits can be lost if the individual with a disability goes to work, all or a portion of income and health benefits may be retained if proper planning is done prior to working and suitable precautions are taken. More information is available from the Social Security office.

What Types of Work Settings Are Available for Youth Leaving the School System?

A variety of employment programming is offered in many states. The school's transition team should be able to describe the options to families. Offerings may include variations on competitive employment and supported employment opportunities.

Competitive employment consists of regular jobs in the community worked by people with and without disabilities. Supported employment refers to paid work for people with disabilities who need special assistance in learning the job requirements and performing the associated tasks. Support can be provided through a job coach (a trainer) for an individual worker in the regular employment setting. Support can also be provided by having a supervisor oversee a crew or enclave of people with disabilities working together at a job site.

Although states also fund segregated work and vocational skills development programs (such as sheltered workshops and work activity centers), many states are de-emphasizing these programs and converting them to programs that help people obtain jobs in integrated settings.

What Types of Living Arrangements Are Available for People with Mental Retardation Who Graduate to Adult Life?

Living arrangements will vary from community to community. Independent living complexes, group homes, or staffed apartments may be available. In some communities, people are able to choose their own homes and receive supports they need to live in their home. Some people will be eligible for rental assistance through a program of the U.S. Department of Housing and Urban Development.

Who Is Going to Provide the Follow-Up and Follow-Along Services to Young Adults after They Graduate?

Some young adults with more severe disabilities may be eligible for services provided by their state agency on mental retardation or rehabilitation services. Young adults who are not eligible for follow-along support from adult services must gain the skills necessary to become their own advocates. The schools should teach them and their families to help them gain an understanding of the adult service systems so that they can gain access to the services they require. These services are often available in their own communities through Job Training Partnership Act programs, state employment agencies, or other adult services.

References

Hasazi, S.B., Collins, M. & Cobb, R.B. (1988). Implementing transition programs for productive employment: New directions, In B.L. Ludlow, A.P. Turnbull & R. Luckasson (Eds.), *Transition to adult life for people with mental retardation — principles and practices.* (pp. 183-189). Baltimore: Paul H. Brookes Publishing Co.

Mitchell, W. (July 1990) *Obtaining Financial Support for Housing for People with Mental Retardation.* (Q&A #101-23). Arlington, TX: The Arc.

Social Security Administration. (June 1991). *Red Book on Work Incentives.* Department of Health and Human Services.

SRI International (Feb. 1991). Youth with Disabilities: How Are They Doing? *The National Longitudinal Transition Study of Special Education Students.* Office of Special Education Programs, U.S. Department of Education.

Part Seven

Specific Health Care Issues

Chapter 34

Physical Fitness and Aging

Author's note: This information is pertinent to many people with other developmental disabilities.

The purpose of this chapter is to provide an overview of what physical fitness is and how it relates to older people with mental retardation. Also provided are some helpful guidelines for family members, support people, service providers, and others interested in starting a program for older individuals with mental retardation.

The Fitness Movement

The fitness movement in this nation has risen to new heights. People today are becoming more aware of the need to participate in regular physical activity. Many Americans are joining fitness centers or purchasing home exercise equipment. This remarkable interest in fitness stems from several research studies that have been published over the last few years demonstrating the enormous health benefits that can be obtained from a higher level of fitness. These studies have shown that the risk of health problems and death from disease, including heart disease, cancer, diabetes, and stroke, drops as a person's fitness level improves.

Reprinted with permission, "Aging, Mental Retardation and Physical Fitness" by James H. Rimmer, Ph.D., © 1997, The Arc.

What Is "Physical Fitness?"

Physical fitness must be defined with consideration for an individual's age and lifestyle. For a younger person, physical fitness is defined as a physical condition that allows an individual to work without becoming overly fatigued, perform daily chores, and have enough energy left over to engage in leisure activities. For example, if an individual is unable to make it through an eight-hour work day or is too tired at the end of the day for leisure or household activities such as gardening, walking, playing tennis, or cleaning, then he or she probably has too low a level of physical fitness. For the older person who may not necessarily be working eight to ten hour days, physical fitness could be defined within the context of being able to conduct the day's chores (e.g., cleaning, dressing, shopping, doing laundry, climbing stairs) without becoming exhausted or tired. Stated another way, the person has enough energy to do daily chores, and still has a reserve of energy left over in order to participate in some type of leisure activity such as gardening or going for a walk. Physical fitness is extremely important for the older population because as a person ages, there is a higher level of fatigue and often pain resulting from arthritis, low back problems, or other ailments. As these conditions worsen over time, many older people become more sedentary thinking that if they rest they will get better. On the contrary, when older people rest and become more inactive, they feel increasingly tired because they have decreased their physical fitness. Thus, it is a vicious cycle: disability and pain cause decreased movement, and decreased movement results in less fitness and a higher level of dysfunction. A good physical fitness level—regardless of the disability—helps older people maintain their quality of life and can reduce their dependence on others to help with activities of daily living such as climbing stairs, bathing, and doing housework.

The second part of the definition for physical fitness can apply to both younger and older individuals. A moderate to high level of fitness reduces the incidence of "hypokinetic" diseases. Hypokinetic basically means a lack of movement or too little movement. When the body doesn't move enough, it slowly deteriorates and becomes vulnerable to disease. In essence, a sedentary lifestyle can contribute to or increase the severity of such problems as hypertension (high blood pressure), obesity (excess fat), adult-onset diabetes, osteoporosis (brittle bones), depression, and low back pain. Individuals who are poorly fit often end up with one or more of these conditions, which impairs the individual's quality of life.

What Are the Different Components of Physical Fitness?

There are four parts to physical fitness:

- Muscle strength and endurance
- Flexibility
- Body composition (body fat)
- Cardiovascular endurance (the ability of the heart, lungs, and blood vessels to transport oxygen to working muscles)

To attain a good level of fitness, your physical fitness routines should focus on each of these areas. Each part of physical fitness directly relates to the health of the individual and to the person's ability to get through the day's activities without becoming overly fatigued.

Importance of Each Part of Fitness to Aging Adults

The four areas of fitness are all very important to a healthy lifestyle. In order for the body to move as efficiently as possible, and in order to prevent those debilitating hypokinetic diseases, all four parts of fitness must be worked on at least on a weekly basis.

Muscle strength and endurance is needed to complete activities of daily living. For example, being able to climb stairs, get in and out of a bathtub or chair without relying too much on the arms, open jars, carry groceries, lift boxes, etc., all depend on an adequate level of muscle strength and endurance. As a person grows older, strength declines and these tasks become more and more difficult. When it gets to the point where the person does not have enough strength to climb stairs or get out of the bathtub, it often means that the person will be dependent on others for assisting them with their activities of daily living. Some experts believe that muscle strength and endurance is the most important component of physical fitness for older adults. Research has shown that there is a significant loss in muscle strength starting at age 45 and continuing up to age 65, and a further decline in the seventh and eighth decades of life. The loss in strength is greater in men than women.

Cardiovascular endurance keeps the circulatory system—the heart, blood vessels, and lungs-in good condition. The number one cause of death in this country is from heart disease. Research has shown that by maintaining good cardiovascular endurance through-out life, you can drastically decrease your chances of having a heart attack, stroke and many other diseases. Good cardiovascular endur-ance also allows people to have lots of energy during the day, so that they don't become fatigued from doing household activities or other physical tasks such as climbing stairs or walking.

Flexibility involves the stretching of connective tissues in our body, which includes the muscles, tendons, and ligaments. Most older adults become very inflexible as they grow older, partly due to a lack of physical activity. When muscles are not moved for a long period of time, they gradually shorten to a point where it becomes difficult to reach for things or bend over to pick something up from the floor. The older a person gets, the tighter his or her muscles become. Flexibility is often neglected in a fitness program. Most people prefer to spend their time doing cardiovascular activities such as riding a stationary bike or walking. However, as a person grows older, flexibility exercises become extremely important for preventing tightness in the joints and muscles.

Body composition is the fourth part of fitness and has to do with the amount of fat that you store in your body. There are numerous research studies that have shown that the more body fat you have the worse your fitness and the quicker your body will age. This is because body fat is "dead weight" and takes a heavy toll on all the systems of the body (e.g., bones, joints, heart, lungs) over time. It's sort of like carrying heavy sandbags in your car. The extra weight puts more stress on the engine and causes a quicker deterioration. Just look around you. There are not too many heavy people living into their 80s and 90s. Most of the very old, including those over 100 years, are lean, and in some cases, just plain skinny! When body fat levels are very high (which is called obesity or overweight), a person is at greater risk for a variety of health problems, including arthritis, diabetes, depression, back pain, heart disease, stroke, and high blood pressure. Body composition has a lot to do with the amount of activity that you get during the day, as well as the type and amount of food you eat.

Do People with Mental Retardation Have Problems in These Areas?

Yes. Research indicates that people with mental retardation have very low levels of cardiovascular endurance. A lack of cardiovascular en-durance often means the individual is unable to sustain long workdays or participate in leisure-time activities (e.g., hiking, swimming, biking) without becoming fatigued. A poor cardiovascular fitness level also translates into a higher risk of disability and death.

The strength levels of adults with mental retardation have also been shown to be very poor. Most studies have indicated that because of a lack of strength at such an early age, it will be very difficult for people at 50 or 60 years of age to perform activities of daily living that require a minimal level of strength. These include climbing stairs, getting up from a chair or the floor, or carrying objects such as a tray filled with food.

Perhaps the most disturbing findings pertain to the fitness levels of adults with mental retardation in regard to their body fat levels. Whereas a third of all Americans are overweight, close to one-half of all people with mental retardation are overweight. When we separate women from men, we find that many more women with mental retardation are overweight compared to men with mental retardation. The high levels of obesity (excess fat) found in people with mental retardation expose them to a higher risk for many different types of diseases that are associated with high levels of body fat. These include Type II diabetes, hypertension, heart disease, stroke, arthritis, respiratory diseases, and cancer.

What Are the Fitness Levels of Older Adults with Mental Retardation?

Although there haven't been any studies completed on aging adults with mental retardation, the research on younger adults with mental retardation has shown that as a group, they have very poor fitness levels. To be quite frank, the fitness levels of adults with mental retardation, in general, are terrible. So, as younger people with mental retardation age, their general lack of physical fitness on top of health problems that older people generally face increases the likelihood that many will have health problems beyond those of their nondisabled peers.

Research (Rimmer, 1994) has noted that adults with mental retardation are at risk for all kinds of hypokinetic diseases that result from physical inactivity. One researcher went as far as saying that people with mental retardation are a "population at risk" because of their sedentary lifestyle (Petetti and Campbell, 1991).

What Happens to the Body as We Age?

The body goes through several changes as we age. First, there is a loss in muscle tissue and a gain in fat tissue. Unfortunately, this is a negative change because fat does not perform a function like your muscles which contract in order to move the body. Therefore, fat just adds to our body weight, making it more difficult to move.

Bones start to lose their mineral content (calcium and phosphorus) as we grow older. This leads to one of the biggest health problems in the elderly, osteoporosis. Osteoporosis causes compression fractures, which are small cracks in the bones. This usually occurs in three areas: the hips, vertebrae (bones in the back), and wrist. When osteoporosis gets progressively worse, a hip fracture can occur.

Our cardiovascular system, consisting of the lungs, heart, and blood vessels, takes a heavy toll as we grow older. A great deal of the deterioration to the cardiovascular system has to do with lifestyle. There is an accumulation of plaque (calcium, cholesterol, fats) inside the blood vessels which over time can lead to a blockage or a ruptured artery. When this occurs, a person will sustain a heart attack or stroke. The number one cause of death in this country is due to cardiovascular disease.

The last thing that slowly starts to deteriorate is the central nervous system. Our reflexes and reactions become slower, and we lose speed in doing things that require agility. Catching ourselves from a slip or fall becomes more difficult.

Should Older People with Mental Retardation Become More Active?

Yes. People with mental retardation who lack physical fitness are more likely to incur other disabling conditions as they age. It is important for these individuals to start to look for opportunities to increase their physical activity. Health care providers, staff, and family members should also take an active role in supporting physical fitness in the aging adult with mental retardation. For example, physical fitness could be included as part of an individual's habilitation plan.

Research has shown that even the frail elderly, which includes people in their 80s or 90s, can improve their fitness level. One study documented large increases in strength and function after a weight-training program in 90-year-old people living in a Boston area nursing home. Other studies have shown significant increases in cardiovascular endurance after performing an exercise program that involved large muscle groups.

Clearly, one of the best ways to get an older person with mental retardation involved in physical activity would be to join a structured exercise program. This would help maintain regularity to the program, and keep the person on a consistent schedule. So often exercise programs are started only to be stopped a short while after they begin. A structured program offers the consistency that so many individuals need in order to continue exercising.

For more information on fitness programs, contact your local YMCA/YWCA, senior center, or private fitness center in your community.

What Are the Steps to Becoming More Fit for the Aging Adult with Mental Retardation?

Here is a list of recommended steps for starting a structured exercise program for an aging adult with mental retardation.

Step 1—Get Physician Approval to Start an Exercise Program

Because of the high risk of injury in starting an exercise program for an older adult who has been inactive for much of his or her life, it is important that the person have a physical to make sure that it is safe to begin an exercise program. Even though a person may have high blood pressure, arthritis, and obesity, an exercise program can and should be started. A precaution is that the physician gives his or her approval before starting the exercise program.

Step 2—Increase Physical Activity Throughout the Day

We often fail to realize that increasing physical activity levels throughout the day can expend a larger number of calories. This is especially important for individuals who won't or do not want to participate in a structured physical fitness program. Some helpful tips include the following:

- Get rid of the remote control and get up and down when changing television channels.

- Use weights (e.g., milk jugs filled with water) to lift and lower several times a day to build strength and flexibility.

- Use stairs instead of the elevator, especially when only going up or down one or two floors.

- While watching television, perform stretching exercises during commercials.

- Go for short five to ten minute walks two to three times a day and work toward increasing pace and duration to benefit cardiovascular endurance.

439

- While lying in bed, lift and lower each leg several times and then lift and lower each arm several times.

- Stand against a wall with arms outstretched and palms flat against the wall. Bend elbows and bring face close to the wall and then extend arms again. This is called a wall push-up.

- Shoot a basketball, play catch, go ice-skating, and participate in other informal sports and physical activities.

- Get involved in community recreation and formal sports programs during the year, such as senior arthritis exercise classes offered by the YMCA/YWCA, low impact aerobic dance, yoga classes, swimming, or Special Olympics International's Unified Sports programs.

Step 3—Choose the Right Exercise Program

There are a variety of exercise programs that are offered in most communities. It is important to select one that fits the specific needs of the individual. Most YMCA/YWCAs offer exercise classes for older adults and so do senior centers. However, these classes are often very structured and may not fit the needs of some older adults with mental retardation. Ask the director of the program if there is a slower moving aerobic dance class, or if a weight training program could be adapted for a group of older adults living in one setting (e.g., group home). It is important that directors of fitness centers understand that they cannot intentionally or unintentionally discriminate against persons with disabilities. If the program doesn't fit the needs of the client, then it's the responsibility of the director to develop a program that does fit the individual's needs. Never take "no" for an answer. There are professionals in adapted physical education or exercise physiology who have a background in developing exercise programs for people with mental retardation. If the YMCA/YWCA or fitness director does not have the expertise to meet the needs of the consumer, then point them to local adapted physical education instructors located in public schools or other experts that can help them develop the program.

Step 4—Exercise a Minimum of Three Days a Week

Once you select the right setting for your exercise program, it's important to exercise at least three days a week. The exercise program should consist of the following components: cardiovascular endurance, muscle strength and endurance, and flexibility. Each of these components should be developed, but more emphasis should be placed on the weakest areas of fitness. For example, if a person has very low levels of arm muscle strength and poor flexibility in the hamstrings, then that person should spend a little more time during each exercise session working on those areas by perhaps lifting light weights or stretching the hamstrings. However, it's important to work on all areas of fitness, so the person would also want to include cardiovascular exercise during each session, perhaps by riding a stationary bike or using a treadmill. Try to also add some extra activity on the days when the person does not go to a structured fitness program. For example, go hiking, swimming, bike riding, or participate in various sports. (Note: There are adult-size tricycles for people unable to ride a bicycle.)

Step 5—Keep the Program Fun and Rewarding

The exercise program must be enjoyable if the person is going to continue with the program for any length of time. If you notice that the person is getting tired of doing the same exercises, ask the fitness instructor to create a new program using different types of equipment and exercises. Sometimes fitness instructors get locked into the same exercise routines and the person gets bored and drops out. There are lots of different ways to develop each area of fitness and a creative instructor can keep people interested in the program. For example, a "before and after" photograph of the person can be taken to help him or her see the progress being made in weight loss, improved posture and increased muscle gain. A good fitness instructor will also notice early signs of burnout or boredom and will modify the program before the person drops out.

Important Information

Many people use a fitness center or exercise program to keep fit. If you are assisting a relative or friend with mental retardation, keep these questions in mind to help locate the most appropriate program.

1. Is the center or program aware of how to accommodate people with disabilities under the Americans with Disabilities Act?

2. Does it have anyone on staff who has a background in working with people who have disabilities?

3. Does it have accessible equipment?

4. Does it offer individualized training sessions at no extra cost or at a minimal cost?

5. Would it be willing to send one of its instructors to a training course or workshop on learning more about fitness and disability?

6. Do instructors have any training in rehabilitation, adapted physical education, or exercise physiology for special populations?

7. Do instructors have a positive attitude toward working with people who have disabilities? Are they open to learning more about a disability?

8. Do instructors put the individual through an assessment to determine the specific strengths and weaknesses of the person in the area of fitness?

9. Do instructors change the program periodically to prevent boredom or burnout?

References

Pitetti, K.H. & Campbell, K.D. (1991). Mentally retarded individuals: A population at risk? *Medicine and Science in Sports and Exercise*: 23, 586-593.

Rimmer, J. H. (1994). *Fitness and rehabilitation programs for special populations*. Dubuque, Iowa: WCB McGraw-Hill. (800) 338-3987.

Professional Associations and Resources

National Consortium for Physical Education and Recreation for Individuals with Disabilities
Adapted Physical Education National Standards
P. O. Box 6639
Charlottesville, Va. 22906-6639
(888) APENS-EX

The Consortium can provide technical support concerning adapted physical education.

American Alliance for Health, Physical Education, Recreation, and Dance (AAHPERD)
American Association for Active Lifestyles and Fitness (AAALF)
Adapted Physical Activity Council (APAC)
1900 Association Drive
Reston, Va. 22091
Toll-free: 800-213-7193
Tel: 703-476-3430
E-mail: aaalf@aahperd.org

APAC is a council within AAALF, a division of AAHPERD. APAC can be contacted at the address, telephone or e-mail address above, and is the primary contact for information on physical fitness and people with mental retardation. APAC can provide materials pertaining to adapted physical fitness education.

Special Olympics International (SOI)
Unified Sports
1325 G Street, N.W., Suite 500
Washington, DC 20005-3104
Tel: 202-628-3630

SOI's Unified Sports program brings athletes of similar ability, with and without mental retardation, together on the same teams.

Eichstaedt, C. B., & Lavay, B. W. (1992). *Physical activity for individuals with mental retardation.* Champaign, Illinois: Human Kinetics Publishers: (800) 747-5698.

Rimmer, J. H. (1994). *Fitness and rehabilitation programs for special populations.* WCB McGraw-Hill. (800) 338-3987.

Sherrill, C. (1998). *Adapted physical activity, recreation and sport.* WCB McGraw-Hill. (800) 338-3987.

Winnick, J. P. (1995). *Adapted physical education and sport.* Champaign, Illinois: Human Kinetics Publishers. (800) 747-5698.

RRTC on Aging with Mental Retardation
Institute on Disability and Human Development
University of Illinois at Chicago
1640 West Roosevelt Road
Chicago, Illinois 60608-6904

Tel: 800-996-8845 (V), 1-800-526-0844 (Illinois Relay Access)
URL: http://www.uic.edu/orgs/rrtcamr/index.html

The Center on Health Promotion Research for Persons with Disabilities

Located in the Institute on Disability and Human Development at the University of Illinois at Chicago, the Center has recently been funded by the Centers for Disease Control and Prevention (CDC) to establish a health promotion program for persons with disabilities. Secondary health conditions will be studied including lack of fitness, obesity, poor nutrition, emotional dependence, depression, behavioral problems, and family stress. The intervention component will be comprised of exercise sessions, nutritional training, cooking instruction, weight management, stress reduction, and peer support. The Center began operation in January 1998 and includes a collaborative project with the RRTC on Aging with Mental Retardation. For more information, contact Dr. Rimmer at the address, telephone number, or e-mail listed below.

James H. Rimmer, Ph.D.
Director of the Center on Health Promotion Research for Persons with Disabilities
Institute on Disability and Human Development
University of Illinois at Chicago
Tel: 312-413-9651
TDD: 312-413-0453
Fax: 312-413-3709
E-mail: jrimmer@niu.edu

The Arc
National Organization on Mental Retardation
1010 Wayne Ave, Suite 650
Silver Spring, MD 20910
Tel: 301-565-3842
Fax: 301-565-3843
E-mail: thearc@metronet.com
URL: http://www.thearc.org

Chapter 35

Sexual Abuse

What Is Sexual Abuse?

Sexual abuse includes a wide range of sexual activities that are forced upon someone. People with mental retardation are often unable to choose to stop abuse due to a lack of understanding of what is happening during abuse, the extreme pressure to acquiesce out of fear, a need of acceptance from the abuser, or having a dependent relationship with the abuser. Sexual abuse consists of sexually inappropriate and non-consensual actions, such as exposure to sexual materials (such as pornography), the use of inappropriate sexual remarks/language, not respecting the privacy (physical boundaries) of a child or individual (e.g., walking in on someone while dressing or in the bathroom), fondling, exhibitionism, oral sex, and forced sexual intercourse (rape).

How Often Are People with Mental Retardation Sexually Abused?

According to research, most people with disabilities will experience some form of sexual assault or abuse (Sobsey & Varnhagen, 1989). The rate of sexual victimization in the general population is alarming, yet largely goes unnoticed. At least 20 percent of females and 5 to 10 percent of males are sexually abused every year in the U.S. Although these figures are disturbingly high, people with mental

Reprinted with permission, "People with Mental Retardation & Sexual Abuse," ©1997, The Arc.

retardation and other developmental disabilities are at an even greater risk of sexual victimization. Victims who have some level of intellectual impairment are at the highest risk of abuse (Sobsey & Doe, 1991).

More than 90 percent of people with developmental disabilities will experience sexual abuse at some point in their lives. Forty-nine percent will experience 10 or more abusive incidents (Valenti-Hein & Schwartz, 1995). Other studies suggest that 39 to 68 percent of girls and 16 to 30 percent of boys will be sexually abused before their eighteenth birthday. The likelihood of rape is staggering: 15,000 to 19,000 of people with developmental disabilities are raped each year in the United States (Sobsey, 1994).

Why Is Sexual Abuse so Common Among People with Mental Retardation?

People with mental retardation may not realize that sexual abuse is abusive, unusual, or illegal. Consequently, they may never tell anyone about sexually abusive situations. People with and without disabilities are often fearful to openly talk about such painful experiences due to the risk of not being believed or taken seriously. They typically learn not to question caregivers or others in authority. Sadly, these authority figures are often the ones committing the abuse. Many special education programs have encouraged students to be compliant in a wide range of life activities, ultimately increasing the child's vulnerability to abuse (Turnbull, et.al., 1994). They often think they have no right to refuse sexually abusive treatment and are not taught risk reduction skills. Risk factors associated with sexual abuse include social powerlessness, communication skill deficits, impaired judgment, family isolation/stress, and living arrangements that increase vulnerability.

Signs of Sexual Abuse[1]

Physical Signs

- Bruises in genital areas
- Genital discomfort
- Sexually transmitted disease
- Signs of physical abuse
- Torn or missing clothing
- Unexplained pregnancy

446

Behavioral Signs

- Depression
- Substance abuse
- Withdrawal
- Atypical attachment
- Avoids specific setting
- Seizures
- Avoids specific adults
- Excessive crying spell
- Regression
- Sleep disturbances
- Disclosure
- Poor self-esteem
- Noncompliance
- Eating disorders
- Resists exam
- Self-destructive behavior
- Headaches
- Learning difficulty
- Sexually inappropriate behavior

Circumstantial Signs

- Alcohol or drug abuse by caregiver
- Devaluing attitudes
- Excessive or inappropriate eroticism
- Isolation of social unit
- Other forms of abuse
- Previous history of abuse
- Seeks isolated contact with children
- Strong preference for children
- Surrogate caregivers
- Unresolved history of abuse
- Pornography usage

[1]Adapted from Violence and Abuse in the Lives of People with Disabilities (1994), D. Sobsey.

What Are the Effects of Sexual Abuse?

Sexual abuse causes harmful psychological, physical, and behavioral effects. Individuals who experience long-term (chronic) abuse by a known, trusted adult at an early age suffer more severe damage compared to those whose abuse is perpetrated by someone not well known to the victim, begins later in life, and is less frequent and non-violent (Tower, 1989). Regardless of the circumstances surrounding sexual abuse (e.g., length of time it occurred, who the abuser is, and the victim's age), all forms of sexual abuse are serious and have the potential to be very damaging to the individual if left unaddressed and unspoken.

Who Is Most Likely to Abuse?

As is the case for people without disabilities who experience sexual abuse, those most likely to abuse are those who are known by the victim, such as family members, acquaintances, residential care staff, transportation providers, and personal care attendants. Research suggests that 97 to 99 percent of abusers are known and trusted by the victim who has developmental disabilities (Baladerian, 1991).

While in 32 percent of cases, abusers were family members or acquaintances, 44 percent had a relationship with the victim specifically related to the person's disability (such as residential care staff, transportation providers, and personal care attendants). Therefore, the delivery system created to meet specialized care needs of those with mental retardation contributes to the risk of sexual abuse.

What Type of Treatment or Therapy Is Available for Victims of Sexual Abuse?

People with developmental disabilities who have been sexually abused typically are not provided a way to "work through" or talk about their traumatic experiences in a treatment or therapeutic setting. Generally, the more severe the disability, the greater the difficulty in accessing services. This may be due to prejudices some people still have about people with disabilities. For example, the benefit of psychotherapy for people with mental retardation is questioned, as well as the impact of the abuse (whether or not abuse impacts people with mental retardation as strongly as others without disabilities).

Yet, all people who experience sexual abuse are affected and can benefit from therapeutic counseling, even if they are non-verbal. Children and adults who suffer abuse need to learn how to tell someone and who to tell. A variety of training techniques that teach self-defense, body integrity, prevention, and reporting should be used.

Human service workers must understand that people with developmental disabilities can and do benefit from therapy.

Locating a qualified therapist may be difficult since the person should be trained in both child/adult sexual abuse, as well as disabilities and sexuality. Payment for the therapy can be obtained through victim witness programs, community mental health centers, or developmental disability centers.

How Can the Incidence of Sexual Abuse of People with Mental Retardation Be Reduced?

Society has been slow to admit that sexual abuse of people with mental retardation is not only possible, but actually happening (Baladerian, 1992).

The first step in reducing the occurrence of sexual abuse is recognizing the magnitude of the problem and confronting the ugly truth that people with mental retardation and other developmental disabilities are more vulnerable to sexual victimization than those without disabilities.

Abusers typically abuse as many as 70 people before ever getting caught. Without reporting, there can be no prosecution of offenders or treatment for victims. Underreporting of sexual abusive incidents involving people with disabilities has in the past, and continues to be, a major obstacle in preventing sexual abuse. Only three percent of sexual abuse cases involving people with developmental disabilities will ever be reported (Valenti-Hein & Schwartz, 1995). Few people ever disclose sexual abuse for a variety of understandable reasons. However, such non-disclosure promotes an environment ripe for continued victimization.

Reporting can be increased through educating individuals with disabilities and service providers, improving investigation and prosecution, creating a safe environment that allows victims to disclose, and finally, employment policies must change to increase safety. For example, background checks on new employees should be conducted on a routine basis; and those with criminal records should be reported to the police, rather than firing the suspected abuser. Otherwise the individual will more than likely continue abusing others while working for future employers.

What Should I Do if I Suspect Sexual Abuse?

All states have laws requiring professionals, such as institutional care providers, police officers, and teachers to report abuse. All states allow the general public to report abuse as well. If you suspect a child is being sexually abused, contact your local child protective agency. If the person is an adult, contact adult protective services. These are also referred to as "Social Services," "Human Services" or "Children and Family Services" in the phone book. You do not need proof to file a report. If you believe the person is in immediate danger, call the police. After a report is made, the incident is referred for investigation to the state social service agency (who handles civil investigations) or to the local law enforcement agency (who handles criminal investigations). For more information on sexual abuse of people with disabilities, contact:

The National Task Force on Abuse and Disabilities
P.O. Box "T"
Culver City, CA 90230
Tel: 310-391-2420
E-mail: abuses@soca.com

The National Committee to Prevent Child Abuse
332 S. Michigan Ave., Ste. 1600
Chicago, IL 60604
Tel:800-555-3748
URL: http://www.childabuse.org/index.html.

The Arc
National Organization on Mental Retardation
1010 Wayne Ave, Suite 650
Silver Spring, MD 20910
Tel: 301-565-3842
Fax: 301-565-3843
E-mail: thearc@metronet.com
URL: http://www.thearc.org

References

Baladerian, N. (1991). Sexual abuse of people with developmental disabilities. *Sexuality and Disability*, 9(4), 323-335.

Baladerian, N. (1992). *Interviewing skills to use with abuse victims who have developmental disabilities*. Washington, D.C.: National Aging Resource Center on Elder Abuse.

Sobsey, D. (1994). *Violence and abuse in the lives of people with disabilities: The end of silent acceptance?* Baltimore: Paul H. Brookes Publishing Co.

Sobsey, D. & Doe, T. (1991). Patterns of sexual abuse and assault. *Sexuality and Disability*, 9 (3), 243-259.

Sobsey, D. & Varnhagen, C. (1989). Sexual abuse and exploitation of people with disabilities: Toward prevention and treatment. In M. Csapo and L. Gougen (Eds.) *Special Education Across Canada* (pp.199-218). Vancouver: Vancouver Centre for Human Developmental and Research.

Tower, C. (1989). *Understanding child abuse and neglect*. Boston: Allyn and Bacon.

Turnbull, H., Buchele-Ash, A., & Mitchell, L (1994). *Abuse and neglect of children with disabilities:* A policy analysis. Lawrence, Kansas: Beach Center on Families and Disability, The University of Kansas.

Valenti-Hein, D. & Schwartz, L. (1995). *The sexual abuse interview for those with developmental disabilities*. James Stanfield Company. Santa Barbara: California.

—by Leigh Ann Reynolds, M.S.S.W., M.P.A.

Leigh Ann Reynolds is a Health Promotion & Disability Prevention Specialist.

This chapter was reviewed by Dick Sobsey, R.N., Ed.D. and Nora Baladerian, Ph.D.

Chapter 36

Alzheimer's Disease

What Is Alzheimer's Disease?

Alzheimer's disease is a slowly progressive, degenerative disorder of the brain that eventually results in abnormal brain function and death (Janicki, 1995). Clinically, Alzheimer's disease is expressed as impairment in the cognitive and adaptive skills necessary for successful personal, community, and occupational functioning.

The initial symptoms often appear very gradually. There may be some minimum memory loss, particularly of recent events. The individual may experience difficulty in finding the right words to use during casual conversations. Work performance may begin to deteriorate, and changes in behavior may become obvious.

As Alzheimer's disease progresses, memory losses become even more pronounced. There may be specific problems with language abilities. Persons affected may have difficulty naming objects or with maintaining a logical conversation. They may have difficulty understanding directions or instructions and become disoriented as to time of day, where they are and who they are with. They may also begin to experience loss of self-care skills, including the ability to use the toilet. Severe changes in personality may begin to become obvious, and their social behavior may be marked by suspiciousness and delusions.

Finally, the disease will progress to the point where all abilities to function normally are lost, and affected individuals need total care.

Reprinted with permission, © 1995, "Alzheimer's Disease and People with Mental Retardation," The Arc.

The stages described may occur over different time periods in different individuals, ranging from 18 months to 20 years.

How Many People Are Affected by Alzheimer's Disease?

Alzheimer's disease accounts for more than 50 percent of the dementias seen in the general adult population. The estimated annual incidence of Alzheimer's disease is approximately 2.4 per 100,000 people age 40 to 60 and 127 per 100,000 people older than age 60. Estimates are that five percent of people over the age of 60 will have Alzheimer's neuropathology, and that this grows to 50 percent for the population age 85 and older. By the year 2000, more than two million Americans will be suffering from various stages of the disease (Janicki, 1994).

How Many People with Mental Retardation Are Affected by Alzheimer's Disease?

Most adults with mental retardation are at the same risk for Alzheimer's disease as are individuals in the general population. However, individuals are at greater risk of developing the disease if they:

- Are over 40 years of age and have Down syndrome.
- Have had some form of head injury, especially severe or multiple injuries.
- Have a history of Alzheimer's disease in their family.

Research from the Center for Aging Policy Studies at the New York State Institute for Basic Research in Developmental Disabilities show that the rate of occurrence of Alzheimer's disease among persons with a developmental disability appears to be about 2 to 3 percent of adults age 40 and older. People with Down syndrome make up about 60 percent of the adults with mental retardation who show signs of probable Alzheimer's disease (Janicki, 1995).

How Are People with Down Syndrome Affected Differently by Alzheimer's disease?

People with Down syndrome have higher rates of Alzheimer's disease. A growing body of research suggests that people with Down syndrome also experience premature aging, perhaps as many as 20 years earlier than would be expected in normal aging (Hawkins and Eklund, 1994). They are often in their mid to late 40s or early 50s when symptoms of Alzheimer's disease first appear, compared to the late 60s for the general population.

Although about 20 to 40 percent of adults with Down syndrome show the behavioral symptoms of dementia, upon autopsy nearly all older adults with Down syndrome show the brain changes associated with Alzheimer's disease. The progression of the disease takes, on the average, about eight years — somewhat less time than among persons in the general population. Men and women seem to be equally susceptible.

The symptoms of the disease may be expressed differently among adults with Down syndrome. For example, at the early stage of the disease, memory loss is not always noted, and not all symptoms ordinarily associated with Alzheimer's disease will occur. Generally, changes in activities of daily living skills are noted, and there may be the onset of seizures when there had been none in the past. Cognitive changes may also be present, but they are often not readily apparent, or they may be ignored because of limitations in the individual's general functional level.

What Are Some Signs That an Older Person with Mental Retardation May Be Developing Alzheimer's Disease?

Recent studies of individuals with mental retardation have shown behavioral symptoms of Alzheimer's dementia in such adults may include, but are not limited to: (1) the development of seizures in previously unaffected individuals, (2) changes in personality, (3) long periods of inactivity or apathy, (4) hyper-reflexitivity, (5) loss of activity of daily living skills, (6) visual retention deficits, (7) loss of speech, (8) disorientation, (9) increase in stereotyped behavior, and (10) abnormal neurological signs (Janicki, Heller, Seltzer & Hogg, 1995).

How Is Alzheimer's Disease Diagnosed in People with Mental Retardation?

There is no single diagnostic test for Alzheimer's disease. If the presence of Alzheimer's disease is suspected, a complete physical examination and more frequent medical, neurological, and psychological evaluations are strongly recommended to establish the progressive nature of the symptoms.

A definitive diagnosis can only be made at the time of autopsy. The numerous test and evaluation procedures will result in a "possible" or "probable" diagnosis of Alzheimer's disease.

To make a probable diagnosis of Alzheimer's disease, it is necessary to observe a well-documented progression of symptoms. Complete evaluation must be performed periodically. Such evaluations or tests are necessary to rule out conditions that are not Alzheimer's disease, or are reversible forms of dementia. A complete evaluation should include:

- A detailed medical history.

- A thorough physical and neurologic examination, including the testing of sensory-motor systems, to rule out other disorders.

- A "mental status test" to evaluate orientation, attention, recent recall, and the ability to calculate, read, write, name, copy a drawing, repeat, understand and make judgments.

- A psychiatric assessment to rule out the presence of a psychiatric disorder, particularly depression.

- Neuropsychological testing to measure a variety of functions that include memory, orientation, language skills, intellectual abilities, and perception.

- Routine laboratory tests, including blood work and urinalysis, and health screenings and other testing such as chest x-ray, electroencephalography (EEG), and electrocardiography (EKG), as well as certain specialized tests as deemed appropriate (Janicki, Heller, Seltzer & Hogg, 1995).

Where Does Someone Go to Be Evaluated for Possible Alzheimer's Disease?

A good place to start is with the person's physician. A neurologist, geriatrician, or an internist can also be a valuable resource.

States may have specialized centers for the evaluation and treatment of people with Alzheimer's disease. These centers may provide geriatric evaluations and assessment procedures plus other services. States may also have specialized services for people with mental retardation who are aging. These may include special clinics of local mental retardation, mental health or aging agencies, and university affiliated programs in developmental disabilities.

What Are the Steps Beyond Diagnosis to Help the Individual?

Once the suspicion of Alzheimer's disease has been clinically confirmed, the person's family, caregiver, or paid providers may need to make changes in the person's daily routine.

First and foremost, the person must feel safe and secure in his or her environment. As a result of the complications associated with Alzheimer's disease, what may have been comfortable and familiar for the individual will become unrecognizable and result in unpredictable behavior.

A few of the tips to help the person cope with the effects of the disease include:

* Emphasize maintaining abilities, particularly those affecting dignity (e.g., toileting, eating), rather than trying to teach new skills.

* Keep changes in environment and daily routine to an absolute minimum.

* Simplify routines and reduce choices to minimize feelings of anxiety and frustration.

* Use patience and redirection, keep verbal requests simple, and provide general supportive care.

Many more tips are contained in the booklet, *Developmental Disabilities and Alzheimer's Disease: What You Should Know*, available from The Arc.

References

Hawkins, B. and Eklund, S. (1994). *Aging-Related Change in Adults with Mental Retardation*. Research Brief. Arlington, Texas: The Arc. (Single copy free with self-addressed stamped envelope.)

Janicki, M.P. (1995). *Developmental Disabilities and Alzheimer's Disease: What You Should* Know. Arlington, Texas: The Arc. (Order from The Arc, Publications Dept., 500 E. Border St., S-300, Arlington, TX 76010.)

Janicki, M.P. (ed.). (1994). *Alzheimer Disease Among Persons with Mental Retardation:* Report from an International Colloquium.

Albany: New York State Office of Mental Retardation and Developmental Disabilities.

Janicki, M.P., Heller, T., Seltzer, G., & Hogg, J. (1995). *Practice Guidelines for the Clinical Assessment and Care Management of Alzheimer and other Dementias among Adults with Mental Retardation*. Washington, DC: American Association on Mental Retardation (444 North Capitol Street, N.W., Suite 846, Washington, DC 20001-1512).

Information in this chapter was provided by Matthew P. Janicki's three publications cited above. He is with the New York State Office of Mental Retardation and Developmental Disabilities.

Additional Information

The Arc
National Organization on Mental Retardation
1010 Wayne Ave, Suite 650
Silver Spring, MD 20910
Tel: 301-565-3842
Fax: 301-565-3843
E-mail: thearc@metronet.com
URL: http://www.thearc.org

Chapter 37

Human Immunodefieciency Virus (HIV) and Acquired Immune Deficiency Syndrome (AIDS)

AIDS stands for Acquired Immune Deficiency Syndrome. It is a disease caused by the Human Immunodeficiency Virus (HIV), sometimes referred to as the AIDS virus. This virus attacks the T-cells, which are part of the body's immune system. The loss of T-cells prohibits the body from fighting off bacteria that it is normally able to destroy before they cause disease. The type of diseases that HIV infection causes are commonly referred to as opportunistic infections. Some examples of these infections are, Pneumocystic carinii pneumonia (PCP), Kaposi's sarcoma (KS), and Candidiasis of the esophagus, trachea, bronchi or lungs. These diseases often prove fatal to the person with AIDS.

A person who is infected with the HIV virus is considered HIV positive. Since HIV may live in a person's body for years before causing any illness, an HIV positive person may look and feel healthy for a long time. In fact, unless people get tested for the HIV antibody, they may not know that they are infected. Once a person is infected with HIV, he is always infected. As yet, there is no cure for AIDS.

The HIV/AIDS epidemic appeared in the 1970s and 1980s. This disease has already infected millions of people, and the numbers are still rising.

Reprinted with permission, © 1997, "HIV/AIDS and Mental Retardation," The Arc.

How Do People Become Infected with HIV?

This virus is fragile and does not live outside the human body for very long. It prefers to live in blood, semen, and vaginal secretions. It is much less likely to be infectious when it is found in other body fluids like tears, saliva, sweat, and urine.

There are three ways for a person to become infected with HIV. First, a person can become infected by having unprotected sexual intercourse with an HIV positive person. The virus may be transmitted in semen, vaginal secretions, or any blood that may be present during sexual activity. Contact with these body fluids during any act of oral, vaginal, or anal sex may result in HIV infection.

Second, an uninfected person may become infected by exposure to the blood of an HIV positive person. This method of transmission is often referred to as blood to blood transmission and includes sharing needles and syringes to inject drugs, tattooing, ear piercing done in an unsanitary setting, biting, and scratching. Other modes of blood to blood transmission include sharing personal care items that may have blood on them and performing any activities that would expose an open wound to blood.

Third, babies of HIV infected women may be born with the infection. HIV can be transmitted before or during birth. This is often referred to as vertical transmission. If the woman breast feeds her baby, she may also transmit HIV during feeding.

What about People with Mental Retardation and HIV?

The HIV/AIDS epidemic also impacts people with mental retardation. Adults with mental retardation may be the victims of sexual abuse and sexual exploitation. In the age of safer sex, some people refuse to take precautions. Sometimes, their sexual partners are adults with mental retardation. One study identified 45 adults with mental retardation and advanced HIV infection or AIDS in 44 states (Marchetti, et al., 1989), but it is estimated that hundreds of such cases already exist. People living in group settings, as well as people living independently, are at risk.

What about Testing?

When a person is infected with HIV, his or her immune system begins producing antibodies to HIV. Blood tests for HIV antibodies are widely available throughout the United States. These blood tests are not "AIDS tests." The two tests that are used to detect the presence of HIV antibodies are the ELISA and the Western Blot. The ELISA test is generally referred to as the screening test, and, if it is "positive," then the Western Blot test is performed. This test confirms the presence of HIV antibodies. Both tests are highly reliable, as they are 99.6 percent accurate.

An important concept to understand about testing is what is referred to as the "window period." This is the time period between a person's being exposed to the virus and having a positive antibody test. This time may extend from a few weeks to several months. Some factors that influence the length of this time period include current health status, presence of other diseases, and method of transmission.

The "window period" means that if someone gets an HIV antibody test within a few weeks of infection, the test results may indicate no sign of antibodies even though the person is infected. It is currently recommended that persons who may have been exposed be repeatedly tested at three month intervals for up to twelve months. These persons should refrain from exposing others during this time.

Counseling by a trained professional should always accompany HIV antibody testing. In most communities, the local health department can provide counseling and testing at little or no cost. Physicians or private health care providers may charge more for the same testing service.

Home collection testing for HIV antibodies is now widely available. Basically, this requires an individual to mail in a sample of blood on a special type of card. These tests are also considered to be highly reliable. However, the cost of this testing procedure may be prohibitive for some persons. There are also concerns that telephone counseling is not adequate for those who test positive. Testing for HIV antibodies does nothing to prevent the spread of the disease. Only behavior changes can stop the spread of HIV and AIDS.

The Centers for Disease Control and Prevention (CDC) strongly recommends counseling and voluntary HIV antibody testing for all pregnant women. This recommendation is based on the finding that vertical or perinatal transmission from an infected mother to her unborn child can be reduced by 67.5 percent by the proper use of the drug AZT during the pregnancy.

Can People with Mental Retardation Protect Themselves from HIV Infection?

Yes. In communities around the country, people with mental retardation are learning how to protect themselves from the AIDS virus and other sexually transmitted diseases. Materials designed by The Arc and other organizations are used to teach safer sex and to reinforce appropriate behaviors. People are learning about their sexual rights and responsibilities. Some people learn faster than others, and others require patience and encouragement as they learn to make safer choices.

Materials should be clear and presented sensitively by trained individuals who are comfortable dealing with this information in an open and non-judgmental manner. Safer sex training should never be forced upon someone who is unwilling to participate. Because of the sensitive nature of the information, training is best offered in small groups or in individual sessions.

What Is Safer Sex?

The only fully "safe" sex is no sex. That is why people use the term "safer" sex. Safer sex involves activities that lower the risk of infection with HIV and other diseases. Safer sex also reduces the risk of unwanted pregnancy.

Safer sex involves limiting the number of one's sexual partners, minimizing the exchange of body fluids, using latex or polyurethane condoms, and using water-based lubricants. Female condoms are available for use by women when their male partner is unwilling to use the male condom. Individuals engaging in sexual activities are encouraged to avoid the use of alcohol and other drugs, as these impair one's ability to use prevention and contribute to poor judgment and decision-making.

Safer sex minimizes the exchange of body fluids containing high concentrations of HIV: semen, vaginal secretions, and blood. The risk of infection from other body fluids is extremely low or nonexistent. Reducing exposure to semen, blood, and vaginal secretions during sex almost eliminates the risk of sexually transmitted diseases.

What Is Dangerous and What Is Safer?[1]

Dangerous Activities include:

- unprotected vaginal, anal, or oral sex with an infected person
- injecting drugs with a used needle
- body piercing with a used needle
- tattooing with a used needle or ink
- vaginal, anal, or oral sex using a condom and an oil based lubricant

462

- inserting unprotected fingers into partner
- reusing condoms

Risky Activities include:

- wet or deep kissing
- mutual masturbation
- cleaning blood spills without wearing latex gloves
- breast feeding by an infected mother
- blood transfusions (especially before March 1985)
- sharing of needles, even if they have been cleaned with bleach
- anal sex, even using a latex condom with water based lubricant

Safer Activities include:

- vaginal sex using a latex condom with water based lubricant
- oral sex using a latex condom or latex dental dam

Much safer activities include:

- abstinence
- dry kissing
- masturbation
- hugging, touching, massage, sharing of fantasies, back rubs, shaking hands, writing love letters, exchanging rings, dancing

[1](adapted from the American Red Cross)

References:

American Red Cross, *Basic HIV/AIDS Instructor's Manual*: Fundamentals, Nov. 1995.

Marchetti, A.G., Nathanson, R.S., Kastner, T.A. (1989). AIDS and developmental disability agencies: A national survey. *American Journal of Public Health.*

Clinical Practice Guidelines, Managing Early HIV Infection, U. S. Department of Health and Human Services, Public Health Service, Jan. 1994.

CDC, Recommendations of the U. S. Public Health Service Task Force for the Use of Zidovudine (AZT) to Reduce Perinatal Transmission of HIV, *MMWR*, Aug. 5, 1994. Vol. 43, No. RR-11.

Resources:

National AIDS Clearinghouse
Tel: 800-485-5231
TDD: 800-243-7012

National Association of People With AIDS (NAPWA)
Tel: 202-898-0414

American Red Cross
Tel: 703-206-7180

The Arc
National Organization on Mental Retardation
1010 Wayne Ave, Suite 650
Silver Spring, MD 20910
Tel: 301-565-3842
Fax: 301-565-3843
E-mail: thearc@metronet.com
URL: http://www.thearc.org

—Jo Anne T. Kowalski, R.N., Ed. D.

Jo Anne Kowalski is part of the Mid-Ohio Valley AIDS Task Force, Parkersburg, W.V.

Chapter 38

Managed Care and Long-Term Services

What Is "Managed Care?"

Until now, the concept of managed care has been used almost solely in the area of acute (not long-term) health care. Basically, it has been defined as the implementation of strategies and actions to contain or limit health care costs. Health maintenance organizations (HMOs) and preferred provider organizations (PPOs) are just two types of managed care models familiar to most people.

Managed care related to long-term services for people with mental retardation generally refers to using similar strategies to contain the costs of publicly-funded residential and other community services and supports. Managed care proponents believe it can be used to curtail health costs. Managed care models may employ various methods of cost containment including controlling prices for health care; providing economic incentives to providers of care to keep costs low; influencing, limiting or controlling the choices of consumers and how they are used; and, coordinating services. (HSRI & NASDDDS, 1995). These managed care strategies, by themselves or in combination, attempt to impact or alter factors that usually drive health care costs: utilization patterns (how much and to what degree services are used); prices charged by suppliers such as doctors and hospitals; and, the share of costs borne by the insured.

Reprinted with permission, © 1995, "Managed Care and Long-Term Services for People with Mental Retardation," The Arc.

Why Might Managed Care Be Necessary for Long-Term Services?

Managed care came about primarily due to costs. Traditionally, increased health care costs related to acute or primary care needs have been driven in large part by the needs of consumers and by health care suppliers who often require and/or provide unchecked and costly services that are usually paid for through insurance, Medicare, out of the person's pocket, or through other sources. Increased insurance costs for care are eventually passed on to consumers in the form of increased premiums. Many of those with no third-party health coverage either have to go without health care or face a severe financial burden paying for care. Even the costs of publicly-funded health care are eventually passed on in the form of higher taxes to meet increasing demand and costs.

Long-term services for many people with mental retardation are paid through Medicaid, a federal/state program that reimburses states for various community living and other services. States are required to provide a certain amount of matching funds to receive federal monies. Similar to acute health care, the costs of long-term services have continued to increase even as cost saving measures have been instituted. States are beginning to look at managed care in long-term services for a number of reasons. The federal budget deficit and the states' financial problems are making it more difficult to fund existing services. Additionally, waiting lists for services have placed a heavy demand on states to provide new and expanded services to people with mental retardation. These factors together are forcing the country to examine strategies to provide long-term services in the most cost efficient manner.

How Would a Managed Care Model Be Utilized to Provide Services?

In a managed acute health care model, a managed care organization (MCO), usually one that is privately operated, is contracted by a company, program or other entity to ensure that adequate and quality health care services are offered to consumers (employees) at a fair and often fixed rate, regardless of what services are provided. This is referred to as "capitation" which basically means that an MCO is expected to provide a full-range of services (whatever the individual may need) at a single, fixed cost. The MCO may have only certain providers that consumers can use and usually reviews what the consumer needs before and during the period of care (i.e., utilization review) to ensure that services and/or costs are controlled. There is usually some risk to the MCO for, if costs of services exceed the agreed upon fixed rate, the MCO may still have to provide the services but take a loss in covering the costs. However, if costs are kept low or within projected limits, then the MCO can operate cost effectively. As briefly described above, an MCO's goal is to successfully utilize strategies of managed care to help ensure that costs are always kept in check or contained so that high quality services are provided and financial risk is avoided.

There is much discussion about how managed care might work with long-term services and how it might resemble or differ from models of managed acute health care. If a state adopted a managed care model, it may very well utilize a similar structure to what is used for acute health. The state's mental retardation agency may utilize one or more MCOs and a capitated system of funding to provide residential and/or other community-based services. A state may adopt its own version of managed care where, for example, it would it be its own MCO or "share" management responsibilities with a private MCO for the provision of services. It may also design a system where only certain services or specific populations of people would fall under a managed care operation. Other variations may include working with several MCOs within a state to ensure that some or all long-term services for people with mental retardation are provided. Any number of managed care variations can exist.

How Will Managed Care Affect Long-term Services for People with Mental Retardation?

Because of the extremely limited experiences to draw on, this question cannot be adequately answered. Of concern to The Arc is that, while managed care is a tool that states can use in controlling costs in their systems as in acute care, there is also potential for substantially undermining the consumer focus and basic values which underlie the various components of long-term supports for people with mental retardation. The basic concept of more cost effective professional decision-making at the heart of managed care is at odds with the principles of consumer and family direction and decision-making which have finally begun to take hold in state long-term services systems.

There is no way to accurately predict managed care's effect on the daily operations of long-term services for people with mental retardation. However, based on the dramatic changes in the general health care field in just the last few years, it could be expected that major change will occur. If it does, vigilance and involvement by consumers and advocates is critical.

How Much Latitude Will States Have in the Delivery of Managed Care Services?

Dependent upon the design of the system and source of funds, there may be some requirements and restrictions that states must continue to follow. For instance, certain state statutory or federal Medicaid requirements for eligibility and quality of care may continue to apply, but then again, they may not if block grants replace entitlements. Generally, states will have a lot of latitude in designing their service delivery systems under managed care. They will have to determine whether there will be one or several different managed care organizations, choose managed care providers, and develop contracts for the management of the system. With the multitude of decisions that will have to be made, there is great potential for significant change in the state's service system.

What Are some of the Potential Problems That May Occur in Managed Long-Term Care Services?

States may turn to using managed acute health care models when planning managed long-term care. So, it is important to understand the problems for people with disabilities in managed acute health care to better understand what similar problems may occur in managed long-term care. Testimony from the Consortium for Citizens with Disabilities (CCD) before Congress noted several problems that Medicaid managed health care has when used with people who have disabilities. CCD drew upon research that indicated managed care leads to a decline in the use of specialist services that are often necessary for the well-being of many individuals with disabilities who have complex and special health problems. In fact, these individuals often depend on specialized care even for services that are considered as primary services. Since states have little experience with managed care for people with disabilities who have these types of health problems, the decline in these services may lead to decline in the health and activity of many individuals with disabilities.

CCD notes that many state Medicaid managed care programs have been allowed to proceed without important quality-of-care standards and consumer protections that have typically been included under Medicaid law. Additionally, it was noted that states may not realize the projected savings from managed care when including people with disabilities in such a system. Due to incentives to keep costs low, managed care plans may determine that it is too expensive, under

468

capitated rates, to serve individuals who have certain health problems, and thus make it difficult for these individuals to receive adequate care (CCD, 1995).

Will Managed Care Result in a Better Quality Service System?

Based on many concerns the disability community has with managed acute health care, it is difficult at this juncture to determine if managed care might improve the developmental disabilities long-term services system. However, a study done by Human Services Research Institute and the National Association of State Directors of Developmental Disabilities Services, Inc. (1995) point out that a well designed managed care system:

- has the potential to allow communities to direct ICF/MR dollars toward better and more widespread use;

- may allow more flexibility in designing supports for individuals versus the individual having to fit into existing services;

- may allow for more flexibility in how supports and services are managed and thus avoid costly over-management of services;

- can focus on the individual's needs and ongoing review to ensure that the individualized services are resulting in desired outcomes;

- may encourage more alliances and partnerships among service agencies;

- can, through capitation, focus on purchasing an array of supports and services tailored to each individual; and,

- can allow state MR/DD authorities to focus on the system's performance and place day-to-day administration on the MCOs.

What Should Be the Role of Consumers and advocates in Managed Care Services?

Given that states may utilize managed acute health care models in establishing managed care for long-term services, it is important that consumers and advocates recognize the issues and become proactive in the planning of state and community long-term services. To ensure that the best interests of consumers with mental retardation and other developmental disabilities are considered throughout the planning and design of a managed care system, it will be critical that advocates become involved in all state level discussions and decisions regarding this systems change. Each subsequent decision takes the state further down a path toward a particular model of care, so advocates should be involved before the state takes its first step toward managed care or as early in the process as possible. Additionally, all information about the process should be accessible (understandable) to people with mental retardation.

Advocates in the state should be involved at the state level when key decisions are being made regarding:

- basic structure of the long-term services program;

- who will be guaranteed eligibility for services;

- what services will be covered and how they will be defined;

- which state agency will oversee the program;

- procedures for ensuring consumer involvement and choice in service coverage decisions;

- procedures for ensuring consumer and family involvement in determining quality;

- establishment of grievance mechanisms;

- development of the provisions of the state's contract with the managed care organization; and,

- the criteria by which the managed care organization will be judged.

Managed care has primarily focused on the provision of acute health care services and, to some degree, long-term services to people who are elderly. Advocates must ensure that the managed care system is forced to focus on the ongoing, everyday needs of individuals participating in their communities and acquiring and maintaining skills. Advocates must focus on the need to provide both acute and ongoing, long-term services which assist people in acquiring and maintaining skills or increased independence. Service systems cannot be allowed to return to custodial models of care or provide inappropriate services for individuals because they may be cheaper or more convenient for the managed care provider. Advocates must be a strong force in ensuring that systems do not lose sight of the hard-won values of individualized planning and support, community inclusion, and consumer involvement and choice. Finally, advocates must ensure that states maintain a key role in oversight and quality assurance.

References:

Human Services Research Institute, Inc. (HSRI) & National Association of State Directors of Developmental Disabilities Services, Inc. (NASDDDS) (in press). *Managed Care and People with Developmental Disabilities: A Guidebook*. (1995) from NASDDDS, 113 Oronoco St., Alexandria, VA 22314, (703) 683-4202 (contact for price).

Consortium for Citizens with Disabilities Health Task Force Testimony submitted to the U.S. Senate Finance Committee on Medicaid revisions. Washington, D.C. July 13, 1995.

Part Eight

Important Economic Matters for Mentally Retarded Individuals

Chapter 39

Employment

How Many People Have Mental Retardation?

Based on the 1990 census, an estimated 6.2 to 7.5 million people in the United States have mental retardation. Mental retardation is 12 times more common than cerebral palsy and 30 times more prevalent than neural tube defects such as spina bifida. It affects 100 times as many people as total blindness.

Mental retardation cuts across the lines of racial, ethnic, educational, social, and economic backgrounds. It can occur in any family. One out of ten American families is directly affected by mental retardation.

How Does Mental Retardation Affect a Person's Ability to Work?

The effects of mental retardation vary considerably among people, just as the range of abilities varies considerably among people who do not have mental retardation. About 87 percent will be mildly affected and will be only a little slower than average in learning new information and skills. As adults, they are capable of performing a variety of jobs.

Reprinted with permission "Employment of People with Mental Retardation," © 1994, The Arc, and "Supported Employment" by Alicia A. Cone, © 1999, American Association on Mental Retardation, reprinted with permission.

The remaining 13 percent of people with mental retardation have serious limitations in functioning. However, with care in assessing their work skills and finding them a job that matches their skills, even those individuals have demonstrated employment success.

What Kinds of Jobs Can People with Mental Retardation Do?

A few jobs where workers with mental retardation have proven themselves competitively include: animal caretakers, laundry workers, building maintenance workers, library assistants, data entry clerks, mail clerks, textile machine tenders, carpenters, medical technicians, store clerks, nursery workers, messengers, cooks, automobile mechanics' helpers, engineering aides, printers, assemblers, factory workers, furniture refinishers, radio and TV repair helpers, photocopy operators, grocery clerks, sales personnel, hospital attendants, nursing aides, cashiers, housekeepers, statement clerks, automobile detail workers, and clerical aides. Other jobs in which individuals with mental retardation can perform successfully are continually being identified.

Don't People with Mental Retardation Need More On-the-Job Training and Supervision Than Other Workers?

In some cases, it does take people with mental retardation longer to master the tasks associated with a job. Supervisors may need to spend some extra time with these workers during the first few days or weeks on the job. However, once trained, workers with mental retardation have demonstrated effective job performance.

In many communities, a job coach may be available to help the person. A job coach is a specialist who accompanies the individual with mental retardation to the job to assist in the initial training period. The job coach may assist the worker in learning tasks or make recommendations to the employer about suitable changes to the job to help accommodate the worker. As the new worker becomes familiar with the job, the job coach gradually fades from being present in the work place, but is often available for consultation if ever necessary.

Employers who hire individuals with mental retardation may be eligible to receive on-the-job training reimbursement from The Arc, the state's rehabilitation agency, or a local Job Training Partnership Act (JTPA) program. Employers may also receive tax credits under the Targeted Jobs Tax Credit provisions of the IRS.

[handwritten annotations across top margin]

Are Workers with Mental Retardation Dependable?

People with mental retardation have a lot to offer employers. In a recent survey (Blanck, 1993), employers in Oklahoma were generally positive about the contributions and abilities of their employees with mental retardation. Almost all (96%) reported they were very satisfied with their employee's work attendance. More than three-fourths (78%) were satisfied with the employee's dedication to work, and 95 percent said that employees with mental retardation do not have higher turnover rates than employees without disabilities performing similar jobs. Finally, more than half of the employers were very satisfied with the worker's productivity (59%) and initiative (58%).

Studies by the E.I. duPont Company (1990) revealed similar positive results. Their workers with mental retardation were comparable to employees without disabilities in performance, attendance and tenure.

People with mental retardation typically are not "job hoppers." They reward their employers with loyalty and diligence—qualities that are sometimes hard to find in today's working population.

Do Workers with Mental Retardation Have More Accidents on the Job?

In the Oklahoma survey, 93 percent of the employers reported that employees with mental retardation did not create a safety risk at the workplace (Blanck, 1993). DuPont (1983) and the President's Committee on Mental Retardation (1983) report safety records equivalent to employees without disabilities.

Do Health and Other Employee Benefit Costs Go Up When a Company Hires People with Mental Retardation?

In general, group health plans and related employee benefit programs are not adversely affected by hiring people with mental retardation—a statement confirmed by 95 percent of the employers in the Oklahoma study (1993).

Do Most Adults with Mental Retardation Have Jobs?

No. Recent studies indicate that only 7 to 23 percent of adults with mental retardation are employed full-time. While an additional small percentage (9-20%) are employed part-time, most are either unemployed or not in the labor force. The National Consumer Survey of adults with mental retardation reported 81 percent not working (Temple University Developmental Disabilities Center/UAP, 1990). Another survey of youth out of school three to five years found 63 percent not working (Wagner, et al, 1992). While today's youth appear to be doing better in the job market, they still are unemployed to a greater extent than youth with most other disabilities and those without disabilities.

Why Aren't More People with Mental Retardation Employed?

Obviously, there is a great untapped reservoir of workers in this country—people who can work, people who want jobs. A number of barriers contribute to the low employment rate of people with mental retardation. They may not receive vocational training and work experience while in school. Due to being segregated in special education programs, they may not learn about career options, have experiences to develop appropriate social skills required for successful employment, and may not be encouraged to look forward to work.

After leaving school, many adults with mental retardation find there are no services in their communities to assist them in obtaining and maintaining employment. Most need some support in learning a job and interventions when they have trouble with job performance.

Employers may hesitate to recruit, hire, and train individuals with mental retardation because they are not sure that they know how to accommodate their disability. Parents may have low expectations of work for their sons and daughters with mental retardation. They may worry that going to work may cause their son or daughter to lose entitlements which provide a monthly income and health coverage. Transportation to work is often a problem for people with mental retardation, especially since many do not drive. Public transportation is not universally available. Finally, they may have difficulty in finding work when the unemployment rate is high in their community.

What Is Being Done to Help More People with Mental Retardation to Become and Stay Employed?

Perhaps the most positive change to opening employment and other opportunities for people with disabilities, including those with mental retardation, is the Americans with Disabilities Act (ADA). Signed into law July 26, 1990, the ADA prohibits discrimination based on disability. It covers employment, public accommodations, transportation, state and local government services, and telecommunication relay services. In employment, it specifically states that employers cannot discriminate against a "qualified individual with a disability" who can perform the "essential functions" of a job "with or without reasonable accommodations."

In the area of direct services, new employment options and services to assist people with mental retardation have been developed in recent years. Included in these options are new models for providing supported employment where workers receive ongoing assistance as necessary in performing their jobs.

Where Can Employers Go to Recruit Potential Workers with Mental Retardation?

To tap this pool of workers, employers can contact local chapters of The Arc, their local secondary school, or rehabilitation agencies in their area. Or, they can contact The Arc's National Employment and Training Program at the National Headquarters' office. Staff will be able to direct the employer to an appropriate source.

What Is Supported Employment?

Supported employment is paid, competitive employment for people who have severe disabilities and a demonstrated inability to gain and maintain traditional employment. Supported employment occurs in a variety of normal, integrated business environments.

Further, supported employment includes:

• Paid minimum wage or better

• Support provided to obtain and maintain jobs; and

• Promotion of career development and workplace diversity.

Facts about Employment

Prior to 1986, people with disabilities had few employment options. They were either unemployed or placed in segregated employment. Today, nationwide, there are over 105,000 individuals with multiple and profound disabilities experiencing independence, integration, and empowerment in competitive, community-based careers accessed through supported employment.

Supported employment is funded by the Rehabilitation Act Amendments of 1992, Title I and Title VI.

Benefits of Supported Employment

The benefits of supported employment include:

- Real employment provides an opportunity for long-term dignity, a chance at upward mobility, and an opportunity to break out of the perpetual problem of unemployment and underemployment.

- It is estimated that supported employment participants earn nearly $600 million annually and pay over $100 million each year in federal, state, and local taxes.

- The percentage of people dependent on public assistance/disability benefits as their primary source of income drops dramatically as a result of participation in supported employment. The result is that 52% of participants' primary income is their paycheck, rather than public assistance or disability benefits.

- Individuals with disabilities participating in supported employment increased their annual earnings 490%. On average, hourly earnings increased from $0.84 to $4.13.

Is Supported Employment Cost Effective?

Yes. Supported employment is cost effective.

- The average cost of a supported employment placement to the federal/state vocational rehabilitation program is $4,000; half of all placements cost less than $3,000 per individual.

- The cost of placing an individual into competitive employment with support is $4,200 compared to the $7,400 annual cost of keeping an individual in a day program.

- A state-by-state comparison indicates that costs for supported employment are from 40% to 80% of the costs of other day services, such as sheltered workshops or work activity centers.

American Association on Mental Retardation (AAMR) believes supported employment programs should be encouraged in the following ways:

- Employment must be viewed as a real option for people with disabilities. Preparation for career selection must be part of all educational programs.

- Individuals with disabilities need to be involved in all aspects of decision making that affect their work lives.

- Federal and state legislative and administrative initiatives must include job development and creation. Federal and state initiatives must reflect an emphasis on inclusion and integrated work settings rather than on segregated and non-work settings.

- Work by people with disabilities needs to happen within and as a part of the regular work force in typical work settings.

- Workers with disabilities should be protected by applicable state and federal statutes with regard to work rules and pay rates. Basic worker benefits and opportunities for upward and lateral mobility need to be available.

- Employment supports should be based on individual needs and preferences and should be flexible.

References

Blanck, P.D. (1993). *The Americans with Disabilities Act: Putting the Employment Provisions to Work*. Northwestern University: The Annenberg Washington Program.

E. I. duPont de Nemours and Company. (1990). *Equal to the task II*. Wilmington, DE.

President's Committee on Mental Retardation. (1983). *The Mentally Retarded Worker _ An Economic Discovery*. U. S. Department of Health and Human Services, Washington, D.C.

Temple University Developmental Disabilities Center/UAP. (July 1990). *The Final Report on the 1990 National Consumer Survey of People with Developmental Disabilities and Their Families*. Philadelphia.

Wagner, M., D'Amico, R., Marder, C., Newman, L. & Blackorby, J. (December 1992). *What Happens Next? Trends in Postschool Outcomes of Youth with Disabilities*. The Second Comprehensive Report from the National Longitudinal Transition Study of Special Education Students. SRI International.

Brooke, V., Wehman, P., Inge K. & Parent, W. (1995). *Toward a customer-driven model of supported employment*. Manuscript submitted for publication.

Rehabilitation Research and Training Center on Supported Employment (1995). Supported employment fact sheet. Richmond, VA: VCU-RRTC.

Revell, G. (1993). P.L.102-569: The Rehabilitation Act Amendments of 1992. *VCU-RRTC Newsletter*. Richmond, VA: VCU-RRTC.

Wehman, P. (1996, January). Supported employment saves dollars and makes good sense. *Richmond Times Dispatch*.

Wehman, P. (1988). *Supported employment: Toward equal employment opportunity for persons with severe disabilities*. Mental Retardation, 26(6), 57-361.

Additional Information

VCU/RRTC on Supported Employment
1314 West Main Street
P.O. Box 94201
Richmond, Virginia 23284-2011
Tel: 804-828-1851
Fax: 804-828-2193

Association for People in Supported Employment (APSE)
1627 Monument Avenue,
Richmond, Virginia, 23220
Tel: 804-278-9187

The Arc
National Organization on Mental Retardation
1010 Wayne Ave, Suite 650
Silver Spring, MD 20910
Tel: 301-565-3842
Fax: 301-565-3843
E-mail: thearc@metronet.com
URL: http://www.thearc.org

Chapter 40

Housing

Older Adults and Their Aging Caregivers

There are an estimated 526,000 adults age 60 and older with mental retardation and other developmental disabilities (e.g., cerebral palsy, autism, epilepsy). Their numbers will double to 1,065,000 by 2030 when all of the post World War II "baby boom" generation, born between 1946 and 1964, will be in their sixties.

People with mental retardation age the same when compared to the general population. They age the same in that the general life expectancy and age-related medical conditions of adults with mental retardation are similar to those of the general population.

They age differently if they have severe levels of cognitive impairment, Down Syndrome, cerebral palsy, or have multiple disabilities. Research indicates that sensory, cognitive, and adaptive skill losses associated with aging may occur earlier with these individuals.

Individuals with Down Syndrome appear to have a higher incidence of Alzheimer's Disease occurring at an earlier age. For these adults symptoms of dementia may often be caused by other conditions that are treatable, such as hypo/hyperthyroidism, depression, and visual and hearing impairments. People with a life-long history of taking certain medications (e.g., psychotropic, anti-seizure) are at a

---

This chapter contains the text from "Aging," © 1999 American Association on Mental Retardation; "Community Living," © 1997 The Arc, reprinted with permission; and "Home Ownership," © 1999 American Association on Mental Retardation, reprinted with permission.

483

higher risk of developing secondary conditions (e.g., osteoporosis, tardive dyskinesia).

What Are the Age-Related Concerns of Adults with Mental Retardation and Their Families?

They are the concerns of all aging adults—securing housing, living independently, getting help when its needed, leading productive and meaningful lives, and staying healthy.

Is There Enough Housing for Aging Adults with Mental Retardation?

No. A recent national survey estimated that 60,876 people with mental retardation and other developmental disabilities are on waiting lists for residential services in 37 states. As adults age, there is a growing need for housing options outside of the family home.

In the last twenty years, there has been a 70% decrease in the number of residents of all ages in large institutions and widespread institutional closures. Concurrently, there has been a large increase in the use of community-based smaller homes and supported living arrangements. Also, over 10,000 adults with mental retardation/developmental disabilities have moved out of nursing homes since 1987.

These trends are expected to continue. Many of the residents who have moved out of institutions and nursing homes and into community residences are older adults. Research has shown that both younger and older adults are able to benefit from living in community settings.

Can Aging Adults with Mental Retardation Remain in Their Homes? Can They "Age in Place?"

They can with the proper support. There will be an increased need for services and supports for older adults with mental retardation, whether they are living with their families or in other residential settings. These services and supports, which can enable them to maintain functioning and live as independently as possible, include personal care services, assistive technologies, home health care, and other in-home supports. Assistive technologies could include mobility and communication devices, home modifications, and techniques for maintaining and improving functioning.

What Are the Key Aging Service Programs?

The Older Americans Act funds comprehensive support services for adults age 60 years and older that can benefit older adults with mental retardation and their older family caregivers. The services include senior centers, nutrition sites, home-delivered meals, homemaker services, and case coordination. Area Agencies on Aging are a starting point for getting information about local services. The Older Americans Act and other federal agencies fund employment opportunities and volunteer programs for older adults.

Community Living

Community-living refers to the programs, services and other supports that enable children and adults with mental retardation and related disabilities to live much the same way that people without disabilities live. For children, this usually means living with their family in their own home and in their own communities. For adults, it usually means having opportunities and supports to live independently, or as independently as possible, in their own home or apartment, or perhaps in a small group home. Community living may also include a variety of other supports and services. For example, a family that is caring for a child with mental retardation may need occasional respite services so that they can take a break from caregiving or attend to other needs. Or, an adult living in a small group home may require help finding a job through an employment program.

What Types of Community Services Are Available?

Community services can take a number of different forms. Community programs in which adults with mental retardation live are usually called supported living or small group home programs.

- **Supported living**: Usually individuals living in homes or apartments of their own. The person may live alone or choose to live with a roommate versus being placed with others. Supported living often involves partnerships between individuals with disabilities, their families and professionals in making decisions about where and how the person wishes to live. Focus is on giving utmost attention to the desires of the person with a disability in how he or she would like to live, and to support the individual in having control over choices of lifestyle. People in supported living may need little or no services from professionals, or they may need 24-hour personal care. The kind and amount of supports are tailored to the individual's needs.

- **Small group homes**: Small group homes are living environments where six or fewer individuals live, usually with 24-hour staff support. In 1996, Prouty & Lakin found that an average of 3.8 people with mental retardation and related developmental disabilities lived in each residential setting in the U.S. The average number was 22.5 people in 1977, and so has continued to drop over the past 19 years.

Community services also include other non-residential types of services that support adults in their own homes, supplement services to individuals who live in the community, and support families in keeping their child with a disability at home. These include, but are not limited to:

- crisis intervention services: on-call support to assist in dealing with crisis situations;

- respite care: temporary relief for full-time, at-home care providers;

- other family support services: states offer a variety of services, from cash subsidies to families so they can purchase their own services, to transportation that enables families to get to services;

- service coordination (case management): professionals that serve as coordinators or "brokers" between services, assisting families and individuals with accessing and benefiting from various programs; and,

- employment programs: services which help adults with mental retardation find jobs.

How Much Care/Support Do People with Mental Retardation Need?

Mental retardation affects each individual differently. While some may need 24-hour care, others are able to live independently or with minimal supports. That is why it is so important for individuals and families to be able to choose flexible programs and services that best meet their needs.

486

Why Is It so Important for People with Mental Retardation to Be Able to Live in Their Own Homes and/or Communities?

Study after study has shown that community living enables people with disabilities to live happier, healthier, and more productive lives. Giving people a real sense of home and community, along with a feeling of independence, can go a long way to contributing to their sense of self-worth and well being. In many cases, community support enables people to live with or near their families. This is particularly important to maintaining a more stable and comforting environment.

Do People with Mental Retardation Have the Power to Make Decisions about Institutionalization Versus Community Living? Do Their Families Decide? The State?

People with mental retardation and/or their families are, in theory, free to decide what type of living situation they desire and is best for them. Adults with mental retardation, not under guardianship, are legally responsible for making decisions about and agreeing to participate in certain programs. In some cases, the state may involuntarily commit someone with mental retardation to a program if there is a life-threatening, emergency, or similar situation. A family or individual's choice about certain community services is often severely hampered by the lack of availability of community programs in many states. If the services and supports an individual needs are not available, these options suddenly become very few.

Aren't There Some People with Mental Retardation so Severe That Institutions Provide the Only Real Viable Option?

Absolutely not. As with anything else, the degree of care needed varies from person to person. Some people with mental retardation manage very well on their own with minimal supports, while others may require 24-hour care. Many communities that are committed to not relegating people with mental retardation to institutions have found that people with the most significant disabilities can safely and happily reside in community, noninstitutional settings. There are community options to meet the needs of all individuals.

What Are the Economic Benefits of Community Living Alternatives?

Community support can save taxpayers a substantial amount of money. In 1996, the average annual cost for a person in a community setting served under the Home and Community Based Services program (flexible Medicaid funding) was $24,783. The annual average cost per resident in large, state-run institutions in 1996 averaged $92,345 (Prouty & Lakin, 1997).

Won't Increased Funding for Community Programs and Supports Mean Bigger Government and Higher Spending?

Not at all. In fact, just the opposite is true. Community living programs represent an alternative to institutionalization, not an added expense. Further, community alternatives generally save money by providing more cost-effective care. And since the whole point of community support is allowing people with mental retardation to live more independently, either with their families or in small homes, it actually requires fewer state resources.

What about Those States That Have Closed Their Institutions? How Has It Affected Services for People with Mental Retardation?

Of the four New England states that have closed institutions, Maine, New Hampshire and Vermont have reduced the size of their waiting lists; Rhode Island has no waiting list. In Connecticut and Massachusetts, states that maintain institutions, the waiting list has increased in numbers.

Trends That Affect the Availability and Use of Community Services

There are several trends that affect the availability and use of community services. Many of these trends inter-relate in how they impact individuals with mental retardation and their families.

Perhaps the most significant trend is the increasing waiting list for community services. Hayden (1992) found an estimated 186,000 people in the U.S. waiting for residential, employment, and other services. As states either cap or cutback the number and kinds of services, more and more individuals end up on long waiting lists for necessary services. Many individuals with mental retardation do not receive the full array of services they need to increase their independence, and there are many who still reside with their families and receive no services whatsoever.

The number of adults with mental retardation still residing with their parents, especially aging parents or parent, is another area of concern. Many parents provide some or all care for an adult son or daughter with mental retardation, but these families increasingly recognize the need to plan for the time when the parents can no longer provide care. As these families begin to explore community residential and other services, they are finding waiting lists for services, sometimes up to several years long. Compounding this problem is the fact that some of these families do not even have access to a support system for providing information and assistance. A recent study in New York found that many of these families are neither in the aging service system or the mental retardation/developmental disabilities service system.

Deinstitutionalization of people with mental retardation has been an extremely positive trend. However, this trend has also increased the need for community services to serve individuals with mental retardation and their families. Many states are not allowing funds to "follow" individuals from institutions to the community. Thus, costly institutions continue to exist while states struggle with funding quality community services.

Dramatic changes in how the service-delivery system for people with mental retardation operates is having a major impact. States are experimenting with service delivery measures—often referred to as "managed care"—in an effort to reduce costs for health and long-term care. While managed care and other systemic changes have the potential to reduce costs and improve the quality and quantity of services, the speed and degree at which states are changing systems may create service gaps or result in less than optimal services for some or all people with mental retardation.

References

Hayden, M.F. (1992). *Adults with mental retardation and other developmental disabilities waiting for community-based services in the U.S.* (Policy Research Brief, Vol. 4., No.3). Minneapolis, MN: University of MN, Institute on Community Integration.

Prouty, R.W. & Lakin, K.C. (Eds.) (1997). *Residential Services for Persons with Developmental Disabilities: Status and Trends Through 1996.* Minneapolis: University of Minnesota, Research and Training Center on Community Living, Institute on Community Integration.

Home Ownership

Home ownership and consumer controlled housing refer to a place to really call a home, that belongs to an individual, and for which the individual is responsible. Unfortunately, for individuals with disabilities, "home" often refers to a program with numerous regulations, paid staff, and restrictions. Control of one's housing and ownership of real estate is power, not only within the individual's immediate community, but within the larger American society.

Barriers to Home Ownership and Control

There are physical, economic, social, and institutional barriers, which include:

1. Lack of personal financial resources;

2. Systemic dependence on programs that limit personal choices;

3. Limited capacity to create innovative housing and support options;

4. Limited involvement of people with disabilities in these efforts; and

5. Limited perspective of the community to envision home ownership.

Issues to Consider When Developing Housing

1. Assist builders/developers in identifying individuals with special housing needs, the best strategies for meeting those needs, and the most effective approaches to marketing the housing to individuals with special housing needs.

2. Assess amount of income available for rent or a mortgage.

3. Determine level of support services required.

4. Determine architectural modifications required.

5. Assess the type of housing that best meets the needs of the individual.

6. Look at other housing initiatives that are meeting the needs of people with disabilities and learn from their experiences.

7. If there are support needs not currently being met, determine how to meet those needs.

8. If the house will be shared with others, decide on how to choose housemates.

9. Look into whether or not a homestead exemption or a tax break is available.

10. Consider maintenance issues.

11. If staff will be in the house, consider issues related to their hiring, training, and firing.

12. Determine the type of legal structure to be used to develop this housing (e.g., limited or general partnerships, corporations, housing cooperatives).

13. Establish linkages with any person, business, advocacy organization that may be helpful in developing the housing.

Options Available for Home Owners

1. Habitat for Humanity (HFH)—helps individuals learn about the responsibility of owning a home, helps individuals build the home through a process known as "sweat equity", and keeps home ownership affordable through paying for only the actual cost of the home and the use of small monthly payments over 7 to 10 years (donation of supplies and labor helps keep costs down).

2. Use of Home and Community Based Waiver Services to keep individuals at home and out of residential programs.

3. Development of community condominium units (please see Specialized Housing Inc., under the Additional Information section).

4. Housing Cooperatives—a group of people organized for the purpose of owning, building, or rehabilitating housing for its members.

5. Single family dwellings.

6. Duplexes and other multiple dwellings.

Housing Ownership Options

1. Tenant Owned—individuals with disabilities own their homes.

2. Parent Owned—parent buys the home for the individual, but individual controls other aspects of the home (e.g., maintenance, housemates).

3. Corporation Owned—parents and others set up corporation to purchase, own, and maintain housing.

4. Partnerships—parents combine resources with other parents to buy a house.

5. Shared Equity—individual makes a purchase with another and gradually buys out the other person.

6. Trust Owned—ownership assigned to a "living trust" set up by parents.

Funding Sources Available for Housing

Federal Sources:

- Section 202 Direct Loan Program
- HUD Rental Rehabilitation Program
- HUD Permanent Housing for Handicapped Homeless Persons
- HUD Community Development Block Grants
- HUD Rental Assistance—Housing Vouchers and Section 8 Certificates
- Low-Income Housing Tax Credit

State/Local Sources:

- Tax-Exempt Bonds for Multi-Family Housing
- Tax-Exempt Bonds for Single Family Mortgages
- Housing Trust Funds

References

1. *Institute on Community Integration*, (1990). Feature issue on consumer controlled housing. IMPACT, 3(1) 612-624-4848.

2. *Capabilities Unlimited*, (1997). Feature issue on housing. Community Advocacy Press, 2(1) 800-871-2181.

3. O'Conner, S., Racino, J., (1989). *New directions in housing, for people with severe disabilities: A collection of resource materials*. Syracuse, NY Center on Human Policy. 315 443-3851.

Additional Information

Habitat for Humanity International
121 Habitat Street
Americus, Georgia, 31709-3498
Tel: 912-924-6935

Specialized Housing, Inc.
45 Bartlett Cres.
Brookline, MA 02446
Tel: 617-277-1805

Hammer Residence
1909 E. Wayzata Blvd.
Wayzata, MN 55391

Center for Community Change through Housing and Support at Trinity College of Vermont
208 Colchester Avenue
Burlington, VT, 05401-6110
Tel: 802-653-1205

National Home of Your Own Alliance
University of New Hampshire, Institute on Disability/UAP
7 Leavitt Lane, Suite 101
Durham, NH 03824-3522
Toll-free: 800-220-8770

The Arc
National Organization on Mental Retardation
1010 Wayne Ave, Suite 650
Silver Spring, MD 20910
Tel: 301-565-3842
Fax: 301-565-3843
E-mail: thearc@metronet.com
URL: http://www.thearc.org

Chapter 41

Social Security Income (SSI) Disability Benefits

This information is written primarily for the parents and caregivers of children with disabilities and adults disabled since childhood. It illustrates the kinds of Social Security and Supplemental Security Income (SSI) benefits a child with a disability might be eligible for and explains how disability claims are evaluated.

Millions of children already get benefits from Social Security. This information will help you decide if your child, or a child you know, is eligible for Social Security or SSI.

The Three Ways a Child Can Get Benefits from Social Security or SSI

There are three ways a child might be eligible for benefits from Social Security or SSI. The three kinds of benefits are:

1. **SSI Benefits for Children**—These are benefits payable to disabled children under age 18 who have limited income and resources, or who come from homes with limited income and resources.

2. **Social Security Dependents—Benefits.** These are benefits payable to children under the age of 18 on the record of a parent who is collecting retirement or disability benefits from Social

"Benefits for Children with Disabilities," Social Security Administration, Publication No. 05-10026, March 1997.

Security, or survivors benefits payable to children under the age of 18 on the record of a parent who has died.

Although children under age 18 who are eligible for these benefits might be disabled, we do not need to consider their disability to qualify them for benefits.

Note: A child can continue receiving dependents or survivors benefits until age 19 if he or she is a full-time student in elementary or high school.

3. **Social Security Benefits For Adults Disabled Since Childhood**—The benefits explained in the previous section normally stop when a child reaches age 18 (or 19 if the child is a full-time student). However, those benefits can continue to be paid into adulthood if the child is disabled. To qualify for these benefits, an individual must be eligible as the child of someone who is getting Social Security retirement or disability benefits, or of someone who has died, and that child must have a disability that began prior to age 22.

Although most of the people getting these benefits are in their 20's and 30's (and some even older), the benefit is considered a "child's" benefit because of the eligibility rules.

SSI Benefits for Children with Disabilities

Non-Medical Rules

SSI is a program that pays monthly benefits to people with low incomes and limited assets who are 65 or older, blind, or disabled. Children can qualify if they meet Social Security's definition of disability and if their income and assets fall within the eligibility limits.

As its name implies, Supplemental Security Income supplements a person's income up to a certain level. The level varies from one state to another and can go up every year based on cost-of-living increases. Check with your local Social Security office to find out more about the SSI benefit levels in your state.

Rules for Children under 18

Most children do not have their own income and do not have many assets. However, when children under age 18 live at home (or are away at school but return home occasionally and are subject to parental control), SSI administration considers the parent's income and assets when deciding if the child qualifies. This process is called "deeming" of income and assets.

Check with your Social Security office for information about your child's specific situation and for a full explanation of the "deeming" process.

Rules for Children 18 and Older

When a child turns 18, parent's income and assets are no longer considered in deciding if he or she can get SSI. A child who was not eligible for SSI before his or her 18th birthday because a parent's income or assets were too high may become eligible at 18. On the other hand, if a child with a disability who is getting SSI turns 18 and continues to live with his or her parent(s), but does not pay for food or shelter, a lower payment rate may apply.

Deciding if a Child Is Disabled for SSI

While your local Social Security office decides if your child's income and assets are within the SSI limits, all documents and evidence pertaining to the disability are sent to a state office, usually called the Disability Determination Service (DDS). There, a team, comprised of a disability evaluation specialist and a doctor, reviews your child's case to decide if he or she meets the Social Security Administration's definition of disability.

If the available records are not thorough enough for the DDS team to make a decision, you may be asked to take your child to a special examination that Social Security will pay for. It is very important that you do this, and that your child puts forth his or her best effort during the examination. The results of the examination will not be considered valid unless your child puts forth his or her best effort. Failure to attend the examination, or invalid results due to poor effort, could result in an unfavorable decision.

Deciding SSI Disability for Children under 18

The law states that a child will be considered disabled if he or she has a physical or mental condition (or a combination of conditions) that results in "marked and severe functional limitations." The condition must last or be expected to last at least 12 months or be expected to result in the child's death. And, the child must not be working at a job that is considered to be substantial work.

To make this decision, the disability evaluation specialist first checks to see if the child's disability can be found in a special listing of impairments that is contained in Social Security's regulations, or if the condition is medically or functionally equal to an impairment that is on the list. These listings are descriptions of symptoms, signs, or laboratory findings of more than 100 physical and mental problems, such as cerebral palsy, mental retardation, or muscular dystrophy, that are severe enough to disable a child, but the child's condition does not have to be one of the conditions on the list. If the symptoms, signs, or laboratory findings of the child's condition are the same as, or medically equal in severity to, the listing, the child is considered disabled for SSI purposes. He or she also will be considered disabled if the functional limitations from his or her condition or combination of conditions are the same as the disabling functional limitations of any listed impairment.

To determine whether the child's impairment causes "marked and severe functional limitations," the disability evaluation team obtains evidence from a wide variety of sources who have knowledge of your child's condition and how it affects his or her ability to function on a day-to-day basis and over time. These sources include, but are not limited to, the doctors and other health professionals who treat your child, teachers, counselors, therapists, and social workers. A finding of disability will not be based solely on your statements or on the fact that your child is, or is not, enrolled in special education classes.

A Special Message to Parents of Children with Severe Disabilities

The disability evaluation process generally takes several months. But the law includes special provisions for people (including children) signing up for SSI disability whose condition is so severe that they are presumed to be disabled. In these cases, SSI benefits are paid for up to six months while the formal disability decision is being made. (Of course, these payments can only be made only if the child meets the other eligibility factors explained above.)

Following are some of the disability categories in which it can presumed the child is disabled and make immediate SSI payments:

- HIV infection
- Blindness
- Deafness (in some cases)

- Cerebral Palsy (in some cases)
- Down Syndrome
- Muscular Dystrophy (in some cases)
- Significant mental deficiency
- Diabetes (with amputation of one foot)
- Amputation of two limbs
- Amputation of leg at the hip

If these special payments are made, and it is later decided that the child's disability is not severe enough to qualify for SSI, the benefits do not have to be paid back.

Children with HIV Infection

Children with HIV infection may differ from adults in the way the infection is acquired and in the course of the disease. DDS disability examiners and doctors have been provided with extensive guidelines to use when evaluating claims for children involving HIV infection.

Some children may not have the conditions specified in the current guidelines for evaluating HIV infection, but may have other signs and symptoms that indicate an impairment that results in marked severe functional limitations. As indicated earlier, this kind of evidence may help show that your child is disabled for SSA purposes.

Social Security Benefits for Older Children with Disabilities and for Adults Disabled Since Childhood

Non-Medical Rules

As indicated earlier, although children under 18 who are eligible for benefits might be disabled, their disability does not need to be considered when deciding if they qualify for Social Security dependent's or survivor's benefits.

However, when a child who is getting a dependent's or survivor's benefit from Social Security reaches 18, those benefits generally stop unless one of the following conditions is met:

- The child is a full-time student in an elementary or high school. In this case, benefits continue until age 19; or

- The child is disabled. In this case benefits can continue as long as the child remains disabled, even into his or her adult years.

Many times, an individual doesn't become eligible for a disabled child's benefit from Social Security until later in life. Here's an example: John Jones starts collecting Social Security retirement benefits at the age of 62. He has a 38-year-old son, Ben, who has had cerebral palsy since birth. Ben will start collecting a disabled "child's" benefit on his father's Social Security record.

How We Decide if an "Adult Child" Is Disabled

Social Security Administration will evaluate the disability of an adult child (age 18 or older) who is applying for Social Security for the first time, or who is being converted from a Social Security dependent child's benefit, by using adult disability criteria. Briefly, to qualify for disability, an adult must have a physical or mental impairment, or combination of impairments, that is expected to keep him or her from doing any "substantial" work for at least a year or is expected to result in death. (Generally, a job that pays $500 or more per month is considered substantial.)

The individual's condition is compared to a listing of impairments that are considered to be severe enough to prevent an individual from working for a year or more. If the individual is not working and has an impairment that meets or is equal to a condition on the list, then he or she is considered disabled for Social Security purposes.

If the person's impairment cannot match with one of the listings, then his or her ability to perform the same type of work he or she did in the past (if any) is assessed. If the person cannot do that work, or does not have any past work history, then SSA consider his or her ability to do any kind of work he or she is suited for (based on age, education, and experience). If, considering all these factors, a person is found to be unable to do any substantial work, then he or she would qualify for disability benefits from Social Security.

Applying for Social Security or SSI Benefits—and How to Expedite the Process

You can apply for Social Security or SSI benefits for your child by calling or visiting your local Social Security office. You should have the child's Social Security number and birth certificate available when you apply. If you're signing up your child for SSI, you also will need to provide records that show your income and your assets, as well as those of the child.

500

The medical evaluation specialists at the DDS need thorough and detailed medical records to help them decide if your child is disabled. You can speed up the claims process by providing the medical records or helping SSA get them. When you file, you will be asked to provide names, addresses, and telephone numbers of all doctors, hospitals, clinics, and other specialists your child has visited.

In addition, if your child is under age 18 and applying for SSI, you will be asked to describe how your child's disability affects his or her ability to function on a day-to-day basis. Therefore, SSA may ask you to provide the names of teachers, day care providers, and family members who can give information about how your child functions. If you have any school records, you should bring them with you to the interview.

Please be as specific and thorough as possible when you answer these questions. This means that you should give the dates of visits to doctors or hospitals, the account numbers, and any other information that will help to get your child's medical records as soon as possible. If you do not have all of this information, tell the interviewer as much as you know.

In many communities, special arrangements have been made with medical providers, social service agencies, and schools to help get the evidence needed to process your child's claim. Most DDS's have Professional Relations Officers who work directly with these organizations to facilitate this process. However, your additional cooperation in obtaining records and evidence will help decide your claim faster.

Medicaid and Medicare

Medicaid is a health care program for people with low incomes and limited assets. In most states, children who get SSI benefits qualify for Medicaid. In many states, Medicaid comes automatically with SSI eligibility. In other states, you must sign up for it. And some children can get Medicaid coverage even if they don't qualify for SSI. Check with your local Social Security office or your state or county social services office for more information.

Medicare is a federal health insurance program for people 65 or older, and for people who have been getting Social Security disability benefits for two years. Because children, even those with disabilities, do not get Social Security disability benefits until they turn 18, no child can get Medicare coverage until he or she is 20 years old.

The only exception to this rule is for children with chronic renal disease who need a kidney transplant or maintenance dialysis. Children in such a situation can get Medicare if a parent is getting Social Security or has worked enough to be covered by Social Security.

Other Health Care Services

If it is decided that a child is disabled and eligible for SSI, SSA refers him or her for health care services under the Children with Special Health Care Needs (CSHCN) provisions of the Social Security Act. These programs are generally administered through state health agencies.

Although there are differences, most CSHCN programs help provide specialized services through arrangements with clinics, private offices, hospital-based out- and in-patient treatment centers, or community agencies.

CSHCN programs are known in the states by a variety of names, including Children's Special Health Services, Children's Medical Services, and Handicapped Children's Program. Even if your child is not eligible for SSI, a CSHCN program may be able to help you. Local health departments, social services offices, or hospitals should be able to help you contact your CSHCN program.

Chapter 42

Future Planning: Making Financial Arrangements with a Trust

Why Is Careful Financial Planning Important for Someone with Mental Retardation?

Our current service delivery system often requires that individuals who receive publicly funded mental retardation services be poor in order to receive funded services. Usually people with mental retardation receiving services, such as those paid for by Medicaid, must contribute toward the cost of their care with the proceeds from their earnings, Supplemental Security Income (SSI) or Social Security Disability Insurance checks. They are then left with only a small personal care allowance (as low as $30 in many states) to cover the cost of clothing, toiletries, and related items. Parents often subsidize the costs of these items because the personal care allowance is insufficient.

If a parent dies and leaves their son or daughter an inheritance to help cover these personal costs, the inheritance will be considered an asset and the individual receiving the inheritance will be charged "cost-of-care." Publicly funded residential costs can be expensive, sometimes amounting to several thousand dollars per month. So, having to pay even some of these costs can quickly deplete funds needed for other purposes.

Careful financial planning enables a parent to provide help in purchasing personal care needs after the parent dies without exposing their son or daughter to cost-of-care charges. The local or state mental

Reprinted with permission, © 1997, The Arc.

503

retardation services agency can provide information about how that state handles cost-of-care issues.

If My Child Is Receiving Medicaid-Funded Services, Won't He or She Continue to Receive Supplemental Security Income?

Many individuals with mental retardation receive SSI, a monthly monetary allowance that usually makes the person eligible for Medicaid health benefits. Adults are eligible for SSI if they have a disability that prevents them from working and earning a self-sufficient wage, and they do not have more than a certain amount of assets. Children also are eligible for SSI if they have "marked and severe functional limitations" from a physical or mental condition.

Medicaid often pays the cost of certain services for people with mental retardation. In order to remain eligible for Medicaid, a person cannot have more than $2,000 in cash assets or assets which can be converted to cash. In some cases items such as a home, car, or a burial plot may not count as available assets.

If an SSI/Medicaid recipient has access to more than $2,000 in available assets, he or she would lose eligibility for SSI and Medicaid. An inheritance or gift above that amount would, therefore, generally disqualify a person from receiving SSI and Medicaid. The recipient would have to spend down the amount to below $2,000 before he or she could reapply for SSI or Medicaid. The inheritance or gift will not have benefited the recipient if the result is the loss of SSI and Medicaid.

How Can I Ensure Financial Security and Not Jeopardize my Family Member's Benefits?

There are ways that parents can help ensure a degree of financial security for a son or daughter with mental retardation without jeopardizing the individual's SSI and related benefits. Some parents have chosen to disinherit the child with mental retardation and leave another sibling an additional share with the hope the non-disabled sibling will use the money to benefit the sibling with a disability. This is sometimes referred to as a "morally obligated" gift. Unfortunately, the assets often intended to benefit the child with mental retardation may not be spent on this person, and if the non-disabled sibling is divorced or dies prematurely, the extra funds may be distributed to a divorced or widowed spouse or another heir.

A more reliable method of providing for financial security without jeopardizing government benefits is through the use of a trust. Trusts hold money or property that the grantor (the person who sets up the trust) leaves for the beneficiary's economic benefit. Unlike an outright gift or inheritance through a will, trusts usually contain carefully written instructions on when and how to use the trust's contents.

Parents or others can set up a trust while they are alive or as part of a will. If parents set up a trust while still alive, they can be the trustee (the person who manages the trust). They can also assign someone else to be trustee. A trustee can be a person or a financial institution.

A trust may be designed to distribute assets to one or more beneficiaries at certain times or under certain conditions. Some trusts make distributions to the beneficiary (or beneficiaries) over time. Others instruct the trustee to distribute just the trust's earnings or the amount the trustee thinks the beneficiary needs. Some trusts may require the accumulation of all income for distribution at a future time.

What Kinds of Trusts Are Most Commonly Used for This Type of Planning?

There are many different types of trusts that serve different purposes. Laws that affect trusts also vary from state to state. However, most states offer some form of supplemental, discretionary, or even cooperative master trust. These are the types of trusts usually recommended when parents want to protect their child's government benefits that the person needs. Some of these are referred to as "special needs" trusts.

Supplemental trusts—Supplemental trusts are designed so the principal and its earnings supplement the beneficiary's care and does not replace the funds required to pay for this same care. This kind of trust is good for the SSI and Medicaid recipient whose assets cannot exceed specific levels. The trust grantor can carefully direct the trust not replace the cost of services covered by Medicaid. Instead, the trust would require the trustee to only provide funds for certain items, services or other expenses not covered by SSI and Medicaid. Supplemental trusts can also be set up for someone who is not on SSI and Medicaid.

Discretionary trusts—Some states allow the trust grantor to give the trustee full discretion in how much or how little of the trust to distribute. This kind of trust can also contain provisions that limit distributions so that the person remains eligible for government benefits.

505

The trustee of a discretionary trust must be very careful not to distribute money from the trust for goods and services or outright to the beneficiary in a manner that will disqualify the beneficiary from receiving benefits. There are several drawbacks to a discretionary trust. The trustee must be very knowledgeable about the type of benefits a person is receiving and the related eligibility requirements. The trustee has total power over all distributions and may hold back all trust distributions to the detriment of the beneficiary.

What Is a "Master Cooperative Trust?"

Sometimes referred to as a "pooled trust," these are special trusts that some organizations have created to serve families. Instead of setting up an individual trust account, these types of trusts allow families to pool their resources with other families. The pooled account is usually managed and invested as one large account. This reduces administrative fees as there is only one account and increases the total amount of principal for investments. Beneficiaries of these trusts usually receive earnings based on their share of the principal.

Master cooperative trusts are helpful to parents with smaller estates and parents who have difficulty finding an appropriate trustee. Many chapters of The Arc operate these trusts, so there is more assurance of an informed, sensitive trustee who knows about the care and support of individuals with mental retardation. Additionally, some master cooperative trusts will serve people with disabilities other than mental retardation.

How Do I Go about Setting Up a Trust?

There are basically two ways to set up a legal trust. It can be testamentary or inter vivos (living).

Testamentary—This means the trust is part of a will and does not take effect until after the person who drew up the will dies. Parents can change the trust's terms any time the will is changed. So, if the intended beneficiary should die first, the will and trust can change. Tax-wise, this kind of trust does not require the person to file or pay income tax on it since there are no funds in it until after that person dies.

Inter vivos (or Living)—This means the person sets up a trust before dying. In doing so, the parents and/or others can make regular gifts to such a trust. Grandparents can make testamentary bequests from their will to the trust set up for the child with mental retardation. Parents can be the trustee and manage the trust according to their own discretion. They can also assign someone else to be trustee to see how that person would manage the trust.

Living trusts are either revocable or irrevocable. This means parents can change a revocable trust or end it before they die. With an irrevocable trust, parents set up the trust and give up most power to change or end it. Both ways of setting up trusts have different tax advantages and disadvantages according to the size of the parents' estate, family situation and many other factors. Remember, though, it is important that parents or others consult with an attorney about which kind of trust suits that particular family's financial and tax situation.

Can I Preserve my Child's Eligibility for SSI or Medicaid if my Child Has Already Received an Inheritance?

Recent changes in the Federal Medicaid law allows an individual, in some cases, to transfer an inheritance to a certain type of supplemental trust and immediately qualify or re-qualify for Medicaid. These changes are included in the Omnibus Budget Reconciliation Act of 1993 (OBRA '93). OBRA '93 allows trust planning opportunities only to certain people who are disabled and to their aging parents who may need Medicaid services in the future. OBRA '93 allows a parent of a child with a disability or person with a disability to set aside funds in a supplemental needs trust. The trust must be carefully written to comply with OBRA '93 regulations and requires that the state providing services for the individual with a disability be paid back for the cost of services when the beneficiary dies. It is critical that the attorney drafting the trust is knowledgeable about the OBRA '93 legislation.

Note: This chapter is only a general overview of one part of future planning. Families should work with a knowledgeable attorney or financial planner to explore other options of planning prior to making legally binding decisions. It is highly recommended that readers also review the materials in the Future Planning Resources list before and during planning.

Additional Information

To obtain a copy of The Arc's *Future Planning Resources,* a list of books, agencies, and other resources that address financial and legal planning, send a request and $2 for postage and handling to:

The Arc
National Organization on Mental Retardation
1010 Wayne Ave, Suite 650
Silver Spring, MD 20910
Tel: 301-565-3842
Fax: 301-565-3843
E-mail: thearc@metronet.com
URL: http://www.thearc.org

—Rick Berkobien and Theresa Varnet

Rick Berkobien is assistant director of The Arc's Department of Research and Program Services. Theresa Varnet is an attorney with Spain, Spain, & Varnet and has a daughter with mental retardation.

Lawrence Faulkner, Westchester ARC, New York and Lisa Rivers, The Arc of Texas reviewed this chapter.

Part Nine

Legal Concerns of the Mentally Retarded and Their Families

Chapter 43

Guardianship

What Is Guardianship?

Guardianship is the legal power to care for another person and manage his or her affairs. Each state has its own specific laws on guardianship, but the following generally describes the guardianship laws for adults throughout the United States:

Guardianship is a legal, not medical determination. When people become adults—including people with mental retardation—they get all the legal rights and responsibilities of any adult. Only the courts have the authority to remove these rights. A court makes this decision based on the person's abilities to handle personal decisions, money, property, and similar matters. The incapacity (or legal inability) to handle these matters is grounds for a guardianship, not mental retardation.

How Do I Decide if My Son or Daughter Needs Guardianship?

Appointing a guardian for someone with mental retardation is a serious matter. This legal status deprives the person of some rights and independence, and has the potential for abuse because of the power it gives one individual over another. However, there may be different reasons why a son or daughter with mental retardation may need a guardian. Some common reasons are:

Reprinted with permission © 1997, "Future Planning: Guardianship and People with Mental Retardation," The Arc.

- A person with mental retardation needs medical care or other services that will not be provided unless there is a clear understanding about the person's legal capacity to consent to treatment or services. Health and service providers are becoming more concerned about liabilities when providing services to someone who may not have the capacity to make an informed consent to treatment or services.

- Parents or siblings cannot get access to important records or provide other help without guardianship. As a legal adult, a person with mental retardation must often give consent for the release of health and other records to parents or others. Health and service providers unsure of the person's ability to give consent may require documentation of the person's legal capacity before allowing access to records without the person's consent.

- The person has assets he or she cannot adequately manage. Guardianship is sometimes needed to ensure the assets are secure and used for the intended purpose, and only when money management alternatives (e.g., representative payeeship, etc.) will not provide sufficient protection.

- Before pursuing guardianship, families should first try to determine if this legal protection is necessary. They need to examine why they feel a family member may require a guardian. Then, they need to familiarize themselves with less restrictive options that may meet these needs without resorting to guardianship.

What Are the Different Types of Guardianship?

Most states have different legal protective statuses or types of guardianship. State laws also often differ in defining incapacity, interpreting the guardian's duties and qualifications, terminology, reporting, documentation, costs, and other areas related to guardianship.

In most states, the different types of guardianship are commonly called:

- Guardianship of the person or property
- Full guardianship
- Limited guardianship
- Temporary guardianship

(For specific information on states' laws, confer with an attorney, or contact your chapter of The Arc.)

512

Guardian of the person or property—This type of guardianship is sometimes characterized as "guardian of the person" or "guardian of the estate." In the guardian of the person, the individual needs a guardian to decide personal issues. These decisions may include where to live, consent for medical treatment, and signing for services.

The court will usually identify specific decision-making areas under guardianship of the person. Courts frequently require periodic reports from the guardian about the guardian's actions over the course of the year or other period.

A guardian of the estate, called a conservator in most states, usually has power over the ward's money or property, not the individual's personal matters. Some states also do not require a judgment of the person's incapacity for a guardianship of the estate. The court can base the need for conservatorship by finding the person unable to manage assets or property.

The court requires this type of guardian to protect the person's property and use it for the person's care, support, education, and other areas of general welfare. The guardian of the estate must use the ward's money for the ward's care and to account periodically to the court. This guardian's duties include careful investment of the guardianship assets. Guardians who have foolishly invested their ward's money may have to pay it back from their own money. They must also keep good records and make them available to the court. Some states require this guardian to put up a bond.

Full guardianship—A full or plenary guardianship basically includes guardianship over all the person's personal and property decision-making. It is usually a collection of all the powers and responsibilities mentioned above. Full guardianship is quite common, as it is the kind with which courts are most familiar.

Since full guardianship involves controlling every aspect of the person's life, it is the most restrictive. However, the person under a full guardianship still retains his or her basic civil rights.

Full guardianship is useful for individuals whose mental retardation is so severe that they are not capable of making informed decisions, and should be used only after exploring the alternatives, including limited guardianship.

Limited guardianship—Many states have designed laws for "limited guardianship" to encourage a person to keep as much control as possible over his or her own life. Under this legal approach, the guardian has authority over the ward only in specifically defined matters. Every decision outside of those defined areas remains with the individual who has mental retardation. This form of guardianship allows the legal guardian to decide only in areas where the person is not capable.

Limited guardianship does require more attention from the court, attorneys, and guardians to be sure it is specific to the individual's needs. Limited guardianship also must try to foresee all the individual's future legal needs. For example, an unpredictable legal situation might arise that is not covered under the limited guardianship. The guardian may not have the authority to provide needed protection and may have to return to court to get more decision-making power.

In many states, the court may authorize a mix of guardianships. For example, a person may need full guardianship of the estate and only limited guardianship over personal matters.

Temporary guardianship—Some states allow guardianship for a limited time. If a legal problem arises from a specific situation, the court can issue a "protective order" or temporary guardianship. Under a protective order, the court can give another person, a public guardian, or corporate guardianship program (these last two are discussed later) the legal authority to handle that specific situation. When the problem is resolved, the order usually ends with no permanent guardianship.

Temporary guardianship usually only applies to temporary situations such as those caused by drugs, momentary illness, or special medical situations. It has limited uses for long-term, reoccurring medical situations or incapacities due to a disability. This allows family members or an agency to pursue temporary guardianship if medical or other treatment is necessary but not provided because of questionable ability to consent. Once the person has temporary guardianship and treatment is provided, the guardianship is usually reviewed to determine if it should be removed.

What Is a Public Guardian?

There will not always be a parent, other family member, or friend to act as guardian of a person with mental retardation. For these and other reasons, many states have appointed public guardians that provide guardianship to people with no family available or willing to become guardian. This is referred to as public guardianship. Nonprofit organizations under contract with the state or local government may also provide public guardianship services.

Public guardians often have large caseloads, time-consuming paperwork, and other duties, so must divide their time among responsibilities. These responsibilities can limit the time and resources public guardians have available to assist their wards. Thus, this type of guardianship is often considered as a "last resort," especially for those who can secure an individual guardian or get the services they need elsewhere.

State resources generally finance public guardianship. Although states usually have safeguards that free public guardians to advocate for their wards, a conflict of interest could arise if a public guardian should have to oppose another state-funded agency. If public guardianship is being considered for a person with mental retardation, care should be taken to be sure these guardians have the time, resources ,and latitude to fulfill their responsibilities.

What Is Corporate Guardianship?

Many states allow incorporated agencies to provide guardianship and related services to people with mental retardation. In these agencies, the corporation is the guardian and assigns a professional staff person or volunteer to carry out guardianship responsibilities for the individual. These organizations often provide legal guardianship, individual service coordination, periodic support, and even temporary guardianship. Parents can contract with such an agency to start specific services either after they die or when they can no longer help their child. Some state agencies also contract with these organizations for guardianship services. The organization's revenues may come from advanced funding from parents, bequests from the parent's estate, life insurance, United Way funding, contributions or subsidies from other organizations such as chapters of The Arc.

Before contracting with a corporate guardianship agency, parents should investigate the organization to be sure it is well managed, has stable funding, and provides quality services. There must be adequate proof the program will remain solvent and continue to supply good services throughout the lives of its wards.

Note: This chapter is only a general overview of one part of future planning. Families should explore with a knowledgeable attorney or advocate the alternatives to guardianship and other aspects of planning prior to making legally binding decisions.

Additional Information

The Arc
National Organization on Mental Retardation
1010 Wayne Ave, Suite 650
Silver Spring, MD 20910
Tel: 301-565-3842
Fax: 301-565-3843
E-mail: thearc@metronet.com
URL: http://www.thearc.org

—*Rick Berkobien*

Rick Berkobien is Assistant Director, Department of Research and Program Services at The Arc.

This information was reviewed by Ron Lantz of Guardian Inc., Battle Creek, MI and Marty Ford of The Arc's Governmental Affairs Office.

Chapter 44

Genetic Discrimination

What Is Genetic Discrimination?

Genetic discrimination describes the differential treatment of individuals or their relatives based on their actual or presumed genetic differences as distinguished from discrimination based on having symptoms of a genetic-based disease (Geller, et al, 1996). Genetic discrimination is aimed at people who appear healthy or whose symptoms are so mild that their functioning and health are not affected. Such individuals may include people who carry the gene for fragile X, the most common inherited cause of mental retardation. Twenty percent of people with this gene will never display any form of mental retardation. Yet, because they carry the gene for fragile X, they could be treated as though they had mental retardation even though they do not (Boyle, 1995).

Why Is Concern about Genetic Discrimination Increasing?

The Human Genome Project, a collaboration of scientists worldwide, is conducting research to find the location of the 100,000 or so human genes by the year 2005.[1] Understanding the complete set of genes, known as the human genome, will lead to precise new approaches to the diagnosis, treatment, and prevention of disease. Errors in our genes are responsible for an estimated 3000 to 4000 clearly

Reprinted with permission ©1996, "Facts about Genetic Discrimination," The Arc.

hereditary diseases and conditions. They play a part in cancer, heart disease, diabetes, and many other common conditions, such as mental retardation. Within the next five to ten years we may be able to discover almost all of the diseases we are at risk of inheriting.

Genetic testing can be harmful if the information is used to deny jobs or insurance or if it leads to other forms of discrimination. According to Francis S. Collins, Director, National Center for Human Genome Research (1995),[2] "all of us carry probably four or five really fouled-up genes and another couple of dozen that are not so great and place us at risk for something" (p. 16). However, although everyone has a few defective genes, not everyone will be affected. Multiple factors within the environment have a significant impact on a person's health. These factors, either alone or combined with a disease-causing gene, can increase or decrease an individual's risk of developing a disease (Nelson-Anderson & Waters, 1995).

Where Is Genetic Discrimination Happening?

A recent study which questioned people with defective genes that could lead to a disease, but who had no symptoms, found that genetic discrimination occurred in many settings (Geller, et al, 1996). As a result, people who fear potential genetic discrimination may be discouraged from obtaining genetic information that could bring health benefits to them and their families.

One of the most common forms of discrimination is denial of health insurance based on a person's genes. Insurance companies gather and use medical information to predict a person's risk of illness and death. They use this "risk" information to determine which individuals and groups they will insure and at what price. That information plays a critical role for people in determining access to health care.

Employment is another area with reported cases of discrimination. Many individuals believe they were not hired or were fired because they were at-risk for genetic conditions. In other cases, individuals who were employed were reluctant to change jobs because they feared losing health insurance coverage (Geller, et al, 1996). Having a defective gene could be considered a pre-existing condition by insurance companies who, on that basis, may deny coverage. Recently passed federal legislation places limitations on the exclusion period for pre-existing conditions when people change jobs (The Health Insurance Portability and Accountability Act of 1996).

Discrimination has also occurred when medical professionals counseled individuals about child bearing by urging prenatal diagnostic testing or telling them they should not have children. Similarly, some adoption agencies have unfairly treated prospective parents with a genetic condition by refusing adoption or assuming they should adopt only children at risk of inheriting a disability (Geller, et al, 1996).

Doesn't the ADA Protect People Against Genetic Discrimination?

The Americans with Disabilities Act (ADA) offers protection from discrimination to individuals currently affected by a genetic condition or disease. It also applies to individuals who are regarded as having a disability. The Equal Employment Opportunities Commission, which oversees enforcement of nondiscrimination in employment, has ruled that ADA applies specifically to individuals who are subjected to discrimination on the basis of genetic information relating to illness, disease, condition, or other disorders (EEOC, 1995). This interpretation extends coverage to people who have genes making them predisposed to a disease-causing disability or who have genes for a late-onset disorder. However, it may not protect carriers of genetic disorders who do not yet manifest symptoms of a disease (the "unaffected carrier"). They may be discriminated against based on concerns about health costs of future affected dependents.

The Americans with Disabilities Act does not cover the insurance industry. Insurance companies may deny health, life, disability, and other forms of insurance to people with defective genes if there is a sound basis for determining risks consistent with state law. Health maintenance organizations can also refuse to cover an individual with a genetic diagnosis even if the individual has no symptoms of the genetic disorder, provided there is a sound basis for the decision based on actual risk experience (Alper and Natowicz, 1993).

What Are the Implications of Genetic Information for Family Members?

When people learn that they have a gene that places them at increased risk for certain diseases, they face the dilemma of whether or not to tell other family members about their potential susceptibility to disease. This information is directly relevant to their biological relatives, for other family members may also have the gene and be at increased risk. It also has implications for family members being at risk of genetic discrimination, since genetic information about an individual is also information about that person's family.

Genetic information may profoundly affect people's decisions about having children. There is also evidence that some individuals who have defective genes are stigmatized, suffering a loss of social and economic opportunities (NIH-DOE Working Group on Ethical, Legal, and Social Implications of Human Genome Research, 1993).

What Steps Are Being Taken to Eliminate Genetic Discrimination?

In addition to federal law and regulations, several states have developed and adopted legislation banning discrimination in health insurance and employment. Currently eleven states have laws prohibiting health insurers from denying health care coverage because of a genetic condition. Seven states prohibit employers from requiring genetic tests or using genetic health predictions in employment decisions. Seven other states have bills pending to protect individuals from discriminatory use of genetic information in employment practices or for insurance purposes (Council for Responsible Genetics, 1996).

As noted earlier, the Federal Health Insurance Portability and Accountability Act of 1996 offers protections against discrimination in health insurance by limiting pre-existing condition exclusions. It also prohibits discrimination against individuals based on health status, including their genetic information.[3]

Additional Information

National Human Genome Research Institute
Office of Communications, Bldg. 31, Rm. 4B09
9000 Rockville Pike
Bethesda, MD 20892
Tel: 301-402-0911
Fax: 301-402-2281
E-mail: wsd@cu.nih.gov
URL: http://www.nhgri.nih.gov

Council for Responsible Genetics (CRG)
5 Upland Rd., Suite 3
Cambridge, Mass. 02140
Tel: 617-868-0870
URL: http://www.gene-watch.org

The Genome Action Coalition
317 Massachusetts Ave., N.E., Suite 200
Washington, D.C. 20002
Tel: 202-546-4732
URL: http://www.tgac.org

The HuGEM Project: Issues in Genetic Privacy and Discrimination
Georgetown University
3307 M St. NW, Suite 401
Washington, DC 20007
Tel: 202-687-8245

The Arc
National Organization on Mental Retardation
1010 Wayne Ave, Suite 650
Silver Spring, MD 20910
Tel: 301-565-3842
Fax: 301-565-3843
E-mail: thearc@metronet.com
URL: http://www.thearc.org

References

Alper, J.S. & Natowicz, M.R. (1993). Genetic discrimination and the public entities and public accommodations titles of the Americans with Disabilities Act. *Am. J. Hum.* Genet., 53, 26-32.

Boyle, P.J. (1995). *Shaping priorities in genetic medicine. Hastings Center Report*, 25, S2-S8.

Collins, F.S. (1995). Evolution of a vision: Genome project origins, present and future challenges, and far-reaching benefits. *Human Genome News*, 7, 3 and 16.

Council for Responsible Genetics. (1996). *Laws regarding genetic discrimination*. Cambridge, MA.

Equal Employment Opportunity Commission (EEOC). (March 14, 1995). *Directives Transmittal. Executive Summary: Compliance Manual Section 902*, Definition of the Term Disability.

Geller, L.N., Alper, J.S., Billings, P.R., Barash, C.I., Beckwith, J. & Natowicz, M.R. (1996). Individual, family, and societal dimensions of genetic discrimination: A case study analysis. *Science and Engineering Ethics*, 2, 71-88.

Nelson-Anderson, D.L. & Waters, C.V. (1995). *Genetic connections: A guide to documenting your individual and family health history*. Missouri: Sonters Publishing.

NIH-DOE Working Group on Ethical, Legal, and Social Implications of Human Genome Research. (1993). *Genetic information and health insurance*. (Report of the Task Force on Genetic Information and Insurance). U.S. Department of Health and Human Services: National Center for Human Genome Research.

The Health Insurance Portability and Accountability Act of 1996, Pub.L. No. 104-191, Title 1, Sec. 101 and 102, 104th Cong. (1996).

Editorial Notes

1. In September 1998, the Human Genome Project announced a new plan to finish the DNA sequence of the human genome by the end of the year 2003.

2. In January 1997, the name of the National Center for Human Genome Research was changed to the National Human Genome Research Institute.

3. On February 8, 2000 President Clinton signed an executive order prohibiting federal government agencies from obtaining genetic information from employees or job applicants or from using genetic information in hiring and promotion decisions.

Chapter 45

Justice and Fair Treatment in the Criminal Justice System

What Are Human Rights?

Typically, when people speak of exercising their rights, they are referring to those fundamental rights that are specifically guaranteed by the U. S. Constitution and each state's constitution. But, "human rights" also often refers to the basic respect and dignity that should be afforded each individual.

No one can take away a person's constitutional rights. However, Congress can add to our constitutional rights by passing federal laws. The Voting Rights Act and the Americans with Disabilities Act are examples of federal laws passed by Congress that expanded the rights of citizens. State legislators can also pass laws that expand on or explain the rights and responsibilities of citizens of their states.

Do People with Mental Retardation Have Rights?

People with mental retardation, like all other citizens, have a vast array of protections under the law which must be recognized and protected.

This chapter includes the following *Fact Sheets* reprinted with permission of the American Association on Mental Retardation: "Human Rights" by Jean E. Tuller, © 1999, and "The Death Penalty," © 1999.

Have People with Mental Retardation Always Been Afforded the Same Human Rights as Others?

There has been a long history of oppression and callous disregard for the lives of individuals with mental retardation. This tradition, together with the societal pressure to devalue individuals with mental retardation, make it essential that those charged with their support and care be aware of the increased risks that individuals with mental retardation continue to face. They must be especially vigilant to protect the autonomy and right to equal protection under the law of individuals with mental retardation.

How Did the Concept of Human Rights Originate?

New concept. The idea that every human being has inherent worth and accompanying "rights" is a relatively new concept. Throughout most of recorded history, the only privileges that people had were those that were granted by the emperor or king in power. In many traditional societies, it was believed that the leader ruled by divine right and that the social order was the "will of God." The value of each person was based on his or her place in the social order. Class, race, gender, or religion were considered legitimate justifications for devaluing individuals and entire segments of a society. The result for the person could be exploitation, oppression, persecution, slavery, torture, or even execution.

U.S. contribution. Our own Declaration of Independence was a pivotal event in the evolution of the concept of human rights. Thomas Jefferson eloquently captured the fundamental notion of the innate right to liberty and equality with these revolutionary words: "We hold these truths to be self-evident, that all men are created equal, that they are endowed by their Creator with certain unalienable Rights, that among these are Life, Liberty and the Pursuit of Happiness."

Human rights internationally accepted. It was nearly two centuries later, after World War II, that the modern concept of "human rights"—that each person has inherent worth—gained worldwide acceptance. With the realization that laws had specifically authorized the unspeakable horrors perpetrated on innocent millions during World War II, the world's conscience awoke to the simple notion that some actions are wrong, no matter what. Every human being has a right to basic respect. The 1945 charter of the United Nations begins by reaffirming a "faith in fundamental human rights, in the dignity and worth of the human person, in the equal rights of men and women."

The Universal Declaration of Human Rights. Three years later, in 1948, the General Assembly of the United Nations adopted the Universal Declaration of Human Rights. It is essentially a list of human rights. The Universal Declaration establishes uniform standards for the treatment of all persons. It proclaims that all human beings shall be entitled to:

- equality before the law;
- protection against arbitrary arrest;
- the right to a fair trial;
- freedom from ex post facto criminal law;
- the right to own property;
- freedom of thought, conscience, and religion;
- freedom of opinion and expression;
- freedom of assembly and association;
- the right to work and to choose one's work freely;
- the right to equal pay for equal work;
- the right to form and join trade unions;
- the right to rest and leisure;
- the right to an adequate standard of living; and,
- the right to an education

In the decades that followed the Universal Declaration, the United Nations promulgated resolutions on specific areas of concern in human rights.

In 1971, the United Nations adopted a Declaration on the Rights of Mentally Retarded Persons. A Declaration on the Rights of Disabled Persons followed in 1975.

References and Resources

- Declaration of Independence
- U.S. Constitution

- United Nations

  Universal Declaration of Human Rights

  Declaration on the Rights of Mentally Retarded Persons

  Declaration on the Rights of Disabled Persons

- Americans with Disabilities Act (Rehabilitation Act of 1973, Section 504)

What Are the Facts about the Death Penalty and People with Mental Retardation?

The facts are:

- Six individuals with mental retardation were executed in the United States in 1995.

- Mental retardation is more prevalent (4% to 10%, according to various researchers) in the criminal justice system than it is in the population at large (1.5% to 2.5%).

- People with mental retardation function at lower levels, both adaptively and intellectually, than the population at large.

- Characteristics associated with mental retardation (i.e., easily led; willingness to talk; and poor understanding of cause/effect and consequences of their actions) often put these individuals at higher risk of unjust incarceration.

- People with mental retardation are often impulsive, which may result in acts that people of average abilities could refrain from.

- Individuals with mental retardation will often attempt to hide their disability to avoid the stigma of disability.

- People with mental retardation often exhibit lowered self-esteem, poor tolerance for frustration, and desire to please authority figures, and often will acquiesce to the wishes of other individuals who are perceived to be more influential.

- The death penalty is disproportionate to the level of culpability possible for people with mental retardation.

- Executing people with mental retardation does not serve justice.

What Is the Judiciary's Position?

The U.S. Supreme Court has acknowledged that the majority of the citizenry are in favor of the death penalty, but are against executing people with mental retardation (Penry v. Lynaugh, 1989). The court's acknowledgment did not alter their opinion that the consensus must come from legislative action on the part of the states and the federal government that would lead to a prohibition of execution of people with mental retardation.

What Has Government Done?

Since the decision in Penry, eleven of the forty death penalty states have enacted legislation to prohibit the execution of people with mental retardation (Arkansas, Colorado, Georgia, Indiana, Kansas, Kentucky, Maryland, New Mexico, New York, Tennessee, & Washington). Also, the federal government has enacted legislation that prohibits the execution of people with mental retardation (18 USCA s 3597 © 1994).

What Are the Policy Implications of the Death Penalty for People with Mental Retardation?

The expressed purpose of the death penalty is to exact justice in the form of punishment and retribution, and to act as a deterrent from future criminal acts. Crimes punishable by death vary from state to state, but typically include murder, and special circumstances in crimes such as robbery, torture, kidnapping, treason, and rape.

Since 1976, over 18 people with various levels of mental disabilities have been executed for capital crimes. In 1995, the United States executed over 30 people, six of whom had documented evidence of mental disabilities. One must ask if capital punishment in these cases served the purpose of justice?

The question of whether a person with mental retardation should be held responsible for a criminal act is not debatable. Individuals whose capabilities are greater than those of people whose disabilities require either extensive or pervasive supports must be held responsible, by some form of incarceration, even to potentially drastic levels, inclusive of life imprisonment. Still, the U.S. Supreme Court has consistently held that mental retardation and mental disabilities constitute mitigating circumstances, and evidence of its existence must be included in jury deliberations, both in the guilt/innocence phase and the sentencing phase (see Penry, 1989).

The reasonable assumption that there must always exist an opportunity for active rehabilitation clearly has to extend to those offenders with mental retardation. Given that individuals who have mental retardation often display various characteristics that should necessarily preclude the imposition of the extreme penalty, the American criminal justice system must seriously reconsider the question of executing such individuals. Any rational analysis of this problem would suggest that the level of culpability necessary for the imposition of the extreme (death) penalty does not exist in a person who has mental retardation.

In those states where there is still no ban on the execution of people with mental retardation, an effort must be made to prohibit such executions. The enactment by eleven state legislatures may not constitute sufficient evidence of a national consensus that the Supreme Court could not determine in Penry, but it does show a distinct national trend.

What Are the Implications for People with Mental Retardation?

People with mental retardation should not be eligible for the death penalty. This is not to suggest that people with mental retardation should not be punished when they break the law, nor does it suggest that people with mental retardation are not responsible for their actions. It suggests that people with mental retardation cannot be held culpable for crimes to the extent that the death penalty would be considered an appropriate punishment.

References and Resources

Public Interest Law Center
125 South 9th Street, Suite 700
Philadelphia, PA 19107
Tel: 215-627-7100

Part Ten

Additional Help and Information

Chapter 46

Glossary

A

adaptive development: development of the child in comparison to other children the same age. This might include the child's ability to dress himself, feed himself, toilet training, how he/she plays with other children, how he/she plays alone, understanding dangers in crossing the street, how he/she behaves if mother leaves the room, etc.

advocate: someone who takes action to help someone else (as in "educational advocate"); also, to take action on someone's behalf.

amendment: a change, revision, or addition made to a law.

amniocentesis: a test performed on a pregnant woman, usually between her sixteenth and eighteenth week of pregnancy. The doctor inserts a hollow needle into the woman's abdomen to remove a small amount of amniotic fluid from around the developing fetus. This fluid can be tested to check for genetic problems and to determine the sex of the child. When there is risk of cesarean section or premature birth, amniocentesis may also be done to see how far the child's lungs have

---

This chapter includes text from "Parent Guides Accessing Programs for Infants, Toddlers, and Preschoolers," National Information Center for Children and Youth with Disabilities (NICHCY), and "An Introduction to Genetics and Genetic Testing," from KidsHealth at http://www.KidsHealth.org, © 1999, The Nemours Foundation, used with permission.

matured. Like chorionic villus sampling, amniocentesis carries a slight risk of inducing a miscarriage.

appeal: a written request for a change in a decision; also, to make such a request.

appropriate: able to meet a need; suitable or fitting; in special education, it usually means the most normal situation possible.

assessment: a collecting and bringing together of information about a child's needs, which may include social, psychological, and educational evaluations used to determine services; a process using observation, testing, and test analysis to determine an individual's strengths and weaknesses in order to plan his or her educational services.

assessment team: a team of people from different backgrounds who observe and test a child to determine his or her strengths and weaknesses.

at risk: a term used with children who have, or could have, problems with their development that may affect later learning.

C

cell death: a natural process in which cells die.

cell differentiation: the process during which cells acquire individual characteristics.

cell migration: the process in which nerve cells move from their place of origin to the place where they will remain for life.

cell proliferation: the process in which nerve cells divide to form new generations of cells.

Child Find: a service directed by each state's Department of Education or lead agency for identifying and diagnosing unserved children with disabilities; while Child Find looks for all unserved children, it makes a special effort to identify children from birth to six years old.

Chorionic villus sampling (CVS): a test performed on a pregnant woman, usually between the tenth and twelfth weeks of pregnancy.

In CVS, the doctor removes a small piece of the placenta to check for genetic problems in a child before birth. Because chorionic villus sampling is an invasive test, there is a small risk that it can induce a miscarriage.

cognitive: a term that describes the process people use for remembering, reasoning, understanding, and using judgment; in special education terms, a cognitive disability refers to difficulty in learning.

comprehensive service system: refers to a list of 14 areas each participating state is to provide under early intervention services. These 14 points range from definition of developmentally delayed, to guidelines for identification, assessment, and provision of early intervention services for the child and family, and include timelines and quality control.

cooperative learning: a group of students with diverse skills and traits working together. This promotes collaboration, teamwork and an appreciation of differences while fostering long-term relationships.

counseling: advice or help given by someone qualified to give such advice or help (often psychological counseling).

D

DNA, deoxyribonucleic acid: the molecule that carries the codes for genetic information. DNA is made of linked subunits called nucleotides. Each nucleotide contains a phosphate molecule, a sugar molecule (deoxyribose), and one of four coding molecules called bases (adenine, guanine, cytosine, or thymine). The sequence of these four bases determines the genetic code.

DNA screening: laboratories use molecular probes to check for a specific coding sequence along the length of a person's DNA molecule. This specific coding sequence is usually one that has been linked to causing an inherited disease.

deletions: a deletion happens when part of a chromosome is missing. Several different syndromes have been linked to deletions of specific parts of chromosomes 4, 5, 9, 13, 18, and 21. For example, Wolf-Hirschhorn syndrome is caused by a deletion of part of chromosome 4. Children born with this syndrome can have abnormalities of the head and face, malformations of the heart, and mental retardation.

developmental: having to do with the steps or stages in growth and development before the age of 18 years.

developmental history: the developmental progress of a child (ages birth to 18 years) in such skills as sitting, walking, talking, or learning.

developmental tests: standardized tests that measure a child's development as it compares to the development of all other children at that age.

disability: the result of any physical or mental condition that affects or prevents one's ability to develop, achieve, and/or function in an educational setting at a normal rate.

discretionary trusts: Some states allow the trust grantor to give the trustee full discretion in how much or how little of the trust to distribute. This kind of trust can also contain provisions that limit distributions so that the person remains eligible for government benefits. The trustee of a discretionary trust must be very careful not to distribute money from the trust for goods and services or outright to the beneficiary in a manner that will disqualify the beneficiary from receiving benefits. There are several drawbacks to a discretionary trust. The trustee must be very knowledgeable about the type of benefits a person is receiving and the related eligibility requirements. The trustee has total power over all distributions and may hold back all trust distributions to the detriment of the beneficiary.

Down syndrome: a trisomy of chromosome number 21 affecting one of every 600 to 800 newborns. Children with Down syndrome have a distinct facial appearance, with eyes that slant upwards at the corners, a small flat face, and a large tongue that tends to stick out. Down syndrome causes varying degrees of mental retardation and is associated with an increased risk for certain heart problems, intestinal atresia (part of the intestines shriveled or missing), and acute leukemia.

due process (procedure): action that protects a person's rights; in special education, this applies to action taken to protect the educational rights of students with disabilities.

E

early interventionist: someone who specializes in early childhood development, usually having a Master's degree or Ph.D. in an area related to the development of infants, toddlers, and preschoolers.

early intervention policies: see policy/policies.

early intervention services or programs: programs or services designed to identify and treat a developmental problem as early as possible, before age 3 (services for 3-5 year olds are referred to as pre-school services).

echolalia: to speak in rapid bursts or repeat words.

eligible: able to qualify.

enzymes: proteins that act as natural catalysts. They help to direct and control the chemical reactions that happen within the body.

evaluation: (as applied to children from birth through two years of age) the procedures used to determine if a child is eligible for early intervention services; (as applied to preschool and school-aged children) the procedures used to determine whether a child has a disability and the nature and extent of the special education and related services the child needs.

F

fluorescent in situ hybridization (FISH), a diagnostic test of the DNA that detects the elastin deletion on chromosome #7 in more than 98% of individuals with Williams syndrome.

forebrain: the largest part of the brain consisting mainly of the cerebrum, which is responsible for thinking and coordination.

free appropriate public education [often referred to as FAPE]: one of the key requirements of IDEA, which requires that an education program be provided for all school-aged children (regardless of disability) without cost to families; the exact requirements of "appropriate" are not defined, but other references within the law imply the most "normal" setting available.

H

handicap: see disability.

I

identification: the process of locating and identifying children needing special services.

Individualized Education Program (IEP): a written education plan for a school-aged child with disabilities developed by a team of professionals (teachers, therapists, etc.) and the child's parents; it is reviewed and updated yearly and describes how the child is presently doing, what the child's learning needs are, and what services the child will need; (For children ages birth through 2 years, the IFSP is used).

Individualized Family Service Plan (IFSP): a written statement for an infant or toddler (ages birth through 2 years old) developed by a team of people who have worked with the child and the family; the IFSP must describe the child's development levels; family information; major outcomes expected to be achieved for the child and family; the services the child will be receiving; when and where the child will receive these services; and the steps to be taken to support the transition of the child to another program; the IFSP will also list the name of the service coordinator assigned to the child and his/her family.

inversions: a small portion of a chromosome breaks off, then reinserts backwards. Inversions affect about one out of every 100 newborns and typically cause no malformations or developmental problems in the children who have them. However, when these children grow to adulthood and wish to become parents, they may have an increased risk of miscarriage or chromosome abnormalities in their own children.

K

karyotyping: a laboratory test that shows chromosome number and appearance. In karyotyping, a photo is taken of a person's chromosomes as they appear under a microscope.

L

lead agency: the agency (office) within a state or territory in charge of overseeing and coordinating service systems for children ages birth through 2.

Least Restrictive Environment (LRE): the least restrictive environment provision of the IDEA states that to the maximum extent appropriate, children with disabilities are educated with children who do not have disabilities "and that special classes, separate schooling, or other removal of ... children from the regular educational environment occurs only when the nature or severity of the handicap is such that education in regular classes with the use of supplementary aids and services cannot be achieved satisfactorily."

M

microdeletions: these happen when a very small piece of a chromosome is missing. Often the missing piece is so small that it involves only a single gene. Because microdeletions cannot be seen with a simple light microscope, they must be detected using sophisticated DNA studies. Syndromes caused by microdeletions include: DiGeorge syndrome, Prader-Willi syndrome, Angelman syndrome, and Williams syndrome.

microcephaly: abnormally small head.

multidisciplinary: a team approach involving specialists in more than one discipline, such as a team made up of a physical therapist, a speech and language pathologist, a child development specialist, an occupational therapist, or other specialists as needed.

O

occupational therapy: a therapy or treatment provided by an occupational therapist that helps individual developmental or physical skills that will aid in daily living; it focuses on sensory integration, on coordination of movement, and on fine motor and self-help skills, such as dressing, eating with a fork and spoon, etc.

P

parent training and information programs: programs that provide information to parents of children with special needs about acquiring services, working with schools and educators to ensure the most effective educational placement for their child, understanding the methods of testing and evaluating a child with special needs, and making informed decisions about their child's special needs.

perseveration: the inability to complete a sentence because of continuous repetition of words at the end of a phrase. For males with fragile X this is the primary language difficulty.

physical therapy: treatment of (physical) disabilities given by a trained physical therapist (under doctor's orders) that includes the use of massage, exercise, etc. to help the person improve the use of bones, muscles, joints, and nerves.

placement: the classroom, program, service, and/or therapy that is selected for a student with special needs.

policy/policies: rules and regulations; as related to early intervention and special education programs, the rules that a state or local school system has for providing services for and educating its students with special needs.

private agency: a non-public agency which may be receiving public funds to provide services for some children.

private therapist: any professional (therapist, tutor, psychologist, etc.) not connected with the public school system or with a public agency.

program(s): in special education, a service, placement, and/or therapy designed to help a child with special needs.

psychologist: a specialist in the field of psychology, usually having a Master's degree or Ph.D. in psychology.

public agency: an agency, office, or organization that is supported by public funds and serves the community at large.

Public Law (P.L.) 94-142: a law passed in 1975 requiring that public schools provide a "free appropriate public education" to school-aged children ages 3-21 (exact ages depend on your state's mandate), regardless of disabling condition; also called the Education For All Handicapped Children Act, with recent amendments now called the Individuals with Disabilities Education Act (IDEA).

Public Law (P.L.) 102-119: passed in 1991, this is an amendment to the Individuals with Disabilities Education Act (IDEA), which requires states and territories to provide a "free appropriate public education" to all children ages 3-21; and provides funds for states and territories to plan a comprehensive service system for infants and toddlers (ages birth through 2 years) with disabilities.

R

related services: transportation and developmental, corrective, and other support services that a child with disabilities requires in order to benefit from education; examples of related services include: speech pathology and audiology, psychological services, physical and occupational therapy, recreation, counseling services, interpreters for the hearing impaired, and medical services for diagnostic and evaluation purposes.

S

service coordinator: someone who acts as a coordinator of an infant's or toddler's services, working in partnership with the family and providers of special programs; service coordinators may be employed by the early intervention agency.

services/service delivery: the services (therapies, instruction, treatment) given to a child with special needs.

special education: see special education programs and services.

special education coordinator: the person in charge of special education programs at the school, district, or state level.

special education programs/services: programs, services, or specially designed instruction (offered at no cost to families) for children over 3 years old with special needs who are found eligible for such services; these include special learning methods or materials in the regular classroom, and special classes and programs if the learning or physical problems indicate this type of program.

special needs: (as in "special needs" child): a term to describe a child who has disabilities or who is at risk of developing disabilities and who, therefore, requires special services or treatment in order to progress.

speech/language pathology: a planned program to improve and/or correct communication problems.

Supplemental trusts: Supplemental trusts are designed so the principal and its earnings supplement the beneficiary's care and does not replace the funds required to pay for this same care. This kind of trust is good for the SSI and Medicaid recipient whose assets cannot exceed specific levels. The trust grantor can carefully direct the trust not replace the cost of services covered by Medicaid. Instead, the trust would require the trustee to only provide funds for certain items, services or other expenses not covered by SSI and Medicaid. Supplemental trusts can also be set up for someone who is not on SSI and Medicaid.

T

teaching: a broad term referring to different groupings of teachers. One common method is to have a regular education teacher team up with a general education teacher and together be responsible for all the children of the class. All team teaching is based on shared responsibility and collaboration.

translocations: small bits of chromosomes shift from one chromosome to another. Translocations may either be inherited from a parent or arise spontaneously in a child's own chromosomes. They affect one out of every 500 newborns. Translocations typically cause no malformations or developmental problems in the children who have them. However, when these children grow to adulthood and wish to become parents, they may have an increased risk of miscarriage or chromosome abnormalities in their own children.

Trisomy 13 (Patau) syndrome: Trisomy 13 syndrome affects one out of every 20,000 newborns. This syndrome causes cleft lip, flexed fingers with extra digits, hemangiomas (blood vessel malformations) of the face and neck, and many different structural abnormalities of the skull and face. It can also cause malformations of the ribs, heart, abdominal organs, and sex organs.

Trisomy 18 (Edwards) syndrome: Trisomy 18 syndrome affects one out of every 8,000 newborns. Children with this syndrome have a low birth weight and a small head, mouth, and jaw. Their hands typically form closed fists with abnormal finger positioning. They may also have malformations involving the hips and feet, heart and kidney problems, and mental retardation. Only about five percent of these children live longer than one year.

Chapter 47

Books, Videos, and Newsletters

Newsletters and Bulletins

Down Syndrome News
Newsletter available from the National Down Syndrome Congress.
7000 Peachtree-Dunwoody Road, NE
Building #5, Suite 100
Atlanta, GA 30328
Tel: 800-232-6372

Exceptional Parent
Magazine for parents and professionals published eight times annually by the Psy-Ed Corporation.
Exceptional Parent
P.O. Box 3000, Dept. EP
Denville, NJ 07834
Tel: 877-372-7368

<u>(*Exceptional Parent* continued on next page)</u>

This chapter includes text from "Parent and Professional Information" reprinted with the express consent and approval of the National Down Syndrome Society, © 1999. Through education, research, and advocacy, NDSS works to ensure that all people with Down syndrome have the opportunity to achieve their full potential in community life. For more information call 800-221-4602 or visit www.ndss.org.; "Briefing Paper on Autism and PDD" National Information Center for Children and Youth with Disabilities (NICHCY), Fact Sheet #20; and excerpts from "National Resources and Materials," © 1998 The National Organization on Fetal Alcohol Syndrome, reprinted with permission.

E-mail: mailto:vieprnt@concentric.net
URL: http://www.coast-resources.con/epartne

FANN—Fetal Alcohol Network Newsletter
158 Rosemont Ave.
Coatsville, PA 19320
Tel: 610-384-1133, Call for a listing of national support groups.

Inclusive Education Programs: Advice on Educating Students with Disabilities in Regular Settings
LRP Publications
Dept. 430
747 Dresher Rd.
P.O. Box 980
Horsham, PA 19044-0980
Tel: 800-341-7874, ext. 275
Fax: 215-784-9639.

A monthly publication which offers legal perspectives on the process of inclusion and presents articles on programs, organizations, laws and strategies.

Inclusion News
Inclusion Press
24 Thome Crescent
Toronto, Ontario M6H 2S5
CANADA
Tel: 416-658-5363
Fax: 416-658-5067

An annual publication edited by Marsha Forest and Jack Pearpoint which presents articles, resource listings, poetry, letters, and diagrams devoted to promoting full inclusion.

Inclusion Times
National Professional Resources, Inc.
25 South Regent St.
Port Chester, NY 10573
Tel: 914-937-8879 or 800-453-7461

A quarterly newsletter focusing on serving children and youth with disabilities in regular education and other inclusive learning environments; attempts to present a balanced viewpoint regarding inclusion.

NCERI Bulletin

National Center on Educational Restructuring and Inclusion
The Graduate School and University Center
The City University of New York
33 West 42 St.
New York, NY 10036-8099
Fax: 212-642-1972

A quarterly publication which highlights the activities of the center and provides in-depth coverage of educational issues relating to inclusion.

News & Views

Quarterly, full-color magazine for and by teens and young adults with Down syndrome, edited by actor and NDSS National Goodwill Ambassador, Chris Burke.
Published by the National Down Syndrome Society
666 Broadway
New York, NY 10012
Tel: 212-460-9330

The only magazine written by and for young adults with Down syndrome made its premiere in September 1994. Edited by Chris Burke, this magazine talks about what it is like to have Down syndrome today. People from all parts of the United States and abroad contribute articles, letters, games and opinions on current events. No other magazine tells this story in the same way. Available by subscription through the National Down Syndrome Society.

TASH Newsletter

The Association for Persons with Severe Handicaps
29 Susquehanna Ave., Suite 210
Baltimore, MD 21240
Tel: 410-828-8274
Fax: 410-828-6706

A monthly publication which provides information on all aspects of the education of people who have severe/profound disabilities.

Update

Quarterly newsletter of the National Down Syndrome Society.
666 Broadway
New York, NY 10012
Tel: 212-460-9330

Books, Videos, and Websites about Autism

Autism: Identification, Education, and Treatment
Berkell, D. E. (Ed.). (1992).
Hillsdale, NJ: Lawrence Erlbaum Associates, Inc.
10 Industrial Ave.
Mahwah, NJ 07430
Tel: 201-236-9500

Handbook of Autism and Pervasive Developmental Disorders (2nd ed.)
Cohen, D. J., & Volkmar, F. (1997) New York: John Wiley & Sons.
Orders to: Eastern Distribution Center
1 Wiley Dr.
Somerset, NJ 08875-1272
Tel: 732-469-4400

Targeting Autism
Cohen, S. (1998) Berkeley, CA: University of California Press.
Orders to: California Princeton Fulfillment Service
1445 Lower Ferry Rd.
Ewing, NJ 08618
Tel: 800-777-4726

Indiana Resource Center for Autism
2853 East 10th Street
Indiana University
Bloomington, IN 47408-2601
Tel: 812-855-6508

Several titles are listed which may be helpful for parents and professionals.

- Helpful Responses to Some of the Behaviors of Individuals with Autism, Dalrymple, N. (1992)

- Helping People with Autism Manage Their Behavior, Dalrymple, N. (1992)

- Some Social Communication Skill Objectives and Teaching Strategies for People with Autism, Dalrymple, N. (1992)

- A Sense of Belonging: Including Students with Autism in Their School Community [Video] Davis, K., & Pratt, C. (1997)

- Autism: Being Friends (1991) [Video]

- Introduction to Autism: Self Instruction Module (Rev. ed.) (1992)

Autism Treatment Guide
Gerlach, E. (1996). Eugene, OR.
Four Leaf Press
2020 Garfield St.
Eugene, OR 97405
Tel: 800-322-1883 or 541-485-4938

Siblings of Children with Autism: A Guide for Families
Harris, S. (1994). Bethesda, MD.
Woodbine House
6510 Bells Mill Rd.
Bethesda, MD 20817
Tel: 800-843-7323 or 301-897-3570

A Parent's Guide to Autism: Answers to the Most Common Questions
Hart, C. A. (1993). New York: Simon & Schuster Co.
Attention: Order Department
100 Front Street
Riverside, NJ 08075
Tel: 800-223-2336

Visual Strategies for Improving Communication. Volume 1: Practical Support for School and Home
Hegdon, L. A. (1995). Troy, MI.
Quirk Roberts Publishing
6219 Seminole Drive
Troy, MI 48098-1127
Tel: 248-879-2598

Plenum Publishing Corporation
233 Spring Street
New York, NY 10013
Tel: 800-221-9369 or 212-620-8000

The following titles are available from Plenum Publishing:

- Journal of Autism and Developmental Disorders

- Current Issues in Autism book series Schopler, E., & Mesibov, G.B (Eds.) including:

  Autism in adolescents and adults (1983)

  Effects of autism on the family (1984)

  Communication problems in autism (1985)

  Social behavior in autism (1986)

  High-functioning individuals with autism (1992)

  Preschool issues in autism (1993)

  Learning and cognition in autism (1995)

MAAP: A Newsletter for Families of More Advanced Autistic People
A quarterly publication of MAAP Services Inc.
124 N Main St
Crown Point, IN 46307
Tel: 219-662-1311

New Jersey Center for Outreach and Services for the Autism Community (COSAC) (1995)
Autism: Basic Information
Ewing, NJ: COSAC.
1450 Parkside Ave., Suite 22
Ewing, NJ 08638
Tel: 609-883-8100

Children with Autism: A Parent's Guide
Powers, M. (1989) Bethesda, MD.
Woodbine House
6510 Bells Mill Rd.
Bethesda, MD 20817
Tel: 800-843-7323 or 301-897-3570

Teaching Children with Autism: Strategies to Enhance Communication and Socialization
Quill, K. A. (1996). Albany, NY: Delmar Publishers.
Delmar Publishers/ITP
7625 Empire Drive
Florence, KY 41022
Tel: 800-347-7707

Autism Information and Resources for Parents, Families, and Professionals
Simpson, R., & Ziontz, P. (1992)
Austin, TX: Pro-Ed.
8700 Shoal Creek Blvd.
Austin, TX 75757-6897
Tel: 800-897-3202 or 512-451-3246

Organizations to Contact for Publication Lists about Autism

These organizations do not have the resources to respond personally to individuals from all across the country, but they have a number of helpful publications available.

Indiana Resource Center for Autism
2853 East 10th Street
Indiana University
Bloomington, IN 47408-2601
Tel: 812-855-6508 (V/TTY)
URL: http://www.isdd.indiana.edu

New Jersey Center for Outreach and Services for the Autism Community (COSAC)
1450 Parkside Ave., Suite 22
Ewing, NJ 08638
Tel: 609-883-8100
URL: http://members.aol.com/njautism

Helpful Web Sites about Autism:

Autism at Yale Developmental Disabilities Home Page
URL: http://info.med.yale.edu/chldstdy/autism

Center for the Study of Autism
URL: http://www.autism.com

Division TEACCH Home Page
URL: http://www.unc.edu/depts/teacch

Syracuse University Autism Resource Page
URL: http://autism-resources.com

Books and Videos about Down Syndrome

Babies with Down Syndrome: A New Parents' Guide (2nd edition)
Stray-Gundersen, K. (Ed.) (1995). Rockville, MD: Woodbine House.
Woodbine House
6510 Bells Mill Rd.
Bethesda, MD 20817
Tel: 800-843-7323

Parents and professionals contribute chapters on the medical, emotional, educational, and social issues concerning the development of the child and the family. A first book for anyone wishing to learn more about Down syndrome, especially new parents.

Brothers, Sisters and Special Needs
Lobato, D.J. (1990). Baltimore, MD: Paul H. Brookes Publishing Co.
Paul H. Brookes Publishing Co.
P.O. Box 10624
Baltimore, MD 21285-0624
Tel: 301-337-9580 or 800-638-3775

A book for parents and professionals that provides information and activities to help young siblings of children with developmental disabilities and chronic illnesses.

Brothers & Sisters — A Special Part of Exceptional Families (2nd edition)
Powell, T.H. and Gallagher, P.A. (1993). Baltimore, MD: Paul H. Brookes Publishing Co.
Paul H. Brookes Publishing Co.
P.O. Box 10624
Baltimore, MD 21285-0624
Tel: 301-337-9580 or 800-638-3775

A guide for parents, their older children, and professionals that encourages a better understanding of the dynamics of family relationships and the challenges of relating to a sibling with special needs. The book combines research with personal testimony from siblings.

Children with Down Syndrome: A Developmental Perspective
Cicchetti, D. and Beeghly, M., (Eds.). New York: Cambridge University Press.

Cambridge University Press
40 West 20th Street
New York, NY 10011
Tel: 212-924-3900

A collection of papers addressing the current state of knowledge of psychological development in infants and children with Down syndrome. Linguistic, social, emotional, cognitive, and representational factors in the developmental process are discussed.

Communication Skills in Children with Down Syndrome
Kumin, L. (1994). Rockville, MD: Woodbine House.
Woodbine House
6510 Bells Mill Rd.
Bethesda, MD 20817
Tel: 800-843-7323

A book which focuses solely on speech and language development in children with Down syndrome. Provides information on the development of communication skills and the ways in which physical and cognitive characteristics of children with Down syndrome contribute to communication difficulties.

Down Syndrome: Advances in Medical Care
Lott, I., & McCoy, E. (Eds.) (1992). New York: Wiley-Liss.
Wiley-Liss
1 Wiley Dr.
Somerset, NJ 08875
Tel: 800-225-5945

Proceedings of the NDSS Down Syndrome Health Care Conference which focused entirely on the health care of people with Down syndrome throughout their life span. Chapters are written by leading experts in the field and address such topics as orthopedics, cardiorespiratory disorders, endocrinology, dental problems, and other relevant clinical advances.

Down Syndrome and Alzheimer's Disease
Nadel, L. & Epstein, C.J. (Eds.) (1992). New York: Wiley-Liss.
Wiley-Liss
1 Wiley Dr.
Somerset, NJ 08875
Tel: 800-225-5945

This volume presents the proceedings of the eighth NDSS Science Symposium which focused on Alzheimer disease in the context of Down syndrome. The chapters look at the neurological aspects of Alzheimer disease in Down syndrome; the development and diagnosis of dementia in persons with Down syndrome; the relations between chromosome 21 and Alzheimer disease; and a review of the approaches being used to investigate the pathogenesis of Alzheimer disease in Down syndrome.

Down Syndrome: Birth to Adulthood

Rynders, J.E. & Horrobin, J.M. (1995). Denver, CO: Love Publishing Company.
Love Publishing Company
1777 South Bellaire St.
Denver, CO 80222
Tel: 303-757-2579

A guide for new parents designed to provide information about Down syndrome and knowledge of how other parents of children with Down syndrome have coped with the experience. Medical, social, and educational issues are discussed.

Down Syndrome: Living and Learning in the Community

Nadel, L. & Rosenthal D. (Eds.)(1995). New York: Wiley Liss.
Wiley-Liss
1 Wiley Dr.
Somerset, NJ 08875
Tel: 800-225-5945

Proceedings of the Fifth International Down Syndrome Conference sponsored by NDSS in collaboration with the European Down Syndrome Association. Topics covered by experts in a variety of fields include speech, language, medical care, nutrition, and social life.

Down Syndrome: A Resource Handbook

Tingey, C. (Ed.) (1988). Boston, MA: College-Hill Press.
Pro Ed
8700 Shoal Creek Blvd.
Austin, TX 78758-6897
Tel: 512-451-3246

A guide for new parents of children with Down syndrome. Addresses medical issues, the family, early development, education, and community activities. Chapters are written by professionals of various disciplines.

Etiology and Pathogenesis of Down Syndrome
Epstein, C.J., Hassold, T., Lott, I.T., Nadel, L., and Patterson, D. (Eds.) (1995). New York: Wiley-Liss.
Wiley-Liss
1 Wiley Dr.
Somerset, NJ 08875
Tel: 800-225-5945

Proceedings of the tenth NDSS Science Symposium. This volume covers a broad range of topics in Down syndrome research, with sections focusing on trisomy 21; the molecular structure of chromosome 21; mental retardation and Alzheimer disease; the phenotype of Down syndrome; and models of Down syndrome.

Keys to Parenting a Child with Down Syndrome
Brill, M. (1993). New York: Barron's Educational Series, Inc.
Barron's Educational Series, Inc.
250 Wireless Blvd.
Hauppauge, NY 11788
Tel: 800-645-3476

A practical guide to raising a child with Down syndrome. The book covers a range of key issues in depth and gives practical advice to parents. Areas addressed include initial reactions to diagnosis, managing family dynamics, obtaining educational and medical services, and planning for adulthood.

Medical & Surgical Care for Children with Down Syndrome: A Guide for Parents
Van Dyke, D.C., Mattheis, P., Eberly, S.S., and Williams, J. (Eds.) (1995). Bethesda, MD: Woodbine House.
Woodbine House
6510 Bells Mill Rd.
Bethesda, MD 20817
Tel: 800-843-7323

A comprehensive guide for parents which provides an overview of specific medical conditions that are more common among children with Down syndrome, along with sections on preventive care, medical decision making, anesthesia and surgical concerns, and planning for health care in adulthood.

Molecular Structure of the Number 21 Chromosome and Down Syndrome

Smith, G.F. (Ed.) (1985). New York: The New York Academy of Sciences.
The New York Academy of Sciences
2 East 63 St.
New York, NY 10021
Tel: 212-838-0230

Proceedings of the first NDSS Science Symposium which addressed new findings about the molecular structure of genes and chromosomes through the fields of molecular genetics, genetic engineering and biochemistry. Papers address the relationship between maternal aging and nondisjunction, deficiencies in the immune system, the chemical composition of the brain and more.

The Morphogenesis of Down Syndrome

Epstein, C.J. (Ed.) (1991). New York: Wiley-Liss, Inc.
Wiley-Liss
1 Wiley Dr.
Somerset, NJ 08875
Tel: 800-225-5945

Proceedings of the seventh NDSS Science Symposium which focused on morphogenesis of Down syndrome; specifically, how chromosome imbalance alters morphogenesis. Attention is given to the morphogenetic differences that characterize the craniofacial, brain, heart, and gastrointestinal tract development, as well as dermatoglyphic alterations in Down syndrome.

A Parent's Guide to Down Syndrome: Toward a Brighter Future

Pueschel, S.M. (1990). Baltimore MD: Paul H. Brookes Publishing Co.
Paul H. Brookes Publishing Co.
P.O. Box 10624
Baltimore, MD 21285-0624
Tel: 301-337-9580 or 800-638-3775

A detailed guide for parents and professionals which discusses the nature of the physical, social, mental and emotional development of children with Down syndrome. Emphasis is given to early intervention, with professionals from various disciplines contributing chapters.

The Phenotypic Mapping of Down Syndrome and Other Aneuploid Conditions
Epstein, C.J. (Ed.) (1993). New York: Wiley-Liss.
Wiley-Liss
1 Wiley Dr.
Somerset, NJ 08875
Tel: 800-225-5945

Proceedings of the ninth NDSS Science Symposium. This volume discusses approaches to understanding the genetics and the underlying mechanisms of the different phenotypic characteristics of Down syndrome, as well as animal models of trisomy 21 relevant to the phenotypic mapping of Down syndrome.

The Psychobiology of Down Syndrome
Nadel, L. (Ed.) (1988). Cambridge, MA: MIT Press.
MIT Press
55 Hayward St.
Cambridge, MA 02142
Tel: 617-253-5646

Proceedings of the fourth NDSS Science Symposium covering the neurobiological and cognitive features of Down syndrome. Emphasis is given to the acquisition and use of language skills, as well as the neuropathological aspects of older individuals with Down syndrome.

Teaching the Infant with Down Syndrome: A Guide for Parents and Professionals (2nd edition)
Hanson, M.J. (1987). Austin, TX: Pro Ed Publishers.
Pro Ed
8700 Shoal Creek Blvd.
Austin, TX 78758-6897
Tel: 800-897-3202

A manual which provides teaching ideas and activities that can be used to assist an infant's development. Additional chapters present information on the emotional reactions to the birth of a child with Down syndrome, medical concerns, and parent-child interaction.

Teaching Reading to Children with Down Syndrome: A Guide for Parents and Teachers.
Oelwein, P. (1995). Bethesda, MD: Woodbine House.
Woodbine House
6510 Bells Mill Rd.
Bethesda, MD 20817
Tel: 800-843-7323

A comprehensive instruction manual to aid parents in teaching their child with Down syndrome to read.

Personal Accounts of Down Syndrome

Cara: Growing with a Retarded Child
Jablow, M.M. (1983). Philadelphia, PA: Temple University Press.
Temple University Press
USB Room 305
Broad and Oxford St.
Philadelphia, PA 19122
Tel: 215-204-8787

The author tells of her experiences raising her daughter Cara, who has Down syndrome. She discusses such varied topics as early intervention, special education, emotional support, and family adjustments. The book deals specifically with early childhood.

Count Us In: Growing Up with Down Syndrome.
Kingsley, J. & Levitz, M. (1994). New York: Harcourt Brace & Company.
Harcourt Brace & Company
6277 Sea Harbor Dr.
Orlando, FL 32887
Tel: 800-543-1918

Two young men with Down syndrome speak in their own words about their experiences growing up with Down syndrome. Jason (age 19) and Mitchell (age 22) share their feelings and thoughts about friendship, school, hopes for the future, and dealing with independence in adulthood.

Differences in Common: Straight Talk on Mental Retardation, Down Syndrome and Life

Trainer, M. (1991). Rockville, MD: Woodbine House.
Woodbine House
6510 Bells Mill Rd.
Bethesda, MD 20817
Tel: 800-843-7323

A collection of essays by the mother of an adult son who has Down syndrome. The author talks about such topics as mainstreaming, terminology, parent groups, siblings' coping strategies, self-awareness, finding a job, advocacy, and societal attitudes towards mental retardation.

Show Me No Mercy

Perske, R. (1984). Nashville, TN: Abingdon Press.
Cokesbury
201 8th Avenue South
PO Box 801
Nashville, TN 37202
Tel: 800-836-7802

The father of a young man with Down syndrome relates the inspirational experience of his attempt to be reunited with his son after a family tragedy separates them.

The World of Nigel Hunt

Hunt, N. (1967). New York: Garrett Publications (out of print—check local library).

This is the autobiography of a young English man with Down syndrome who began the book when he was 17. The book is a classic about Down syndrome. Includes an introduction, written by Mr. Hunt's father and section of photographs.

Books for Children

Our Brother Has Down's Syndrome: An Introduction for Children

Cairo, S. (1985). Ontario: Firefly Books, Ltd.
Firefly Books
250 Sparks Ave.
Willowdale M2H 2S4
Ontario, Canada

Tel: 416-499-8412

A book of color photos and text to introduce and explain Down syndrome to young children, especially siblings. It is a personalized account of a young boy, Jai, as told by his two sisters.

Special Kids Make Special Friends
Shalom, D. B. (1984). Bellmore, NY: Association for Children with Down Syndrome, Inc.
Association for Children with Down Syndrome, Inc.
2616 Martin Ave.
Bellmore, NY 11710
Tel: 516-221-4700

A book designed to educate young children about Down syndrome. Children from a pre-school run by the Association for Children with Down Syndrome are shown learning and playing.

Books about Heart Disease and Down Syndrome

"Cardiac Aspects," Marino, B. In: *Biomedical Concerns in Persons With Down Syndrome.* Pueschel, S. & Pueschel, J. (Eds.) (1992). Baltimore, MD: Paul H. Brooks, pp. 91-103.

Paul H. Brookes Publishing Co.
P.O. Box 10624
Baltimore, MD 21285-0624
Tel: 800-638-3775

"Cardiorespiratory Problems in Children with Down Syndrome," Kidd, L. In: *Down Syndrome: Advances in Medical Care.* Lott, I. & McCoy, E. (Eds.) (1992). New York, NY: Wiley-Liss, pp. 61-69.

Wiley-Liss
1 Wiley Dr.
Somerset, NJ 08875
Tel: 800-225-5945

"Heart Disease and Children with Down Syndrome," Cousineau, A. & Lauer, R. In: *Medical & Surgical Care for Children with Down Syndrome: A Guide for Parents.* Van Dyke, D., Mattheis, P., Eberly, S. & Williams, J. (Eds.) (1995). Bethesda, MD: Woodbine House, pp. 35-63.

Woodbine House
6510 Bells Mill Rd.
Bethesda, MD 20817
Tel: 800-843-7323

"The Heart" In: *Medical Care in Down Syndrome: A Preventive Medicine Approach*. Rogers, P. & Coleman, M. (1992). New York, NY: Marcel Dekker, Inc., pp.157-168.

Marcel Dekker, Inc.
270 Madison Ave., 4th Floor
New York, NY 10016
Tel: 212-696-9000

The Heart and Down Syndrome, Kidd, L. & Taussig, H. (1995). New York, NY: National Down Syndrome Society.

National Down Syndrome Society
666 Broadway
New York, NY 10012
Tel: 800-221-4602 or 212-460-9330

Books about Endocrine Conditions in Down Syndrome

Endocrine Conditions in Down Syndrome, McCoy, E. (1995). New York, NY: National Down Syndrome Society.

National Down Syndrome Society
666 Broadway
New York, NY 10012
Tel: 800-221-4602 or 212-460-9330

"Endocrine Function in Down Syndrome," McCoy, E. In: *Down Syndrome: Advances in Medical Care*, Lott, I. & McCoy, E. (Eds.) (1992). New York, NY: Wiley-Liss, pp. 71- 82.

Wiley-Liss
1 Wiley Dr.
Somerset, NJ 08875
Tel: 800-225- 5945

"Endocrinologic Aspects," Pueschel, S. & Bier, J. In: *Biomedical Concerns in Persons with Down Syndrome*, Pueschel, S.&

Pueschel, J. (Eds.) (1992). Baltimore, MD: Paul H. Brookes, pp. 259-272.

Paul H. Brookes Publishing Co.
P.O. Box 10624
Baltimore, MD 21285-0624
Tel: 800-638-3775

"The Endocrine System" In: *Medical Care in Down Syndrome: A Preventive Medicine Approach*. Rogers, P. & Coleman, M. (1992). New York: NY Marcel Dekker, Inc., pp.189-200.

Marcel Dekker, Inc.
270 Madison Ave., 4th Floor
New York, NY 10016
Tel: 212-696-9000

"Thyroid Conditions and Other Endocrine Concerns in Children with Down Syndrome," Foley, T., Jr. In: *Medical & Surgical Care for Children with Down Syndrome: A Guide for Parents*. Van Dyke, D., Mattheis, P., Eberly, S. & Williams, J. (Eds.) (1995). Bethesda, MD: Woodbine House, pp. 85-108.

Woodbine House
6510 Bells Mill Rd.
Bethesda, MD 20817
Tel: 800-843-7323

Books about the Neurology of Down Syndrome

"The Central Nervous System" In: Medical Care in Down Syndrome: A Preventive Medicine Approach. Rogers, P. and Coleman, M. (1992). New York: Marcel Dekker, Inc., pp. 201-224.

Marcel Dekker, Inc.
270 Madison Ave., 4th Floor
New York, NY 10016
Tel: 212-696-9000

"223 Neurologic Abnormalities," Florez, J. In: Biomedical Concerns in Persons with Down Syndrome. Pueschel, S. and Pueschel, J., (Eds.) (1992). Baltimore, MD: Paul H. Brookes Publishing Co., pp. 159-173.

Paul H. Brookes Publishing Co.
P.O. Box 10624
Baltimore, MD 21285-0624
Tel: 800-638-3775

"Neurological and Neurobehavioral Disorders in Down Syndrome,"
Lott, I. In: Down Syndrome: Advances in Medical Care. Lott, I.,
and McCoy, E. (Eds.) (1992). New York, Wiley-Liss, Inc., pp.
103-109.

Wiley-Liss
1 Wiley Dr.
Somerset, NJ 08875
Tel: 800-225-5945

"Neurology of Children with Down Syndrome," Mattheis, P. In:
Medical & Surgical Care for Children with Down Syndrome: A
Guide for Parents. Van Dyke, D., Mattheis, P., Eberly, S., Williams, J. (Eds.) (1995). Bethesda, MD: Woodbine House, Inc., pp.
267-287.

Woodbine House, Inc.
6510 Bells Mill Rd.
Bethesda, MD 20817
Tel: 800-843-7323

The Neurology of Down Syndrome, Lott, I. (1995). New York: National Down Syndrome Society.

National Down Syndrome Society
666 Broadway
New York, NY 10012
Tel: 800-221-4602 or 212-460-9330

Educational Resources on Inclusion

This list will familiarize you with organizations, publications and
other materials that present a commitment to the philosophy and
practice of inclusion. The list is not exhaustive.

The Educational Challenges Program

The Educational Challenges Program is a two-year study of inclusive education examines the nature of the public school experience

for children with Down syndrome. Directed by Gloria Wolpert, Ed.D., this study is the first national survey of inclusion for children with Down syndrome and explores the full spectrum of options that are, or should be, available to all children with Down syndrome. As part of the Educational Challenges Program, NDSS has developed a pamphlet on inclusion and an annotated resource list of organizations and materials available to help parents and professionals.

Teaching Partnership Program

Four color posters bring the message of inclusion, understanding and friendship to classrooms across the U.S. The NDSS teaching partnership program uses posters and educational materials to help students understand what it's like to have a developmental disability and to foster friendship among all students. This program, thanks to the generous support of many people who have an interest in inclusive education, has already placed thousands of posters in schools across the U.S. and prompted hundreds of children to write essays about their new understanding of their classmates with Down syndrome.

The first copy of a poster is free; additional copies are $3 each. The posters are targeted to specific grade ranges and feature the following positive messages:

- Grades 1-3: None of us are the same on the outside. All of us are the same on the inside.
- Grades 4-6: Friendship knows no boundaries.
- Grades 7-9: It's cool to be yourself.
- Grades 10-12: The future rides on the acceptance of all of us!

Posters can be ordered through the online order form or by calling (800) 221-4602, or by email to info@ndss.org. Please help to increase awareness, understanding and acceptance of Down syndrome by ordering a teaching poster and information packet or by telling your local school and teachers about the teaching partnership program. It works!

American Association of University Affiliated Programs (AAUAP)

8630 Fenton St., Suite 410
Silver Spring, MD 20910
Tel: 301-588-8252
URL: http://www.aauap.org

AAUAP is the central office for the 61 University Affiliated Programs (UAPs) and is their representative to the federal government. UAPS are located at major universities and teaching hospitals in all states. These multidisciplinary centers support the independence, productivity, integration and inclusion into the community of individuals with developmental disabilities and their families. Services provided by UAPs vary according to state; but in general, each one provides direct services, conducts research, designs programs and provides practical training. For information on the UAP nearest you, contact the above number.

Center on Human Policy
Syracuse University
805 South Crouse Avenue
Syracuse, NY 13244-2380
Tel: 315-443-3851
Fax: 315-443-4338
E-Mail: thechp@sued.syr.edu
URL: http://soeweb.syr.edu/thechp

The Center on Human Policy is a research, policy and advocacy organization involved in the national movement to insure the rights of people with disabilities. The center distributes a variety of reports and resources on the integration of people with disabilities into community life. Among these materials is an "inclusion packet" which contains sample case studies, reprints of chapters and articles, a list of important factors in inclusion and a bibliography.

Cooke Foundation for Special Education
456 West 52 St.
New York, NY 10019
Tel: 212-245-3376

The Cooke Foundation for Special Education is a not-for-profit organization dedicated to advocating and providing inclusive education placements for children with disabilities in New York City. The Cooke Foundation is the only private program which helps students and their parents locate regular elementary schools (public, private and parochial) interested in including children with disabilities and provides the necessary supports (consulting teachers, teaching assistants, staff development, etc.) to enable these students to succeed in regular school environments.

Down Syndrome Association of Greater Cincinnati (DSAGC)
1821 Summit Rd., Suite G-20
Cincinnati, OH 45237
Tel: 513-761-5400
E-Mail: dsagc@aol.com
URL: http://www.dsagc.com

A parent support organization which distributes an "Inclusion Packet" containing information on the philosophy, laws, strategies and resources pertaining to inclusion.

Expectations Unlimited, Inc.
P.O. Box 655
Niwot, CO 80544
Tel: 303-652-2727

Expectations Unlimited, Inc. distributes video presentations and conference recordings on many aspects of Inclusive Education. Their collection includes the conferences sponsored by the Colorado Coalition for Inclusive Education.

Federation for Children with Special Needs
1135 Tremont Street, Suite 420
Boston, MA 02120
Tel: 617-236-7210 or 800-331-0688
Fax: 617-572-2094
E-Mail: fcsninfo@fcsn.org
URL: http://www.fcsn.org

National office of the federally funded Parent Training and Information Centers. The centers are designed to make parents aware of their legal rights under P.L. 94-142 and to provide information, advocacy and training. Parents can locate their state office by calling the above number.

Inclusion Press/Centre for Integrated Education and Community
24 Thome Crescent
Toronto, Ontario
M6H 2S5 CANADA
Tel: 416-658-5363
Fax: 416-658-5067

Directed by Dr. Marsha Forest and Dr. Jack Pearpoint, this organization and publishing house provides books, videos and printed matter regarding inclusion. In addition, they publish a newsletter called, "Inclusion News" and provide seminars and workshops on the philosophy and practice of inclusion.

Institute on Community Integration
University of Minnesota
150 Pillsbury Dr., S.E.
Minneapolis, MN 55455
Tel: 612-624-4512 (publications)
Tel: 612-624-6300 (general information)

The institute's efforts are directed at facilitating the independence of citizens with disabilities and their social integration into the mainstream of community life. The Institute conducts over 60 projects that provide training, service and consultation, research and information dissemination. Information on inclusion, as well as other topics, is available through newsletters, resource guides, training manuals, research reports, curricula and brochures.

National Center on Educational Restructuring and Inclusion (NCERI)
The Graduate School and University Center
The City University of New York
33 West 42 St.
New York, NY 10036
Tel: 212-642-2656

NCERI promotes and supports educational programs where all students are served effectively in inclusive settings. Toward this goal, NCERI addresses issues of national and local policy, conducts research, provides training and technical assistance, and disseminates information about programs, practices, evaluation and funding of inclusive education programs.

National Information Center for Children and Youth with Disabilities (NICHCY)
P.O. Box 1492
Washington, DC 20013-1492
Toll-free: 800-695-0285
Tel: 202-884-8200
URL: http://www.nichcy.org

NICHCY is a federally funded information clearinghouse that provides free information on disabilities and disability-related issues. Provides clearly written booklets and resource listings regarding special education services.

National Parent Network on Disabilities
1130 17th Street, NW, Suite 400
Washington, DC 20036
Tel: 202-463-2299
Fax: 202-463-9403
E-Mail: NPND@cs.net
URL: http://www.npnd.org

Sponsors "All Children Belong," an inclusion training project, and acts as a national advocacy and lobbying organization on behalf of children and adults with disabilities. Provides written information on inclusion.

Parent Advocacy Coalition for Educational Rights (PACER) Center
4826 Chicago Ave. South
Minneapolis, MN 55417-1098
Tel: 612-827-2966 or 800-53-PACER (in MN)
E-Mail: webmaster@pacer.org
URL: http://www.pacer.org

PACER Center is a coalition of organizations founded on the concept of Parents Helping Parents. The center conducts workshops, provides training and disseminates information related to special education and disabilities.

Parent Education and Assistance for Kids (PEAK) Parent Center, Inc.
6055 Lehman Dr., Suite 101
Colorado Springs, CO 80918
Tel: 719-531-9400
URL: http://www.peakparent.org

PEAK is the Focus Center on Inclusion for the Technical Assistance for Parents Program (TAPP) project of Parent Training and Information Centers nationwide. The center develops and distributes informational materials, curricula, training guides and a newsletter. In addition, PEAK is a co-sponsor of the annual Strategies for Inclusive Education Conference.

Schools Are For Everyone (SAFE)

P.O. Box 9503
Schenectady, NY 12309

National organization whose primary function is to support the placement of children in inclusive settings. Provides general information regarding inclusion: how to advocate for inclusion; how to impact on legislation at the local, state and federal level; and how to locate local SAFE chapters. In addition, provides assistance on legal questions regarding inclusion.

Special Education Resource Center (SERC)

25 Industrial Park Rd.
Middletown, CT 06457
Tel: 860-632-1485

SERC is an information clearinghouse which provides annotated bibliographies and resource listings regarding inclusion. Its mission is to serve as a centralized resource for professionals, families and community members regarding early intervention, special education and pupil services and transition-to-adult life for individuals with special needs.

The Association for Persons with Severe Handicaps (TASH)

29 W Susquehanna Ave., Suite 210
Baltimore, MD 21204
Tel: 410-828-8274
Fax: 410-828-6706
URL: http://www.tash.org

TASH is a national organization which is devoted to promoting the full inclusion of people with disabilities and to eradicating the injustices and inequities experienced by these individuals. TASH gathers and disseminates information; advocates on behalf of people with disabilities; and supports research, education and judicial efforts. A newsletter, journal and other materials are available through the organization.

Additional Reading about Sexuality in Individuals with Developmental Disabilities

"Affection, Love, Intimacy, and Sexual Relationships," Jurkowski, E. & Amado, A. In: Friendships and Community Connections

Between People With and Without Developmental Disabilities. Amado, A. (Ed.) (1993). Baltimore, MD: Paul H. Brookes, pp. 129-151.

Paul H. Brookes Publishing Co.
P.O. Box 10624
Baltimore, MD 21285- 0624
Tel: 800-638-3775

This chapter discusses the need to consider the sexuality of individuals with developmental disabilities, and focuses on the importance of sex education as a means to enhance quality of life and relationships and to prevent sexual abuse. The chapter also includes comments from individuals with disabilities, revealing how they view their own sexuality.

Couples With Intellectual Disabilities Talk about Living and Loving, Schwier, K. (1994). Bethesda, MD: Woodbine House.

Woodbine House
6510 Bells Mill Rd.
Bethesda, MD 20817
Tel: 800-843-7323

This book profiles various people with developmental disabilities who have been involved in meaningful intimate relationships. These first-hand accounts reveal the often-ignored existence of sexuality and the desire for intimate relationships among individuals with intellectual disabilities.

"Sexuality and Community Living," Schwab, W. In: Down Syndrome: Advances in Medical Care. Lott, I. & McCoy, E. (Eds.) (1992). New York, NY: Wiley-Liss, pp. 157-166.

Wiley-Liss
1 Wiley Dr.
Somerset, NJ 08875
Tel: 800-225-5945

This chapter provides a general overview of sexual development in adolescents with Down syndrome. The author stresses the necessity for caregivers and health care providers to acknowledge the innate need of all individuals for personal intimacy, and to therefore consider sex education and opportunities for relationships.

Sexuality Education for Children and Youth with Disabilities, National Information Center for Children and Youth with Disabilities, News Digest, Vol. 1, Number 3 (1992). Washington, DC: NICHCY.

P.O. Box 1492
Washington, DC 20013-1492
Toll-free: 800-695-0285
Tel: 202-884-8200
URL: http://www.nichcy.org

This packet of information includes articles on sexual development, teaching sexuality to children with disabilities, developing social skills and fostering relationships. Also included is a list of resources.

Sexuality in Down Syndrome, Schwab, W. (1995). New York, NY: National Down Syndrome Society.

National Down Syndrome Society
666 Broadway
New York, NY 10012
Tel: 800-221-4602 or 212-460-9330

This booklet answers commonly asked questions about sexuality in individuals with Down syndrome. Information is provided about sexual feelings, physical development, menstruation and reproduction. The importance of sex education appropriate for individuals with Down syndrome is discussed.

SIECUS Report, Volume 23, Number 4, April/May (1995). New York, NY: Sexuality Information and Education Council of the United States (SIECUS).

SIECUS
130 West 42nd Street, Suite 350
New York, NY 10036
Tel: 212-819-9770
Fax: 212-819-9776
E-Mail: siecus@siecus.org
URL: http://www.siecus.org

This report includes articles on sexuality-related issues and sex education for people with developmental disabilities. A comprehensive bibliography of books, teaching aids, curricula and newsletters covering related topics on sexuality is included.

Resources and Materials about Fetal Alcohol Syndrome

Fantastic Antone Succeeds: Experiences in Educating Children with FAS
NOFAS
1819 H Street NW, Suite 750
Washington, DC 20006
Tel: 800-944-9662

A Manual on Adolescents and Adults with FAS with Special Reference to American Indians
FAS Project
5300 Homestead Ave NE
Albuquerque, NM 87109
Tel: 505-837-4228

Training Tapes for Living with F.A.S. and F.A.E.
Altschul Group Corporation
1560 Sherman Ave, Suite 100
Evanston, IL 60201-9971

Working with FAS Children: A Handbook for Caregivers of FAS/FAE Children
Jean Cornish
Minnesota Services Associates
Tel: 612-645-0688

Chapter 48

Directory of Organizations

The organizations listed below are only a few of the many that provide services and information about disability issues to families. When calling or writing an organization, it is always a good idea to be as specific as you can in stating your needs and concerns. For example, state the gender and age of your child, the disability he or she has, and any special needs or interests you have in making your request. This helps organizations provide you with information that is truly helpful and on target.

Clearinghouses, Information Centers, and Government Agencies

Administration on Developmental Disabilities
Administration for Children and Families
U.S. Department of Health and Human Services
Mail Stop: HHH 300-F
370 L'Enfant Promenade, S.W.
Washington, DC 20447
Tel: 202-690-6590
E-Mail: add@acf.dhhs.gov
URL: http://www.acf.dhhs.gov/programs/add/index.htm

ARCH National Resource Center for Crisis Nurseries and Respite Care Services

Chapel Hill Training Outreach Project
800 Eastowne Drive
Suite 105
Chapel Hill, NC 27514
Tel: 800-473-1727; or 919-490-5577
National Respite Locator Service: 800-773-5433
E-Mail: YLayden@intrex.net
URL: http://www.chtop.com/archbroc.htm

Centers for Disease Control and Prevention

Tel: 404-639-3534
Toll-free: 800-311-3435
Website: http://www.cdc.gov

Communication and Information Services (formerly Clearinghouse on Disability Information)

Office of Special Education and Rehabilitative Services (OSERS)
Room 3132, Switzer Building
330 C Street S.W.
Washington, DC 20202-2524
Tel: 202-205-5507
Fax: 202-401-2608
URL: http://www.ed.gov/offices/OSERS

Consumer Product Safety Commission

4330 East-West Highway
Bethesda, Maryland
Tel: 800-638-CPSC
TDD: 800-638-8270
Website: http://www.cpsc.gov

Department of Education

400 Maryland Avenue, SW
Washington, DC 20202
Tel: 800-USA-LEARN
TTY: 800-437-0833
Fax: 202-401-0689
E-Mail: customerservice@inet.ed.gov
URL: http:/www.ed.gov

Emergency Medical Services for Children—National Resource Center
111 Michigan Avenue N.W.
Washington, DC 20010-2979
Tel: 202-884-4927
Fax: 301-650-8045
E-Mail: info@emscnrc.com
URL: http://www.ems-c.org

Environmental Protection Agency's Safe Drinking Water
Hotline: 800-426-4791
Website: http://www.epa.gov/opptintr/lead

ERIC Clearinghouse on Disabilities and Gifted Education
Council for Exceptional Children
1920 Association Drive
Reston, VA 20191-1589
Tel: 800-328-0272
Fax: 703-264-9449
URL: http://ericec.org

Head Start Bureau
330 "C" Street, SW
Washington, D.C. 20447
URL: http://www2.acf.dhhs.gov/programs/hsb

HEATH Resource Center (National Clearinghouse on Postsecondary Education for Individuals with Disabilities)
One Dupont Circle N.W., Suite 800
Washington, DC 20036-1193
Tel: 800-544-3284 (Voice/TTY, outside of DC area); 202-939-9320 (in DC area)
Fax: 202-833-4760

National Association of Protection and Advocacy (P&A) Systems, (NAPAS)
900 Second Street, NE
Suite 211
Washington, D.C. 20002
Tel: 202-408-9514
Fax: 202-408-9520

E-Mail: napas@vipmail.earthlink.net
URL: http://www.protectionandadvocacy.com

National Center for Education in Maternal and Child Health
2000 15th Street North
Suite 701
Arlington, VA 22201-2617
Tel: 703-524-7802
Fax: 703-524-9335
E-Mail: info@ncemch.org
URL: http://www.ncemch.org

National Center for Youth with Disabilities
University of Minnesota
Box 721
420 Delaware Street S.E.
Minneapolis, MN 55455
Tel: 612-626-2825
TTY: 612-624-3939

National Clearinghouse on Family Support and Children's Mental Health
Portland State University
P.O. Box 751
Portland, OR 97207
Toll-free: 800-628-1696
Tel: 503-725-4040

National Clearinghouse on Women and Girls with Disabilities
114 East 32nd Street, Suite 701
New York, NY 10016
Tel: 212-725-1803

National Coalition of Hispanic Health and Human Services Organizations
Washington, DC
Tel: 202-387-5000
E-Mail: cossmho@cossmho.org
URL: http://www.cossmho.org

National Council on Alcoholism and Drug Dependence
12 West 21st Street
New York, NY 10010
Tel: 800-622-2255
Fax: 212-645-1690
E-Mail: national@ncadd.org
URL: http://www.ncadd.org

National Council on Disability
1331 F St. N.W.
Suite 1050, 10th Floor
Washington, DC 20004-1107
Tel: 202-272-2004
TTY: 202-272-2074
Fax: 202-272-2022
E-Mail: mquigley@ncd.gov
URL: http://www.ncd.gov

National Health Information Center (ONHIC)
P.O. Box 1133
Washington, DC 20013-1133
Tel: 800-336-4797; or 301-565-4167

National Highway Traffic Safety Administration (NHTSA) Headquarters
Traffic Safety Programs, NTS-15,
400 Seventh Street, S.W.
Washington, D.C. 20590
Tel: 202-366-1739
Hotline: 888-327-4236
Website: http://www.nhtsa.dot.gov

National Human Genome Research Institute
Office of Communications
Bldg. 31, Rm. 4B09
9000 Rockville Pike
Bethesda, MD 20892
Tel: 301-402-0911
Fax: 301-402-2218
E-Mail: wsd@cu.nih.gov
URL: http://www.nhgri.nih.gov

National Information Center for Children and Youth with Disabilities (NICHCY)
P.O. Box 1492
Washington, DC 20013-1492
Toll-free: 800-695-0285
Tel: 202-884-8200
E-Mail: nichcy@aed.org
URL: http://www.nichcy.org

National Information Center on Deafness
Gallaudet University
800 Florida Avenue N.E.
Washington, DC 20002
Tel: 202-651-5051
TTY: 202-651-5052
E-Mail: nicd@gallux.gallaudet.edu
URL: http://www.gallaudet.edu/~nicd

National Institute on Alcohol Abuse and Alcoholism
6000 Executive Boulevard, Suite 409
Willco Building
Bethesda, MD 20892-7003
Tel: 301-443-3860
URL: http://www.niaaa.nih.gov

National Institute of Child Health and Human Development
Building 31, Room 2A34
Bethesda, MD 20892-2425
Tel: 301-496-5133
E-Mail: nichdwebmaster-r@mail.nih.gov
URL: http://www.nichd.gov

National Institute of Mental Health
6001 Executive Boulevard
Rm. 8184, MSC 9663
Bethesda, Maryland 20892-9663
Tel: 301-443-4513
Fax: 301-433-4279
E-Mail: nimhinfo@nih.gov
Website: http://www.nimh.nih.gov

National Institute of Neurological Disorders and Stroke
Office of Communications and Public Liaison
P.O. Box 5801
Bethesda, Maryland 20824
Toll-free: 800-352-9424
Tel: 301-496-5751
URL: http://www.ninds.nih.gov

National Lead Information Center
Tel: 800-424-LEAD
TDD: 800-526-5456
Website: http://www.nsc.org/ehc/lead.htm

National Organization on Fetal Alcohol Syndrome
1819 H Street, NW, Suite 750
Washington, DC 20006
Tel: 800-944-9662
E-Mail: 4woman@soza.com
URL: http://www.nofas.org

National Organization for Rare Disorders, Inc. (NORD)
P.O. Box 8923
New Fairfield, Connecticut 06812-8923
Tel: 203-746-6518
Toll-free: 800-999-6673
Fax: 203-746-6481
E-Mail: orphan@rarediseases.org
Website: http://www.rarediseases.org

National Rehabilitation Information Center (NARIC)
1010 Wayne Avenue, Suite 800
Silver Spring, MD 20910-5633
Toll-free!: 800-346-2742
TTY: 301-495-5626
Voice/TTY in MD: 301-562-2400
E-Mail: naricinfo@kra.com
URL: http://www.naric.com/naric

The National SAFE KIDS Campaign
1301 Pennsylvania Ave, NW, Suite 1000
Washington, D.C. 20004-1707

Tel: 202-662-0600
Fax: 202-393-2072
E-Mail: program@safekids.org
Website: http://www.safekids.org

Office of Indian Education Programs, Bureau of Indian Affairs (BIA)
1849 C Street N.W.
MS-3512-MIB-OIE-23
Washington, DC 20240
Tel: 202-208-3596

Office of Minority Health Resource Center/DHHS
Rockwell Bldg. 2
5515 Security Lane, 1st Floor
Rockville, MD 20852
Tel: 800-444-6472

Research and Training Center on Family Support and Children's Mental Health
Portland State University
P.O. Box 751
Portland, OR 97207
Tollfree: 800-628-1696
Tel: 503-725-4040

The RESNA Technical Assistance Project
1700 North Moore Street
Suite 1540
Arlington, VA 22209-1903
Tel: 703-524-6686
Fax: 703-524-6630
TTY: 703-524-6639
E-Mail: nbailey@resna.org
URL: http://www.resna.org

Technical Assistance to Parent Programs (TAPP) Network

National Office: Federation for Children with Special Needs
95 Berkeley Street, Suite 104
Boston, MA 02116
Tel: 617-482-2915 (V/TTY)
Fax: 617-695-2939
E-Mail: mziegler@fesn.org
URL: http://www.fesn.org

Regional Offices:

West Region—Washington State PAVE
6316 South 12th Street
Tacoma, WA 98465
Toll-free in WA: 800-572-7368
Tel: 206-565-2266

Midwest Region—PACER Center
4826 Chicago Avenue South
Minneapolis, MN 55417
Toll-free in MN only: 800-537-2737 (V/TTY)
Tel: 612-827-2966 (V/TTY)

Northeast Region—Parent Information Center
P.O. Box 1422
Concord, NH 03302.
Tel: 603-224-7005

South Region—Exceptional Children's Assistance Center
P.O. Box 16
Davidson, NJ 28036
Toll-free in NC: 800-962-6817
Tel: 704-892-1321

Other Organizations

Alliance for Technology Access
2175 East Francisco Boulevard
Suite L
San Rafael, CA 94901
Tel: 415-455-4575
Toll-Free: 800-455-7970
Fax: 415-455-0654
E-Mail: atainfo@ATAcess.org
URL: http://www.ATAcess.org

Alzheimer's Association
919 North Michigan Ave., Suite 1000
Chicago, IL 60611-1676
Tel: 800-272-3900
Fax: 312-335-1110
E-Mail: info@alz.org
URL: http://www.alz.org

American Alliance for Health, Physical Education, Recreation, and Dance (AAHPERD)
American Association for Active Lifestyles and Fitness (AAALF)
Adapted Physical Activity Council (APAC)
1900 Association Drive
Reston, Va. 22091
Toll-free: 800-213-7193
Tel: 703-476-3430
E-Mail: webmaster@aahperd.org

APAC is a council within AAALF, a division of AAHPERD. APAC can be contacted at the address, telephone or e-mail address above, and is the primary contact for information on physical fitness and people with mental retardation. APAC can provide materials pertaining to adapted physical fitness education.

American Academy of Pediatrics
141 Northwest Point Boulevard
Elk Grove Village, Illinois 60007-1098
Tel: 847-228-5005
Fax: 847-228-5097
E-Mail: kidsdocs@aap.org
Website: http://www.aapa.org

American Association on Mental Retardation
444 North Capitol Street, NW
Suite 846
Washington, D.C. 20001-1512
Toll-free: 800-424-3688
Tel: 202-387-1968
Fax: 202-387-2193
URL: http://www.aamr.org

American Camping Association (ACA), Inc.
5000 State Road 67, North
Martinsville, IN 46151-7902
Toll-free: 800-428-2267
Tel: 765-342-8456
URL: http://www.acacamps.org (The current guide is free on the ACA web site)

The Arc
National Organization on Mental Retardation
1010 Wayne Ave
Suite 650
Silver Spring, MD 20910
Tel: 301-565-3842
Fax: 301-565-3843
E-mail: thearc@metronet.com
URL: http://www.thearc.org

Association for the Care of Children's Health
7910 Woodmont Avenue, Suite 300
Bethesda, MD 20814-3015
Toll-free: 800-808-ACCH
Tel: 301-654-6549

Association for People in Supported Employment (APSE)
1627 Monument Avenue,
Richmond, Virginia, 23220
Tel: 804-278-9187

Association for Persons with Severe Handicaps (TASH)
29 W. Susquehanna Avenue, Suite 210
Baltimore, MD 21204

Tel: 410-828-8274
TTY: 410-828-1306
Fax: 410-828-6706
E-Mail: nweiss@tash.org
URL: http://www.tash.org

Association of Birth Defects Children
930 Woodcock Rd.
Suite 225
Orlando, FL 32803
Tel: 407-245-7035
Toll-free: 800-313-ABDC (2232)
E-Mail: abdc@birthdefects.org
Website: http://www.birthdefects.org/MAIN.HTM

Autism National Committee
249 Hampshire Drive
Plainsboro, NJ 08536

Autism Research Institute
4182 Adams Avenue
San Diego, California 92116
Tel: 619-281-7165
Website: http://www.autism.com/ari

Autism Society of America
7910 Woodmont Ave., Suite 300
Bethesda, MD 20814-3015
Toll-free: 800-3-AUTISM
Tel: 301-657-0881
Fax: 301-657-0869
URL: http://www.autism-society.org

Beach Center on Families and Disability
University of Kansas
3111 Haworth Hall
Lawrence, KS 66045
Tel: 913-864-7600 (V/TTY)
Fax: 785-864-7605
E-Mail: beach@dole.lsi.ukans.edu
URL: http://www.lsi.ukans.edu/beach/beachhp.htm

The Bicycle League of America
1612 K Street NW
Washington, D.C. 20006-2082
Tel: 202-822-1330
Fax: 202-922-1334
E-Mail: bikeleague@bikeleague.org
Website: http://www.bikeleague.org

Brain Injury Association (formerly the National Head Injury Foundation)
105 North Alfred Street
Alexandria, VA 22314
Tel: 703-236-6000
Fax: 703-236-6001
E-Mail: FamilyHelpline@biausa.org
URL: http://www.biausa.org

Center for Community Change through Housing and Support at Trinity College of Vermont
208 Colchester Avenue
Burlington, VT, 05401-6110
Tel: 802-653-1260

Center for the Study of Autism
P.O. Box 4538
Salem, OR 97302
URL: http://www.autism.org

Children's PKU Network
1520 State St., Suite #240
San Diego, CA 922101
Tel: 619-233-3202
Fax: 619-233-0838
E-Mail: magol@gfe.net or pkunetwork@aol.com

Council for Exceptional Children
1920 Association Drive
Reston, VA 20191-1589
Tel: 703-620-3660 or 888-CEC-SPED
Fax: 703-264-9494
E-Mail: service@cec.sped.org
URL: http://www.cec.sped.org

Council for Responsible Genetics (CRG)
5 Upland Rd., Suite 3
Cambridge, Mass. 02140
Tel: 617-868-0870
Fax: 617-491-5344
E-Mail: crg@gene-watch.org
URL: http://www.gen-watch.org

Easter Seals—National Office
230 West Monroe Street
Suite 1800
Chicago, IL 60606
Toll-free: 800-221-6827
Tel: 312-726-6200
TT: 312-726-4258
Fax: 312-726-1494
E-Mail: info@easter-seals.org
URL: http://www.easter-seals.org

Epilepsy Foundation—National Office
4351 Garden City Drive
Suite 500
Landover, MD 20785
Tel: 301-459-3700
Toll-free: 800-332-1000
TTY: 800-332-2070
E-Mail: postmaster@efa.org
Web site: http://www.efa.org

Family Caregiver Alliance
690 Market Street, Suite 601
San Francisco, CA 94104
Toll-free: 800-245-6686 (CA only)
Tel: 415-434-3388
Fax: 415-434-3508
E-Mail: info@caregiver.org
URL: http://www.caregiver.org

Family Voices
P.O. Box 769
Algodones, NM 87001

Tel: 505-867-2368
Toll-free: 888-835-5669
Fax: 505-867-6517
E-Mail: kidshealth@familyvoices.org
URL: http://www.familyvoices.org

FRAXA Research Foundation, Inc.
45 Pleasant St.
Newburyport, MA 01950
Tel: 978-462-1866
Fax: 978-463-9985
E-Mail: info@fraxa.org
URL: http://www.fraxa.org

Habitat for Humanity International
121 Habitat Street
Americus, Georgia, 31709-3498
Tel: 912-924-6935
Fax: 912-924-6541
E-Mail: public_info@habitat.org
URL: http://www.habitat.org

Hammer Residence
1909 E. Wayzata Blvd.
Wayzata, MN 55391

Harborview Injury Prevention Research Center
Box 359960
325 Ninth Avenue
Seattle, Washington 98104-2499
Tel: 206-521-1520
Fax: 206-521-1562
E-Mail: hiprc@u.washington.edu
URL: http://depts.washington.edu/hiprc

Head Injury Hotline
212 Pioneer Building
Seattle, WA 98104-2221
Tel: 206-621-8558
E-Mail: brain@headinjury.com
URL: http://www.headinjury.com

The HuGEM Project: Issues in Genetic Privacy and Discrimination
Georgetown University
3307 M St. NW, Suite 401
Washington, DC 20007
Tel: 202-687-8245
Fax: 202-687-6770
E-Mail: medethx@gunet.georgetown.edu
URL: http://www.georgetown.edu/research/nrcbl

Independent Living Research Utilization Project (ILRU)
The Institute for Rehabilitation and Research
2323 South Sheppard
Suite 1000
Houston, TX 77019
Tel: 713-520-0232
TT: 713-520-5136
E-Mail: ilru@ilru.org
URL: http://www.ilru.org

International Rett Syndrome Association
9121 Piscataway, Suite 2B
Clinton, MD 20735
Toll-free: 800-818-7388
Tel: 301-856-3334
Fax: 301-856-3336
E-Mail: irsa@paltech.com
URL: http://www.healthy.net/pan/cso/cioi/IRSA.HTM

Learning Disabilities Association of America (LDA)
4156 Library Road
Pittsburgh, PA 15234
Toll-free: 888-300-6710
Tel: 412-341-1515; 412-341-8077
E-Mail: vldanatl@usaor.ne
URL: http://www.ldanatl.org

The Lissencephaly Network, Inc.
716 Autumn Ridge Lane
Fort Wayne, Indiana 46804-6402
Tel: 219-432-4310

Fax: 219-432-4310
URL: http://www.lissencephaly.org

March of Dimes Birth Defects Foundation
1275 Mamaroneck Avenue
White Plaines, NY 10605
Tel: 914-428-7100
URL: http://www.modimes.org

National Angelman Syndrome Foundation
414 Plaza Drive, Suite 209
Westmont, IL 60550
Toll-free: 800-432-6435
Fax: 630-655-0391
E-Mail: asf@adminsys.com
URL: http://chem-faculty.ucsd.edu/harvey/asfsite

National Autism Hotline
C/O Autism Services Center
P.O. Box 507
605 Ninth Street
Prichard Building
Huntington, West Virginia 25710-0507
Tel: 304-525-8014
Fax: 525-8026

National Consortium for Physical Education and Recreation for Individuals with Disabilities
Adapted Physical Education National Standards
P. O. Box 6639
Charlottesville, Va. 22906-6639
Toll-free: 888-273-6739
E-Mail: Lek@virginia.edu
URL: http://teach.virginia.edu/go/apens

The Consortium can provide technical support concerning adapted physical education.

National Down Syndrome Society
666 Broadway
New York, NY 10012
Toll-free: 800-221-4602

Tel: 212-460-9330
URL: http://www.ndss.org

National Fragile X Foundation
PO Box 190488
San Francisco, CA 94119
Tel: 510-763-6030
Toll-free: 800-688-8765
Fax: 510-763-6223
E-Mail: natlfx@sprintmail.com
URL: http://nfxf.org

National Home of Your Own Alliance
University of New Hampshire, Institute on Disability/UAP
7 Leavitt Lane, Suite 101
Durham, NH 03824-3522
Tel: 800-220-8770

National Parent Network on Disabilities
1130 17th Street, NW, Suite 400
Washington, DC 20036
Tel: 202-463-2299
Fax: 202-463-9403
E-Mail: NPND@cs.net
URL: http://www.npnd.org

National Tuberous Sclerosis Association
8181 Professional Place, Suite 110
Landover, MD 20785-2226
Toll-free: 800-225-NTSA
Tel: 301-459-9888
Fax: 301-459-0394
E-Mail: ntsa@ntsa.org
URL: http://www.ntsa.org

Native American Research and Training Center
1642 E. Helen
Tucson, AZ 85719
Tel: 520-621-5075
TTY: 520-621-5075
Fax: 520-621-9802

E-Mail: lclore@u.arizona.edu
URL: http://www.ahsc.arizona.edu/nartc

The New Jersey Center for Outreach and Services for the Autism Community, Inc. (COSAC)
1450 Parkside Avenue
Suite 22
Ewing, New Jersey 08638
Tel: 609-883-8100
E-Mail: njautism@aol.com
URL: http://members.aol.com/njautism

Research for Rett Foundation
P.O. Box 50347
Mobile, AL 36605
Toll-free: 800-422-7388

Resources for Children with Special Needs
Annual Special Camp Guide
200 Park Avenue, South
Suite 816
New York, NY 10003
Tel: 212-677-4650
$24.50 including shipping and handling (available in English & Spanish)

RRTC on Aging with Mental Retardation
Institute on Disability and Human Development
University of Illinois at Chicago
1640 West Roosevelt Road
Chicago, Illinois 60608-6904
Tel: 312-413-1520
TTY: 312-413-0453
URL: http://www.uic.edu/orgs/rrtcamr/index.html

Sibling Information Network
A.J. Pappanikou Center
University of Connecticut
249 Glenbrook Road, U64
Storrs, CT 06269-2064
Tel: 860-486-5035

Sick Kids (need) Involved People (SKIP)
C/O SKIP of New York
545 Madison Avenue, 13th Floor
New York, NY 10022
Tel: 212-421-9160

Special Olympics International (SOI)
Unified Sports
1325 G Street, N.W., Suite 500
Washington, DC 20005-3104
Tel: 202-628-3630
Fax: 202-824-0200
URL: http://www.specialolympics.org

Specialized Housing, Inc.
45 Bartlett Cres.
Brookline, MA 02446
Tel: 617-277-1805

Spina Bifida Association of America
4590 MacArthur Boulevard, N.W., Suite 250
Washington, D.C. 20007-4226
Toll-free: 800-621-3141
Tel: 202-944-3285
E-Mail: sbaa@sbaa.org
URL: http://www.sbaa.org
Call for a state-by-state listing

United Cerebral Palsy
1660L Street N.W., Suite 700
Washington, D.C. 20036
Toll-free (V/TT): 800-872-5827
Fax: 202-776-0414
E-Mail: ucpanatl@ucpa.org
URL: http://www.ucp.org

VCU/RRTC on Supported Employment
1314 West Main Street
P.O. Box 94201
Richmond, Virginia 23284-2011
Tel: 804-828-1851
Fax: 804-828-2193

Williams Syndrome Association
1316 N. Campbell, Suite 16
Royal Oak, MI 48067
Tel: 248-541-3630
Fax: 248-541-3631
URL: http://www.williams-syndrome.org

Williams Syndrome Foundation
University of California
Irvine, CA 92679-2310
Tel: 949-824-7259
URL: http://www.wsf.org

Zero to Three/National Center for Infants, Toddlers and Families
734 15th Street N.W., Suite 1000
Washington, DC 20005-1013
Tel: 202-638-1144
Toll-free: 800-899-4301
URL: http://zerotothree.org

Index

Index

Index

discretionary trusts 505–6
  defined 534
disintegrative disorder 142–44
Division TEACCH, web site 547
DNA (deoxyribonucleic acid)
  defined 533
  described 233–34
  fragile X syndrome 83
  Williams syndrome 138
  see also chromosomes; genes
DNA methylation
  Angelman syndrome 113
  described 84, 85
DNA screening, defined 533
Down, John Langdon 22
Down syndrome 15, 21–57, 483
  causes 23–25
    mosaicism 24
    nondisjunction 23–24
    translocation 24
  clinical information 35–50
  defined 534
  development 26–27
  diagnosis 25–26
  information resources 33, 548–59
  medical problems 26
  questions and answers 28–33
  research 29–30
  risk factors 24, 28–29
  statistics 22
  Supplemental Security Income benefits 499
Down Syndrome: Advances in Medical Care (Lott, et al.) 549, 556, 557, 559, 566
Down Syndrome: A Resource Handbook (Tingey) 550
Down Syndrome: Birth to Adulthood (Rynders, et al.) 550
Down Syndrome: Living and Learning in the Community (Nadel, et al.) 550
Down Syndrome and Alzheimer's Disease (Nadel, et al.) 549–50
Down Syndrome Association of Greater Cincinnati (DSAGC) 562
Down Syndrome News 33, 541
Do you really know what is best for me? OR how to help your board of directors become whole (Bales) 354

drowning, near and mental retardation 16
drug abuse
  birth defects 217–20
  mental retardation 228
drug use
  birth defects 214–15
  mental retardation 4
  pregnancy 243–44
Ducharme, G. 332
Duchenne muscular dystrophy 100
due process 384–87
  defined 534
"Due Process: Procedural Safeguards in P. L. 94-142" 379n
duPont Company, abilities of mentally retarded persons 477
Dybwad, G. 353, 354
dysplastic ears, Down syndrome 26

E

early intervention 397–411
  services 297–98
    defined 535
  Down syndrome 27
early interventionist, defined 535
ear shape, Down syndrome 26
Easter Seals Camping and Recreation List 363
Easter Seal Society
  camping and recreation list 363
  contact information 187, 192, 196, 582
  respite services 334
Eberly, S. 556, 558, 559
Eberly, S. S. 551
echocardiograms, Down syndrome 38
echolalia, defined 535
economic hardship, mental retardation 221–25
Edelson, Stephen M. 161n, 173
education 373–430
  Angelman syndrome 112–13
  assistive technology 420–21
  autism 165–67
  child care centers 222–23
  Down syndrome 27

Z

Health Reference Series
COMPLETE CATALOG

AIDS Sourcebook, 1st Edition

Basic Information about AIDS and HIV Infection, Featuring Historical and Statistical Data, Current Research, Prevention, and Other Special Topics of Interest for Persons Living with AIDS

Along with Source Listings for Further Assistance

Edited by Karen Bellenir and Peter D. Dresser. 831 pages. 1995. 0-7808-0031-1. $78.

"One strength of this book is its practical emphasis. The intended audience is the lay reader . . . useful as an educational tool for health care providers who work with AIDS patients. Recommended for public libraries as well as hospital or academic libraries that collect consumer materials."
— *Bulletin of the Medical Library Association, Jan '96*

"This is the most comprehensive volume of its kind on an important medical topic. Highly recommended for all libraries." — *Reference Book Review, '96*

"Very useful reference for all libraries."
— *Choice, Association of College and Research Libraries, Oct '95*

"There is a wealth of information here that can provide much educational assistance. It is a must book for all libraries and should be on the desk of each and every congressional leader. Highly recommended."
— *AIDS Book Review Journal, Aug '95*

"Recommended for most collections."
— *Library Journal, Jul '95*

AIDS Sourcebook, 2nd Edition

Basic Consumer Health Information about Acquired Immune Deficiency Syndrome (AIDS) and Human Immunodeficiency Virus (HIV) Infection, Featuring Updated Statistical Data, Reports on Recent Research and Prevention Initiatives, and Other Special Topics of Interest for Persons Living with AIDS, Including New Antiretroviral Treatment Options, Strategies for Combating Opportunistic Infections, Information about Clinical Trials, and More

Along with a Glossary of Important Terms and Resource Listings for Further Help and Information

Edited by Karen Bellenir. 751 pages. 1999. 0-7808-0225-X. $78.

"Recommended reference source."
— *Booklist, American Library Association, Dec '99*

"A solid text for college-level health libraries."
— *The Bookwatch, Aug '99*

Cited in *Reference Sources for Small and Medium-Sized Libraries, American Library Association, 1999*

Alcoholism Sourcebook

Basic Consumer Health Information about the Physical and Mental Consequences of Alcohol Abuse, Including Liver Disease, Pancreatitis, Wernicke-Korsakoff Syndrome (Alcoholic Dementia), Fetal Alcohol Syndrome, Heart Disease, Kidney Disorders, Gastrointestinal Problems, and Immune System Compromise and Featuring Facts about Addiction, Detoxification, Alcohol Withdrawal, Recovery, and the Maintenance of Sobriety

Along with a Glossary and Directories of Resources for Further Help and Information

Edited by Karen Bellenir. 650 pages. 2000. 0-7808-0325-6. $78.

SEE ALSO Drug Abuse Sourcebook, Substance Abuse Sourcebook

Allergies Sourcebook

Basic Information about Major Forms and Mechanisms of Common Allergic Reactions, Sensitivities, and Intolerances, Including Anaphylaxis, Asthma, Hives and Other Dermatologic Symptoms, Rhinitis, and Sinusitis

Along with Their Usual Triggers Like Animal Fur, Chemicals, Drugs, Dust, Foods, Insects, Latex, Pollen, and Poison Ivy, Oak, and Sumac; Plus Information on Prevention, Identification, and Treatment

Edited by Allan R. Cook. 611 pages. 1997. 0-7808-0036-2. $78.

Alternative Medicine Sourcebook

Basic Consumer Health Information about Alternatives to Conventional Medicine, Including Acupressure, Acupuncture, Aromatherapy, Ayurveda, Bioelectromagnetics, Environmental Medicine, Essence Therapy, Food and Nutrition Therapy, Herbal Therapy, Homeopathy, Imaging, Massage, Naturopathy, Reflexology, Relaxation and Meditation, Sound Therapy, Vitamin and Mineral Therapy, and Yoga, and More

Edited by Allan R. Cook. 737 pages. 1999. 0-7808-0200-4. $78.

Alzheimer's, Stroke & 29 Other Neurological Disorders Sourcebook, 1st Edition

Basic Information for the Layperson on 31 Diseases or Disorders Affecting the Brain and Nervous System, First Describing the Illness, Then Listing Symptoms, Diagnostic Methods, and Treatment Options, and Including Statistics on Incidences and Causes

Edited by Frank E. Bair. 579 pages. 1993. 1-55888-748-2. $78.

"Nontechnical reference book that provides reader-friendly information."
—*Family Caregiver Alliance Update, Winter '96*

"Should be included in any library's patient education section." —*American Reference Books Annual, 1994*

"Written in an approachable and accessible style. Recommended for patient education and consumer health collections in health science center and public libraries." —*Academic Library Book Review, Dec '93*

"It is very handy to have information on more than thirty neurological disorders under one cover, and there is no recent source like it." —*Reference Quarterly, Reference and User Services Association, Fall '93*

SEE ALSO Brain Disorders Sourcebook

Alzheimer's Disease Sourcebook, 2nd Edition

Basic Consumer Health Information about Alzheimer's Disease, Related Disorders, and Other Dementias, Including Multi-Infarct Dementia, AIDS-Related Dementia, Alcoholic Dementia, Huntington's Disease, Delirium, and Confusional States

Along with Reports Detailing Current Research Efforts in Prevention and Treatment, Long-Term Care Issues, and Listings of Sources for Additional Help and Information

Edited by Karen Bellenir. 524 pages. 1999. 0-7808-0223-3. $78.

"Recommended reference source."
—*Booklist, American Library Association, Oct '99*

Arthritis Sourcebook

Basic Consumer Health Information about Specific Forms of Arthritis and Related Disorders, Including Rheumatoid Arthritis, Osteoarthritis, Gout, Polymyalgia Rheumatica, Psoriatic Arthritis, Spondyloarthropathies, Juvenile Rheumatoid Arthritis, and Juvenile Ankylosing Spondylitis

Along with Information about Medical, Surgical, and Alternative Treatment Options, and Including Strategies for Coping with Pain, Fatigue, and Stress

Edited by Allan R. Cook. 550 pages. 1998. 0-7808-0201-2. $78.

"... accessible to the layperson."
—*Reference and Research Book News, Feb '99*

Asthma Sourcebook

Basic Consumer Health Information about Asthma, Including Symptoms, Traditional and Nontraditional Remedies, Treatment Advances, Quality-of-Life Aids, Medical Research Updates, and the Role of Allergies, Exercise, Age, the Environment, and Genetics in the Development of Asthma

Along with Statistical Data, a Glossary, and Directories of Support Groups and Other Resources for Further Information

Edited by Annemarie S. Muth. 650 pages. 2000. 0-7808-0381-7. $78.

Back & Neck Disorders Sourcebook

Basic Information about Disorders and Injuries of the Spinal Cord and Vertebrae, Including Facts on Chiropractic Treatment, Surgical Interventions, Paralysis, and Rehabilitation

Along with Advice for Preventing Back Trouble

Edited by Karen Bellenir. 548 pages. 1997. 0-7808-0202-0. $78.

"The strength of this work is its basic, easy-to-read format. Recommended."
—*Reference and User Services Quarterly, American Library Association, Winter '97*

Blood & Circulatory Disorders Sourcebook

Basic Information about Blood and Its Components, Anemias, Leukemias, Bleeding Disorders, and Circulatory Disorders, Including Aplastic Anemia, Thalassemia, Sickle-Cell Disease, Hemochromatosis, Hemophilia, Von Willebrand Disease, and Vascular Diseases

Along with a Special Section on Blood Transfusions and Blood Supply Safety, a Glossary, and Source Listings for Further Help and Information

Edited by Karen Bellenir and Linda M. Shin. 554 pages. 1998. 0-7808-0203-9. $78.

"Recommended reference source."
—*Booklist, American Library Association, Feb '99*

"An important reference sourcebook written in simple language for everyday, non-technical users. "
—*Reviewer's Bookwatch, Jan '99*

Brain Disorders Sourcebook

Basic Consumer Health Information about Strokes, Epilepsy, Amyotrophic Lateral Sclerosis (ALS/Lou Gehrig's Disease), Parkinson's Disease, Brain Tumors, Cerebral Palsy, Headache, Tourette Syndrome, and More

Along with Statistical Data, Treatment and Rehabilitation Options, Coping Strategies, Reports on Current Research Initiatives, a Glossary, and Resource Listings for Additional Help and Information

Edited by Karen Bellenir. 481 pages. 1999. 0-7808-0229-2. $78.

"Recommended reference source."
—*Booklist, American Library Association, Oct '99*

SEE ALSO Alzheimer's, Stroke & 29 Other Neurological Disorders Sourcebook, 1st Edition

Breast Cancer Sourcebook

Basic Consumer Health Information about Breast Cancer, Including Diagnostic Methods, Treatment Options, Alternative Therapies, Help and Self-Help Information, Related Health Concerns, Statistical and Demographic Data, and Facts for Men with Breast Cancer

Along with Reports on Current Research Initiatives, a Glossary of Related Medical Terms, and a Directory of Sources for Further Help and Information

Edited by Edward J. Prucha. 600 pages. 2000. 0-7808-0244-6. $78.

SEE ALSO *Cancer Sourcebook for Women, 1st and 2nd Editions, Women's Health Concerns Sourcebook*

Burns Sourcebook

Basic Consumer Health Information about Various Types of Burns and Scalds, Including Flame, Heat, Cold, Electrical, Chemical, and Sun Burns

Along with Information on Short-Term and Long-Term Treatments, Tissue Reconstruction, Plastic Surgery, Prevention Suggestions, and First Aid

Edited by Allan R. Cook. 604 pages. 1999. 0-7808-0204-7. $78.

"Recommended reference source."
—Booklist, American Library Association, Dec '99

SEE ALSO *Skin Disorders Sourcebook*

Cancer Sourcebook, 1st Edition

Basic Information on Cancer Types, Symptoms, Diagnostic Methods, and Treatments, Including Statistics on Cancer Occurrences Worldwide and the Risks Associated with Known Carcinogens and Activities

Edited by Frank E. Bair. 932 pages. 1990. 1-55888-888-8. $78.

Cited in *Reference Sources for Small and Medium-Sized Libraries, American Library Association, 1999*

"Written in nontechnical language. Useful for patients, their families, medical professionals, and librarians."
—Guide to Reference Books, 1996

"Designed with the non-medical professional in mind. Libraries and medical facilities interested in patient education should certainly consider adding the *Cancer Sourcebook* to their holdings. This compact collection of reliable information . . . is an invaluable tool for helping patients and patients' families and friends to take the first steps in coping with the many difficulties of cancer."
—Medical Reference Services Quarterly, Winter '91

"Specifically created for the nontechnical reader . . . an important resource for the general reader trying to understand the complexities of cancer."
—American Reference Books Annual, 1991

"This publication's nontechnical nature and very comprehensive format make it useful for both the general public and undergraduate students." *—Choice, Association of College and Research Libraries, Oct '90*

New Cancer Sourcebook, 2nd Edition

Basic Information about Major Forms and Stages of Cancer, Featuring Facts about Primary and Secondary Tumors of the Respiratory, Nervous, Lymphatic, Circulatory, Skeletal, and Gastrointestinal Systems, and Specific Organs; Statistical and Demographic Data; Treatment Options; and Strategies for Coping

Edited by Allan R. Cook. 1,313 pages. 1996. 0-7808-0041-9. $78.

"An excellent resource for patients with newly diagnosed cancer and their families. The dialogue is simple, direct, and comprehensive. Highly recommended for patients and families to aid in their understanding of cancer and its treatment." *—Booklist Health Sciences Supplement, American Library Association, Oct '97*

"The amount of factual and useful information is extensive. The writing is very clear, geared to general readers. Recommended for all levels." *—Choice, Association of College and Research Libraries, Jan '97*

Cancer Sourcebook, 3rd Edition

Basic Consumer Health Information about Major Forms and Stages of Cancer, Featuring Facts about Primary and Secondary Tumors of the Respiratory, Nervous, Lymphatic, Circulatory, Skeletal, and Gastrointestinal Systems, and Specific Organs

Along with Statistical and Demographic Data, Treatment Options, Strategies for Coping, a Glossary, and a Directory of Sources for Additional Help and Information

Edited by Edward J. Prucha. 1,100 pages. 2000. 0-7808-0227-6. $78.

Cancer Sourcebook for Women, 1st Edition

Basic Information about Specific Forms of Cancer That Affect Women, Featuring Facts about Breast Cancer, Cervical Cancer, Ovarian Cancer, Cancer of the Uterus and Uterine Sarcoma, Cancer of the Vagina, and Cancer of the Vulva; Statistical and Demographic Data; Treatments, Self-Help Management Suggestions, and Current Research Initiatives

Edited by Allan R. Cook and Peter D. Dresser. 524 pages. 1996. 0-7808-0076-1. $78.

". . . written in easily understandable, non-technical language. Recommended for public libraries or hospital and academic libraries that collect patient education or consumer health materials."
—Medical Reference Services Quarterly, Spring '97

"Would be of value in a consumer health library. . . . written with the health care consumer in mind. Medical jargon is at a minimum, and medical terms are explained in clear, understandable sentences."
—Bulletin of the Medical Library Association, Oct '96

"The availability under one cover of all these pertinent publications, grouped under cohesive headings, makes this certainly a most useful sourcebook."
— *Choice, Association of College and Research Libraries, Jun '96*

"Presents a comprehensive knowledge base for general readers. Men and women both benefit from the gold mine of information nestled between the two covers of this book. Recommended."
— *Academic Library Book Review, Summer '96*

"This timely book is highly recommended for consumer health and patient education collections in all libraries."
— *Library Journal, Apr '96*

SEE ALSO Breast Cancer Sourcebook, Women's Health Concerns Sourcebook

■

Cancer Sourcebook for Women, 2nd Edition

Basic Consumer Health Information about Specific Forms of Cancer That Affect Women, Including Cervical Cancer, Ovarian Cancer, Endometrial Cancer, Uterine Sarcoma, Vaginal Cancer, Vulvar Cancer, and Gestational Trophoblastic Tumor; and Featuring Statistical Information, Facts about Tests and Treatments, a Glossary of Cancer Terms, and an Extensive List of Additional Resources

Edited by Edward J. Prucha. 600 pages. 2000. 0-7808-0226-8. $78.

SEE ALSO Breast Cancer Sourcebook, Women's Health Concerns Sourcebook

■

Cardiovascular Diseases & Disorders Sourcebook, 1st Edition

Basic Information about Cardiovascular Diseases and Disorders, Featuring Facts about the Cardiovascular System, Demographic and Statistical Data, Descriptions of Pharmacological and Surgical Interventions, Lifestyle Modifications, and a Special Section Focusing on Heart Disorders in Children

Edited by Karen Bellenir and Peter D. Dresser. 683 pages. 1995. 0-7808-0032-X. $78.

". . . comprehensive format provides an extensive overview on this subject."
— *Choice, Association of College and Research Libraries, Jun '96*

". . . an easily understood, complete, up-to-date resource. This well executed public health tool will make valuable information available to those that need it most, patients and their families. The typeface, sturdy non-reflective paper, and library binding add a feel of quality found wanting in other publications. Highly recommended for academic and general libraries. "
— *Academic Library Book Review, Summer '96*

SEE ALSO Healthy Heart Sourcebook for Women, Heart Diseases & Disorders Sourcebook, 2nd Edition

Communication Disorders Sourcebook

Basic Information about Deafness and Hearing Loss, Speech and Language Disorders, Voice Disorders, Balance and Vestibular Disorders, and Disorders of Smell, Taste, and Touch

Edited by Linda M. Ross. 533 pages. 1996. 0-7808-0077-X. $78.

"This is skillfully edited and is a welcome resource for the layperson. It should be found in every public and medical library."
— *Booklist Health Sciences Supplement, American Library Association, Oct '97*

■

Congenital Disorders Sourcebook

Basic Information about Disorders Acquired during Gestation, Including Spina Bifida, Hydrocephalus, Cerebral Palsy, Heart Defects, Craniofacial Abnormalities, Fetal Alcohol Syndrome, and More

Along with Current Treatment Options and Statistical Data

Edited by Karen Bellenir. 607 pages. 1997. 0-7808-0205-5. $78.

"Recommended reference source."
— *Booklist, American Library Association, Oct '97*

SEE ALSO Pregnancy & Birth Sourcebook

■

Consumer Issues in Health Care Sourcebook

Basic Information about Health Care Fundamentals and Related Consumer Issues, Including Exams and Screening Tests, Physician Specialties, Choosing a Doctor, Using Prescription and Over-the-Counter Medications Safely, Avoiding Health Scams, Managing Common Health Risks in the Home, Care Options for Chronically or Terminally Ill Patients, and a List of Resources for Obtaining Help and Further Information

Edited by Karen Bellenir. 618 pages. 1998. 0-7808-0221-7. $78.

"The editor has researched the literature from government agencies and others, saving readers the time and effort of having to do the research themselves. Recommended for public libraries."
— *Reference and User Services Quarterly, American Library Association, Spring '99*

"Recommended reference source."
— *Booklist, American Library Association, Dec '98*

Contagious & Non-Contagious Infectious Diseases Sourcebook

Basic Information about Contagious Diseases like Measles, Polio, Hepatitis B, and Infectious Mononucleosis, and Non-Contagious Infectious Diseases like Tetanus and Toxic Shock Syndrome, and Diseases Occurring as Secondary Infections Such as Shingles and Reye Syndrome

Along with Vaccination, Prevention, and Treatment Information, and a Section Describing Emerging Infectious Disease Threats

Edited by Karen Bellenir and Peter D. Dresser. 566 pages. 1996. 0-7808-0075-3. $78.

Death & Dying Sourcebook

Basic Consumer Health Information for the Layperson about End-of-Life Care and Related Ethical and Legal Issues, Including Chief Causes of Death, Autopsies, Pain Management for the Terminally Ill, Life Support Systems, Insurance, Euthanasia, Assisted Suicide, Hospice Programs, Living Wills, Funeral Planning, Counseling, Mourning, Organ Donation, and Physician Training

Along with Statistical Data, a Glossary, and Listings of Sources for Further Help and Information

Edited by Annemarie S. Muth. 641 pages. 1999. 0-7808-0230-6. $78.

Diabetes Sourcebook, 1st Edition

Basic Information about Insulin-Dependent and Non-insulin-Dependent Diabetes Mellitus, Gestational Diabetes, and Diabetic Complications, Symptoms, Treatment, and Research Results, Including Statistics on Prevalence, Morbidity, and Mortality

Along with Source Listings for Further Help and Information

Edited by Karen Bellenir and Peter D. Dresser. 827 pages. 1994. 1-55888-751-2. $78.

". . . very informative and understandable for the layperson without being simplistic. It provides a comprehensive overview for laypersons who want a general understanding of the disease or who want to focus on various aspects of the disease."
— *Bulletin of the Medical Library Association, Jan '96*

Diabetes Sourcebook, 2nd Edition

*Basic Consumer Health Information about Type 1 Diabetes (Insulin-Dependent or Juvenile-Onset Diabetes), Type 2 (Noninsulin-Dependent or Adult-Onset Diabetes), Gestational Diabetes, and Related Disorders, Including Diabetes Prevalence Data, Management Issues, the Role of Diet and Exercise in Con-*trolling Diabetes, Insulin and Other Diabetes Medicines, and Complications of Diabetes Such as Eye Diseases, Periodontal Disease, Amputation, and End-Stage Renal Disease

Along with Reports on Current Research Initiatives, a Glossary, and Resource Listings for Further Help and Information

Edited by Karen Bellenir. 688 pages. 1998. 0-7808-0224-1. $78.

"**Recommended reference source.**"
— *Booklist, American Library Association, Feb '99*

"**. . . provides reliable mainstream medical information . . . belongs on the shelves of any library with a consumer health collection.**" — *E-Streams, Sep '99*

"**Provides useful information for the general public.**"
— *Healthlines, University of Michigan Health Management Research Center, Sep/Oct '99*

Diet & Nutrition Sourcebook, 1st Edition

Basic Information about Nutrition, Including the Dietary Guidelines for Americans, the Food Guide Pyramid, and Their Applications in Daily Diet, Nutritional Advice for Specific Age Groups, Current Nutritional Issues and Controversies, the New Food Label and How to Use It to Promote Healthy Eating, and Recent Developments in Nutritional Research

Edited by Dan R. Harris. 662 pages. 1996. 0-7808-0084-2. $78.

"**Useful reference as a food and nutrition sourcebook for the general consumer.**"
— *Booklist Health Sciences Supplement, American Library Association, Oct '97*

"**Recommended for public libraries and medical libraries that receive general information requests on nutrition. It is readable and will appeal to those interested in learning more about healthy dietary practices.**"
— *Medical Reference Services Quarterly, Fall '97*

"**An abundance of medical and social statistics is translated into readable information geared toward the general reader.**" — *Bookwatch, Mar '97*

"**With dozens of questionable diet books on the market, it is so refreshing to find a reliable and factual reference book. Recommended to aspiring professionals, librarians, and others seeking and giving reliable dietary advice. An excellent compilation.**"
— *Choice, Association of College and Research Libraries, Feb '97*

SEE ALSO *Digestive Diseases & Disorders Sourcebook, Gastrointestinal Diseases & Disorders Sourcebook*

633

Diet & Nutrition Sourcebook, 2nd Edition

Basic Consumer Health Information about Dietary Guidelines, Recommended Daily Intake Values, Vitamins, Minerals, Fiber, Fat, Weight Control, Dietary Supplements, and Food Additives

Along with Special Sections on Nutrition Needs throughout Life and Nutrition for People with Such Specific Medical Concerns as Allergies, High Blood Cholesterol, Hypertension, Diabetes, Celiac Disease, Seizure Disorders, Phenylketonuria (PKU), Cancer, and Eating Disorders, and Including Reports on Current Nutrition Research and Source Listings for Additional Help and Information

Edited by Karen Bellenir. 650 pages. 1999. 0-7808-0228-4. $78.

"Recommended reference source."
—*Booklist, American Library Association, Dec '99*

SEE ALSO *Digestive Diseases & Disorders Sourcebook, Gastrointestinal Diseases & Disorders Sourcebook*

Digestive Diseases & Disorders Sourcebook

Basic Consumer Health Information about Diseases and Disorders that Impact the Upper and Lower Digestive System, Including Celiac Disease, Constipation, Crohn's Disease, Cyclic Vomiting Syndrome, Diarrhea, Diverticulosis and Diverticulitis, Gallstones, Heartburn, Hemorrhoids, Hernias, Indigestion (Dyspepsia), Irritable Bowel Syndrome, Lactose Intolerance, Ulcers, and More

Along with Information about Medications and Other Treatments, Tips for Maintaining a Healthy Digestive Tract, a Glossary, and Directory of Digestive Diseases Organizations

Edited by Karen Bellenir. 335 pages. 1999. 0-7808-0327-2. $48.

SEE ALSO *Diet & Nutrition Sourcebook, 1st and 2nd Editions, Gastrointestinal Diseases & Disorders Sourcebook*

Disabilities Sourcebook

Basic Consumer Health Information about Physical and Psychiatric Disabilities, Including Descriptions of Major Causes of Disability, Assistive and Adaptive Aids, Workplace Issues, and Accessibility Concerns

Along with Information about the Americans with Disabilities Act, a Glossary, and Resources for Additional Help and Information

Edited by Dawn D. Matthews. 616 pages. 2000. 0-7808-0389-2. $78.

Domestic Violence & Child Abuse Sourcebook

Basic Information about Spousal/ Partner, Child, and Elder Physical, Emotional, and Sexual Abuse, Teen Dating Violence, and Stalking, Including Information about Hotlines, Safe Houses, Safety Plans, and Other Resources for Support and Assistance, Community Initiatives, and Reports on Current Directions in Research and Treatment

Along with a Glossary, Sources for Further Reading, and Governmental and Non-Governmental Organizations Contact Information

Edited by Helene Henderson. 600 pages. 2000. 0-7808-0235-7. $78.

Drug Abuse Sourcebook

Basic Consumer Health Information about Illicit Substances of Abuse and the Diversion of Prescription Medications, Including Depressants, Hallucinogens, Inhalants, Marijuana, Narcotics, Stimulants, and Anabolic Steroids

Along with Facts about Related Health Risks, Treatment Issues, and Substance Abuse Prevention Programs, a Glossary of Terms, Statistical Data, and Directories of Hotline Services, Self-Help Groups, and Organizations Able to Provide Further Information

Edited by Karen Bellenir. 600 pages. 2000. 0-7808-0242-X. $78.

SEE ALSO *Alcoholism Sourcebook, Substance Abuse Sourcebook*

Ear, Nose & Throat Disorders Sourcebook

Basic Information about Disorders of the Ears, Nose, Sinus Cavities, Pharynx, and Larynx, Including Ear Infections, Tinnitus, Vestibular Disorders, Allergic and Non-Allergic Rhinitis, Sore Throats, Tonsillitis, and Cancers That Affect the Ears, Nose, Sinuses, and Throat

Along with Reports on Current Research Initiatives, a Glossary of Related Medical Terms, and a Directory of Sources for Further Help and Information

Edited by Karen Bellenir and Linda M. Shin. 576 pages. 1998. 0-7808-0206-3. $78.

"Overall, this sourcebook is helpful for the consumer seeking information on ENT issues. It is recommended for public libraries."
—*American Reference Books Annual, 1999*

"Recommended reference source."
—*Booklist, American Library Association, Dec '98*

Endocrine & Metabolic Disorders Sourcebook

Basic Information for the Layperson about Pancreatic and Insulin-Related Disorders Such as Pancreatitis, Diabetes, and Hypoglycemia; Adrenal Gland Disorders Such as Cushing's Syndrome, Addison's Disease, and Congenital Adrenal Hyperplasia; Pituitary Gland Disorders Such as Growth Hormone Deficiency, Acromegaly, and Pituitary Tumors; Thyroid Disorders Such as Hypothyroidism, Graves' Disease, Hashimoto's Disease, and Goiter; Hyperparathyroidism; and Other Diseases and Syndromes of Hormone Imbalance or Metabolic Dysfunction

Along with Reports on Current Research Initiatives

Edited by Linda M. Shin. 574 pages. 1998. 0-7808-0207-1. $78.

"Recommended reference source."
— *Booklist, American Library Association, Dec '98*

Environmentally Induced Disorders Sourcebook

Basic Information about Diseases and Syndromes Linked to Exposure to Pollutants and Other Substances in Outdoor and Indoor Environments Such as Lead, Asbestos, Formaldehyde, Mercury, Emissions, Noise, and More

Edited by Allan R. Cook. 620 pages. 1997. 0-7808-0083-4. $78.

"Recommended reference source."
— *Booklist, American Library Association, Sep '98*

"This book will be a useful addition to anyone's library." — *Choice Health Sciences Supplement, Association of College and Research Libraries, May '98*

". . . a good survey of numerous environmentally induced physical disorders . . . a useful addition to anyone's library."
— *Doody's Health Sciences Book Reviews, Jan '98*

". . . provide[s] introductory information from the best authorities around. Since this volume covers topics that potentially affect everyone, it will surely be one of the most frequently consulted volumes in the *Health Reference Series.*" — *Rettig on Reference, Nov '97*

Ethical Issues in Medicine Sourcebook

Basic Information about Controversial Treatment Issues, Genetic Research, Reproductive Technologies, and End-of-Life Decisions, Including Topics Such as Cloning, Abortion, Fertility Management, Organ Transplantation, Health Care Rationing, Advance Directives, Living Wills, Physician-Assisted Suicide, Euthanasia, and More; Along with a Glossary and Resources for Additional Information

Edited by Helene Henderson. 600 pages. 2000. 0-7808-0237-3. $78.

Family Planning Sourcebook

Basic Information about Planning for Pregnancy and Contraception, Including Traditional Methods, Barrier Methods, Permanent Methods, Future Methods, Emergency Contraception, and Birth Control Choices for Women at Each Stage of Life

Along with Statistics, Glossary, and Sources of Additional Information

Edited by Amy Marcaccio Keyzer. 600 pages. 2000. 0-7808-0379-5. $78.

SEE ALSO *Pregnancy & Birth Sourcebook*

Fitness & Exercise Sourcebook

Basic Information on Fitness and Exercise, Including Fitness Activities for Specific Age Groups, Exercise for People with Specific Medical Conditions, How to Begin a Fitness Program in Running, Walking, Swimming, Cycling, and Other Athletic Activities, and Recent Research in Fitness and Exercise

Edited by Dan R. Harris. 663 pages. 1996. 0-7808-0186-5. $78.

"A good resource for general readers."
— *Choice, Association of College and Research Libraries, Nov '97*

"The perennial popularity of the topic . . . make this an appealing selection for public libraries."
— *Rettig on Reference, Jun/Jul '97*

Food & Animal Borne Diseases Sourcebook

Basic Information about Diseases That Can Be Spread to Humans through the Ingestion of Contaminated Food or Water or by Contact with Infected Animals and Insects, Such as Botulism, E. Coli, Hepatitis A, Trichinosis, Lyme Disease, and Rabies

Along with Information Regarding Prevention and Treatment Methods, and Including a Special Section for International Travelers Describing Diseases Such as Cholera, Malaria, Travelers' Diarrhea, and Yellow Fever, and Offering Recommendations for Avoiding Illness

Edited by Karen Bellenir and Peter D. Dresser. 535 pages. 1995. 0-7808-0033-8. $78.

"Targeting general readers and providing them with a single, comprehensive source of information on selected topics, this book continues, with the excellent caliber of its predecessors, to catalog topical information on health matters of general interest. Readable and thorough, this valuable resource is highly recommended for all libraries."
— *Academic Library Book Review, Summer '96*

"A comprehensive collection of authoritative information." — *Emergency Medical Services, Oct '95*

Food Safety Sourcebook

Basic Consumer Health Information about the Safe Handling of Meat, Poultry, Seafood, Eggs, Fruit Juices, and Other Food Items, and Facts about Pesticides, Drinking Water, Food Safety Overseas, and the Onset, Duration, and Symptoms of Foodborne Illnesses, Including Types of Pathogenic Bacteria, Parasitic Protozoa, Worms, Viruses, and Natural Toxins

Along with the Role of the Consumer, the Food Handler, and the Government in Food Safety; a Glossary, and Resources for Additional Help and Information

Edited by Dawn D. Matthews. 339 pages. 1999. 0-7808-0326-4. $48.

Forensic Medicine Sourcebook

Basic Consumer Information for the Layperson about Forensic Medicine, Including Crime Scene Investigation, Evidence Collection and Analysis, Expert Testimony, Computer-Aided Criminal Identification, Digital Imaging in the Courtroom, DNA Profiling, Accident Reconstruction, Autopsies, Ballistics, Drugs and Explosives Detection, Latent Fingerprints, Product Tampering, and Questioned Document Examination

Along with Statistical Data, a Glossary of Forensics Terminology, and Listings of Sources for Further Help and Information

Edited by Annemarie S. Muth. 574 pages. 1999. 0-7808-0232-2. $78.

"A wealth of information, useful statistics, references are up-to-date and extremely complete. This wonderful collection of data will help students who are interested in a career in any type of forensic field. It is a great resource for attorneys who need information about types of expert witnesses needed in a particular case. It also offers useful information for fiction and nonfiction writers whose work involves a crime. A fascinating compilation. All levels."
— *Choice, Association of College and Research Libraries, Jan 2000*

Gastrointestinal Diseases & Disorders Sourcebook

Basic Information about Gastroesophageal Reflux Disease (Heartburn), Ulcers, Diverticulosis, Irritable Bowel Syndrome, Crohn's Disease, Ulcerative Colitis, Diarrhea, Constipation, Lactose Intolerance, Hemorrhoids, Hepatitis, Cirrhosis, and Other Digestive Problems, Featuring Statistics, Descriptions of Symptoms, and Current Treatment Methods of Interest for Persons Living with Upper and Lower Gastrointestinal Maladies

Edited by Linda M. Ross. 413 pages. 1996. 0-7808-0078-8. $78.

". . . very readable form. The successful editorial work that brought this material together into a useful and understandable reference makes accessible to all readers information that can help them more effectively under-

stand and obtain help for digestive tract problems."
— *Choice, Association of College and Research Libraries, Feb '97*

SEE ALSO Diet & Nutrition Sourcebook, 1st and 2nd Editions, Digestive Diseases & Disorders Sourcebook

Genetic Disorders Sourcebook

Basic Information about Heritable Diseases and Disorders Such as Down Syndrome, PKU, Hemophilia, Von Willebrand Disease, Gaucher Disease, Tay-Sachs Disease, and Sickle-Cell Disease, Along with Information about Genetic Screening, Gene Therapy, Home Care, and Including Source Listings for Further Help and Information on More Than 300 Disorders

Edited by Karen Bellenir. 642 pages. 1996. 0-7808-0034-6. $78.

"Recommended for undergraduate libraries or libraries that serve the public."
— *Science & Technology Libraries, Vol. 18, No. 1, '99*

"Provides essential medical information to both the general public and those diagnosed with a serious or fatal genetic disease or disorder."
— *Choice, Association of College and Research Libraries, Jan '97*

"Geared toward the lay public. It would be well placed in all public libraries and in those hospital and medical libraries in which access to genetic references is limited." — *Doody's Health Sciences Book Review, Oct '96*

Head Trauma Sourcebook

Basic Information for the Layperson about Open-Head and Closed-Head Injuries, Treatment Advances, Recovery, and Rehabilitation

Along with Reports on Current Research Initiatives

Edited by Karen Bellenir. 414 pages. 1997. 0-7808-0208-X. $78.

Health Insurance Sourcebook

Basic Information about Managed Care Organizations, Traditional Fee-for-Service Insurance, Insurance Portability and Pre-Existing Conditions Clauses, Medicare, Medicaid, Social Security, and Military Health Care

Along with Information about Insurance Fraud

Edited by Wendy Wilcox. 530 pages. 1997. 0-7808-0222-5. $78.

"Particularly useful because it brings much of this information together in one volume. This book will be a handy reference source in the health sciences library, hospital library, college and university library, and medium to large public library."
— *Medical Reference Services Quarterly, Fall '98*

Awarded "Books of the Year Award"
by the American Journal of Nursing, 1997

636

Health Resources Sourcebook

Basic Consumer Health Information about Sources of Medical Assistance, Featuring an Annotated Directory of Private and Public Consumer Health Organizations and Listings of Other Resources, Including Hospitals, Hospices, and State Medical Associations

Along with Guidelines for Locating and Evaluating Health Information

Edited by Dawn D. Matthews. 500 pages. 2000. 0-7808-0328-0. $78.

Healthy Aging Sourcebook

Basic Consumer Health Information about Maintaining Health through the Aging Process, Including Advice on Nutrition, Exercise, and Sleep, Help in Making Decisions about Midlife Issues and Retirement, and Guidance Concerning Practical and Informed Choices in Health Consumerism

Along with Data Concerning the Theories of Aging, Different Experiences in Aging by Minority Groups, and Facts about Aging Now and Aging in the Future; and Featuring a Glossary, a Guide to Consumer Help, Additional Suggested Reading, and Practical Resource Directory

Edited by Jenifer Swanson. 536 pages. 1999. 0-7808-0390-6. $78.

SEE ALSO *Physical & Mental Issues in Aging Sourcebook*

Healthy Heart Sourcebook for Women

Basic Consumer Health Information about Cardiac Issues Specific to Women, Including Facts about Major Risk Factors and Prevention, Treatment and Control Strategies, and Important Dietary Issues

Along with a Special Section Regarding the Pros and Cons of Hormone Replacement Therapy and Its Impact on Heart Health, and Additional Help, Including Recipes, a Glossary, and a Directory of Resources

Edited by Dawn D. Matthews. 336 pages. 2000. 0-7808-0329-9. $48.

SEE ALSO *Cardiovascular Diseases & Disorders Sourcebook, 1st Edition, Heart Diseases & Disorders Sourcebook, 2nd Edition, Women's Health Concerns Sourcebook*

Heart Diseases & Disorders Sourcebook, 2nd edition

Basic Consumer Health Information about Heart Attacks, Angina, Rhythm Disorders, Heart Failure, Valve Disease, Congenital Heart Disorders, and More, Including Descriptions of Surgical Procedures and Other Interventions, Medications, Cardiac Rehabilitation, Risk Identification, and Prevention Tips

Along with Statistical Data, Reports on Current Research Initiatives, a Glossary of Cardiovascular Terms, and Resource Directory

Edited by Karen Bellenir. 612 pages. 2000. 0-7808-0238-1. $78.

SEE ALSO *Cardiovascular Diseases & Disorders Sourcebook, 1st Edition, Healthy Heart Sourcebook for Women*

Immune System Disorders Sourcebook

Basic Information about Lupus, Multiple Sclerosis, Guillain-Barré Syndrome, Chronic Granulomatous Disease, and More

Along with Statistical and Demographic Data and Reports on Current Research Initiatives

Edited by Allan R. Cook. 608 pages. 1997. 0-7808-0209-8. $78.

Infant & Toddler Health Sourcebook

Basic Consumer Health Information about the Physical and Mental Development of Newborns, Infants, and Toddlers, Including Neonatal Concerns, Nutritional Recommendations, Immunization Schedules, Common Pediatric Disorders, Assessments and Milestones, Safety Tips, and Advice for Parents and Other Caregivers

Along with a Glossary of Terms and Resource Listings for Additional Help

Edited by Jenifer Swanson. 600 pages. 2000. 0-7808-0246-2. $78.

Kidney & Urinary Tract Diseases & Disorders Sourcebook

Basic Information about Kidney Stones, Urinary Incontinence, Bladder Disease, End Stage Renal Disease, Dialysis, and More

Along with Statistical and Demographic Data and Reports on Current Research Initiatives

Edited by Linda M. Ross. 602 pages. 1997. 0-7808-0079-6. $78.

Learning Disabilities Sourcebook

Basic Information about Disorders Such as Dyslexia, Visual and Auditory Processing Deficits, Attention Deficit/Hyperactivity Disorder, and Autism

Along with Statistical and Demographic Data, Reports on Current Research Initiatives, an Explanation of the Assessment Process, and a Special Section for Adults with Learning Disabilities

Edited by Linda M. Shin. 579 pages. 1998. 0-7808-0210-1. $78.

"Readable . . . provides a solid base of information regarding successful techniques used with individuals who have learning disabilities, as well as practical suggestions for educators and family members. Clear language, concise descriptions, and pertinent information for contacting multiple resources add to the strength of this book as a useful tool."
— *Choice, Association of College and Research Libraries, Feb '99*

"Recommended reference source."
— *Booklist, American Library Association, Sep '98*

"This is a useful resource for libraries and for those who don't have the time to identify and locate the individual publications."
— *Disability Resources Monthly, Sep '98*

Liver Disorders Sourcebook

Basic Consumer Health Information about the Liver and How It Works; Liver Diseases, Including Cancer, Cirrhosis, Hepatitis, and Toxic and Drug Related Diseases; Tips for Maintaining a Healthy Liver; Laboratory Tests, Radiology Tests, and Facts about Liver Transplantation

Along with a Section on Support Groups, a Glossary, and Resource Listings

Edited by Joyce Brennfleck Shannon. 591 pages. 2000. 0-7808-0383-3. $78.

Medical Tests Sourcebook

Basic Consumer Health Information about Medical Tests, Including Periodic Health Exams, General Screening Tests, Tests You Can Do at Home, Findings of the U.S. Preventive Services Task Force, X-ray and Radiology Tests, Electrical Tests, Tests of Blood and Other Body Fluids and Tissues, Scope Tests, Lung Tests, Genetic Tests, Pregnancy Tests, Newborn Screening Tests, Sexually Transmitted Disease Tests, and Computer Aided Diagnoses

Along with a Section on Paying for Medical Tests, a Glossary, and Resource Listings

Edited by Joyce Brennfleck Shannon. 691 pages. 1999. 0-7808-0243-8. $78.

"This is an overall excellent reference with a wealth of general knowledge that may aid those who are reluctant to get vital tests performed."
— *Today's Librarian, Jan 2000*

Men's Health Concerns Sourcebook

Basic Information about Health Issues That Affect Men, Featuring Facts about the Top Causes of Death in Men, Including Heart Disease, Stroke, Cancers, Prostate Disorders, Chronic Obstructive Pulmonary Disease, Pneumonia and Influenza, Human Immunodeficiency Virus and Acquired Immune Deficiency Syndrome, Diabetes Mellitus, Stress, Suicide, Accidents and Homicides; and Facts about Common Concerns for Men, Including Impotence, Contraception, Circumcision, Sleep Disorders, Snoring, Hair Loss, Diet, Nutrition, Exercise, Kidney and Urological Disorders, and Backaches

Edited by Allan R. Cook. 738 pages. 1998. 0-7808-0212-8. $78.

"Recommended reference source."
— *Booklist, American Library Association, Dec '98*

Mental Health Disorders Sourcebook, 1st Edition

Basic Information about Schizophrenia, Depression, Bipolar Disorder, Panic Disorder, Obsessive-Compulsive Disorder, Phobias and Other Anxiety Disorders, Paranoia and Other Personality Disorders, Eating Disorders, and Sleep Disorders

Along with Information about Treatment and Therapies

Edited by Karen Bellenir. 548 pages. 1995. 0-7808-0040-0. $78.

"This is an excellent new book . . . written in easy-to-understand language." — *Booklist Health Sciences Supplement, American Library Association, Oct '97*

". . . useful for public and academic libraries and consumer health collections."
— *Medical Reference Services Quarterly, Spring '97*

"The great strengths of the book are its readability and its inclusion of places to find more information. Especially recommended." — *Reference Quarterly, Reference and User Services Association, Winter '96*

". . . a good resource for a consumer health library."
— *Bulletin of the Medical Library Association, Oct '96*

"The information is data-based and couched in brief, concise language that avoids jargon. . . . a useful reference source." — *Readings, Sep '96*

"The text is well organized and adequately written for its target audience."
— *Choice, Association of College and Research Libraries, Jun '96*

". . . provides information on a wide range of mental disorders, presented in nontechnical language."
— *Exceptional Child Education Resources, Spring '96*

"Recommended for public and academic libraries."
— *Reference Book Review, 1996*

Mental Health Disorders Sourcebook, 2nd Edition

Basic Consumer Health Information about Anxiety Disorders, Depression and Other Mood Disorders, Eating Disorders, Personality Disorders, Schizophrenia, and More, Including Disease Descriptions, Treatment Options, and Reports on Current Research Initiatives

Along with Statistical Data, Tips for Maintaining Mental Health, a Glossary, and Directory of Sources for Additional Help and Information

Edited by Karen Bellenir. 605 pages. 2000. 0-7808-0240-3. $78.

Mental Retardation Sourcebook

Basic Consumer Health Information about Mental Retardation and Its Causes, Including Down Syndrome, Fetal Alcohol Syndrome, Fragile X Syndrome, Genetic Conditions, Injury, and Environmental Sources

Along with Preventive Strategies, Parenting Issues, Educational Implications, Health Care Needs, Employment and Economic Matters, Legal Issues, a Glossary, and a Resource Listing for Additional Help and Information

Edited by Joyce Brennfleck Shannon. 642 pages. 2000. 0-7808-0377-9. $78.

Obesity Sourcebook

Basic Consumer Health Information about Diseases and Other Problems Associated with Obesity, and Including Facts about Risk Factors, Prevention Issues, and Management Approaches

Along with Statistical and Demographic Data, Information about Special Populations, Research Updates, a Glossary, and Source Listings for Further Help and Information

Edited by Wilma Caldwell. 400 pages. 2000. 0-7808-0333-7. $48.

Ophthalmic Disorders Sourcebook

Basic Information about Glaucoma, Cataracts, Macular Degeneration, Strabismus, Refractive Disorders, and More

Along with Statistical and Demographic Data and Reports on Current Research Initiatives

Edited by Linda M. Ross. 631 pages. 1996. 0-7808-0081-8. $78.

Oral Health Sourcebook

Basic Information about Diseases and Conditions Affecting Oral Health, Including Cavities, Gum Disease, Dry Mouth, Oral Cancers, Fever Blisters, Canker Sores, Oral Thrush, Bad Breath, Temporomandibular Disorders, and other Craniofacial Syndromes

Along with Statistical Data on the Oral Health of Americans, Oral Hygiene, Emergency First Aid, Information on Treatment Procedures and Methods of Replacing Lost Teeth

Edited by Allan R. Cook. 558 pages. 1997. 0-7808-0082-6. $78.

"**Unique source which will fill a gap in dental sources for patients and the lay public. A valuable reference tool even in a library with thousands of books on dentistry. Comprehensive, clear, inexpensive, and easy to read and use. It fills an enormous gap in the health care literature.**" — Reference and User Services Quarterly, American Library Association, Summer '98

"**Recommended reference source.**" — Booklist, American Library Association, Dec '97

Osteoporosis Sourcebook

Basic Consumer Health Information about Primary and Secondary Osteoporosis, Juvenile Osteoporosis, Related Conditions, and Other Such Bone Disorders as Fibrous Dysplasia, Myeloma, Osteogenesis Imperfecta, Osteopetrosis, and Paget's Disease

Along with Information about Risk Factors, Treatments, Traditional and Non-Traditional Pain Management, and Including a Glossary and Resource Directory

Edited by Allan R. Cook. 600 pages. 2000. 0-7808-0239-X. $78.

SEE ALSO Women's Health Concerns Sourcebook

Pain Sourcebook

Basic Information about Specific Forms of Acute and Chronic Pain, Including Headaches, Back Pain, Muscular Pain, Neuralgia, Surgical Pain, and Cancer Pain

Along with Pain Relief Options Such as Analgesics, Narcotics, Nerve Blocks, Transcutaneous Nerve Stimulation, and Alternative Forms of Pain Control, Including Biofeedback, Imaging, Behavior Modification, and Relaxation Techniques

Edited by Allan R. Cook. 667 pages. 1997. 0-7808-0213-6. $78.

"**The text is readable, easily understood, and well indexed. This excellent volume belongs in all patient education libraries, consumer health sections of public libraries, and many personal collections.**" — American Reference Books Annual, 1999

"**A beneficial reference.**" — Booklist Health Sciences Supplement, American Library Association, Oct '98

"**The information is basic in terms of scholarship and is appropriate for general readers. Written in journalistic style . . . intended for non-professionals. Quite thorough in its coverage of different pain conditions and summarizes the latest clinical information regarding pain treatment.**" — Choice, Association of College and Research Libraries, Jun '98

"**Recommended reference source.**" — Booklist, American Library Association, Mar '98

Pediatric Cancer Sourcebook

Basic Consumer Health Information about Leukemias, Brain Tumors, Sarcomas, Lymphomas, and Other Cancers in Infants, Children, and Adolescents, Including Descriptions of Cancers, Treatments, and Coping Strategies

Along with Suggestions for Parents, Caregivers, and Concerned Relatives, a Glossary of Cancer Terms, and Resource Listings

Edited by Edward J. Prucha. 587 pages. 1999. 0-7808-0245-4. $78.

◼

Physical & Mental Issues in Aging Sourcebook

Basic Consumer Health Information on Physical and Mental Disorders Associated with the Aging Process, Including Concerns about Cardiovascular Disease, Pulmonary Disease, Oral Health, Digestive Disorders, Musculoskeletal and Skin Disorders, Metabolic Changes, Sexual and Reproductive Issues, and Changes in Vision, Hearing, and Other Senses

Along with Data about Longevity and Causes of Death, Information on Acute and Chronic Pain, Descriptions of Mental Concerns, a Glossary of Terms, and Resource Listings for Additional Help

Edited by Jenifer Swanson. 660 pages. 1999. 0-7808-0233-0. $78.

"Recommended reference source."
— Booklist, American Library Association, Oct '99

SEE ALSO Healthy Aging Sourcebook

◼

Plastic Surgery Sourcebook

Basic Consumer Health Information on Cosmetic and Reconstructive Plastic Surgery, Including Statistical Information about Different Surgical Procedures, Things to Consider Prior to Surgery, Plastic Surgery Techniques and Tools, Emotional and Psychological Considerations, and Procedure-Specific Information

Along with a Glossary of Terms and a Listing of Resources for Additional Help and Information

Edited by M. Lisa Weatherford. 400 pages. 2000. 0-7808-0214-4. $48.

◼

Pregnancy & Birth Sourcebook

Basic Information about Planning for Pregnancy, Maternal Health, Fetal Growth and Development, Labor and Delivery, Postpartum and Perinatal Care, Pregnancy in Mothers with Special Concerns, and Disorders of Pregnancy, Including Genetic Counseling, Nutrition and Exercise, Obstetrical Tests, Pregnancy Discomfort, Multiple Births, Cesarean Sections, Medical Testing of Newborns, Breastfeeding, Gestational Diabetes, and Ectopic Pregnancy

Edited by Heather E. Aldred. 737 pages. 1997. 0-7808-0216-0. $78.

"A well-organized handbook. Recommended."
— Choice, Association of College and Research Libraries, Apr '98

"Reecommended reference source."
— Booklist, American Library Association, Mar '98

"Recommended for public libraries."
— American Reference Books Annual, 1998

SEE ALSO Congenital Disorders Sourcebook, Family Planning Sourcebook

◼

Public Health Sourcebook

Basic Information about Government Health Agencies, Including National Health Statistics and Trends, Healthy People 2000 Program Goals and Objectives, the Centers for Disease Control and Prevention, the Food and Drug Administration, and the National Institutes of Health

Along with Full Contact Information for Each Agency

Edited by Wendy Wilcox. 698 pages. 1998. 0-7808-0220-9. $78.

"Recommended reference source."
— Booklist, American Library Association, Sep '98

"This consumer guide provides welcome assistance in navigating the maze of federal health agencies and their data on public health concerns."
— SciTech Book News, Sep '98

◼

Rehabilitation Sourcebook

Basic Consumer Health Information about Rehabilitation for People Recovering from Heart Surgery, Spinal Cord Injury, Stroke, Orthopedic Impairments, Amputation, Pulmonary Impairments, Traumatic Injury, and More, Including Physical Therapy, Occupational Therapy, Speech/Language Therapy, Massage Therapy, Dance Therapy, Art Therapy, and Recreational Therapy

Along with Information on Assistive and Adaptive Devices, a Glossary, and Resources for Additional Help and Information

Edited by Dawn D. Matthews. 531 pages. 1999. 0-7808-0236-5. $78.

◼

Respiratory Diseases & Disorders Sourcebook

Basic Information about Respiratory Diseases and Disorders, Including Asthma, Cystic Fibrosis, Pneumonia, the Common Cold, Influenza, and Others, Featuring Facts about the Respiratory System, Statistical and Demographic Data, Treatments, Self-Help Management Suggestions, and Current Research Initiatives

Edited by Allan R. Cook and Peter D. Dresser. 771 pages. 1995. 0-7808-0037-0. $78.

"Designed for the layperson and for patients and their families coping with respiratory illness. . . . an exten-

sive array of information on diagnosis, treatment, management, and prevention of respiratory illnesses for the general reader."
— *Choice,*
Association of College and Research Libraries, Jun '96

"A highly recommended text for all collections. It is a comforting reminder of the power of knowledge that good books carry between their covers."
— *Academic Library Book Review, Spring '96*

"A comprehensive collection of authoritative information presented in a nontechnical, humanitarian style for patients, families, and caregivers."
— *Association of Operating Room Nurses, Sep/Oct '95*

■

Sexually Transmitted Diseases Sourcebook

Basic Information about Herpes, Chlamydia, Gonorrhea, Hepatitis, Nongonoccocal Urethritis, Pelvic Inflammatory Disease, Syphilis, AIDS, and More

Along with Current Data on Treatments and Preventions

Edited by Linda M. Ross. 550 pages. 1997. 0-7808-0217-9. $78.

■

Skin Disorders Sourcebook

Basic Information about Common Skin and Scalp Conditions Caused by Aging, Allergies, Immune Reactions, Sun Exposure, Infectious Organisms, Parasites, Cosmetics, and Skin Traumas, Including Abrasions, Cuts, and Pressure Sores

Along with Information on Prevention and Treatment

Edited by Allan R. Cook. 647 pages. 1997. 0-7808-0080-X. $78.

". . . comprehensive, easily read reference book."
— *Doody's Health Sciences Book Reviews, Oct '97*

SEE ALSO Burns Sourcebook

■

Sleep Disorders Sourcebook

Basic Consumer Health Information about Sleep and Its Disorders, Including Insomnia, Sleepwalking, Sleep Apnea, Restless Leg Syndrome, and Narcolepsy

Along with Data about Shiftwork and Its Effects, Information on the Societal Costs of Sleep Deprivation, Descriptions of Treatment Options, a Glossary of Terms, and Resource Listings for Additional Help

Edited by Jenifer Swanson. 439 pages. 1998. 0-7808-0234-9. $78.

"Recommended reference source."
— *Booklist, American Library Association, Feb '99*

"A useful resource that provides accurate, relevant, and accessible information on sleep to the general public. Health care providers who deal with sleep disorders patients may also find it helpful in being prepared to answer some of the questions patients ask."
— *Respiratory Care, Jul '99*

Sports Injuries Sourcebook

Basic Consumer Health Information about Common Sports Injuries, Prevention of Injury in Specific Sports, Tips for Training, and Rehabilitation from Injury

Along with Information about Special Concerns for Children, Young Girls in Athletic Training Programs, Senior Athletes, and Women Athletes, and a Directory of Resources for Further Help and Information

Edited by Heather E. Aldred. 624 pages. 1999. 0-7808-0218-7. $78.

Substance Abuse Sourcebook

Basic Health-Related Information about the Abuse of Legal and Illegal Substances Such as Alcohol, Tobacco, Prescription Drugs, Marijuana, Cocaine, and Heroin; and Including Facts about Substance Abuse Prevention Strategies, Intervention Methods, Treatment and Recovery Programs, and a Section Addressing the Special Problems Related to Substance Abuse during Pregnancy

Edited by Karen Bellenir. 573 pages. 1996. 0-7808-0038-9. $78.

"A valuable addition to any health reference section. Highly recommended."
— *The Book Report, Mar/Apr '97*

". . . a comprehensive collection of substance abuse information that's both highly readable and compact. Families and caregivers of substance abusers will find the information enlightening and helpful, while teachers, social workers and journalists should benefit from the concise format. Recommended."
— *Drug Abuse Update, Winter '96/'97*

SEE ALSO Alcoholism Sourcebook, Drug Abuse Sourcebook

■

Traveler's Health Sourcebook

Basic Consumer Health Information for Travelers, Including Physical and Medical Preparations, Transportation Health and Safety, Essential Information about Food, Water, Sun Exposure, Insect and Snake Bites, Camping and Wilderness Medicine, and Travel with Physical or Medical Disabilities

Along with International Travel Tips, Vaccination Recommendations, Geographical Health Issues, Disease Risks, a Glossary, and a Listing of Additional Resources

Edited by Joyce Brennfleck Shannon. 650 pages. 2000. 0-7808-0384-1. $78.

■

Women's Health Concerns Sourcebook

Basic Information about Health Issues That Affect Women, Featuring Facts about Menstruation and Other Gynecological Concerns, Including Endometriosis, Fibroids, Menopause, and Vaginitis; Reproductive Concerns, Including Birth Control, Infertility, and Abortion; and Facts about Additional Physical, Emotional, and Mental Health Concerns Prevalent among Women Such as Osteoporosis, Urinary Tract Disorders, Eating Disorders, and Depression

Along with Tips for Maintaining a Healthy Lifestyle

Edited by Heather E. Aldred. 567 pages. 1997. 0-7808-0219-5. $78.

"Handy compilation. There is an impressive range of diseases, devices, disorders, procedures, and other physical and emotional issues covered . . . well organized, illustrated, and indexed." —*Choice, Association of College and Research Libraries, Jan '98*

SEE ALSO *Breast Cancer Sourcebook, Cancer Sourcebook for Women, 1st and 2nd Editions, Healthy Heart Sourcebook for Women, Osteoporosis Sourcebook*

Workplace Health & Safety Sourcebook

Basic Information about Musculoskeletal Injuries, Cumulative Trauma Disorders, Occupational Carcinogens and Other Toxic Materials, Child Labor, Workplace Violence, Histoplasmosis, Transmission of HIV and Hepatitis-B Viruses, and Occupational Hazards Associated with Various Industries, Including Mining, Confined Spaces, Agriculture, Construction, Electrical Work, and the Medical Professions, with Information on Mortality and Other Statistical Data, Preventative Measures, Reproductive Risks, Reducing Stress for Shiftworkers, Noise Hazards, Industrial Back Belts, Reducing Contamination at Home, Preventing Allergic Reactions to Rubber Latex, and More

Along with Public and Private Programs and Initiatives, a Glossary, and Sources for Additional Help and Information

Edited by Chad Kimball. 600 pages. 2000. 0-7808-0231-4. $78.

■

Health Reference Series Cumulative Index, 1st Edition

A Comprehensive Index to the Health Reference Series, 1990-1999

1,500 pages. 2000. 0-7808-0382-5. $78.